PYTHON

NOVICE TO NINJA

AF885327

Raspberry Pi Edition

Bruce Smith

the coding press
www.codingpress.com.au

Raspberry Pi:
PYTHON UNLEASHED

ISBN: 9 780648 098768
Editor: Alan Ford Edits
Cover: Sumit Shringi, Graphic Designer (Book Cover-Design)
Typeset by The Coding Press using Affinity Publisher
Thanks to: Joshua Jones, Tom Racy Annie James

The python is not swift, yet it succeeds by persistence.

Nature has endowed it with strength that overcomes all.

– Aristotle, philosopher and natural scientist

CONTENTS

IMPORTANT NOTE

Python programs follow a style guideline known as PEP8, which will be covered later in this book. Although PEP8 helps maintain consistency, it is not required for a program to run correctly. One of the guidelines suggests including two blank lines between certain sections of code, but this will not always be followed in the listings here. This is to reduce whitespace.

PROGRAMS AND QUESTIONS

There are over 250 programs in this book. I suggest that you type in as many of these as you can, rather than loading them in from the files. Typing is the best way to learn and get a feeling for the commands, syntax and flow of a Python program. Learn how to correct and ensure your coding is correct and works. Bear in mind that some program lines extend longer than the space available across the width of the book. As such they will often 'wrap-around' onto the next line. That said the programs are available to download from the website at:

```
www.brucesmith.info/PUD.html
```

QUESTIONS AND EXERCISES

Most chapters, not all, contain questions at the end. These questions are related to the text in the chapter just read. There are up to 15 questions. No answers are provided in the book, they are there for you to answer or review the contents of the chapter prior to answering. Exercises include answers, but remember my solution may be different to yours, but as long as you get the right result that's it! You'll also find more exercises on the downloads file.

00: Novice to Ninja

What does **novice** and **ninja** mean regarding learning to program Python on the Raspberry Pi? There are many books for programmers who are starting their Python experience. But they cover the basics and **don't** actually get under the 'hood' and into the detail. They leave you in the hallway, and don't show the rest of the house. Within these pages I seek to correct that and take you to those places beyond the hallway, providing a higher level of knowledge and expertise to transform you from a complete beginner (or intermediate), who's just learning the ropes, to a skilled and confident Python coder. Merriam-Webster defines each word thus:

- A **novice** in computer terms can be defined as a beginner or someone who has no previous experience in a particular field or activity.
- On the other hand, **ninja** isn't typically defined in the same way in dictionaries. In popular usage, it's often used to describe someone who has achieved a high level of skill or expertise. An expert, maybe someone to be feared?

You may not be a novice in use of the Raspberry Pi, and may have some programming knowledge, but this tome will just accelerate your learning. Being a '**Python ninja**' doesn't mean you've mastered every single aspect of the language, after all, there's always more to learn. Instead, it means you've reached a point where you're comfortable and efficient with the language, can solve problems creatively, and write clean, effective code. You know how to handle different challenges, think like a programmer, and confidently create your own projects or collaborate with others.

Programs

There are a **lot** of programs in this book. You can download the source from the authors website at:

```
www.brucesmith.info/PUD.html
```

They are there for your convenience. andI would **strongly** suggest that you **type these programs in yourself.** Unless you do you won't start to understand how a Python program goes together. How it is structured and what goes where as well as why? Most of demo programs are not that long, so it shouldn't be overly difficult. As you progress through the book then they will become much longer, so you could delve into the download at that point.

Typing is another key skill. If you can't type, to whatever degree, in today's world then things become long-winded. It is the biggest skill you can master and is starting to become part of the school curriculum here.

I'm always pleased to hear from readers, please feel free to contact me at:

`feedback@brucesmith.info`

Use the Website Please

If you didn't buy this through **The Coding Press** website, I'd be grateful if you consider purchasing any more of my books from there. You will find a larger choice of book formats, and help support me directly as a creative. I am one of a few independent publishers and certainly the only one writing seriously about the Raspberry Pi.

This means I can fully reap the benefits of my efforts in writing and publishing. Supporting creators directly allows us to continue producing more great content. People often think of the cost of the final project but not the six plus months or so it takes to go from first word to finish article!

Raspberry Pi Versions

The contents of this book have been tested on the Raspberry Pi 3, 4, 400 and 5, 500 and any future Pi releases running Python 3. There are some differences in the application here and there, but it is remarkably consistent across all these versions. Where differences occur, and these relate mainly to implementation issues, then I have noted this and provided the **relevant** information for each model. In general, this book should work for any Raspberry Pi that can run Python 3. Below is a guide to how Python 3 reacts to being run on various Raspberry Pi models.

Raspberry Pi 1 (2012): Python 3 can run on this model, but due to its limited processing power and memory (512 MB RAM), it may not perform well for more complex programs, such as graphics and use of high intensity modules such as NumPy.

Raspberry Pi 2 (2015): Python 3 runs smoothly on this Raspberry Pi. It features more processing grunt (Quad-core 900 MHz CPU) and 1 GB of RAM, allowing for better performance with Python applications.

Raspberry Pi 3 (2016): Python 3 runs very well on the Raspberry Pi 3, which has a Quad-core 1.2 GHz CPU and 1 GB RAM, making it suitable for more demanding Python applications, including GUI-based ones.

Raspberry Pi 3B+ (2018): Python 3 runs smoothly on this model, which has improved performance over the Pi 3 supporting a 1.4 GHz CPU.

Raspberry Pi 4 (2019): Python 3 comes into its own on the Pi 4. This model offers 8 GB of RAM, making it ideal for larger Python programs, and can handle graphics with ease.

Raspberry Pi 400 (2020): Python 3 works well on the 400. This model is a keyboard-integrated Raspberry Pi 4 with a 1.8 GHz CPU. It is effectively a 4 inside a keyboard!

Raspberry Pi 5/500 (2024) Python 3 is impressive on the 5. This model offers up to 8 GB of RAM, making it ideal for memory intensive programs.

Raspberry Pi Zero and Zero W (2015 and 2017): Python 3 runs on the Raspberry Pi Zero, but given the limited processing power (single-core 1 GHz CPU) and RAM (512 MB), performance may be slow.

Raspberry Pi Zero 2 W (2021): Python 3 runs on this model. It has improved performance over the original Zero with a Quad-core CPU and 512 MB RAM, making it more capable for Python tasks.

Raspberry Pi Pico: This is a different type of device compared to the standard Raspberry Pi models. It is a **microcontroller**, not a single-board computer, so it doesn't run a full operating system like Raspberry Pi OS. Instead, it runs programs directly on the hardware but uses a derivative of Python called MicroPython. This is discussed in Chapter 45.

Operating Systems: All Raspberry Pi versions running Raspberry Pi OS (formerly Raspbian and updated to Bookworm from Raspberry Pi 5), which come pre-installed with Python 3, will support Python 3 out of the box. Raspberry Pi OS maintains support for Python 3.x.

Python Types

Technically, there is only one Python programming language, but there are multiple implementations of Python that cater to different needs and environments. The most common Python implementations are:

Python: The standard implementation of Python edition and the one we are learning herein.

CPython: The reference implementation of Python, written in the C programming language. CPython = Python (the language) + C-based implementation.

Jython: Python implementation written in Java. Useful when you need to integrate Python with Java programs or Java-based frameworks.

PyPy: A Python implementation focused on speed, written in RPython (a restricted subset of Python). PyPy is discussed in Chapter 44.

IronPython: A Python implementation targeting the .NET framework and Mono (cross-platform implementation of .NET.)

MicroPython: A lean and efficient Python implementation designed to run on microcontrollers and small embedded systems.

Stackless Python: A Python implementation based on CPython but with added support for microthreads.

Brython: A Python implementation that runs entirely in the browser, converting Python code into JavaScript.

01: Hello

Python, alongside JavaScript and Java, is one of the most widely used programming languages in the world. Some might even say it's the most popular and significant, especially in the business world where it's the go-to software. If you're aiming to become a commercial programmer and haven't yet explored Python, you might find fewer doors open—**it's that essential**.

As a taster, look at these famous organisations and their uses of Python:

YouTube: the world's largest video-sharing platform, extensively uses Python for back-end services, including video sharing, website operation, and system administration. Python is known for being simple and easy to maintain, making it ideal for a platform like YouTube, which requires handling massive amounts of data and user interactions efficiently. Its strong libraries for web development, and support for data handling allow YouTube engineers to scale the platform easily.

Instagram: one of the most popular social media platforms, relies heavily on Python and its modules, for handling millions of active users and managing its back-end services. Instagram chose Python for its simplicity and ability to help developers write clean, maintainable code. It also helps Instagram scale its infrastructure efficiently. Python's scalability and speed in development cycles allowed Instagram to keep up with its explosive growth without compromising performance.

Spotify: the popular music streaming service uses Python for data analysis, back-end services, and machine learning to provide personalised recommendations. Python excels at handling large amounts of data, which Spotify needs for features like personalised music recommendations and user behaviour analysis. Its data science libraries for analytic and machine learning tasks. Additionally, Python's asynchronous framework capabilities, like Tornado and asyncio, enable Spotify to handle multiple concurrent connections (such as streaming requests) efficiently.

Reddit: is one of the largest online communities, is primarily written in Python. It uses Python for its back-end to manage user submissions, interactions, and content. Reddit originally started with Lisp but migrated to Python for its simplicity and wide range of libraries. Python allows Reddit to scale easily, handle millions of daily interactions, and manage a large amount of content without sacrificing performance. Python's versatility and Reddit's use of frameworks enable it to support its massive user base while remaining flexible for future growth. Reddit's decision to use Python also makes it easier to maintain and add new features over time.

Google: has used Python since its early days, and it plays a significant role in various parts of Google's infrastructure, including search algorithms, system management tools, and back-end services. Google values Python for its simplicity, speed of development, and readability. These attributes allow developers to write and maintain code quicker, which is crucial in a large-scale environment like Google. Python's flexibility also allows it to be used in everything from system administration to machine learning. For example, Google's internal systems (like parts of Google Search) and tools like YouTube Data API rely on Python. In fact, Guido van Rossum, the creator of Python, worked at Google for several years, and Google actively supports Python's development.

Netflix: utilises Python for content delivery, data analytic, and automation, playing a critical role in its recommendation algorithms and internal systems. Netflix uses Python for data streaming and analysis to track user preferences and optimise content recommendations. Python's powerful libraries, such as NumPy, Pandas, and TensorFlow. Additionally, Python helps Netflix automate content delivery and infrastructure management, making their systems more efficient and scalable.

NASA uses Python in various scientific computing and space research applications, including data analysis and simulations. Python's extensive scientific libraries (like SciPy and NumPy) and its ease of integration with other technologies make it ideal for complex scientific tasks. Python is widely used in scientific research because of its readability and vast array of scientific libraries. Python's ease of integration with other languages (such as C or Fortran for performance-critical code) also makes it an ideal choice for NASA, where various specialised tools and systems need to work together seamlessly.

Uber: uses Python for back-end services and data science tasks, helping manage its large-scale ride-sharing operations. Python's ease of use and ability to handle large-scale, real-time data processing makes it a natural fit for Uber's, fast-paced environment. Uber processes millions of ride requests, driver updates, and trip calculations in real-time, and Python's capabilities help manage these concurrent processes efficiently. Python also plays a critical role in Uber's data science efforts, where it's used for calculating estimated time of arrival (ETA), optimising routes, and pricing algorithms.

Pi Space

No wonder, then, that Python has found a cosy spot on the Raspberry Pi; it comes bundled with your Raspberry Pi OS installation at no extra charge!

So, what makes Python so special? It's known as a high-level language, which means it's designed with us humans in mind—**easy to read and write**. High-level languages are user-friendly and more abstract compared to low-level languages. Programmers love them because the code is easy to understand and maintain. Fun fact: another high-level language, C, was used to create Python itself, which is why Python's official name is C Python.

And no, the name has nothing to do with snakes. Python is named after a cult 70s British comedy show, *Monty Python's Flying Circus*. Remember John Cleese's 'Ministry of Silly Walks'? Classic! (If you haven't seen it, give it a search on YouTube.) There are more nods to the show sprinkled throughout the language.

At first glance, Python code might look a bit intimidating. Don't let that fool you. Despite its appearance, it's all about **readability**. Python emphasises 'structured programming,' nudging you to write clean and tidy code. It's like the language itself is helping you craft perfect programs. Structure is key in every aspect of life, so why should a programming language be any different?

One of Python's biggest charms is the availability of ready-made building blocks for writing programs, kind of like assembling a house from bricks. Think of these bricks as the building blocks of the language. In Python terms, they're called **libraries** and **modules**. They do exactly what they say on the tin—libraries of code with specific functions, and modules that provide exactly what you need.

The best part? You don't need to create each step from scratch. You simply pick the blocks you need and snap them together. Python's popularity ensures there are plenty of these resources available, all designed to make your coding life easier.

Python's syntax is simple and readable, making it a breeze for beginners. The way Python uses **line indentation** to define code blocks makes it easy to spot different parts of a program at a glance. Plus, Python allows you to execute commands and segments of code 'on the fly' thus allowing you see results immediately when typing commands at the prompt. You can almost test your code on the fly.

And let's not forget about the massive **'standard library'** that comes with Python—a treasure trove of pre-written code. You don't have to worry much about getting access to these tools because the standardised interface between them makes it super easy.

The standard library itself is ever **expanding**, or added to in the case of Bookworm on the Raspberry Pi 5. Modules such as NumPy that have normally had to be installed, is now part of the library, so well worth checking if its installed first.

This not only saves you time but also keeps your programs lightweight by only using what you need. Python's **cross-platform compatibility** means your programs can run smoothly on various operating systems like Windows, macOS, and Linux. Write it once, use it many times.

So, as we move forward, the code we write on the Raspberry Pi will be, for the most part, transferable to other environments. How great is that?

Python Uses

On the first page of this chapter, I outlined just some of the large multi-nationals who make use of Python everyday, indeed you could say it underpins a large chunk of their business functionality.

Python plays a pivotal role in the educational landscape of the Raspberry Pi, offering versatility beyond just coding for learning. Some of the remarkable applications of Python on the Raspberry Pi include:

Home Automation: Python is a go-to for automating and controlling smart home devices, enabling users to script interactions with sensors, cameras, lights, and more.

Making: With an extensive array of add-on like hats, robots, displays, and weather monitors, Python's libraries control these attachments seamlessly.

Web Development: Python serves as a capable tool for crafting web applications, making it ideal for web-based projects on the Raspberry Pi.

Game Development: Crafting simple games using Python and libraries like PyGame on the Raspberry Pi provides an enjoyable introduction to programming and game development.

IoT (Internet of Things): Python finds its niche in IoT projects, connecting sensors, actuators, and other IoT devices to the Raspberry Pi, facilitating communication with cloud services.

Data Science and Analytics: Many of the Python libraries support data science, machine learning, and analytics on the Raspberry Pi, empowering users to analyse data and run machine learning models.

Robotics: Python's prowess extends to programming robots and robotic systems on the Raspberry Pi, with add-on modules like 'GPIO Zero' simplifying hardware control.

Network Programming: Python's networking capabilities make it apt for projects involving device communication over a network, such as building a networked media centre or a file server.

Security and Penetration Testing: Python is an asset for security-related tasks, offering tools and libraries for penetration testing and network security on the Raspberry Pi.

Python on the Raspberry Pi is not just a programming language; it's a gateway to a multitude of exciting possibilities across various domains. The applications are endless.

Home Help

I personally use Python for a lot of things at home. It's so easy to use. Anything that involves, sorting, figures, text etc. For example, I use it for pulling together all my account data for the end of year tax return.

For this book, I typeset it using an application called *Affinity Publisher*. I created a program that extracts all the programs in the text and then test each one of them. Any errors are logged and changes can be made. This would otherwise be a time consuming copy and paste process.

It's up to you to come up with the ideas…

Learning

So, how do you go about learning Python? Well if you have this book you're well on your way. Given that fact there are some things to help:

Set Clear Goals

Decide why you want to learn Python: Do you want to use it for web development, data analysis, automation, or game development? Or do you just want to **learn**? Knowing your end goal will help guide your learning path.

Small Steps. For example, aim to write a small Python script within the first week, then move to more complex projects over time.

Get the Basics Right

Understand fundamental programming concepts. It's important, especially for Python. Keep an open mind and ensure you understand one chapter before jumping to the next one. Answer any questions and try a programming example. Get though correct. Then move on. Take existing programs and rework them for something you need.

Modify existing code: Try tweaking open-source code to see how things work. It helps you understand how small changes affect the program.

Practice, Practice, Practice

Consistent coding is the key. Even 20–30 minutes a day will build your skills faster than cramming once a week.

Stay Curious

Be open to learning new things as Python is vast and versatile. Try solving problems. Get online and check out the Python communities and forums. Keep in touch with the Raspberry Pi Python community.

Python 32-bit or 64-bit?

Python will run on either version of the ARM microprocessor. This is due to something called the Python Virtual Machine, which we'll look at later. So you are covered either way. There are some speed advantages with using A64 especially dealing with large sets of data.

02: Python Interactive

Open the Terminal window (that's the black box in the top left of your screen with '>_' inside it). Once you've got that open, type:

```
python3
```

And press the **<Enter>** key.

The Python Interpreter interactive command line will materialise, and include details such as the version of Python in use. You should see a prompt that looks like this:

```
>>>
```

This confirms that you're in the right spot. Just to be sure you're not mixing it up, the standard Terminal prompt is '>_'. Similar, but different enough to keep you on your toes! Note that the standard Terminal prompt will normally include details of your log-in such as:

```
pi@raspberrypi:~$
```

or similar

Now that you're in the **Python Interactive Shell** (no need to abbreviate here), you're ready to type in and execute Python code on the fly. Go ahead and type:

```
print("G'day mate")
```

Then press **<Enter>**. The code will run immediately, and the output will pop up on the line below. (Any guesses on what it might be?) I'm not Australian but living down under makes **"G'day mate"** a common term!

While the Python command line is super handy for quick tests and playing around with code, there's an even better way to work with Python as we shall see shortly.

To exit the interactive shell, just type:

```
exit()
```

at the **>>>** prompt, and hit the <Enter> key again.

You'll be whisked back to the Command Line of the Terminal, still in the same window.

Checking In

Some Raspberry Pi setups come with two versions of Python installed. On my Raspberry Pi 4B, when I typed:

```
python --version
```

(Note: That's **two** hyphens.)

It returned:

```
Python 2.7.2
```

However, when I typed:

```
python3 --version
```

It produced:

```
Python 3.7.3
```

Depending on your Raspberry Pi, you might see the same version for both commands, and it is probably different from mine. Python is constantly being updated, so you may have a newer version. Using **python3** ensures that version 3.x.x—the latest version on your Raspberry Pi—is used.

For those running the Bookworm version of the OS, you might only have one version of Python installed. Python 3.

This book focuses on Python version 3 and above. So, if you happen to have multiple versions installed, just remember to use Python 3, and I'll show you how to make sure of that shortly.

To ensure you have the latest version of Python, at the Terminal prompt type:

```
sudo apt update
```

and press <Enter>. Let everything update, and if it asks you anything, just reply with 'Y'.

When the cursor returns, type:

```
sudo apt full-upgrade
```

This command updates all the software 'packages' on your system, making sure they're the latest versions available for your OS, including those all-important Python packages. (You can check for any changes afterwards using the '**--version**' command.) Note that version numbers after 3.x can change quickly.

```
sudo apt install python3
```

Would ensure that Python3 was installed.

Don't worry if you don't have the absolute latest version of Python. Like I mentioned earlier, it's horses for courses. The version you have is almost certainly the right one for your version of the Raspberry Pi OS. Older versions of the Pi often run older versions of Python—makes sense, right?

Equally, as you upgrade your installation as the Raspberry Pi often suggest you do, you may well get an update on the version of Python you're using.

IDE

An **Integrated Development Environment**—what we in programming speak call an IDE—is pure bliss, like the best thing since **apple pie** and custard. So, let's get set up for some coding comfort. I recommend creating a directory in your Home folder. Maybe give it a name like 'PYTHON'. The name doesn't really matter, but something specific will help keep your coding projects organised. If you've downloaded the program files from my website, pop them into this folder.

Python programs are simply text files, a bunch of statements that, when combined just right, perform tasks. We group these statements into sets, each set handling a specific job. Bundle them together, and bingo—you've got a program.

The IDE is the hero of our coding adventure. Think of it as a magical space where you can create, run, and fix your programs, all within one window.

For this journey, our IDE of choice is 'Thonny', which is just perfect for beginners. You can find it under the Raspberry menu, nestled in the Programming drop-down menu. Once you open it, a screen like that shown in Figure 2a greet you.

(Don't worry if your screen looks a bit different. Looks and layout can vary slightly from version to version. I've put the numbers there for descriptive purposes!)

Maximise the Thonny window to fill your screen if you like, or just keep it as a normal floating window that you can resize as needed. The choice is yours. Thonny's interface is all about simplicity, designed to keep things smooth and easy as you write and run your Python code. While it might not be the top pick for larger projects, it works perfectly for our purposes..

Let's break down the Thonny window into three handy mini windows, each with its own job. I've numbered them 1, 2, and 3 for easy reference:

1. **Script Editor**: This is where the magic happens. Write your Python code here. It's clean, it's spacious, and it's your coding canvas.

2. **Shell**: Just below the Script Editor is the Interactive Python Shell. This is your playground for testing snippets of code on the fly, like what we did in the command line earlier. We call this a REPL (Read-Eval-Print Loop).

3. **Assistant**: On the right, this window gives you feedback about your program when it runs. If there's an error, it'll offer some hints on what might need fixing.

You can resize any of these windows individually by dragging their borders.

Across the very top of the window (Figure 2b), you'll find the menus as drop-downs and icons. These are laid out in a standard format, so they should feel familiar. Most are intuitive, but a few might make you pause—no worries, we'll explore their purposes as we go along. If you hover your pointer over the icons, a tool tip will pop up explaining what they do.

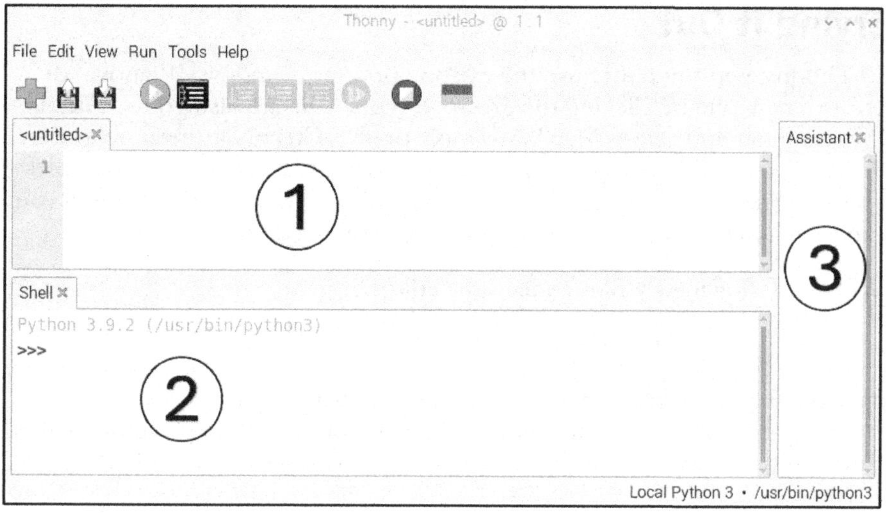

Figure 2a. Typical Thonny start-up screen.

Figure 2b The Thonny Menu Bar.

Now, if you glance at the bottom right-hand side of the Thonny window, you'll see something like this:

```
/usr/bin/python3
```

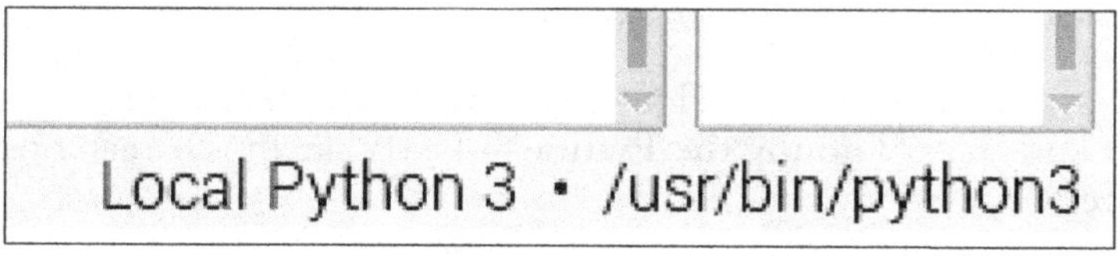

Figure 2c. Python version being used by Thonny, and its location.

This shows the version of Python that Thonny is using. The address following the version points to the location of the system version of Python.

Now, you're all set. The interface of Thonny. is a model of clarity, uncluttered and honed to the essential elements for Python coding. Thonny's user-friendly design boasts simplicity to ensure smooth writing and running of your programs. While it might not be the go-to IDE for larger, more complex programs, those are likely beyond the scope of this book.

Trying It Out

In Thonny, you can either use the existing program window ('1' above) or create a new one by clicking the green '+' icon. You can also go to "File" in the menu bar and select 'New', or simply press **<Ctrl+N>** (meaning press the 'Ctrl' and 'N' keys together). There are so many ways to start—just pick one and get going! This action will open a new tab in the code area, and you can switch between tabs by clicking the one you need.

Type the following Python code in the editor:

```
print("Hello from Thonny!")
```

Save the file by clicking on 'File' and selecting 'Save', or by pressing <Ctrl+S>. Choose a filename and location for your Python program, making sure to give it a **.py** extension. For example, you could save it as: **hello.py**

You'll see the name and directory of the file in the Thonny bar at the very top of the window.

To run the program, click on the green 'Run' button in the toolbar, select 'Run' from the menu bar, or simply press the 'F5' key as a shortcut. I've put a small yellow sticker on my F5 key—it makes it easy to find . Well worth doing. But any method is fine to run a program.

Thonny will execute the Python program, and you should see the output "Hello from Thonny!" displayed in the Shell pane at the bottom of the Thonny window.

If you look at the program window, you'll notice that the small tab might say **<untitled>*** at the top. This indicates that the file hasn't been saved yet. If it had the files name would be displayed here.

In case you're curious, Thonny draws its name from a fictional snake character known as **'Thonny the Python'**—kinda like the character on the front cover!

When writing Python programs, you can use either uppercase or lowercase characters, but there are some general conventions for when to use each. As we delve deeper into Python, we'll uncover and define these conventions.

A Real Program

Open a new code editor window by pressing the big green cross. Click in the Code Editor window and carefully enter the following:

```
#Filename: start1.py
import datetime
now = datetime.datetime.now()
print(now)
```

If you've downloaded the programs then this isn't included. You need to type it in. Now, let's bring this Python program to life. Hit the green '**Run**' button at the top of the window, and watch the result unfold in the '**Shell**' window. You should see the current date and time displayed down to six decimal points of a second!

Take a peek at the Assistant window—you should find a reassuring message confirming that your program is working perfectly, which is great considering we just ran it successfully!

Figure 2d. Date and Time in the Shell window.

You can also run this program in the Shell window of the IDE. Follow these steps:

1. In the Code Editor, select all three lines of the program by clicking and pressing <Ctrl-A>. Then, press <Ctrl-C> to copy.

2. Navigate to the Shell window, click inside to select it, and press <Ctrl-V> to paste the program there.

3. Finally, press <Enter> to run the program.

The same process applies when using the Python Interpreter in the Terminal window. Select the Terminal window, choose 'Paste' from the 'Edit' menu, and press <Enter> to execute the program.

In both scenarios, every line you enter in either the Thonny Shell or the Python Interpreter in the Terminal window gets executed immediately. You'll see an output whenever a line involves an action that displays a result.

Things to Note: Here' are a few things to note about the program above.

- The first line starts with a **hash symbol, '#'**. A Python program ignores anything after a line that starts with a hash symbol. This allows you to put comments or notes in your programs. As you can see, I use this to denote the filename of the program. Thus, the program here is called 'start1.py'. You'll find it listed as such in the download programs. You can use as many comment lines as you wish. Don't go overboard otherwise you lose the program within the comments. And for the scope of this book, you don't need to type them in, if you are doing that.
- The program shows how we have used an imported item, by the name of **datetime**. This item is called a 'module' and contains the routines we needed to retrieve and print the date and time. A module is a file that contains Python code—which you can use in your own programs. For example, the datetime module helps you work with dates and times."
- The last lines gather information required and then displays it, and while you might now know the exact syntax of the rest of the program means you can read it and understand what is happening.

Thonny Windows

Thonny is flexible because it has several additional windows you can open and display. You can explore these by selecting the 'View' menu at the top of the window. A good one to add is the 'Files' window. You can navigate to your programs and load them with a double click, as shown in Figure 2e below. Note how the 'Files' window that the Python logo signifies Python programs.

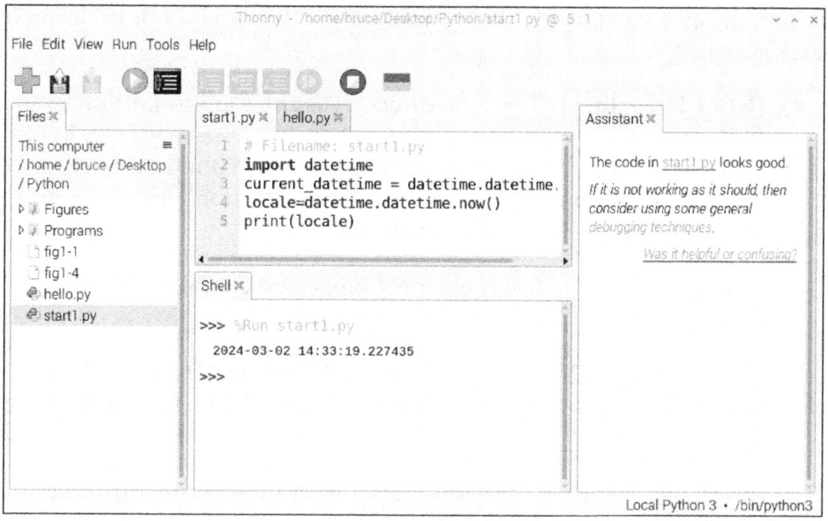

Figure 2e. Additional Thonny windows. Files is useful to keep open.

The Raspberry Pi File System

Understanding the file system on your Raspberry Pi is essential for any programmer. The system files are in what's known as the '**root**' directory, which is the starting point of the operating system. If you want to explore these files on Raspberry Pi OS, just open a Desktop window and use the **File Explorer** to check out the root directories.

Familiarising yourself with these system files helps you understand the structure of your Pi and makes customisation easier. Trust me, this knowledge will come in handy later, as we'll see in Chapter 03.

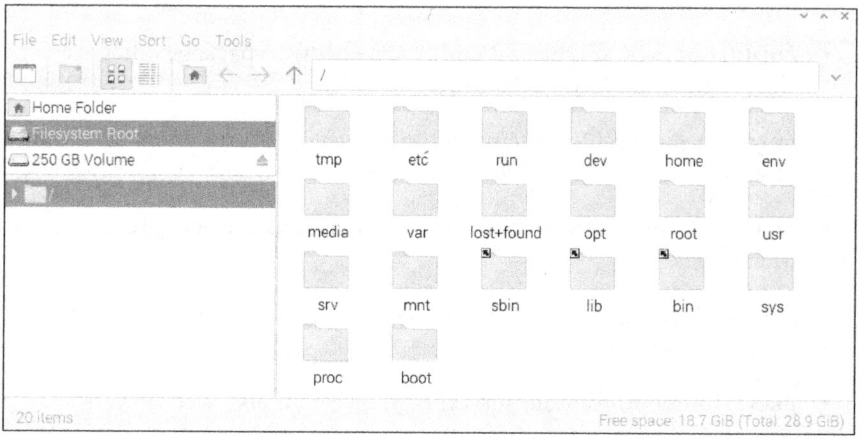

Figure 2f. Folders in the root directory.

Don't be shy about exploring these folders—just be careful not to delete or change anything.

- **/ (Root Directory):** The root directory is the top-level directory in the file system. Everything in the file system branches out from here. Note in **/root**, it's the home directory for the root user, but you should understand that regular users typically don't interact with it unless using administrative privileges.
- **/bin**: This directory holds essential binary executables (commands) necessary for system recovery and repair.
- **/boot**: Here, you'll find the files needed for your Raspberry Pi to boot up, including the bootloader, configuration files like '**config.txt**,' and the kernel.
- **/dev**: Contains device files that represent physical and virtual devices like disks, serial ports, and even random number generators.
- **/etc**: A treasure trove of system-wide configuration files and scripts. If you need to tweak installed software, you'll likely find its config files here.
- **/home**: This is where user home directories live. Each user on the system has their own sub-directory under '/home.'
- **/lib and /lib64**: These directories store essential shared library files that both the system and applications rely on.
- **/media**: If you plug in a USB drive or other removable media, it often gets mounted here.
- **/mnt**: This is a common spot for temporarily mounting file systems.
- **/opt**: Here, you might find additional software packages that aren't part of the default installation.
- **/proc**: A virtual file system offering a wealth of information about processes and system status.
- **/run**: This directory contains run-time data like process IDs and socket files.
- **/sbin**: Home to system binaries (commands) typically used by the system administrator.
- **/srv**: Intended for data served by the system, like web servers.
- **/sys**: Another virtual file system, exposing kernel and device information.

- **/tmp**: A temporary storage area for files, often wiped clean when the system reboots.
- **/usr**: This directory is packed with user-related programs, libraries, documentation, and other files.
- **/var**: This is where you'll find variable data files, like logs, spool files, and temporary files that stick around even after a reboot.

In the **/home** directory, you'll find a folder with your username—your personal space on the Pi. This is where all your folders and files live. If you need, you can create additional users, each with their own separate environment, allowing you to compartmentalise your Pi experience.

Head over to your **/home/username** directory to access all your data. Here, you'll come across folders like **Desktop**, **Pictures**, **Documents**, **Downloads**, and more. This is the ideal place to organise your programming world. Jumping back to Figure 2c you'll remember that the Python version we're using is located in: **usr/bin/.**

Important Line Wraps

Many of the lines of Python code in the rest of these books are too long to sit on one line. They therefore wrap into a second or more. If your type a program in and there is an error when you run the program than look at the error message and see if you can solve the issue for yourself. This may simply be deleting the <Enter> you have inserted as part of the line wrap.

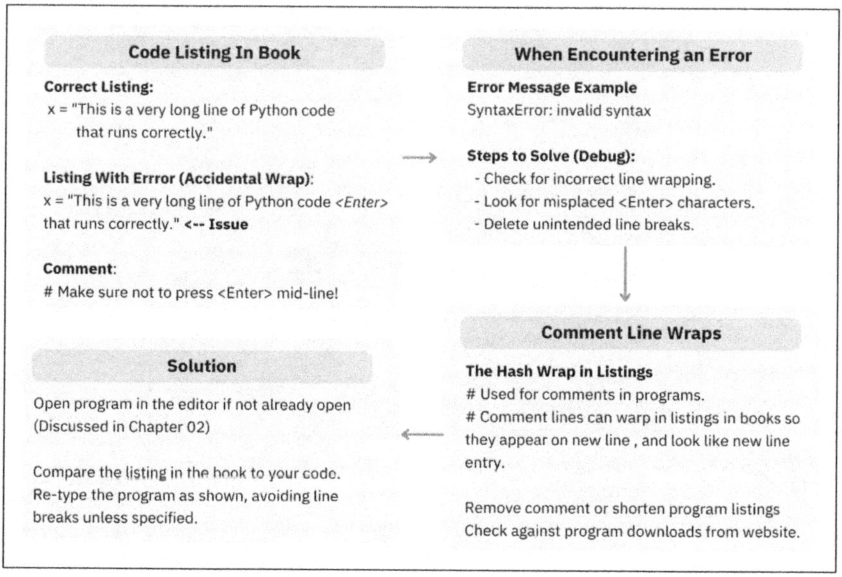

Figure 2g. Investigating Line Wraps

Questions

1. What command do you use to start the Python interactive shell from the Terminal window? And how do you exit the Python interactive shell and return to the regular Terminal prompt?
2. Which command should you run to check the version of Python 3 on your Raspberry Pi?
3. Why is it important to use the command 'python3' instead of 'python' when running Python code in this book?
4. What command updates the software packages, including Python, to the latest version on your Raspberry Pi?
5. What is displayed in the bottom-right corner of the Thonny window, and why is it important?
6. What is the purpose of a Python module? Give an example of a module used in the text.

03: A Matter of Style

Okay. You might find the opening section of this chapter requires some head-scratching—especially the terminology. But give it a go, work through the chapter, and then maybe come back here a second time to understand it better. It may not seem like it now, but these concepts will become second nature without you even noticing. Many people will shudder at me putting this chapter here, and many will simply ignore it. But I just want you to know how important it is. Feel free to skip it if you are confused, but do come back to it when you have completed the first dozen or so chapters.

Object-Oriented Programming

OOP is a style of programming that uses, as its name suggests, "objects" to construct programs. It allows you to model and manage the properties and behaviour of program code as 'real-world' concepts, making them more 'lifelike.' In your mind's eye, you can start to draw comparisons. Terms such as **inheritance** and **encapsulation** may seem complex at first, but they become clear with understanding and practice. They mean the same as they do in real life. You inherit something. You encapsulate something. Other terms, such as polymorphism and abstraction, may not be as intuitive but shouldn't impede understanding or, more importantly, your learning of Python programming.

What's important are the key building blocks of OOP. In Python, there are four fundamental concepts to grasp:

- Class
- Object
- Attributes
- Methods

The Block

Think of a **class** as a blueprint for a house. The blueprint outlines the structure, layout, and characteristics of the house, such as the number of bedrooms, the number of restrooms, and how many parking spaces there are. Is there a pool? These are the **attributes** of the class. A class contains attributes that define the characteristics of the object it creates.

From this blueprint, you can create multiple houses, each an **instance** of the class. For example, you could use the blueprint to construct a dozen identical houses on a street—a "block." However, not everyone wants an identical house. Some families might modify theirs: one might forgo a pool, another might convert the basement into an entertainment room, and so on.

To make these changes, you can adjust the **attributes** directly or use a **method** to do so. For example, if you want to convert a room into an entertainment room, you might create a method like **convert_to_entertainment_room()** that updates the relevant attributes. This is an example of **encapsulation**: bundling data (attributes) and methods (actions) within the class, so the class manages its own state and behaviours. **Abstraction** also plays a role here, as the method hides the complexity of the conversion, exposing a simple action for the user to call.

In this analogy:

- A **class** is the blueprint of the house.
- **Attributes** are the features of the house (e.g., number of bedrooms, presence of a pool).
- **Methods** are actions that can be performed by or on the house (e.g., unlocking a door, turning on the lights).

There are three methods here: **unlock_door():** A method to unlock the front door; **turn_on_lights()**: A method to turn on the house's lights; and **convert_to_entertainment_room()**: A method to re-purpose a room.

Changing a room's purpose is called modifying the state of the object. If done via a method like convert_to_entertainment_room(), it showcases how classes manage changes to their internal attributes or state.

In this case, modifying an attribute or changing the state of an object would be a way to describe the process of adapting the class to make a room into an entertainment room. If you are creating a specific method like `convert_to_entertainment _room()`, it's an example of encapsulation, where the logic to make the change is handled within the class itself. Encapsulation refers to bundling the data (attributes) and methods (actions) within a class, ensuring that the object manages its own state and behaviours. **Abstraction** also plays a role here because the method hides the complexity of how the room is converted, only exposing a simple action for the user to call.

Think of a **method** as something the house can do or an action that can be performed on the house. Just like living in a house involves doing certain things, like unlocking the door, turning on the lights, or opening the garage, methods are actions that can be performed by an object created from a class.

This house blueprint can be used to construct multiple houses with shared features and design principles-but all based on the same plan, with adjustments as needed. Attributes are the ingredients in this 'House' recipe.

Constructor and Attributes

When creating an object, its attributes are set up using a **constructor**, a special method typically named **__init__** in Python. The constructor initialises the object's attributes with specific values. For example:

```
class House:
    def __init__(self, bedrooms, restrooms, garage,
basement, pool):
        self.bedrooms = bedrooms
        self.restrooms = restrooms
        self.garage = garage
        self.basement = basement
        self.pool = pool
```

This constructor initialises the object's attributes with values. A constructor is a method.

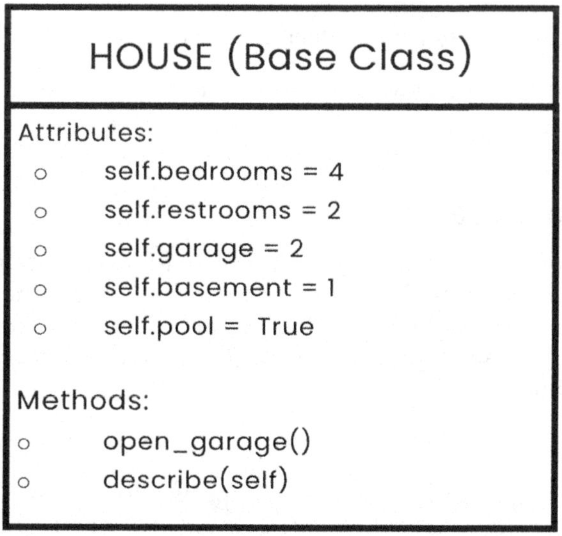

Figure 3a. The House Base Class blueprint.

Encapsulation ensures that these attributes are controlled and accessed only through specific methods, hiding the internal data from external modification. Each instance variable (e.g., self.bedrooms) belongs to a specific object, allowing each house (object) to have unique features.

Inheritance and Polymorphism

Inheritance allows us to extend the blueprint of a base class to create specialised versions. For instance, we might create subclasses like TownHouse, Bungalow, or Villa. These subclasses inherit attributes and methods from the base House class but can also add new ones or override existing ones. For example, a TownHouse class might inherit the bedrooms and restrooms attributes but introduce a new **number_of_floors** attribute. Inheritance allows us to reuse and extend the blueprint without rewriting everything from scratch.

Polymorphism allows these subclasses to define methods with the same name as those in the base class but with different behaviours. For instance, a **describe()** method in the House class might provide a generic description of a house, while the TownHouse class overrides it to include details like the number of floors. This flexibility makes OOP wonderfully flexible, enabling different classes to share a common interface while behaving differently.

- The **class** is the blueprint.
- **Attributes** are the features of the house.
- **Methods** are the actions the house can perform.
- **Inheritance** extends the blueprint for new types of houses.
- **Polymorphism** allows subclasses to implement shared methods in their own way.

Class Instance

The diagram opposite (Figure 3b) builds on the previous one and aims to provide a visual representation of how this works. We have the **House Base Class**, which lists the attributes of the class inside the box. This serves as a blueprint for all houses in a development. The base class house includes the following attributes:

- Four bedrooms, two restrooms, double garage, basement and pool

Next to the base class diagram, we have a specific house that is an instance created from this base class/blueprint. This individual house has the following attributes:

- Four bedrooms, two restrooms, double garage, no basement, no pool

This means it is based on the blueprint (the **base class**) but with altered attributes, demonstrating how instances of a class can have their own unique attribute values.

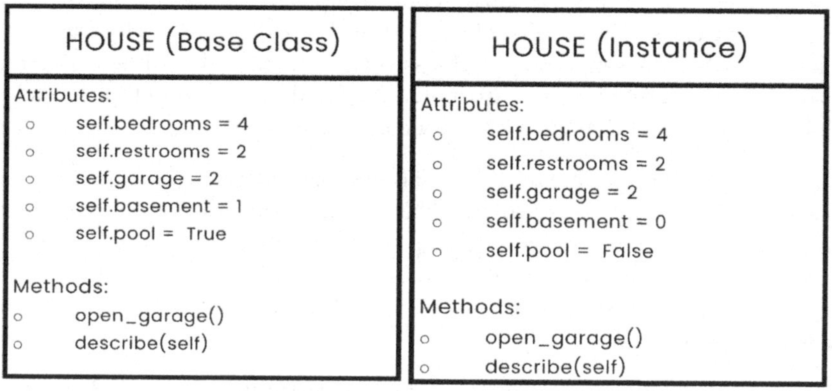

Figure 3b. Base class and an instance of a class.

As mentioned earlier, the attributes are defined using a special method called a constructor, typically named __init__ in Python. The constructor is a method that is automatically called when a new object of the class is created. It allows attributes to be customised during object creation by accepting parameters. For example:

```
class House:
    def __init__(self, bedrooms, restrooms, garage,
basement, pool):
        self.bedrooms = bedrooms
        self.restrooms = restrooms
        self.garage = garage
        self.basement = basement
        self.pool = pool
```

In this example, the constructor initialises the attributes of the house using the values provided as arguments when the object is created. For example:

```
house1 = House(4, 2, “double”, False, True)
house2 = House(3, 1, "single", True, False)
```

Here, house1 and house2 are two different **instances** of the House class, each with their own unique attributes.

These attributes are known as **instance variables** because they are specific to each instance (or object) of the House class. Each object has its own set of these variables, meaning no two objects share attribute values unless explicitly programmed to do so. This allows for the creation of multiple houses with different attributes. For example, one house might have a pool while another does not.

Derived Classes

Using House as a base class, we can create more specific types of houses like Townhouses, Bungalows, or Villas. These classes are derived from the original base class. They are still houses, but they differ in structure and behaviour while sharing some of the same attributes and methods. These derived classes can inherit the attributes and methods of the House class while also introducing their own unique characteristics.

For example, we might create a TownHouse class as a derived class of House. A townhouse shares many of the same attributes as a generic house (e.g., bedrooms, restrooms, garage) but has additional or modified characteristics, such as driveway_parking or end_of_row. These new attributes reflect the specific features of a townhouse that aren't present in the base House class.

In some cases, the derived class may override attributes or methods from the base class to better represent its specific type. For instance, while a generic House might have a describe() method that provides a basic description of the house, the TownHouse class could override this method to include details like "end-of-row" status or "shared walls."

Key Concepts

- **Inheritance**: Derived classes reuse attributes and methods from the base class, avoiding code duplication.
- **Overriding**: Derived classes can redefine methods or attributes to customise their behaviour.
- **Extensibility**: The base class (House) provides a foundation, while derived classes (TownHouse, Bungalow, etc.) add or modify features to create specific types of houses.

Methods in Derived Classes

Derived classes can override methods from the base class or define their own unique methods. For example, a **TownHouse** class might override the **describe()** method to exclude information about a pool (since townhouses typically don't have pools) and include details specific to townhouses, such as their position in a row of houses. Here's an example

```
class TownHouse(House):
    def describe(self):
        return f"This townhouse has {self.bedrooms}
bedrooms, {self.restrooms} restrooms, and is part of a
row of houses."
```

In this method, the placeholders (**{self.bedrooms}** and **{self.restrooms}**) are replaced with the values of the respective attributes. For instance, if self. bedrooms is 3, the output will show "This townhouse has 3 bedrooms...".

This structure exemplifies the principles of OOP, where objects (houses) have both data (attributes) and behaviour (methods) that model real-world entities.

Polymorphism Example

Polymorphism allows objects of different derived classes to be treated as instances of the base class. Even though each derived class implements its own version of methods (like describe()), they can all be used through a common interface. Here's an example:

```
house = House(4, 2, "double", False, True)
townhouse = TownHouse(3, 2, "single")

print(house.describe())
# Output: A house with 4 bedrooms, 2 restrooms, and a
double garage.

print(townhouse.describe())
# Output: This townhouse has 3 bedrooms, 2 restrooms,
and is part of a row of houses.
```

In this example:

- The describe() method behaves differently depending on the type of object calling it (a House or a TownHouse), demonstrating polymorphism in action.

- Both objects can use the describe() method through the shared interface of the base class, but each provides behaviour specific to its class.

Additional Examples: Classes Galore

To further understand inheritance and method customisation, let's consider a **Vehicle** base class. This class might have attributes like **make, seats, model, colour,** and **year.** It could also have methods like **power(), refuel(), drive(), stop(),** and **reverse()**. A derived class called **ElectricVehicle** could inherit most of these attributes and methods but replace the **refuel()** method with **charge()** to represent how electric vehicles operate.

Another Example: Shapes

Here's an analogy using shapes to illustrate inheritance and customisation:

- **Base Shape**: A generic shape with common characteristics, such as length and width. It might include a method to calculate the area (length * width).
- **Derived Shape (Rectangle)**: A rectangle is a specific kind of shape. It inherits the attributes length and width from the base shape and calculates the area using the base method.
- **New Shape (Circle):** A circle doesn't have length and width; it has a radius. While it may still use the concept of area, it overrides the method to calculate the area using the formula for a circle (π * radius^2

Here:

- **Inheritance**: Allows new shapes (e.g., Rectangle) to reuse and extend features of the base class (Shape) without rewriting everything.
- **Customisation**: New shapes (e.g., Circle) can override or define their own methods while remaining conceptually related to the base class.
- **Polymorphism**: Objects of different derived classes (Rectangle, Circle) can be treated uniformly as instances of the base class (Shape), but each implements its own specific behaviour.

Programming with OOP

Here's how you might typically construct a program to represent the OOP concepts we've discussed. These code snippets might not make sense immediately, but take your time to examine each one closely—you'll see how they fit together. The terminology used is intentionally simple and clear.

Example 1: The House Class

```
class House:
    def __init__(self, bedrooms, bathrooms, has_pool):
        self.bedrooms = bedrooms  # Attribute
        self.bathrooms = bathrooms  # Attribute
        self.has_pool = has_pool  # Attribute

    def unlock_door(self):  # Method
        print("The door is unlocked.")

    def turn_on_lights(self):  # Method
        print("The lights are turned on.")

    def fill_pool(self):  # Method
        if self.has_pool:
            print("The pool is being filled.")
        else:
            print("This house doesn't have a pool.")
```

In this example:

Attributes like bedrooms, bathrooms, and has_pool describe the house's characteristics.

Methods like unlock_door(), turn_on_lights(), and fill_pool() describe actions that can be performed by or on the house.

Example 2: Converting a Room to an Entertainment Room

We can add functionality to convert a room into an entertainment room:

```
class House:
    def __init__(self, bedrooms, bathrooms, has_pool,
rooms):
        self.bedrooms = bedrooms
        self.bathrooms = bathrooms
        self.has_pool = has_pool
        self.rooms = rooms

    def convert_to_entertainment_room(self, room):
        if room in self.rooms:
            self.rooms[self.rooms.index(room)] =
'entertainment room'
            print(f"The {room} has been converted into
an entertainment room.")
        else:
            print(f"There is no {room} to convert.")
```

Here, he convert_to_entertainment_room() method modifies the rooms list. It checks if the specified room exists and, if so, updates it to "entertainment room."

Example 3: Adding a Garage

```
class House:
    def __init__(self, bedrooms, bathrooms, garage_
size, has_garage):
```

```
            self.bedrooms = bedrooms
            self.bathrooms = bathrooms
            self.garage_size = garage_size
              # Number of cars the garage can hold
            self.has_garage = has_garage
              # Boolean to indicate if house has a garage

        def open_garage(self):
            if self.has_garage:
                print(f"The garage door is opening... This
    garage can fit {self.garage_size} cars.")
            else:
                print("This house does not have a garage.")
```

You can create an instance of the House class and call its methods:

```
my_house = House(bedrooms=3, bathrooms=2, garage_
size=2, has_garage=True)
my_house.open_garage()
```

Output:

```
The garage door is opening... This garage can fit 2
cars.
```

You can expand this by adding more methods, such as:

```
def close_garage(self):
    if self.has_garage:
        print("The garage door is closing...")
    else:
        print("This house does not have a garage.")
```

Combining Snippets into a Full Program

You may feel that this chapter is way to advanced to be at the front of the book. It probably is. But OOP is essential to life on Python. Some of what you have read will stick, and as I've said, and promise, these concepts will go almost unnoticed by you and everything will fall into place as you continue on. Re-read this chapter every few chapters of the book. More will stick.

These snippets of code can be combined to create a comprehensive program. While we won't combine them here, I encourage you to experiment and build on these examples as you progress through the book. Keep tripping back here until you can create the completed program. Then you'll fully understand OOP! I promise it will happen.

04: Foundations

I like to think of the key components that make up a Python program as "wrappers." These wrappers are like containers for the code you write, and when you put them together in the right order, you create a fully functioning program. Imagine it like **Ferrero Rocher** chocolates—each one wrapped in shiny gold foil. In this analogy, the chocolates represent your code, and the box of chocolates is the complete program. Each wrapper (or section of your program) encapsulates a piece of code, just like those gold foils enclose a delicious treat.

In Python, these wrappers are known as **functions**, and they're created using the **def** keyword (short for define). This def keyword is essential because each function you create needs a unique name. Technically, you could have two functions with different names doing the same thing, but having multiple functions doing the same thing is not a great practice due to redundancy and maintainability issues. Plus it's just plain silly. Here's the basic syntax for defining a function:

```
def function_name(parameters):
    #Function body
    #Perform desired operations
    #Return a value if needed
```

Let's break it down:

- **def**: This keyword starts your function definition. This normally occurs inside a class definition.
- **function_name**: This is the name you give your function.
- **parameters or arguments:** These are the optional values you can pass into your function. They're enclosed in parentheses and separated by commas if there's more than one.

- **:** (colon): This signals the end of the function declaration and the start of the function's code.
- **#** (hash): This symbol allows you to place comments in the code. Everything after it on that line is ignored by Python. Note the hash is not part of the function definition. It's just a comment.
- **Function body**: This is where the magic happens—the code inside the function executes, possibly using the arguments you provided.
- **return**: If your function needs to return a value, you use this keyword. If not, you can skip it.

Using the def keyword to define functions helps you keep your code organised, making it easier to reuse sections later. Once you've defined a function, you can call it by its name followed by parentheses, which triggers the function to run and return a result if necessary. And the best part? You can call your function as many times as you like.

Here's a conceptual look at how a Python program might operate:

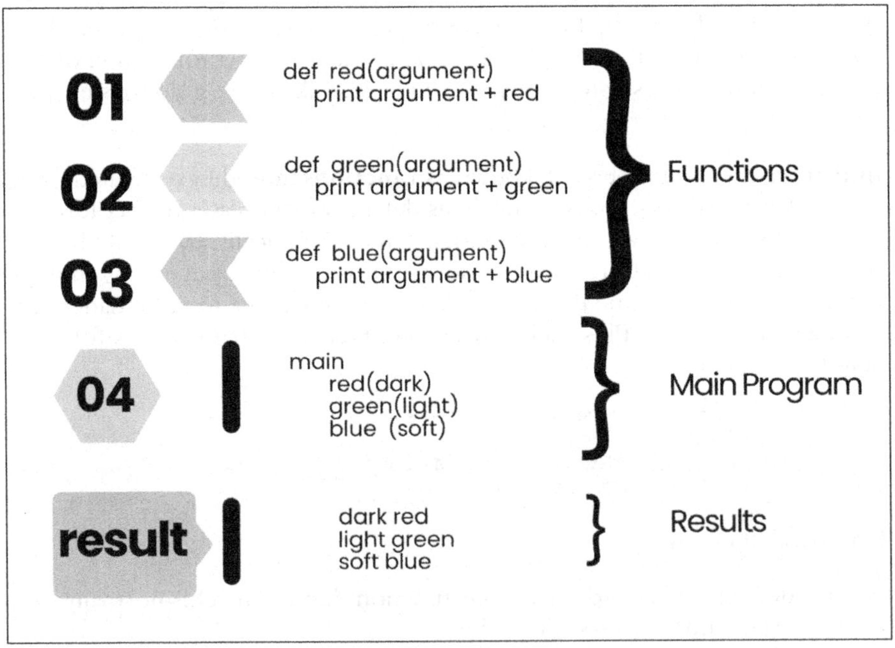

Figure 4a. Stylised version of a Python programs' operation.

In this diagram, we enter at 'main,' with each function being called and passing an argument to the next. It's not necessary to have functions right at the start of a program, but it helps keep things organised.

Each function takes its argument, performs its task (maybe even adding its own flair), and when the program finishes, it outputs the result. Hopefully, this gives you a clear sense of how a structured Python program works and makes the whole thing easier to understand. Any Python program can be organised this way, giving your code a neat, logical flow (The numbers are the start of each line are from reference only and should not be typed in.).

```
1        #Filename: function1.py
2        def greet(name):
3                return f"Hello, {name}!"

4        message = greet("John")
5        print(message)
6        #Output: Hello, John!
```

In this example, we define a function named 'greet' with a parameter called 'name' (2). The function simply appends the value of 'name' to the word 'Hello' and then returns the combined words (3). This returned value is then stored in the container '**message**' (4), which is finally printed on the screen (5). In this specific case, the value passed as the 'name' parameter is 'John'. (Item 1 is a comment depicting the filename in the downloadable programs.)

When you run the program, it displays:

```
Hello, John
```

Let's break this down using Object-Oriented Programming (**OOP**) concepts:

Function Definition (Method):

def greet(name): defines a function called 'greet'. In OOP, functions that belong to classes are known as methods. Here, 'greet' is a method that takes a parameter called 'name'.

Function Call (Object Instantiation):

message = greet("John") is like creating an instance of an object in OOP. By calling the 'greet' method with the argument "John," you're essentially creating an instance of that function, and the result is stored in the variable container 'message'.

Printing the Output (Object Interaction):

print(message) can be thought of as interacting with an object. You're using the print command to display the result stored in 'message'. In OOP terms, this could be analogous to accessing an object's properties or calling its methods.

So, in a nutshell, this program involves defining a method ('greet'), creating an instance with specific data ("John"), and then interacting with that instance by printing the result. While this example doesn't fully dive into class-based OOP, it does touch on some core OOP principles like encapsulation (the function), instantiate (creating an instance with data), and interaction (printing the result).

Modules and Libraries

Think of a module as a single file of Python code—a Python program, really. It's like a toolbox that holds a bunch of related tools, organising and wrapping up your code nicely. For instance, remember that time we used the 'datetime' module in a previous program (Page 28)? This module has a whole set of functions specifically for working with dates and times. Once you've imported the datetime module, you can access all these handy tools whenever you need them.

A library is like a bigger toolbox that holds multiple modules. It's a collection of related modules that work together to help you with various tasks. You often see these libraries getting installed when you add new software to your Raspberry Pi or update your programs.

Let's break it down with a simple diagram (imagine a neat little sketch here) to show how modules and libraries relate to each other:

- **Module**: the module itself, which acts like a container holding code. Inside a module, you'll find classes and functions just some of the building blocks that give the module its functionality. (There are others but…)
- **Library**: a collection of modules. Each module in the library handles a specific set of tasks.

This setup describes how a library bundles multiple modules, each packed with different elements, to provide a wide range of tools for your programming projects.

Libraries are super useful because they save you from reinventing the wheel every time you need to solve a common programming problem. Python comes with a '**standard library**' a base set of modules that offer all sorts of functionality right out of the box. And then there are third-party libraries created by the Python community that take things even further. For example, the Math and Science folks often use these four modules:

- **NumPy**: For numerical operations and array manipulation.
- **SciPy**: For scientific and technical computing.
- **SymPy**: For symbolic mathematics.
- **Pandas**: For data manipulation and analysis.

Here's the code for **datetime** again:

```
import datetime
locale = datetime.datetime.now()
```

In this case:

Module: The datetime module is part of Python's standard library and is used for handling date and time operations (first datetime).

Class: Within the datetime module, the datetime class represents date and time (second datetime). For the time being think of 'class' as being a function.

(Dot/Period): The period separates the module (datetime) from the class (datetime) and then from the method **now()**. (We want the date and time right now!)

So, in this example, datetime is the **module**. When you write import datetime, you're importing the datetime module from Python's standard library. Then, when you use **datetime.datetime.now()**, you're calling an 'action' from the datetime 'function' (class) within that module to get the current date and time. The datetime module contains other utilities too, such as date and time.

Here's another example, but this time with a simple Python function:

```
#Filename: function2.py
def add_numbers(a, b):
    result = a + b
    print(result)

#Example use:
add_numbers(3, 5)
```

In this snippet, we define a function called '**add_numbers**' that takes two inputs, 'a' and 'b'. The function adds the two numbers that are represented by 'a' and 'b' (remember algebra?) together, stores the result in a mystical container called 'result', and then prints it on the screen. When you call this function with 'add_numbers(3, 5)', it will return 8.

This code doesn't require a module, as this addition is handled within the standard Python release. More complex math does though. For example, when calculating a square route, as this modified program shows:

```
#Filename: function3.py
import math
def sq_root(a, b):
    result = math.sqrt(a + b)
    print(result)

#Example use:
sq_root(14, 2)
```

Could you organise the above two programs as a single class? Answer at the end of this chapter with example.

Modules and libraries are great for organising your code and collaborating with others. By importing the right modules and libraries into your project, you can tap into their functionality and boost your productivity without bloating your software. This modular approach means you can bring in only the components you need and easily remove them when you don't. And the great thing is that these modules and libraries don't cost a penny. Just help yourself.

Python Interactive Shell

You can run programs directly in the Thonny shell, whether they're just one-liners or longer programs. Thonny evaluates each line as you type it, giving you instant feedback. You can also do this kind of "dynamic" typing in the Python Shell from the Terminal window, as we talked about earlier. But if you need to quickly check something or do a bit of calculation, Thonny is super handy since it's "right there".

Let's try a simple three-line program in the Thonny Shell that shows you the current directory you're working in. Type these three lines one after the other and watch how the colours change—purple for 'import', 'pink' for dir and 'print', and 'green' for "Current Directory". This makes it easier to see the structure of your program and is easier on the eyes:

```
import os
dir = os.getcwd()
print("Current Directory:", dir)
```

When you hit <Enter> after the last line, Thonny will show you the directory you're currently working in. For me, it looks something like this:

```
/home/bruce/Desktop/Python
```

Now, let's switch to the Terminal and open the Python shell by typing:

```
python3
```

Want to see what files are in your current directory? Just type these lines one after the other:

```
import os
dir = os.getcwd()
files = os.listdir(dir)

for file in files:
    print(file)
```

Notice that when you press <Enter> after the second-to-last line, the shell shows **three dots (...)** instead of the usual **>>>** prompt. This happens because the next command needs to be indented, so just press the <Tab> key before typing the last line, 'print(file)'. After that, press <Enter> twice to run the program. You should see a listing of the files in your current directory—probably your 'raspberrypi' folder unless you've changed it. (Mine's 'bsb'.)

Quick tip: you don't need to use import the os module again if you've already used it earlier in the same session (meaning you haven't closed the shell window). This command just brings in a module of extra commands that work with the operating system—hence, os.

We've introduced a couple of new commands here. Just roll with them for now. We'll dive deeper into what they do later. To exit the Python shell, simply type **exit()** or **quit()** and press <Enter>.

Terminal Shell

We've dabbled with the Terminal a few times now, but what exactly is it? Think of the Terminal as your direct line to the Raspberry Pi's **brain**. It's a text-based interface that lets you communicate with the operating system using commands. This interface is often called the **command-line interface**, or CLI for short. By typing in commands, you can perform all sorts of tasks, from basic file management to running programs.

Now, behind the scenes, lurking under the bonnet of the Raspberry Pi, there's something called **Bash**. Bash is like the translator between you and the Raspberry Pi. It's a command processor, or shell, that interprets whatever you type into the Terminal and then makes the **magic** happen. Bash is the default shell on the Raspberry Pi, so it's the one doing all the heavy lifting when you use the Terminal.

When you open a Terminal window, you'll see a prompt where you can start typing commands. Once you hit <Enter>, the Terminal sends your command over to Bash, which processes it and shows you the results right there in the same window. Bash is like the middleman, ensuring that what you say gets understood and acted upon by the computer, or generates an error if you type incorrectly.

On systems like Raspberry Pi OS, Bash is the main go-to for this kind of interaction. It takes your command, does its thing, and shows you the results in the same window. To put it simply, the Terminal is where you do the talking, and Bash is the one who makes sure the computer gets the message.

We've seen this in action a few times, especially when playing around with the Python interpreter. The CLI is a handy tool, not just for Python, but for doing all sorts of things. You can even run your Python programs directly from the CLI.

Remember that PYTHON folder we created for our programs? Go ahead and right-click on it from the Desktop and choose the **'Open in Terminal'** option. Now, the CLI is pointing right to that folder. If you want to see what files are inside, just type:

```
ls
```

And to run a Python program, simply use this command:

```
python3 function3.py
```

Where 'function3.py' is the name of your program. And there you go!

Bytecode

Python on a Raspberry Pi works pretty much the same way it does on any other computer, but programmers often tweak things to suit the Pi's unique features. The Raspberry Pi provides a great environment for running Python applications, making it popular for education, prototyping, and all sorts of DIY projects.

But how does a simple text file—the program—turn into something that computers as different as a Raspberry Pi, Windows PCs, and Macs can run? To get there, we need to understand how the two main types of program execution work: using an **interpreter** or a **compiler**.

Interpreted Languages

With interpreted languages, not surprisingly, an interpreter reads your program code, line by line and performs the actions on the fly. This means the interpreter **translates** and executes the code in real-time, giving you flexibility. One big plus is that interpreted languages are platform-independent—your code can run on any system that has the interpreter installed. However, the trade-off is that this can slow things down a bit since the translation happens as the program runs, every time. This also means that errors pop up while running the program, but once you fix them, the program will flow smoothly.

An analogy is a chef who has a recipe book and cooks by working through the instructions one by one. Retrieving what he needs at each step and carrying out any actions required -get four eggs and break the eggs into a bowl.

The interpreter is typically installed on your Raspberry Pi as part of the development environment for the language you are using. Many IDEs come with built-in support for interpreters. They allow you to run code directly within the IDE, using the interpreter you've installed.

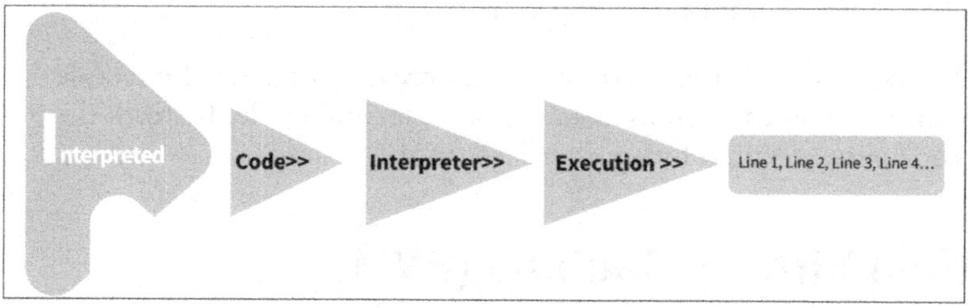

Figure 4b. Interpreting a language process.

Compiled Languages

Compiled languages work a bit differently. Before you can run the program, a compiler is used to translate it into machine code. This process involves converting the entire program into an executable file that the computer's hardware can run directly. The advantage here is performance—compiled programs run faster because they don't need to be translated on the fly. However, this comes at the cost of flexibility and development time, as any changes to the code mean you need to recompile the program.

Continuing the chef analogy above. In this case the chef gets everything together he required and in one action creates the recipe.

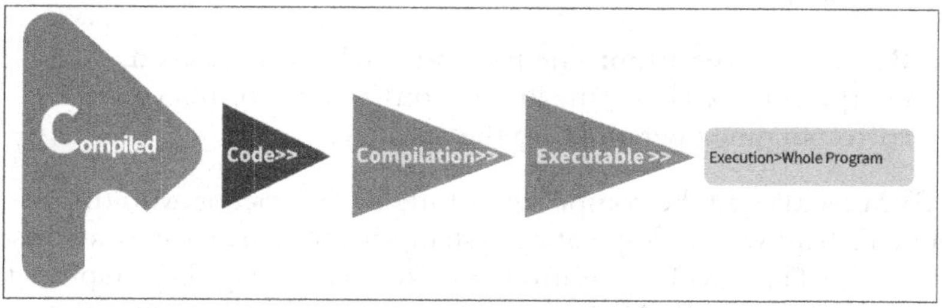

Figure 4c. Compiling a language process.

Key Differences

So, the main difference between interpreted and compiled languages lies in how they execute code. Interpreted languages translate and execute code line by line, offering immediate feedback and easier debugging, but often at the cost of speed. Compiled languages require a separate compilation step, resulting in faster execution but requiring more time during development. (Interestingly a program to be compiled must first be interpreted!)

Where Does Python Fit In?

Python is considered an interpreted language, so it has all the characteristics we mentioned above. But instead of translating the program into machine code line by line, Python takes a slightly different approach. It converts the program into an intermediate format called **bytecode**. This bytecode is then read and converted into a form that the computer's processor can run, essentially turning it into machine code.

The key point here is that Python doesn't create a final machine code program that you can run as a standalone executable file. Instead, the Bytecode gets executed by another layer in the system.

Python Virtual Machine (PVM)

The PVM is a crucial part of the Python interpreter. It's the run-time engine that executes the bytecode generated from your Python source code. The PVM makes sure your Python programs can run on any system with a compatible Python interpreter. Because bytecode is platform-independent, the PVM can take that bytecode and turn it into the correct machine code for whatever computer you're using. This is what makes Python so portable.

How It All Comes Together

So, to sum it up, running a Python program involves two main steps:

1. **Source Code to Bytecode:** When you write Python code in a .py file and run it, the Python interpreter first compiles the source code into bytecode. This bytecode is a lower-level, representation of your program.

2. **Bytecode Execution:** The PVM then takes this bytecode and interprets it, executing the instructions and performing the corresponding operations on the machine.

The PVM handles all the complicated stuff, like interacting with the computer's hardware and operating system, so you don't have to worry about those details. That's why it's relatively easy to create things like graphics in Python—because the PVM abstracts away the hardware complexities.

Two chapters in and although we haven't looked at any real specific Python programs yet, we have examined in quite some detail how Python works and how things are structured. We have done that using Thonny, the Python Interactive Shell and the Terminal.

The Answer

I asked earlier if you could combine the two functions into class?. The answer is yes.

```
#Filename: function4.py
import math

class MathOperations:
```

```
    def add_numbers(self, a, b):
        result = a + b
        print(result)

    def sq_root(self, a, b):
        result = math.sqrt(a + b)
        print(result)

#Example use:
math_ops = MathOperations()
math_ops.add_numbers(3, 5)  # This will print 8
math_ops.sq_root(14, 2)     # This will print 4.0
```

MathOperations: This is the class that contains both the add_numbers and sq_root methods.

add_numbers(self, a, b): This method adds the two numbers and prints the result.

sq_root(self, a, b): This method calculates the square root of the sum of the two numbers and prints the result.

math_ops = MathOperations(): Creates an instance of the MathOperations class.

The methods are then called on the **math_ops** object, which will perform the operations and print the results.

In this case, the **MathOperations** class is actually not really worth having because it doesn't take advantage of OOP principles like state, encapsulation, or inheritance. The methods are essentially standalone functions, and the class adds unnecessary complexity without providing additional value. Here's why:

No State: The class does not maintain any data or state. Both methods (add_numbers and sq_root) simply perform operations using input parameters and don't rely on or modify attributes of the class.

No Encapsulation: The methods could be implemented as standalone functions instead of being part of a class since there's no hidden logic or need for abstraction.

Extra Boilerplate: Creating an instance of the class (math_ops = MathOperations()) adds unnecessary steps when you could just call functions directly.

In object-oriented programming, the **state** of an object refers to the data it holds at any given time. This data is stored in the object's attributes (like **self.history** in the example. The object *remembers* what it has done. For example, you can review the operation history at any time without recalculating.

In this case we're better off to use the code as standalone functions, which are simpler and more readable:

```
#Filename: function5.py
import math

def add_numbers(a, b):
    result = a + b
    print(result)
def sq_root(a, b):
    result = math.sqrt(a + b)
    print(result)

# Example use:
add_numbers(3, 5)   # This will print 8
sq_root(14, 2)      # This will print 4.0
```

This approach eliminates the need to define and instantiate a class and keeps the code straightforward. So classes, while being important, are not needed everywhere.

A class would be useful if you added functionality that required state or re-usability. For example:

- Store frequently used values as attributes.
- Extend behaviour through inheritance or encapsulation.

```
#Filename: function6.py
import math

class MathOperations:
    def __init__(self):
        self.history = []  # Store operation history

    def add_numbers(self, a, b):
        result = a + b
        self.history.append(f"Added {a} and {b}:
{result}")
        print(result)

    def sq_root(self, a, b):
        result = math.sqrt(a + b)
        self.history.append(f"Square root of {a} + {b}:
{result}")
        print(result)

# Example use:
math_ops = MathOperations()
math_ops.add_numbers(3, 5)
math_ops.sq_root(14, 2)
print(math_ops.history)  # Access stored operation
history
```

Here, the **history** attribute provides state, which makes the class more meaningful. In essence use a class **only** if you have state, re-usability, or complex behaviour to encapsulate.

05: Environments

Imagine your Raspberry Pi Python setup as a bustling marketplace, full of different stalls, each specialising in something unique. You've got a fruit and veg stand, a hardware store, and maybe even a bakery. Each of these stalls represents a its own **environment.** They're all running their own businesses, keeping everything neat and orderly, without stepping on each others toes. You move from one stall to another (Maybe edging to the Bakery first.) If you are shopping online these are virtual environments.

In Python, a virtual environment is just like one of these stalls. It's a dedicated space where you can install and manage all the bits and bobs needed for a particular project. This way, each project has everything it needs, without causing a muddle with other projects or your main Python setup.

Think of the 'system' Python that comes pre-installed as **the main market square.** By creating virtual environments, you're setting up separate stalls where each project can have its own space. It's like making sure each stall has its own signboard and stockroom, so they can run smoothly without mixing up their goods.

In this analogy, these shops are your **'virtual environments'.** And just like the shelves in these shops—much like the dependencies in your Python projects—everything needs to be well-organised. Python software repositories like **PyPi (Python Package Index)** act like a giant library of modules, ensuring you can always find the right package version, just like pulling the right book off a shelf.

And, just like in any busy marketplace, things change. **Python and its libraries get updated,** and somctimes these updates don't play nicely with your existing code, especially when jumping between major versions (like from Python 2 to 3). This is where virtual environments really shine! They act as a cosy little bubble around your project, preserving the exact setup you used—say, Python 3.9.2—so your code keeps working just as it should, even as the Python world moves on.

Virtual environments provide each project with its own haven, complete with its own set of dependencies, **which never interfere with others.** This keeps everything running smoothly, without any nasty surprises from conflicting packages.

So, what's the takeaway? **Avoid tinkering too much with the 'system' Python.** Just as a plumber's toolbox is different from an electrician's, your projects might need different versions of packages. Virtual environments let you tailor each project's toolbox without worrying about clashing with others. Usually, you won't need different versions of Python for each environment, but it's good to know you can if you run into compatibility issues between releases. This, if likely, may come if you pursue a Python programming career.

They also make sharing your setup with someone else a breeze. **It's like handing over your secret recipe to a friend—no matter who follows it, the result should be spot on** (well, unless it's me in the kitchen!). And as we'll see much later on, you can even provide these recipes to anyone who wants them. (And they'll come with all the ingredients needed!)

In short, virtual environments help you manage the quirks of working with different Python versions and libraries, ensuring your projects run smoothly and consistently.

We'll keep popping back to this subject as we move through the book, acquiring the relevant knowledge as we go.

Version Numbers

This following figure shows naming conventions in Python software, and software in general. It's good to know what an update means.

The version of Thonny on your Raspberry Pi can vary a bit depending on your OS and Python version. Different systems might have slight variations, but don't worry—the core functionality stays consistent. You might just find that certain features are tucked away in different menus—nothing a bit of poking around won't solve.

When you fired up Thonny, you saw the Python location address:

```
/usr/bin/python3
```

It's preceded by the text: **'Local Python 3'.** The '/usr/bin/' part means you're using the 'system' Python, even though it's not explicitly labelled that way—it's just implied. As we mentioned earlier when we talked about root directories, we'll be changing this location to point to our custom virtual environment once we set it up.

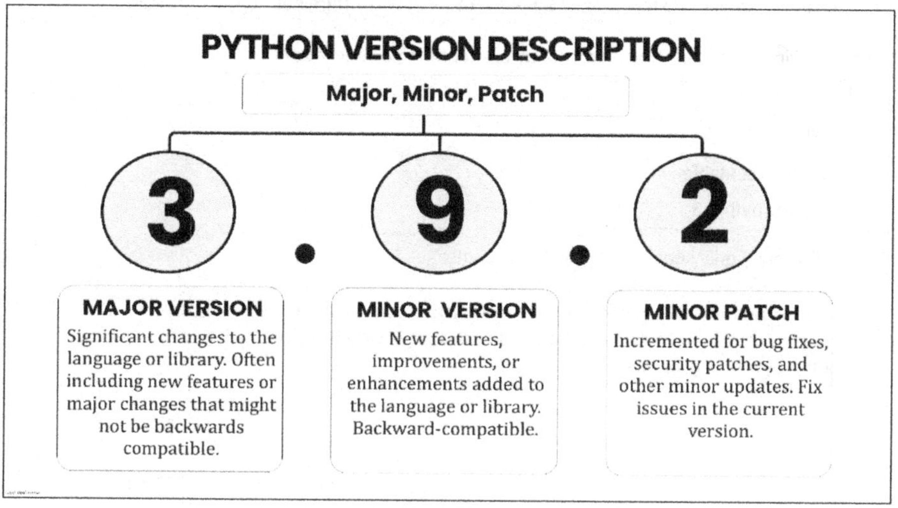

Figure 5a. Understanding version numbers.

Virtual Environments with Thonny

Setting up a virtual environment is very practical, especially if you're just tinkering around daily without a specific project in mind. Personally, I keep my virtual environment in a directory called 'PyDaily' on my Desktop. This is one of only two folders I keep there; the other is 'PiHome', which holds everything else that would otherwise clutter up my work space. The 'Pi' and 'Py' at the beginning of the folder names are little reminders of what they're for. (Actually I don't - as there's a much better method as we'll learn later is this book. But for now we'll use PyDaily. Sorry for the fib.)

You'll need to create the PyDaily (or whatever you want to call it) where you want it. At this point I suggest you create it one the Desktop. Up to you though, and there are other options suggested too.

To set up your virtual environment in Thonny, go to its **'Tools'** menu and select **'Options'.** In the Thonny Options window, head to the **'Interpreter'** tab. As you'll see in Figure 5b (over), the **'Python executable'** drop-down box shows the same address we saw earlier.

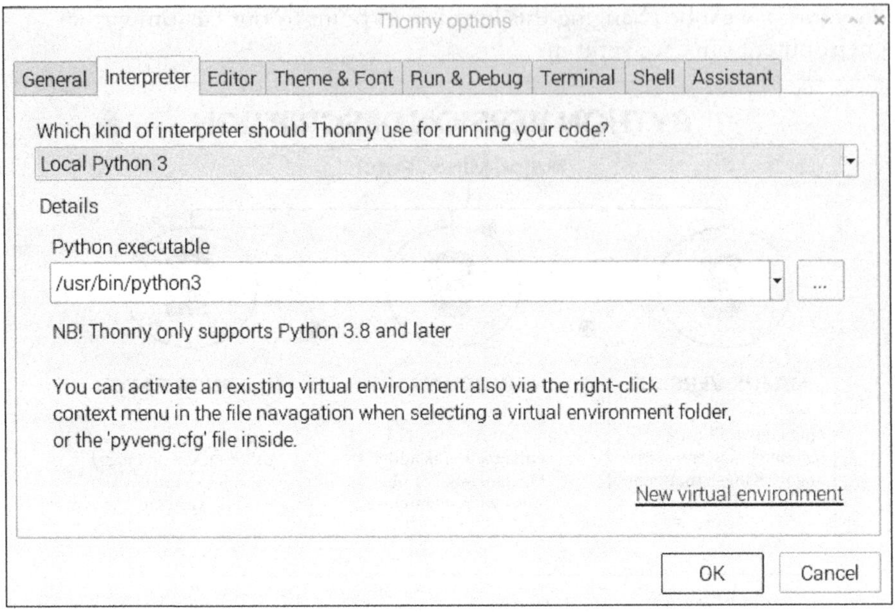

Figure 5b. The Interpreter window in Thonny.

Now, click on **'New virtual environment'** at the bottom right side of the window. You'll be asked to navigate to an empty folder where the virtual environment will be created, as shown.

Once you've done that, you'll see that the Python executable is now located within the PyDaily folder, as shown in Figure 5d. Notice that the upper window indicates that the **'Local Python 3'** is in use, but now it's the local version created in your virtual environment. Close Thonny and open it again - restarting it to make sure these changes stick. From now on, the Python interpreter in the PyDaily environment will handle any actions you take.

Instructions for Different Raspberry Pi Models:

- Raspberry Pi 4: Look for the 'New virtual environment' link in the bottom right-hand corner of the Thonny window. Click it, then click 'OK' when the prompt appears. Navigate to the 'Home' icon in the left-hand panel, select the 'PyDaily' folder, and click 'OK'.

- Raspberry Pi 5: Click the '+folder' icon on the far right side of the window. In this new window, create a directory called 'PyDaily' and hit 'Create'. Enter the folder, press 'OK', and after a moment, you'll be back in the 'Interpreter' window. You'll notice that the 'Python executable' drop-down now points to the environment we just set up.

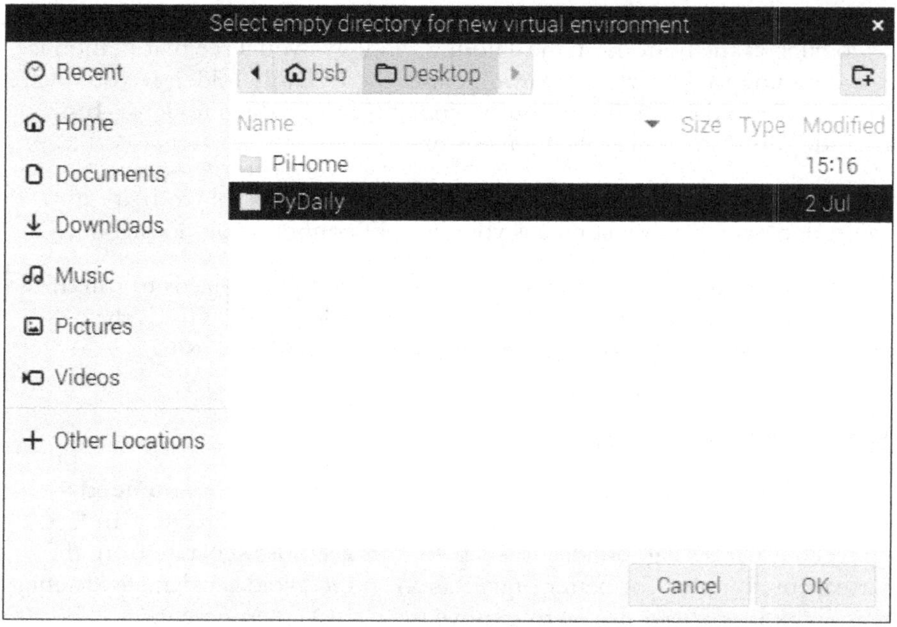

Figure 5c. Select the directory where you want to create the virtual environment.

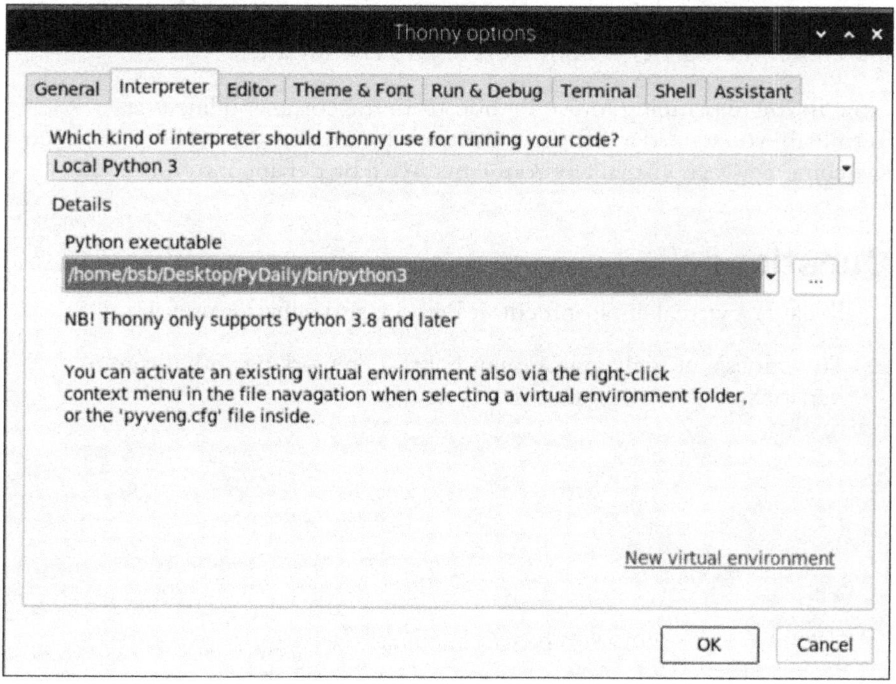

Figure 5d. The Python executable drop down now points to the virtual environment.

These changes should remain in place even after any reboot. You can check by looking at the bottom of the Thonny window—you'll see that Python is now pointing to the virtual environment in the **PyDaily** folder. If you open the PyDaily folder, you'll find four main items inside: three folders—**bin, include, lib**—and a file called **pyvenv.cfg.**

Sometimes, in older setups, you might also see a **'Share'** folder. If it's not there, don't worry—it just means your current configuration doesn't need it.

These folders and files are the nuts and bolts that Python needs to run. If you open the 'lib' folder, you'll find a Python folder inside. This is the specific version of Python that your virtual environment is using.

Keeping Separate

When you're using a virtual environment with Python, there's **no need** to stash your programs right inside the virtual environment directory. In fact, some consider it's a good idea to keep your project files separate from the virtual environment for better organisation and to avoid accidentally deleting your work if you ever decide to remove the virtual environment.

If you have more than one virtual environment created using Thonny you can switch between them simply by selecting it from the drop-down menu in the Thonny interpreter window. Just restart Thonny after.

Now, if you're planning to use Python from the command line (via Terminal), you'll need a different approach for creating, activating, and even switching between virtual environments. We'll be delving into this later.

Questions

1. What is a virtual environment in Python, and why is it useful?
2. How does a virtual environment help when working with different versions of Python or libraries?

06: Variables & Strings

Variables are the heart and soul of programming. The magical tools that let your programs come to life, handling all the data as the program runs. Whether it's text, like what you'd type in a word processor, or numbers, like you'd crunch in a spreadsheet, **variables are the unsung heroes** making everything possible. No variables, no programs.

Variables are containers where you store different kinds of information. You toss the info into these containers using an **assignment operator**—which is just a fancy way of saying the '=' sign. Here's a quick example:

```
my_name = "Bruce"
my_age = 25
```

Here, my_name is holding the string "Bruce", and my_age is holding the number 25. (Wishful thinking on the age, right?)

They're called 'variables' **because they can change!** The cool thing about Python is that you don't have to worry about declaring what type of variable you're using ahead of time. Python's smart enough to figure it out based on what you give it. So, **my_name** is a string (which is just tech-speak for text), and my_age is a number. No need to specify types—Python's got you covered.

Here's another quick example (you can try these in the Python Interactive Shell):

```
message = "Hello"   # string type
count = 10          # integer type
pi = 3.14           # float type
```

Strings (text) need to be wrapped in quotes—single or double, but they must match at each end. If you accidentally put a number in quotes, Python will treat it as text, not a number, and that's a surefire way to trip up your code.

When it comes to **naming your variables,** there are a few simple rules. They must start with a letter or an underscore, and they can only include letters, numbers, and underscores. Plus, **variable names are case-sensitive**, so 'name' and 'Name' would be seen as completely different variables.

Once your variables are set up, you can use them pretty much anywhere in your code:

```
total = price * quantity
print("The total cost is:", total)
```

You can also change what's inside a variable whenever you like:

```
count = 10
count = count + 1
print(count)
#Output: 11
```

Now, let's talk about **scope**. This is just a fancy word for where your variable exists in the code. If you define a variable inside a function, it's **local** to that function—you can't use it outside. But if you define it outside a function, it's **global** and you can use it anywhere in your code. The topic of scope is very important for Python. *Chapter 24 Advanced Functions* details the use of scope.

Python programmers often use **lowercase letters with underscores between words** for variable names, like this:

```
first_name = "John"
```

You can also assign **multiple variables in one go**:

```
x, y, z = 1, 2, 3
```

This simply means that x, y, and z now hold the values 1, 2, and 3, respectively. It's kind of like those algebra exercises we all did:

```
a = 1
b = 2
c = a + b    # c now equals 3
```

Variables let you store and juggle data, making your programs flexible and dynamic.

Constants are variables that shouldn't change—they're, well, constant. You usually write them in **uppercase** to remind yourself not to mess with them, though Python doesn't enforce this. **Constants are fixed values** that are crucial to how your program behaves.

```
PI=3.14
```

As we've seen, you can display the value of a variable using the **print()** function:

```
name = "Alice"
print("Hello", name)
```

The output here would be **Hello Alice**

And if you ever need to remove a variable or constant, you can use the **del** statement:

```
x = 10
del x
```

After running **del x**, the variable x is gone, and trying to use it will cause an error.

In short, **variables are the workhorses of your code,** storing values and results that you can reuse throughout your program. They also let your programs talk to different parts of your code or other modules.

String Theory

In computer programming, a "string" is a sequence of characters, like letters, numbers, or symbols, that are treated as a single item of data.

The different arrangements of characters in a computer string can form different words or sentences, In this case, these "strings" serve as building blocks in programming, for text and data.

Back in **Chapter 03**, when we dabbled in **Object-Oriented Programming (OOP),** you might remember bumping into strings here and there, showing that some variables were expecting a string as input.

So, what's the deal with **methods** and strings in Python? A method is basically a function that's attached to an object. In the case of strings, these methods let you perform operations on your text. For example, with string methods, you can split a string, search for a specific character, or join a bunch of strings together. Strings can also be displayed in all sorts of ways, which makes them handy for generating formatted output like reports, logs, or messages.

A Simple Example

Let's check out an example to see strings in action:

```
#Filename: string1a.py
def greet(name):
    return f"Hello, {name}!"

message = greet("Oliver")
print(message)
```

When you run this code, it'll give you the output: **Hello, Oliver!**

We saw a similar example earlier, but in the context of this chapter what's happening here? First, we've defined a function called 'greet'. Inside the parentheses, there's a parameter called **name**, which we expect to be a string variable. Now, this name parameter isn't anything special in Python—you could call it whatever you like, whether it's 'Constantinople' or 'tin'. **In Python, variables aren't stuck with a specific type**; they just take on the type of whatever value you assign to them.

When you call the greet function, it's looking for a string to be passed in, and we give it **"Oliver"**:

```
message = greet("Oliver")
```

Now, 'message' is another string variable. The line above is basically saying, "Hey Python, call the greet function and pass the string "Oliver" into it." Notice how we've used **double quotes** (" ") here, but you could totally use **single quotes** (' ') instead—Python doesn't care either way.

Then we get to this part:

```
return f"Hello, {name}!"
```

This line uses what's called an **f-string** to create a formatted string that includes the value of the **name** variable. These **f-strings**, are a super neat and efficient way to create formatted strings. They let you drop expressions right inside curly braces { }. In this case, the expression inside the braces is name, which, as you guessed, holds some text—probably a name. Note also that the '!' mark is printed as part of the string after the **name** argument.

f-strings are a more efficient and readable way to format strings, as they allow you to include expressions directly within curly braces { }, which Python evaluates at run-time.

When the function gets called with a name argument, it returns a greeting message that includes whatever text is in the name variable. The **return statement** sends this result back to wherever the function was called from, letting that part of your code use or tweak the returned value. The little program on the previous page is a great example of how to define and call a simple function in Python.

The function greet(name) encapsulates (or wraps) the behaviour of taking a name as input and returning a greeting message. Encapsulation, in a broader sense, means bundling data (the name) and the logic that operates on it (the greeting) inside the function. This keeps the logic contained and reusable.

While the function-based approach demonstrates encapsulation on a smaller scale, the OOP example with the **Greeter** class (below) demonstrates encapsulation at a higher level, where both data (name) and behaviour (greet()) are bundled together within a class. This is a more formal use of encapsulation in Object-Oriented Programming."

Interaction

The interaction happens when the greet("Oliver") function is called, and the result is assigned to message. The print(message) statement is another form of interaction, where the program outputs the result of the function call.

While this code demonstrates encapsulation (by grouping functionality in the greet() function) and interaction (by calling the function and printing the result), a more formal example of encapsulation in the context of OOP would involve encapsulating data and behaviour inside a class and controlling access to that data through methods.

For example, in an OOP context:

```
#Filename: string1b.py
class Greeter:
    def __init__(self, name):
        self.name = name  # This is encapsulated data

    def greet(self):
        return f"Hello, {self.name}!"  # This is
encapsulated behaviour

greeter = Greeter("Oliver")
message = greeter.greet()
print(message)
```

Not withstanding the note made about when to use a class in the previous chapter, this OOP example shows encapsulation by keeping both the data (name) and the behaviour (greet()) inside the class **Greeter**, and interaction happens when the object greeter calls its greet() method.

How Long Can a String Be?

As for how long a string can be, that really depends on how much memory your Raspberry Pi has. For most everyday purposes, you can work with strings of just about any length, if you've got enough memory to store them. But be careful—if you're working with really **huge strings,** they can gobble up a lot of memory and potentially slow down your program.

Chopping Up Made Easy

Splitting strings in Python is like slicing up a loaf of bread—you get nice slices that are easier to handle than the whole loaf. To do this, you use the **split()** method, which breaks up a string into multiple pieces (or "sub-strings") based on a **delimiter** you specify. Let's dive into an example:

```
#Filename: string2.py
string = "Hello, there!"
parts = string.split(", ")
print(parts)
```

Output:

```
['Hello', 'there!']
```

In this case, the string "Hello, there!" gets split wherever it finds ", " (a comma followed by a space). The split() method then returns a **list** containing the split pieces. As you can see, the output is ['Hello', 'there!'].

By default, if you don't give split() a specific delimiter, it'll use a space to chop up the string. But what if you want to store those split parts in separate variables? Easy! Just make sure you have the right number of variables to match the number of pieces, and assign as you split:

```
#Filename: string3.py
string = "Hello, there!"
part1, part2 = string.split(", ")
print(part1)  # Output: Hello
print(part2)  # Output: there!
```

Here, **part1** grabs the first piece, and **part2** snags the second. The output on your screen will be:

```
Hello
there!
```

Notice there are no brackets around the outputs here—they're just printed as separate strings. You can even get clever and **concatenate** (fancy word for "join together") the parts to form a new string or replace the original one: Also not that the process doesn't add spaces so you will need to include these in your concatenation if required.

```
rearranged_string = part2 + part1
print(rearranged_string)
```

Want to split the string using something other than a comma and space? **The delimiter can be any string**—even if it's more than one character:

```
#Filename: string4.py
string = "apple,banana,orange"
fruits = string.split(",")
print(fruits)
#Output: ['apple', 'banana', 'orange']
```

In this example, we've split the string "apple,banana,orange" into three parts using a **comma** (,) as the delimiter.

Haystack Needle

Now, what if you want to search for a **specific character or sub-string** within a string? Python's got a few tricks up its sleeve for that, too.

First up is the **in** operator. This handy tool checks if a particular character or sub-string is hanging out in your string. It gives you a **Boolean value—True** if it finds what you're looking for, and **False** if it doesn't. Here's how it works:

```
#Filename: string5.py
string = "Hello, there!"
if "o" in string:
    print("The string contains the letter 'o'.")
```

This produces:

```
The string contains the letter 'o'.
```

In this example, the **in** operator is on the hunt for the character "o" in the string. Since it's there, the output statement gets displayed.

Next up is the **find()** method, which is like a little detective that finds the index (position) of the first occurrence of a character or sub-string in your string. If it can't find what you're looking for, it returns **-1**. Here's how to use it:

```
#Filename: string6.py
string = "Hello, there!"
index = string.find("t")
print(index)  # Output: 7
```

In this example, the find() method tracks down the index of the character "t" in the string. The output will be 7, which is the position of "t" (Python starts counting at 0, so "H" is at position 0). The space is also counted as part of the overall length.

The Dynamic Duo

You can get even more precise by combining the **in** and **find()** methods. First, you check if the letter exists in the string, and if it does, you then display its index:

```
#Filename: string7.py
string = "Hello, there!"
if "o" in string:
    index = string.find("o")
    print(f"The letter 'o' is at index: {index}")
#Using f-string for clean formatting
```

This will produce:

```
The string contains the letter 'o' at index: 4
```

That's the fifth item in the string, 'cause we start counting from zero. Keep in mind that the find() method only returns the index of the **first occurrence** of the character, even if it shows up multiple times in the string. So, if "o" appears more than once, find() will only tell you the location of the first.

The Other Dynamic Duo

When it comes to joining strings in Python, you've got two main tools in your toolbox: the **join()** method and the **+ operator**. Each one is great in different situations, so let's look at when and how to use them.

The join() Method: Efficient and Flexible

The **join()** method is like the Swiss Army knife of string concatenation—it's super-efficient, especially when you need to combine a bunch of strings with a specific separator. You've got a list of words, and you want to turn them into a single sentence. That's where **join()** really shines. It calculates the total length of the final string just once and then performs the concatenation in a single step, making it perfect for handling a lot of strings.

Here's a quick example:

```
#Filename: string8.py
strings = ["Hello", "there!"]
result = " ".join(strings)
print(result)
#Output: Hello there!
```

In this case, **join()** takes the list of strings and glues them together with a space in between. The result? A nicely formatted sentence.

On the other hand, the **+ operator** is your go-to for smaller, simpler tasks. If you've got just a couple of strings you want to combine, **+** is quick, easy, and keeps your code readable. It's perfect for situations where you want to, say, greet someone by combining a greeting and a name. Check it out:

```
#Filename: string9.py
string1 = "Hello"
string2 = "there!"
result = string1 + " " + string2
print(result)
#Output: Hello there!
```

Here, the **+** operator does the job of combining string1, a space, and string2. The result is stored in the result variable, and when you print it out, you get a nice, clean sentence.

Sometimes, you might want to use both **join()** and **+** together**,** especially when you need to concatenate multiple strings in a more complex way. Here's an example that shows how you can combine these methods for maximum flexibility:

```
#Filename: strings10.py
#Define a list of strings
words = [
    "When", "using", "the", "join()", "method", "you",
"need", "to", "provide","the", "strings", "to", "be",
"concatenated", "as", "an", "iterable"
]

#join() method to concatenate with a space separator
sentence_join = " ".join(words)
print("Using join():")
print(sentence_join)

#Define additional strings
additional_strings = ["(e.g.,", "a", "list,", "tuple,",
"or", "set)."]

#Concatenate additional strings using the + operator
sentence_plus = sentence_join + " " + "
".join(additional_strings)
print("\nUsing + operator and join():")
print(sentence_plus)

#extend expression with more strings
extended_strings = [
    "We", "specify", "the", "string", "on", "which",
"we", "will", "join", "the",
    "elements", "as", "the", "separator", "(in",
"this", "case,", "\" \")."
]

#Extend the sentence using the join() method
sentence_extended = " ".join([sentence_plus] +
extended_strings)
print("\nExtended using join():")
print(sentence_extended)
#Final concatenation use both methods for more strings
final_addition = [
    "As", "you", "might", "have", "guessed",
```

```
"already,", "you", "can", "concatenate", "over", "two",
"strings", "using", "both", "the", "+", "operator",
"and", "the", "join()", "method."
]
final_sentence = sentence_extended + " " + "
".join(final_addition)
print("\nFinal concatenation:")
print(final_sentence)
```

Inside the Program:

- **Using join():** We start by creating a list of words and use **" ".join(words)** to concatenate them into a single string with spaces between each word.
- **Using + Operator and join():** Next, we create another list of additional strings and combine them with the initial sentence using both the + operator and join().
- **Extending the Expression:** We take it a step further by joining the already-concatenated sentence with even more strings.
- **Final Concatenation:** Finally, we show how to concatenate even more strings using both methods, giving you a comprehensive example of just how flexible these tools can be.
- **Line Length:** You may notice that some of the lines are split across lines using <Enter> characters. This is because the Python standard suggest lines should not be more than 79 characters in length. This is a guidance, not a requirement.

This program shows you just how flexible and efficient both the join() method and the **+** operator are when it comes to string concatenation.

Case Swapping

Ever wanted to flip the case of every letter in a string? Of course you have, many times! Well, Python's got a nifty trick up its sleeve called **swapcase()** that does just that. This handy method takes every uppercase letter and turns it into lowercase, and vice versa—basically flipping the case of each character in the string.

Example 1: A Case Flip

Let's dive into an example:

```
#Filename: string11.py
string = "Hello, there!"
flipped_string = string.swapcase()
print(flipped_string)
#Output: hELLO, THERE!
```

The **swapcase()** method is called on the string "Hello, there!". It turns all the uppercase letters lowercase, and all the lowercase letters are now uppercase. So "Hello, there!" becomes "hELLO, THERE!". **Note** that this affects the original variable.

Example 2: Keeping the Original String Safe

Now, what if you want to flip the case but still hang on to the original string? No problem. Just assign the flipped version to a new variable, and your original string stays exactly as it was.

Here's how you do it:

```
#Filename: string12.py
string = "Hello, there!"
flipped_string = string.swapcase()
print(flipped_string)
print(string)
#Output: hELLO, THERE!
```

Output:

```
hELLO, THERE!
Hello, there!
```

In this example, **flipped_string** holds the **case-flipped** version of your original string. Meanwhile, the string variable keeps its original value intact. This way, you can easily compare the two or use them both in different parts of your program without any worries.

Why This Is Useful

Using swapcase() and storing the result in a new variable is real handy when you want to experiment with different versions of a string while still keeping the original around. Whether you're working on text manipulation, creating case-insensitive comparisons, or just having fun with string transformations, **swapcase()** gives you the flexibility to play around with text without losing your original data

Reversing a String

If you want to reverse the letters in a string? Well, Python makes it a breeze with its handy slicing feature. In just one line of code, you can flip a string backwards, as if you were reading it in a mirror. Here's how you achieve it:

```
#Filename: string13.py
string = "Hello, there!"
reversed_string = string[::-1]
print(reversed_string)
```

Output:

```
ereht ,olleH
```

What's going on here? The **slicing** syntax **[::-1]** is the secret sauce. It tells Python to take the string and step through it in reverse order. The -1 step value is what does the magic, flipping the entire string so "Hello, there!" becomes "!ereht ,olleH".

Here's another example:

```
#Filename: string14.py
string = "HannaH"
string = string[::-1]
print(string)
```

Keeping the Original String Safe

As before if you want to keep your original string just as it is while still getting a reversed version. Again, you simply store the reversed string in a new variable. That way, your original string stays untouched, and you have the reversed version ready to go.

Here's how you do it:

```
#Filename: string15.py
string = "Hello, there!"
reversed_string = string[::-1]
print(reversed_string)
print(string)
#The original string remains unchanged
```

Output:

```
!ereht ,olleH
Hello, there!
```

In this example, **reversed_string** holds the flipped version, while the original string variable stays exactly the same.

Why This Is Handy

Reversing strings can be incredibly useful in various scenarios—whether you're working on palindromes, creating fun text effects, or just need to flip some text around for a specific task. Using slicing with [::-1] gives you a quick and easy way to get the reversed string without losing the original.

Passing Multiple Arguments

Passing multiple arguments to **functions** in Python is straightforward. This isn't a shouting match or dispute, it's referring to the values or inputs you pass to a function or method when you call it. These values are used by the function to perform operations or calculations. Arguments allow you to customise the behaviour of a function by providing different inputs.

You just separate them with commas, and there are several ways to handle those arguments depending on what you need your function to do. Let's explore a few approaches together.

Positional Arguments: Keep It Simple

The most straightforward way to pass arguments to a function is by using **positional arguments**. With this method, you pass the arguments in the exact order they're defined in the function's parameter list:

```
#Filename: string16.py
def add_numbers(a, b):
    return a + b

result = add_numbers(5, 3)
print(result)
#Output: 8
```

In this case, 5 and 3 are passed as positional arguments to add_numbers, and the function simply adds them together. That was "lemon squeezy".

What? I come from the east end of London and some of us older ones speak a dialect called **Cockney Rhyming Slang**. Lemon squeezy! means *easy*! Other examples of CRS are 'Plates of Meat – feet, Apples and Pears – stairs. Frog and Toad – road. It's unique. I digress…

Keyword Arguments: Specify and Conquer

With **keyword arguments**, you get a little more flexibility. You can specify the parameter names along with their values when calling the function. This way, you can even pass the arguments out of order—Python knows what goes where!

```
#Filename: string17.py
def greet(name, message):
    print(f"{message}, {name}!")
greet(message="Hello", name="John")
# Output: Hello, John!
```

Here, we used **keyword arguments** to specify that "Hello" should go to message and "John" should go to name, regardless of the order.

Default Arguments: A Handy Backup

Sometimes, you might want a parameter to have a **default value** in case it isn't provided. That's where **default arguments** come in handy. If you don't provide a specific value, Python will use the default; if you do provide one, it'll override the default:

```
#Filename: string18.py
def exponentiate(base, exponent=2):
    return base ** exponent
result1 = exponentiate(3)
#Uses default exponent=2. Result: 9
result2 = exponentiate(2, 4)
#Overrides default exponent. Result: 16

print(result1, result2)
```

In this example, if you don't pass an argument, Python assumes it's 2, but if you do, it'll use whatever you specify.

Arbitrary Arguments: Go with the Flow

What if you don't know how many arguments will be passed to your function? Python lets you handle **arbitrary arguments** with ***args** for a variable number of positional arguments, and ****kwargs** for keyword arguments. Just remember, ***args** comes before ****kwargs** if you're using both. Here's an example:

```
#Filename: string19.py
def multiply(*args):
    result = 1
    for num in args:
        result *= num
    return result

product = multiply(2, 3, 4)
#Multiply 2 * 3 * 4.
print("Product is:", product)
#Output: Product is: 24
```

And another example:

```
#Filename: string20.py
def print_person_info(**kwargs):
    for key, value in kwargs.items():
        print(f"{key}: {value}")

print_person_info(name="John", age=25, city="New York")
#Output:
#name: John
#age: 25
#city: New York
```

Unpacking Arguments: Spread It Out

Let's say you've got a list of values, and you want to pass them as individual arguments to a function. You can **unpack** them using the * syntax. This spreads the values out, so they fit into the function's parameters just right.

Here's the example:

```
#Filename: string21.py
def calculate_sum(a, b, c):
    return a + b + c
```

```
values = [1, 2, 3]
result = calculate_sum(*values)
#Unpack the list into individual arguments
print(result)
#Output: 6
```

In this case, the list [1, 2, 3] is unpacked and passed to calculate_sum as individual arguments.

Object Type

In Python, figuring out the type of an object can be done, thanks to the handy **type()** function. This function lets you peek under the hood to see what kind of data you're working with at any given moment.

As mentioned before, one of the great things about Python is that you don't have to declare the type of a variable ahead of time. Python just knows. It's smart like that—it infers the type automatically based on the value you assign:

```
#Filename: string22.py
x = 10
y = "Hello, World!"
z = [1, 2, 3]
print(type(x))  # Output: <class 'int'>
print(type(y))  # Output: <class 'str'>
print(type(z))  # Output: <class 'list'>
```

Here's what's happening: x is assigned the number 10, so Python knows x is an integer. y gets the string "Hello, World!", making y a string. And z, which is a list of numbers, is recognised as a list. When you use the type() function, it returns the type of the variable as a type object, which you can then use to check what kind of data you're dealing with.

This ability helps you make sure you're handling the right type of data, especially when you're performing operations on variables. For instance, trying to add a string to a number won't work—it's a mismatch. But with **type()**, you can double-check what you're working with first.

Remember, Python is a **dynamically typed language**, which means variables aren't tied down to a specific type. They can change their type on the fly during run-time, depending on what values you assign to them. So, a variable that's an integer at one moment could easily become a string in the next. This flexibility is useful, but it also makes it important to know the type of your variables as you go along. A few other things you should know:

Strings are immutable: In Python, strings cannot be changed after they are created. If you modify a string, Python creates a new string object with the modified value, rather than altering the original string. (Note that the variable, which points to the string, is mutable.)

Variable references: In Python, variables are essentially references to objects in memory. When you assign a value to a variable, you're creating a reference to an object. Understanding this can help clarify why modifying one variable doesn't affect another, even if they initially seem to hold the same value.

Garbage collection: Python automatically manages memory using *garbage collection*, which reclaims memory occupied by objects that are no longer referenced by any variable. In other words throw them out with the garbage.

f-strings: While you've already encountered f-strings for embedding expressions within strings, it's worth exploring advanced f-string features like formatting numbers, aligning text, and including expressions directly inside curly braces.

```
length = 5
width = 3
area = f"The rectangles area is length {length} and width
{width} is {length * width}."
print(area)
```

format() method: This is another powerful way to format strings, offering control over how values are represented (e.g., specifying the number of decimal places for a float, or formatting numbers with commas).

```
# Filename: string23.py
# Formatting floating-point numbers
pi = 3.14159265359

# Display pi rounded to 2 decimal places
result = "The value of pi is approximately {:.2f}".
format(pi)

print(result)
```

Old-style formatting: The % operator is the oldest method for string formatting, still found in some legacy code. Understanding it can be helpful for reading and maintaining older Python scripts.

```
#Filename: string24.py
name = "Alice"
age = 30
# Using % operator for string formatting
greeting = "Hello, my name is %s and I am %d years
old." % (name, age)
print(greeting)
```

Local vs. Global scope: Variables defined inside a function are local to that function and can't be accessed outside it. Global variables, on the other hand, are accessible from any part of the code. Understanding how Python manages scope and how to use the global and non-local keywords can prevent unintended side effects.

Variable lifetime: The lifetime of a variable refers to the duration during which it exists in memory. Local variables are destroyed after the function in which they are defined finishes executing, while global variables persist throughout the program's execution.

String methods: Beyond the basics, Python provides many string methods like **strip(), replace(), startswith(), endswith(), partition()**, and more. Each of these methods can be used to perform common string operations.

```
#Filename: string25.py
text = "Python is fun to learn"

# Using partition() to split the string at
# the first occurrence of "is"

before, separator, after = text.partition("is")

print("Before:", before)
print("Separator:", separator)
print("After:", after)

#Output
#Before: Python
#Separator: is
#After:  fun to learn
```

Dynamic typing and **type checking:** Although Python is dynamically typed, you can use the **isinstance()** function to check the type of a variable before performing operations on it. This can help prevent run-time errors.

f-strings

Python's f-strings (formatted string literals) don't have specific functions, but they support embedding expressions and leveraging Python's standard string methods, functions, and formatting capabilities. Here's a list of common usage patterns and tools that work with f-strings:

String Methods You Can Use in f-strings

These are just some of the standard string methods that can be applied within an f-string:

Case Conversion:

```
.lower()         #Convert to lowercase.
.upper()         #Convert to uppercase.
.capitalize()    #Capitalise the first letter.
.title()         #Capitalise the first letter of each word.
.swapcase()      #Swap the case of characters

#Demo example
name = "john"
```

```
print(f"Hello, {name.upper()}!")  #Output: Hello, JOHN!
```

Alignment and Padding

```
.center(width, fillchar)     #Center align with padding
.ljust(width, fillchar)      #Left-align with padding
.rjust(width, fillchar)      #Right-align with padding

#Demo example:
name = "John"
print(f"{name.center(10, '*')}")  #Output: ***John***
```

Trimming and Replacing

```
.strip()         #Remove whitespace from both ends
.lstrip()        #Remove whitespace from the left
.rstrip()        #Remove whitespace from the right
.replace(old, new)    #Replace occurrences of substring

#Demo example
name = "  John  "
print(f"{name.strip()} is here.")
# Output: John is here.
```

Formatting Expressions

f-strings support formatting options directly using : (colon). These options are commonly used with numbers, strings, and other data types.

Numbers

```
Decimal places: {value:.2f} (2 decimal places).
Thousands separator: {value:,}.
value = 12345.6789

#Demo examples
print(f"Formatted: {value:.2f}")     #Formatted: 12345.68
print(f"With commas: {value:,}")     #12,345.6789
```

Alignment

```
Left-align: {value:<10}
Right-align: {value:>10}
Center-align: {value:^10}

#Demo examples
name = "John"
print(f"{name:<10}")  # Output: John
print(f"{name:>10}")  # Output: John
print(f"{name:^10}")  # Output: John
```

Built-in Functions

```
len()
round()
max()/min()
sum()

#Demo Example
name = "John"
print(f"Length of name: {len(name)}")
#Output: Length of name: 4
```

This is just a sample of what is available in f-strings formatting and functions. You can find plenty more

07: Loops

Loops are the engine that drives your code**,** allowing you to repeat a section of code based on a specific condition or for a set number of times. They're simple yet incredibly versatile, helping you move through elements, perform calculations, and automate those tedious tasks. Loops are a great way to add a dynamic element to your program, especially when you don't know in advance how many times something needs to happen. The two most commonly used types of loops are **for loops** and **while loops.**

For Loop

A **for** loop lets you loop over a sequence of items a certain number of times. Say you want to print numbers from one to ten—this is a perfect job for a for loop:

```
for i in range(0, 10):
    print(i)
```

In this code, the **range()** function generates a sequence of numbers starting from the specified value (0 in this case) and goes up to, but doesn't include, the end value (10 here). The **for** loop then moves through this sequence, and the **print() statement** displays each number during each pass. The result? A neat column of printed numbers. Of course, this loop could contain many more lines of code that would all be executed 10 times.

If you want to print the numbers in a single row, you can use **end=** like this:

```
#Filename: loop1.py
for i in range(0, 10):
    print(i, end=' ')
```

Output:

```
0 1 2 3 4 5 6 7 8 9
```

By using **end=** in this example, we're telling Python to use a space character at the end of each print statement instead of the default newline character, making the numbers print in a single row with spaces between them.

Don't want a space between the numbers? Use **end=''.** Prefer commas? Try **end=','.** Just keep in mind that this will add a comma after the last number too. To fix that, you can tweak the code a bit:

```
#Filename: loop2.py
for i in range(0, 10):
    print(i, end=', ' if i < 9 else '')
```

Here, the **end=', ' if i < 9 else ''** construct ensures a comma and space are added after each value—except the last one.

Here's another approach:

```
#Filename: Loop3.py
for i in range(0, 10):
    if i < 9:
        print(i, end=', ')
    else:
        print(i, end='\n')
```

In this version, if **i** is less than nine, it prints the number followed by a comma and a space **end=', '**. Otherwise, it prints the number followed by a newline **end='\n**.' Here \n is the newline character code.

You can start and end a loop with any value:

```
#Filename: loop4.py
for i in range(30, 40):
    print(i, end=' ')
```

Here's a different example using a list:

```
fruits = ["apple", "banana", "cherry"]
for fruit in fruits:
    print(fruit)
```

Output:

```
apple
banana
cherry
```

This loop moves through a list of fruits, printing each one. We'll dive deeper into lists in the next chapter, but you can probably already grasp how it works.

While Loop

A **while loop** keeps running a block of code as long as a specified condition is true. It's perfect for situations where you want something to keep happening until a condition changes, donated by **<=**.

The basic structure looks like this:

```
while condition:
    # code block
```

The code block runs as long as the condition remains true. If the condition becomes false, the loop stops, and the program moves on to the next part of the code. For example, this loop keeps going as long as the **count** variable is less than or equal to nine:

```
#Filename: loop5.py
count = 0
while count <= 9:  # Less than or equal to 9
    print(count)
    count += 1
```

This will print the numbers in a column. If you want them in a row, use **end=** again:

```
#Filename: Loop6.py
counter = 0
while counter <= 9:
    print(counter, end=' ')
    counter += 1
```

You can also add commas and newline characters:

```
#Filename: loop7.py
counter = 0
while counter <= 9:
    if counter < 9:
        print(counter, end=', ')
        counter += 1
```

Loop Control Statements

Loop control statements let you manage the flow within loops—whether that means exiting early, skipping certain iterations, or repeating based on conditions. Here are the three main types of loop control statements:

break: This statement exits a loop immediately, regardless of whether the loop has completed. Control then moves to the next statement after the loop.

```
#Filename: loop8.py
for i in range(0, 10):
    print(i)
    if i == 7:
        break
```

In this example, the loop prints the numbers 0 to 7 because it breaks when **i** equals seven. (Here, == compares the value of objects, not their memory location.)

continue: This statement skips the current iteration of a loop and jumps to the next one, ignoring any remaining code in that iteration.

```
#Filename: loop9.py
for i in range(0, 10):
    if i == 7:
        continue
    print(i)
```

Here, the loop prints all the numbers except 7.

pass: This is a placeholder for code you haven't written yet. It does nothing but serves as a reminder that something will go there eventually.

```
for i in range(3):
    pass
```

Looping with an Index

Sometimes, you need to access both the index and the value of each item in a sequence. The **enumerate()** function in a **for loop** is perfect for this:

```
#Filename: Loop10.py
fruits = ["apple", "banana", "cherry"]
for index, fruit in enumerate(fruits):
    print(f"Index: {index}, Fruit: {fruit}")
```

Output:

```
Index: 0, Fruit: apple
Index: 1, Fruit: banana
Index: 2, Fruit: cherry
```

enumerate() returns the index and the corresponding item in the sequence. This is great for situations where you need both.

In Python, **enumerate** is a built-in function that allows you to loop over an iterable and get both the index and the value of each item simultaneously. This is especially handy when you need to keep track of the position of elements in a list while iterating.

Nested Loops

You can place loops inside other loops—this is known as **'nested'** loops. It's useful when you need to work with multiple sequences or perform repetitive tasks within tasks:

```
#Filename: loop11.py
for i in range(1, 4):
    for j in range(1, 4):
        print(i, j)
```

Output:

```
1 1
1 2
1 3
2 1
2 2
2 3
3 1
3 2
3 3
```

Here, for each value of **i** in the outer loop, the inner loop goes through all values of **j**. This creates a grid-like pattern of iterations.

You can nest as many loops as you need, though keep in mind that excessive nesting can make your code harder to read and maintain. The correct indentation is key to keeping everything clear and avoiding strange bugs.

Else and Elif Statements

The **else** and **elif** statements allow you to define alternative blocks of code when the preceding if condition is not met.

- The else statement runs when all previous conditions are False.
- The elif (short for "else if") statement checks additional conditions sequentially when the initial **if** condition is False.

This structure is useful for handling multiple conditions cleanly and efficiently.

An **else** or **elif** statement is a great way to handle situations where the preceding **if** conditions are met. They provide alternative blocks of code to execute when all the previous conditions are false:

```
#Filename: loop12.py
x = 5

if x > 10:
    print("x is greater than 10")
else:
    print("x is not greater than 10")
```

In this example, the **if** condition checks if **x** is greater than 10. Since it's not (because **x** is 5), the code in the **else** block runs, printing "x is not greater than 10".

You can also nest multiple **else** statements using the **if-elif-else** structure to handle multiple conditions:

```
#Filename: loop13.py
x = 5

if x > 10:
    print("x is greater than 10")
elif x > 5:
    print("x is greater than 5 but not greater than
10")
else:
    print("x is not greater than 5")
```

This structure checks the conditions one by one, executing the block of code that matches the first **true** condition. If the first if condition (x > 10) is **false**, the program moves to the elif condition (x > 5). Since x is 5, this condition is also **false**, so the else block executes.

Using range() to Step

The **range() function** generates a sequence of numbers you can loop through. It gives you the flexibility to define the starting value, ending value, and step size.

The basic syntax is:

```
range(start, end, step)
```

Here are a few examples:

```
#Filename: loop14.py
#step size of '1' - the default
for i in range(1, 6):
    print(i)
```

Output:

```
1
2
3
4
5
```

In this example, the loop goes from one to five with a step size of one. The sequence excludes the end value. Looping with a specified step size:

```
#Filename: loop15.py
#specified step size: 2
for i in range(0, 10, 2):
    print(i)
```

Output:

```
0
2
```

```
4
6
8
```

This loop goes from zero to 10 with a step size of two, printing even numbers from zero to eight. You can also loop in reverse order using a step size of -1.

```
#Filename: loop16.py
#Looping in reverse with a negative step:
for i in range(10, 0, -1):
    print(i)
```

However, **range()** doesn't support floating-point numbers for the step argument:

```
#Filename: loop17.py
#Attempting to loop with a step size of 0.5 (float):
for i in range(0, 5, 0.5):
    print(i)
```

Output:

```
TypeError: 'float' object cannot be interpreted as an
integer.
```

To achieve a similar effect, you can manually increment the loop variable within the loop. You can also create custom loops using different step sizes:

```
#Filename: loop18.py
#Looping with a step size of 3:
for i in range(0, 10, 3):
    print(i)
```

This loop goes from zero to 10 with a step size of three, printing multiples of three.

Remember, **range()** generates numbers up to, but not including, the end value. The step size can be positive or negative, but it must be an integer.

Looping with an Index

Sometimes, you might want to loop through a sequence while also keeping track of the index of each element. This is where the **enumerate()** function comes in, as it lets you access both the index and the value of each item during each iteration:

```
#Filename: loop19.py
fruits = ['apple', 'banana', 'orange']

for index, fruit in enumerate(fruits):
    print(f"Index: {index}, Fruit: {fruit}")
```

Output:

```
Index: 0, Fruit: apple
Index: 1, Fruit: banana
Index: 2, Fruit: orange
```

In this example, **enumerate()** is used to loop over the list of fruits. It returns a **tuple** containing the index and the corresponding element of the sequence. The loop variable **index** captures the index, and **fruit** captures the element value. (A **tuple** in Python is an ordered, immutable collection of items, typically used to store a fixed set of values. More shortly.)

You can customise the starting index:

```
#Filename: loop20.py
#Looping with a custom starting index:
fruits = ['apple', 'banana', 'orange']
for index, fruit in enumerate(fruits, start=1):
    print(f"Index: {index}, Fruit: {fruit}")
```

Output:

```
Index: 1, Fruit: apple
Index: 2, Fruit: banana
Index: 3, Fruit: orange
```

Here, the **start** parameter of the **enumerate()** function is set to one, so the index starts at 1 instead of the default 0.

You can also perform selective operations based on the index:

```
#Filename: loop21.py
#Selective operations based on the index:
fruits = ['apple', 'banana', 'orange']
for index, fruit in enumerate(fruits):
    if index % 2 == 0:
        print(f"Index: {index}, Fruit: {fruit}")
```

Output:

```
Index: 0, Fruit: apple
Index: 2, Fruit: orange
```

In this example, the **if** statement checks if the index is even by using the modulo operator (**%**). The program only prints elements with even indices.

You can even loop through the sequence in reverse order:

```
#Filename: loop22.py
#Looping with reversed index order
fruits = ['apple', 'banana', 'orange']
for index, fruit in reversed(list(enumerate(fruits))):
    print(f"Index: {index}, Fruit: {fruit}")
```

Output:

```
Index: 2, Fruit: orange
Index: 1, Fruit: banana
Index: 0, Fruit: apple
```

Here, the **reversed()** function is used to reverse the order of the enumerated elements. The **list()** function converts the reversed iterate back into a list for iteration.

These examples show how looping with an index can be useful for customising the starting index, performing selective operations, or reversing the order of iteration.

Nested Loops

When you place one loop inside another loop, you create a **nested loop.** Nested loops are great for handling more complex tasks, like working with multiple dimensions or performing repetitive tasks within tasks:

```
#Filename: loop23.py
#Nested loops
for i in range(1, 4):
    for j in range(1, 4):
        print(f"i: {i}, j: {j}")
```

Output:

```
i: 1, j: 1
i: 1, j: 2
i: 1, j: 3
i: 2, j: 1
i: 2, j: 2
i: 2, j: 3
i: 3, j: 1
i: 3, j: 2
i: 3, j: 3
```

In this example, the outer loop iterates over the range of values from one to four, and for each iteration of the outer loop, the inner loop also iterates from one to four. The result is a grid-like pattern of iterations, which can be useful for working with two-dimensional data or performing tasks that require interaction between two variables.

You can have multiple levels of nested loops in Python, allowing you to tackle even more complex scenarios. Just make sure your indentation is correct—this will help you define the nested structure clearly and avoid any strange results or errors.

Nested loops are often used for tasks like matrix operations, pattern generation, and searching through multidimensional data. They're a handy tool when you need to handle repetitive tasks.

Here's an example of nested loops with different ranges:

```
#Filename: loop24.py
#Nested loops with different ranges
for i in range(1, 4):
    for j in range(1, i+1):
        print(j, end=' ')
    print()
```

Output:

```
1
1 2
1 2 3
```

In this example, the number of iterations in the inner loop is determined by the value of **i** from the outer loop. In each iteration, the inner loop prints the numbers from one to **i**, creating a pattern of increasing numbers.

And here's an example of using nested loops to generate a pattern:

```
#Filename: loop25.py
#Nested loops for pattern generation
for i in range(5):
    for j in range(i):
        print('*', end=' ')
    print()
```

Output:

```
*
* *
* * *
* * * *
```

In this example, the inner loop prints asterisks based on the current iteration of the outer loop, creating a simple pattern.

Note that loop control statements only affect the loop in which they appear. If you had Loop A inside Loop B and these have loops of 10 and 5 respectively. Then Loop B would complete before going back to Loop A.

Loops come with a lot of perks, but like anything, there are a few downsides too. Let's dive into the pros and cons of using loops in your code.

Advantages of Loops

- **Efficiency Boost:** Loops make your code way more efficient by letting you write a set of instructions once and then run them over and over. This not only saves you from repeating the same lines of code manually but also makes your code cleaner and easier to manage.

- **Automation of Repetitive Tasks:** Loops are perfect for automating those repetitive tasks that would otherwise be a headache to handle manually. Whether you need something done a set number of times or until a particular condition is met, loops have got you covered.

Without them, you'd be stuck copying and pasting code, which is a recipe for mistakes.

- **Handling Variable Data Sets:** One of the best things about loops is how they let you work with variable data sets. You can iterate over collections and perform operations on each item individually. This flexibility makes it easy to process large amounts of data and perform complex operations efficiently.

- **Scalability:** Loops make your code scalable. Instead of hard-coding repetitive operations, loops allow your code to handle larger data sets or adapt to changing requirements without needing a massive overhaul. It's like having a code base that grows with your needs.

Disadvantages of Loops

- **Risk of Infinite Loops:** If you're not careful, you can accidentally create an infinite loop—where the loop's condition never becomes false. This can cause your program to hang or become unresponsive, forcing you to shut it down. It's crucial to define exactly when your loop should stop and make sure there's a clear exit strategy.

- **Performance Overhead:** While loops are great, they can come with a performance cost, especially when you're dealing with large data sets or have nested loops. These can slow down your program's execution time. In such cases, it might be worth optimising your loop or even considering a different approach.

- **Readability and Maintainability Issues:** Overusing loops or implementing them poorly can make your code harder to read and maintain. Complex loop structures with nested loops or tricky conditions can confuse anyone trying to understand your code—especially if they're not familiar with it. It's important to write loops that are clear and straightforward.

- **Potential for Bugs:** Loops introduce the possibility of errors, like off-by-one errors or incorrect loop conditions. If your loop control variables or conditions aren't set up correctly, you could end up with unintended behaviour or incorrect results. That's why it's so important to thoroughly test your loops and implement them carefully to ensure they do what you expect.

Questions

1. What are loops in programming, and why are they useful?

2. What are the two main types of loops commonly used in Python?

3. How does a for loop work in Python, and when would you use it?

4. How can you make a for loop print values in a single line instead of separate lines?
5. What does the range() function do in a for loop?
6. How does a while loop differ from a for loop in Python?
7. What are loop control statements, and name the three main types?
8. How does the break statement affect loop execution?
9. What does the continue statement do in a loop?
10. What is the purpose of the enumerate() function in a for loop?
11. What are nested loops, and when might you use them?
12. How can you avoid creating an infinite loop in Python?
13. What are some advantages and disadvantages of using loops in programming?

08: Lists

Lists, Dictionaries, and Tuples are essential in Python programming. Knowing how to use them correctly is very important because they're all closely connected. And when you start using them together—like having lists of dictionaries or dictionaries of lists—you'll see just how handy they can be.

Getting the hang of these data structures is key to being a great Python programmer because they make it easier to store, tweak, and pull-out data whenever you need it.

In the next few chapters, we're going to dive into each one and how to use them. But first, here's a quick overview of what each one is all about.

Lists: Lists are **ordered collections** of items, meaning they keep everything in the order you **put** them into a list. They're great because you can store different types of data all in one place and easily add, remove, or change things whenever you like. They're incredibly flexible and dynamic, which is why they're a go-to for tasks like storing sequences of values, and looping through elements, (or even creating stacks or queues which we'll cover in due course). Lists are a staple in Python because they make data manipulation a breeze.

Dictionaries: Dictionaries are **unordered ordered collections** of key-value pairs, which means you can quickly find what you need based on a specific key. Unlike lists that use numbers (indexes) to find items, dictionaries use keys, making them very convenient for tasks like storing data that needs to be mapped. **The fact that you can access values quickly by their keys** makes dictionaries a must-have when you're dealing with data retrieval and mapping out relationships between things. Real life mapping include things such as, names to phone numbers, words to definitions and product IDs to details. Of course there are zillions more.

Tuples: Tuples are collections of ordered elements, but with a twist—they **can't be changed** once you've created them. They're perfect for when you need to represent fixed sequences of values that shouldn't be messed with, like coordinates, database records, or what a function returns. **Tuples are lightweight and memory-efficient**, making them a great choice when you need something that's both fast and safe from accidental changes. While they might not be as flexible as lists, their benefits include protection from unintended edits and quicker iteration.

So, how are these data structures related? Well, they all help you store and work with collections of values, but each one has its own special features and ideal use cases:

- **Lists** are mutable and ordered, making them perfect for when you need to store and manage sequences of items that might change.
- **Dictionaries** are mutable and ordered, offering quick access to values based on keys, which is great for mapping and associating data.
- **Tuples** are immutable and ordered, giving you fixed sequences of values that won't change, which is ideal when you need reliability.

In Python programming, knowing when to reach for a list, dictionary, or tuple is crucial for writing **efficient, expressive code**.

Common Lists

Lists are a go-to for programmers in Python, and for good reason—they come with a bunch of handy methods that let you tweak and play with your data in almost any way you can think of. In fact, with lists, dictionaries, and tuples, there's pretty much nothing you can't do with data.

A list is like a magical container that lets you store and organise a bunch of items (let's not get too deep into Russell's Paradox here!). It's **ordered and mutable**, which means you can change the items inside and even shuffle them around. Just like variables, lists can hold all sorts of data—numbers, strings, you name it. And here's the cool part: lists can even contain other lists, and yes, lists of lists!

Lists have a few key characteristics that make them useful:

- **Ordered**: The elements in a list follow a specific order, which is determined by an index value. This index is like a label that tells you where each item is so you can easily access and manipulate them.
- **Mutable**: You can change, add, or remove elements after you've created the list. It's all very flexible.

- **Heterogeneous**: Lists can hold different types of data. Want to mix numbers and strings in the list? Go right ahead.
- **Dynamic**: When you add or remove elements, lists automatically grow or shrink to fit. No need to worry about running out of space (unless you literally run out of memory, but that's another story).

To create a list, just pop a comma-separated sequence of items inside square brackets, like this:

```
my_list = [99, 98, 97, 96, 95]
```

Here, **my_list** holds five integer elements. And remember, the elements in my_list are ordered, starting from index 0. It's important to keep in mind that the first item in a list is at position 0 (zero).

Let's break it down a bit further: in the example above, the index starts at 0, which holds the value 99. The value 96 is stored at index 3. So, when you want to refer to the first element in my_list, you'd use:

```
my_list[0]
```

This would point you to 99. And if you want the element 96, you'd use:

```
my_list[3]
```

Your list should not be so long as to make it unwieldy. A very long list might affect how efficient your code is. Also, as your list grows, operations like adding or removing items can start to take more time and space. So, if you're working with a giant list, you might want to think about breaking it up into smaller chunks.

There is a bunch of ways to access and work with lists. If you get a good grasp of how lists work and how they're indexed, you'll be all set to tackle these examples with ease.

Working with List Operators

Remember those operators we talked about with variables earlier on? Well, they work with lists too. But, as always, the outcome depends on what's inside the list. Let's dive into an example using the + operator:

```
#Filename: list1.py
#Adding lists
list1 = [1, 2, 3]
list2 = [4, 5, 6]
result = list1 + list2
print(result)
```

Now, you might expect the result to be [5, 7, 9], right? But hold on, it doesn't do a summation here? Instead, it **joins one list to another**, like sticking two pieces of wood together. So, what you actually get is:

```
[1, 2, 3, 4, 5, 6]
```

But what about the subtraction operator?

```
#Filename: list2.py
#Subtract list2 from list1
list1 = [1, 2, 3, 4, 5]
list2 = [3, 4, 5, 6, 7]
result = list1 - list2
print(result)
```

Uh-oh! If you try to subtract lists like this, you'll run into a **TypeError** because Python doesn't support - for lists. If you want to subtract one list from another, you'll need to step through each item and subtract them one by one. This is where a technique called **list comprehension** comes in handy:

```
#Filename: list3.py
list1 = [1, 2, 3, 4, 5]
list2 = [3, 4, 5, 6, 7]
result = [x - y for x, y in zip(list1, list2)]
print(result)
#Output: [-2, -2, -2, -2, -2]
```

Here's what's happening:

- We're using a for loop to go through each item in the lists.
- The **zip function** pairs up corresponding elements from list1 and list2.
- Then, the list comprehension subtracts these pairs element by element. (By the way, as you've probably gathered already, 'zip' here doesn't mean compressing files—it's just grouping pairs together. We'll talk more about it in the chapter on Tuples.)

Let's break it down step by step. Start by defining the lists:

```
list1 = [1, 2, 3, 4, 5]
list2 = [3, 4, 5, 6, 7]
```

Zip the lists together

```
Step 1:  Pair corresponding elements from each list.
    (1, 3)
    (2, 4)
    (3, 5)
    (4, 6)
    (5, 7)
```

```
Step 2: Subtraction operation in list comprehension
    (1 - 3) = -2
    (2 - 4) = -2
    (3 - 5) = -2
    (4 - 6) = -2
    (5 - 7) = -2
```

And that gives us the result: [-2, -2, -2, -2, -2].

If you want to **add** the elements of two lists together, it works the same way:

```
#Filename: list4.py
list1 = [1, 2, 3, 4, 5]
list2 = [3, 4, 5, 6, 7]

result = [x + y for x, y in zip(list1, list2)]
print(result)
#Output: [4, 6, 8, 10, 12]
```

As with subtraction, this assumes the lists are the same length. You can also multiply and divide corresponding elements by using * and /. For instance, replace the + with a * in the result line and you get:

```
[3, 8, 15, 24, 35]
```

If you flip back to the subtraction example, there's a way to get a list of elements that are in list1 but not in list2. Check this out:

```
#Filename: list5.py
list2 = [1, 2, 3, 4, 5]
list1 = [3, 4, 5, 6, 7]
# Subtract elements of list2 from list1
result_list = [item for item in list1 if item not in
list2]

print(result_list)
#Output: [6, 7]
```

But if both lists are identical:

```
#Filename: list6.py
list1 = [1, 2, 3, 4, 5]
list2 = [1, 2, 3, 4, 5]
#Subtract elements of list2 from list1
result_list = [item for item in list1 if item not in
list2]

print(result_list)
#Output: []
```

You'll end up with an empty list ([]). So, remember, the order in which you subtract lists can **drastically change the result**. It's easy to trip up here, so always double-check if things aren't adding up as expected!

What if you want to compare lists? That's straightforward:

```
#Filename: list7.py
#Comparing lists
list1 = [1, 2, 3]
list2 = [1, 2, 3]
result = list1 == list2
print(result)  # Output: True
```

Here, the **==** operator checks if the lists have the same values in the same order. If they do, you get True. If not, you get False.

Subtracting numbers in a list isn't always straightforward, and lists might not be the best tool for this specific job. But hang in there, we'll circle back to this later.

In the first example, we used the + operator to add one list to the end of another. You can also do this with the **extend()** method:

```
#Filename: list8.py
list1 = [1, 2, 3]
list2 = [56, 65]

#Extend the list
list1.extend(list2)
print(list1)
#Output: [1, 2, 3, 56, 65]
```

There's also an append method, but it works a little differently:

```
#Filename: list9.py
#Append an element to the end of the list
list1 = [1, 2, 3]
list1.append(4)

print(list1)
#Output: [1, 2, 3, 4]
```

But what happens if you attach a list to another list?

```
#Filename: list10.py
#List within list
list1 = [1, 2, 3]
list2 = [56, 65]
list1.append(list2)
print(list1)
```

The output is:

```
[1, 2, 3, [56, 65]]
```

So, instead of adding list2 as individual elements, it gets added as a single item—a list within a list.

Now, what if we do this?

```
#Filename: list11.py
list1 = [1, 2, 3]
list2 = [56, 65]

#Append lists
list1.append(list2)
list3 = list1
list1.append(list3)
print(list1)
print(list2)
print(list3)
```

The result would be:

```
[1, 2, 3, [56, 65], [...]]
[56, 65]
[1, 2, 3, [56, 65], [...]]
```

In Python, **[...]** isn't a special list notation. It just shows there's a recursive reference—a list pointing back to itself. To see this in action, you can iterate through the list and print each item:

```
#Filename: list12.py
list1 = [1, 2, 3]
list2 = [56, 65]

#Append lists
list1.append(list2)
list3 = list1
list1.append(list3)

for item in list1:
    print(item)
```

And the output would be:

```
1
2
3
[56, 65]
[1, 2, 3, [56, 65], [...]]
```

So why does this happen? It's because when you append list3 to list1, which already contains list1, you create a **circular reference**. It's like a snake eating its tail! This isn't common practice and can lead to some pretty confusing behaviour, so it's something to watch out for.

To avoid this, you can create a new list and copy the elements over:

```
#Filename: list13.py
list1 = [1, 2, 3]
list2 = [56, 65]

#Create a new list and copy elements
new_list1 = list1.copy()
```

```
#Append list2 to the new list
new_list1.append(list2)

#Append the new list to list1
list1.append(new_list1)

for item in list1:
    print(item)
```

This way, you avoid circular references and get a cleaner output:

```
1
2
3
[1, 2, 3]
[56, 65]
```

Again, it's a subtle difference but easy to mix up.

Working With Different Lengths

The examples we've looked at so far all used lists of the same length. But what if they're not? Enter the **zip_longest** function from the un-ordered iterators module. It lets you fill in the gaps with whatever value you want—like a 0 in this case:

```
#Filename: list14.py
from itertools import zip_longest

list1 = [1, 2, 3, 4, 5]
list2 = [3, 4, 5, 6, 7, 8, 9]

result = [x + y for x, y in zip_longest(list1, list2,
fillvalue=0)]
print(result)
#Output: [4, 6, 8, 10, 12, 8, 9]
```

Here, **zip_longest** pairs up elements from list1 and list2, and **fillvalue**=0 fills in any missing values. It's like making list1 [1, 2, 3, 4, 5, 0, 0].

But if you want to handle lists of different lengths without filling in extra values, you can use a loop:

```
#Filename: list15.py
list1 = [1, 2, 3, 4, 5]
list2 = [3, 4, 5, 6, 7, 8, 9]

#Find the minimum length of the two lists
min_length = min(len(list1), len(list2))

#Perform addition up to the minimum length
result = [list1[i] + list2[i] for i in range(min_
length)]

#Append the remaining elements from the longer list
```

```
result += list1[min_length:] + list2[min_length:]

print(result)
#Output: [4, 6, 8, 10, 12, 8, 9]
```

Here, the loop adds corresponding elements up to the length of the shorter list, then appends any remaining elements from the longer list. This flexibility is one of the many reasons that lists are so useful!

There are lots of ways to work with lists, whether they're the same length or not. We're just scratching the surface of what you can do.

When to Use List Comprehension

List comprehension is one of those neat Python tricks that can really save you time and make your code cleaner. But when exactly would you want to use it? Let's look at a few scenarios where list comprehension really shines:

- **Element-wise Operations Between Two Lists**: Imagine you've got two lists of numbers—maybe actual expenses and budgeted amounts. You want to perform an operation like subtraction, addition, or multiplication on each pair of elements from these lists. List comprehension is perfect for this! You might subtract actual expenses from budgeted amounts to find out how well you stuck to your budget or who you need to metaphorically kick if overspent.
- **Filtering and Conditional Processing**: Say you want to filter out or conditionally process elements from one list based on elements in another. For instance, you could create a list that only shows the differences where the first list has higher values than the second, ignoring the rest. This is dead handy when you're dealing with data and only want to focus on certain conditions.
- **Maintaining Immutability**: In some cases—like functional programming or when you want to avoid changing your existing lists—you can use list comprehension to create a new list without altering the originals. This is great when you need to keep your original data intact but still want to do some calculations or comparisons. For example, if you have two lists representing stock prices over two different weeks, you could calculate the weekly changes in price without messing up your original data. This lets you quickly see how prices changed from one week to the next.

Here's a short program to tackle that last example:

```
#Filename: lists16.py
week1_prices = [100, 102, 105, 107, 110]
week2_prices = [103, 101, 106, 108, 109]

price_changes = [w2 - w1 for w1, w2 in zip(week1_
prices, week2_prices)]
print(price_changes)
#Output: [3, -1, 1, 1, -1]
```

This program helps you analyse how the prices have changed over the course of the week in a straightforward and efficient way. Just by looking at the output, you can quickly see the differences from one week to the next.

Changing List Elements

One of the great things about lists is that they're mutable, meaning you can change them around as much as you like! If you want to swap out an item for something else, it's as easy as assigning a new value to a specific index. For example:

```
#Filename: list17.py
my_list = [99,98,97,96,95]
my_list[2] = 10
print(my_list)
#Output: [99,98, 10, 96, 95]
```

Here, the item at index 2 (which is actually the third item in the list, thanks to our trusty zero-based indexing) is replaced with 10. It overwrites the item it is replacing. Simple enough, as shown below in Figure 8a.

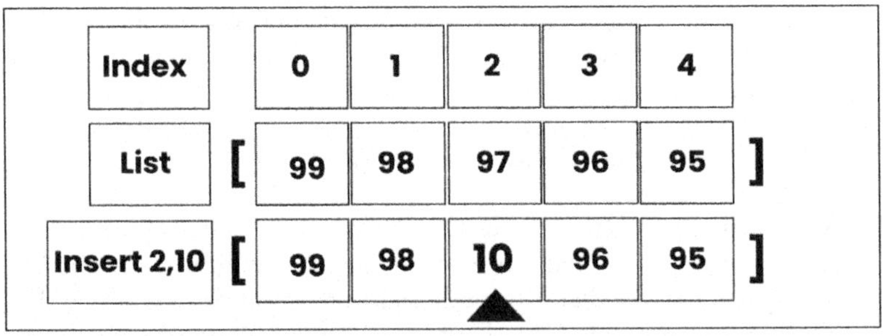

Figure 8a. Inserting '10' in the list at index '2'2.

You can also slice out a section of a list to create a sub-list. **Slicing** lets you specify a range of indices, separated by a colon, to grab a chunk of the list and put it into a new one—all without touching the original list:

```
#Filename: list18.py
my_list = [99,98,97,96,95]
sub_list = my_list[1:4]
#Extracts elements at indices 1, 2, and 3
print(sub_list)  # Output: 98, 97, 96
```

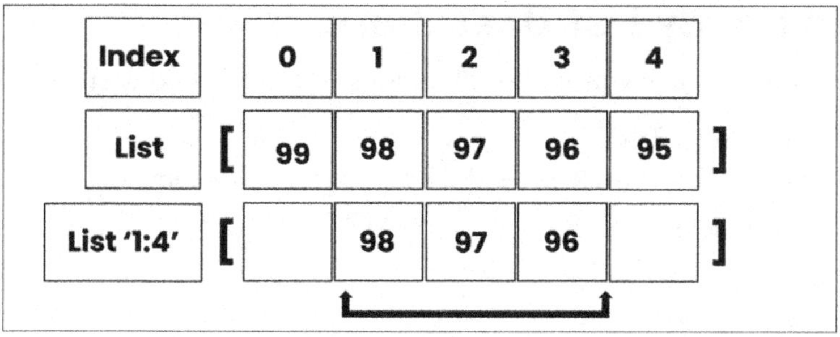

Figure 8b. The slicing ends before the last index value.

Want to know how many elements are in your list? The **len()** function has got you covered:

```
#Filename: list19.py
my_list = [99, 98, 97, 96, 95]
length = len(my_list)
print(length)
#Output: 5
```

And if you're looking to combine two or more lists, the **+** operator makes it a breeze:

```
#Filename: list20.py
my_list = [99, 98, 97, 96, 95]
combined_list = my_list + [6, 7, 8]
print(combined_list)
#Output: [99, 98, 97, 96, 95, 6, 7, 8]
```

Adding Elements to a List

You've got a couple of options here: use the **append()** function to add something to the end of the list, or use **insert()** to slip an element into a specific spot. Here's your example:

```
#Filename: list21.py
my_list = [99, 98, 97, 96, 95]

my_list.insert(2, 100)
print(my_list)
my_list.append(200)
print(my_list)
#Output:
#[99, 98, 100, 97, 96, 95]
#[99, 98, 100, 96, 96, 95, 200]
```

Here, we inserted 100 at index 2, which nudged the existing elements to the right, and then we tacked 200 onto the end of the list with append().

Some Handy List Operations

Let's run through a few more list operations you might find useful:

Appending to a List

Adding an element to the end of the list is a snap with append().

```
#Filename: list22.py
#Handy List Operations
my_list = [1, 2, 3]
my_list.append(4)
print("Updated List:", my_list)
#Output: Updated List: [1, 2, 3, 4]

#Accessing List Elements:
#Grab an element using its index.
#Here's how you'd get the first element
my_list = [1, 2, 3, 4]
first_element = my_list[0]
print("First Element:", first_element)
#Output: First Element: 1

#Slicing a List:
#Want just a part of the list? Slice away!
my_list = [1, 2, 3, 4, 5]
sliced_list = my_list[2:4]
print("Sliced List:", sliced_list)
#Output: Sliced List: [3, 4]

#List Concatenation:
#Join two lists together using +.
list1 = [1, 2, 3]
list2 = [4, 5, 6]
concat_list = list1 + list2
print("Concatenated List:", concat_list)
```

And the output from all these operations would be:

```
Updated List: [1, 2, 3, 4]
First Element: 1
Sliced List: [3, 4]
Concatenated List: [1, 2, 3, 4, 5, 6]
```

With these simple operations, you can start to do some really clever things in Python.

Removing Elements from a List

When it comes to removing elements from a list, Python gives you several tools to get the job done: **remove(), pop(),** and **del()**. But each one has its own way of handling the task, so let's break them down.

The **remove()** method is your go-to when you want to get rid of the first occurrence of a specific value in a list. It hunts down the value, removes it if it finds it, and if the value isn't in the list? Well, it throws a ValueError and lets you know it couldn't find it. Here's an example:

```
#Filename: list23.py
#Using remove()
numbers = [1, 2, 3, 4, 3, 5, 3, 6]
numbers.remove(3)
print(numbers)
#Output: [1, 2, 4, 3, 5, 3, 6]
```

Notice how only the **first occurrence** of 3 is removed? If remove() does its thing, all the other elements shuffle along to fill the gap. But if there's more than one 3, like in our list, only the first one gets the boot.

The pop() Method

This one's a bit more precise because it lets you remove an element at a specific index and even returns the removed element. If you don't give it an index, it'll just **pop** off the last element. And yes, it changes the original list. For example:

```
#Filename: list24.py
numbers = [1, 2, 3, 4, 5]
removed_element = numbers.pop(2)
print(removed_element)
#Output: 3 (element at index 2)
print(numbers)
```

By running pop() again, we can remove yet another element, further shortening the list:

```
#Filename: list25.py
numbers = [1, 2, 3, 4, 5]
removed_element = numbers.pop(2)
print(removed_element)  #Output: 3 (element at index 2)
print(numbers)          #Output: [1, 2, 4, 5]
removed_element = numbers.pop(2)
print(removed_element)  #Output: 4 (new element at
index 2)
print(numbers)          #Output: [1, 2, 5]
```

The del Statement

Then there's the **del** statement, a more general-purpose tool that can remove elements or slices from a list, delete entire lists, or even get rid of variables. Unlike pop(), it doesn't return the removed element, but it directly modifies the list.

```
#Filename: list26.py
numbers = [1, 2, 3, 4, 5]
del numbers[2]
print(numbers)  # Output: [1, 2, 4, 5]
```

Clearing an Entire List

And if you ever need to wipe out an entire list in one go, the **clear()** method is your best friend:

```
#Filename: list27.py
my_list = [1, 2, 3, 4, 5]
my_list.clear()
print(my_list)
#Output: []
```

Just like that, the list is cleared out, leaving you with an empty list ([]).

Counting, Finding, Sorting & Multidimensional

You can count the occurrences of an element in a list using the **count()** method. To find the index of the first occurrence of an element, you can use the **index()** method as follows:

```
#Filename: list28.py
numbers = [1, 2, 3, 4, 5]
count = numbers.count(2)
#Counts the occurrences of the number 2

index = numbers.index(4)

print(count)    #Find number of the number 2.
print(index)    #Finds the index of number 4
```

A ValueError will be raised if the element is not found in the list.

Sorting Lists in Place

The **sort()** method sorts the list in place (modifies the original list).

```
#Filename: list29.py
my_list = [3, 1, 4, 2, 5]
my_list.sort()
print(my_list)  # Output: [1, 2, 3, 4, 5]
```

Sorting with sorted():

The **sorted()** function returns a new sorted list without changing the original list.

```
#Filename: list30.py
my_list = [3, 1, 4, 2, 5]
sorted_list = sorted(my_list)
print(sorted_list)  # Output: [1, 2, 3, 4, 5]
print(my_list)  # Output: [3, 1, 4, 2, 5]
```

Accessing Elements in Nested Lists

How to access and manipulate elements in a list of lists.

```
#Filename: list31.py
list_of_lists = [
    [1, 2, 3],
    [4, 5, 6],
    [7, 8, 9]
]
print(list_of_lists[1][2])
#Output: 6
```

Flattening a List of Lists

Convert a nested list into a single list.

```
#Filename: list32
nested_list = [[1, 2], [3, 4], [5, 6]]
flat_list = [item for sublist in nested_list for item in
sublist]
print(flat_list)
#Output: [1, 2, 3, 4, 5, 6]
```

Exercise: Putting It All Together

Write a program that does the following:

- Takes a list of numbers as input from the user.
- Prints each number in the list along with its index (use enumerate()).
- Calculates the sum of all even numbers in the list (use a for loop with an if condition).
- Stops processing the list if it encounters a number greater than 100 (use break).

Solution over the page.

```
# Filename: 08-exercise-01.py
# Step 1: Take a list of numbers as input from the user
# The user will enter numbers separated by spaces, and
we'll convert them to integers
user_input = input("Enter a list of numbers separated
by spaces: ")
numbers = list(map(int, user_input.split()))

# Step 2: Print each number in the list along with its
index (using enumerate)
print("\nNumbers and their indices:")
for index, number in enumerate(numbers):
    print(f"Index {index}: {number}")

# Step 3: Calculate the sum of all even numbers in the
list
even_sum = 0
for number in numbers:
    if number % 2 == 0:  # Check if the number is even
        even_sum += number

print(f"\nThe sum of all even numbers in the list is:
{even_sum}")

# Step 4: Stop processing the list if a number greater
than 100 is encountered
print("\nProcessing the list with a 'break'
condition:")
for number in numbers:
    if number > 100:
        print(f"Number greater than 100 encountered:
{number}")
        break
    print(f"Processing number: {number}")

print("\nProgram complete.")
```

Explanation

User Input: The program takes a space-separated list of numbers and converts it to integers. **Enumerate**: Each number and its index are printed using enumerate(). **Sum of Evens**: The program uses a for loop and an if statement to add only even numbers. **Break Condition**: The loop stops processing as soon as a number greater than 100 is encountered, demonstrating the use of the break statement.

09: Dictionaries

A dictionary is a data structure and a way to organise and store information. Dictionaries are flexible, **unordered,** and can contain **various types** of data. They let you link or tie unique keys to specific values. You might also hear this called an associative array or a hash table.

Every entry in a dictionary comprises a **key** paired with its matching value. This 'key' acts like a special tag, helping you fetch the right value. Curly braces, {}, enclose the key-value pairs in a dictionary, and a colon, :, separates each key from its corresponding value.

```
#Filename: dict1.py
#Create a dictionary
person = {
    'name': 'John',
    'age': 25,
    'country': 'USA'
}
#Access dictionary values
print(person['name'])      #Output: John
print(person['age'])       #Output: 25
print(person['country'])   #Output: USA
```

In this example, the person dictionary adds a new key-value pair **country**: **USA** and updates the value for the existing key **age**.

To retrieve values from a dictionary, you use square brackets '[]' to enclose the desired key. For instance, 'person['name']' yields 'John,' 'person['age']' provides 25, and 'person['country']' gives 'USA.'

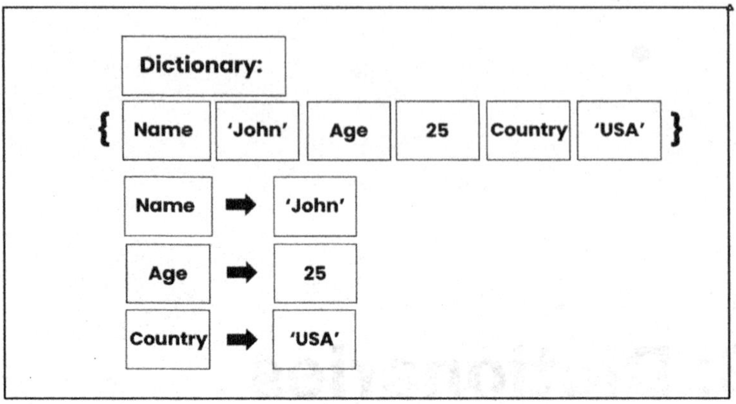

Figure 9a. Every entry in a dictionary comprises a 'key' paired with its matching value.

Like lists, you can also change the items within the dictionary by re-assigning them thus:

```
#Filename: dict2.py
#Add or Modify Elements:
person = {'name': 'John', 'age': 25}
#Add a new key-value pair
person['country'] = 'USA'
#Modify the value for an existing key
person['age'] = 26
print(person['name'])
print(person['age'])
print(person['country'])


#Remove Elements:
person = {'name': 'John', 'age': 25, 'country': 'USA'}
#Remove a specific key-value pair
del person['age']
#Remove and return the value for a specific key
person.pop('country')
#Remove all key-value pairs, emptying the dictionary
person.clear()
```

Dictionaries find widespread use when there's a need to associate and retrieve values using **distinct keys**. They provide an efficient mechanism for data access and present a well-structured approach to store and manage information.

You can generate multiple dictionaries, each identified by a unique name. Within dictionaries, the number of elements is flexible, constrained only by the memory, much like lists.

Dictionaries offer a range of operations and data extraction capabilities. Many of these operations parallel those explored in the preceding chapter on lists.

The following examples show the manipulation of data stored in variables of **different data types**. By using methods and operations, you can change, access, and combine this data in a variety of ways. #

```
#Filename: dict3.py
#Adding Key-Value Pairs to a Dictionary

my_dict = {"name": "John", "age": 30}
my_dict["country"] = "USA"
print("Updated Dictionary:", my_dict)
#Accessing Dictionary Values
my_dict = {"name": "John", "age": 30}
name = my_dict["name"]
print("Name:", name)
#Removing Key-Value Pairs from a Dictionary
my_dict = {"name": "John", "age": 30}
del my_dict["age"]
print("Updated Dictionary:", my_dict)
```

Add or Change Elements

You can add additional elements to a dictionary and adjust the existing elements.

```
#Filename: dict4.py
#Create a dictionary
person = {'name': 'John', 'age': 25}
#Add a new key-value pair
person['country'] = 'USA'
#Change the value for an existing key
person['age'] = 26

# Access dictionary values
print(person['name'])
print(person['age'])
print(person['country'])
print(person['age'])
```

In this example, the person dictionary appends a new key-value pair 'country: 'USA', and updates the value for the existing key 'age'.

Remove Elements

Different methods can remove elements from a dictionary. The **del** statement removes a specific key-value pair, the **pop()** method removes and returns the value for a specific key, and the **clear()** method removes all key-value pairs, leaving the dictionary empty.

```
#Filename dict5.py
person = {'name': 'John', 'age': 25, 'country': 'USA'}
#Remove a specific key-value pair
del person['age']
#Remove and return the value for a specific key
person.pop('country')
#Remove all key-value pairs, emptying the dictionary
person.clear()
print (person)
```

We create a dictionary in the usual way in the example below. We define them as strings by placing the key-value pairs in double quotes. The second half of the program shows how we can perform various functions, including string concatenation.

```
#Filename: dict6.py
#Create a dictionary with strings as values
person = {
    "name": "John",
    "age": "30",
    "occupation": "Engineer"
}
# Concatenate the name and occupation strings
full_name_occupation = person["name"] + ", " +
person["occupation"]

print(full_name_occupation)
#Output: "John, Engineer"
```

Check for Key Existence

It is also possible to check if a key exists in a dictionary using the **in** operator. Likewise the **not in** operator can be used to check if a key does not exist. The **in** operator returns **True** if the key exists and **False** otherwise.

```
#Filename: dict7.py
person = {'name': 'John', 'age': 25}
print('name' in person)        #True
print('country' not in person)  #True
```

Accessing Keys and Values

In this example, the **keys()** method returns a list of keys in the dictionary, and the **values()** method returns a list of values.

```
#Filename: dict8.py
person = {'name': 'John', 'age': 25}
keys = person.keys()       #Get a list of keys
values = person.values()   #Get a list of values

print(keys)
print(values)
```

Length of a Dictionary

The **len()** operator allows you to find out the length of a dictionary. It is simple enough to get the number of items:

```
#Filename: dict9.py
person = {'name': 'John', 'age': 25}
#Get the number of key-value pairs
count = len(person)
print(count)  #Output: 2
```

It can also determine the number of key-value pairs in the dictionary by iterating over keys and values:

```
#Filename: dict10.py
person = {'name': 'John', 'age': 25}

#Iterate over keys
for key in person:
    print(key)

#Iterate over values
for value in person.values():
    print(value)

#Iterate over key-value pairs
for key, value in person.items():
    print(key, value)
```

In these examples, you can sweep over the keys, values, or key-value pairs using a for loop. The **items()** method returns an iterable of key-value pairs.

Dictionaries and OOP

Dictionaries share conceptual similarities with objects in OOP by providing a flexible and dynamic structure for organising and managing data.

While dictionaries lack the explicit behaviour (**methods**) associated with OOP objects, they do provide a way to structure data, which is a fundamental aspect of object-oriented design.

In OOP, objects are instances of classes, and each object can have attributes (data) and methods (functions) associated with it.

In OOP, objects have attributes that define their properties. Dictionaries, with keys representing attributes and values containing corresponding data, provide a similar structure. For example:

```
#Filename: dict11.py
car_price = {'BMW': 98000, 'Lexus': 102000, 'Holden': 35000}
#Adding 2000 more to the existing value of BMW
car_price["BMW"] += 2000

#Access dictionary values
print(car_price['BMW'])
print(car_price['Lexus'])
print(car_price['Holden'])
print(car_price)

# Filename: dict12.py
# Create a dictionary with strings as values
cars = {
    "make": "Lexus",
    "price": "98000",

    "size": "5 seats"
}

#Concatenate the make, size, and price strings
```

```
full_details = cars["make"] + ", " + cars["size"] + ", $" + cars["price"]
print(full_details)
```

Encapsulation in OOP involves bundling data and methods that operate on that data within a unit.

```
#Filename: dict12.py
#OOP Example
class Car:
    def __init__(self, make, model):
        self.make = make
        self.model = model


    def start_engine(self):
        print("Engine started.")

#Dictionary representation
car_dict = {'make': 'Toyota', 'model': 'Camry'}
print (car_dict)
```

Dictionaries are dynamic and allow for the addition, modification, or removal of key-value pairs during run-time. This flexibility reflects some aspects of the dynamic nature of OOP.

```
#Filename: dict13.py
class Person:
    def __init__(self, name, age):
        self.name = name
        self.age = age

#Creating an instance of Person class
person = Person('Alice', 30)

#Initialising empty dictionary
person_dict = {}

# Adding a new attribute to the person object
person.height = 170


#Adding a new key-value pair to person_dict dictionary
person_dict['height'] = 170
print(person.height)
print (person_dict)
```

Dictionaries provide a convenient way to represent objects and their attributes in a serialised format for data storage.

The hash function in Python generates a **hash value** for each key used in a dictionary. This function converts the keys into unique (**hash**) values, which are essentially integers. Hash values decide the indices where the corresponding values are placed.

Here's the **magic**: The hash function ensures that similar keys produce unique hash values, reducing the chances of **collisions** where different keys producing the same hash. This is crucial for the dictionary to work smoothly.

The key to maintaining unique hash values lies in the design of the hash function. A good hash function ensures that even minor changes in the input (the keys) result in significantly unique hash values.

Think of it like a secret recipe: a change in the ingredients (the key) results in a completely different task meal.

This property minimises the chances of what we call **collisions**, where different keys produce the same hash.

Similar But Different

Lists and dictionaries serve different purposes and have distinct features. This chapter builds on concepts introduced previously, providing examples to illustrate the differences and uses of each.

Differences Between Dictionaries and Lists

Having looked at some example programs, you might ask what is the difference between a dictionary and a list? So, let's answer that now, if you haven't already had an inkling.

- They are both fundamental data structures, with several differences
- A list is an ordered collection of elements that can be of any data type.
- A dictionary is an unordered collection of key-value pairs
- Square brackets '[]' enclose lists, and commas separate the elements.
- A list preserves the order of its elements and assigns each element an index starting from 0.
- Dictionaries have each key-value pair separated by a colon ':' and enclosed in curly braces '{}'.
- Keys are unique within a dictionary, and they are used to retrieve the corresponding values.
- Unlike lists, dictionaries do not maintain any inherent order.
- To access elements in a list, you need to specify their position using square brackets. For instance, **my_list[0]** retrieves the **first** element.
- To access elements in a dictionary, you use their keys. By specifying

the corresponding key within square brackets, like my_dict['key'], you can retrieve the associated value.

- Lists are mutable, meaning you can alter their elements after creating the list. You can make changes, additions, or removals of elements using various list methods or indexing operations.
- Dictionaries are also mutable. You can change values, add new key-value pairs, or remove existing entries from the dictionary.
- Lists **maintain** the order of elements as they are added. The position of each element within a list is determined by its index.
- Dictionaries **do not** maintain a specific order. They do not guarantee the order of key-value pairs, which may not match the order of insertion.

We opt for dictionaries over lists when:

- **Key-Value Mapping:** The need arises to associate values with unique keys and perform lookups based on those keys.
- **Flexible Data Structure:** There is a requirement for flexible storage and organisation of data. Dictionaries permit keys of various data types, and values can encompass complex objects.
- **Dynamic Data Updates:** Dynamic updates are crucial, allowing the addition, alteration, or deletion of key-value pairs during run-time. Great if your program involves frequent changes or updates to data based on specific keys.
- **Unique Key Enforcement:** There is a necessity to enforce unique keys, ensuring that each key within the dictionary is distinct.

The program provides an example of this:

```
#Filename: dict14.py
#Using a dictionary for key-value mapping
student_info = {
    'name': 'John Doe',
    'age': 22,
    'major': 'Computer Science',
    'grades': {'math': 90, 'English': 85, 'history':
75}
}

#Flexible Data Structure:  objects as values
flexible_data = {
    42: 'Answer to the Ultimate Question of Life, the
Universe, and Everything',
    'list_example': [1, 2, 3],
    'nested_dict': {'key1': 'value1', 'key2': 'value2'}
}
```

```
#Dynamic Data: Adding, changing deleting key-valuepairs
student_info['grades']['science'] = 88
# Adding a new subject

student_info['major'] = 'Data Science'
# Changing the major

del student_info['grades']['history']
# Deleting a subject

# Unique Key Enforcement: Enforcing unique keys
unique_keys = {
    'id_001': 'Data Entry 001',
    'id_002': 'Data Entry 002',
    'id_003': 'Data Entry 003'
}

#Displaying the dictionaries
print("Student Info:", student_info)
print("Flexible Data:", flexible_data)
print("Unique Keys:", unique_keys)
```

You would prefer a **list** over a dictionary when:

- **Sequential Access:** When your need involves accessing elements based on their position or performing operations reliant on element order, such as sorting or indexing, a list becomes the more appropriate choice. Lists uphold a specific order, facilitating element access through indices.

- **Duplicate Elements:** Opt for a list if you wish to permit duplicate values in your data structure. Lists support multiple elements sharing the same value, while dictionaries mandate key uniqueness.

- **Memory Efficiency:** Lists exhibit a smaller memory footprint compared to dictionaries, especially when dealing with a substantial number of elements. If memory efficiency is a priority and key-based access or key uniqueness isn't necessary, a list proves more efficient.

- **Simple Data Storage:** For straightforward data collections devoid of key-value mappings or specific lookup requirements, a list offers a simpler and more straightforward structure for storing and accessing the data.

- **Data Indexing:** In scenarios involving a large data-set and the need for swift value lookup based on specific keys, dictionaries shine. They ensure efficient and rapid retrieval through key-based indexing.

- **Mapping Relationships:** Dictionaries stand out for representing relationships or associations between entries. For instance, mapping student names to their corresponding grades or associating user IDs with user information is well-suited for dictionaries.

- **Configuration Settings:** Commonly employed for storing and accessing configuration settings in applications, dictionaries shine bright. Keys in dictionaries represent the settings' names, while values store their corresponding configurations.
- **Grouping Data:** Dictionaries prove valuable for grouping data based on shared attributes. For example, you can use a dictionary to group students by their age or employees by department.

```
#Filename: dic15.py
#Sequential Access with Lists
print("Sequential Access with Lists:")
my_list = [10, 20, 30, 40, 50]
print("Original List:", my_list)
print("Element at index 2:", my_list[2])  # Accessing
element by index
my_list.sort()  # Sorting the list
print("Sorted List:", my_list)
print()

#Duplicate Elements in Lists
print("Duplicate Elements in Lists:")
my_list_with_duplicates = [10, 20, 30, 20, 40, 50, 30]
print("List with Duplicates:", my_list_with_duplicates)
print()

#Memory Efficiency with Lists
print("Memory Efficiency with Lists:")
import sys
large_list = list(range(1000000))  # Creating a large
list
print("Memory used by the list:", sys.getsizeof(large_
list), "bytes")
print()

#Data Indexing with Dictionaries
print("Data Indexing with Dictionaries:")
student_grades = {'Alice': 90, 'Bob': 85, 'Charlie':
95, 'Alice': 88}
print("Grades Dictionary:", student_grades)
print("Grade for Alice:", student_grades['Alice'])  #
Accessing value by key
print()

#Mapping Relationships with Dictionaries
print("Mapping Relationships with Dictionaries:")
employee_department = {'John': 'HR', 'Jane': 'IT',
'Bob': 'Finance', 'Alice': 'IT'}
print("Employee Department Mapping:", employee_
department)
print()
#Configuration Settings with Dictionaries
print("Configuration Settings with Dictionaries:")
app_settings = {'theme': 'dark', 'font_size': 14,
'debug_mode': True}
print("App Settings:", app_settings)
print("Theme Setting:", app_settings['theme'])
print()
```

```
#Grouping Data with Dictionaries
print("Grouping Data with Dictionaries:")
students_by_age = {20: ['Alice', 'Bob'], 22:
['Charlie'], 25: ['David', 'Eva']}
print("Students Grouped by Age:", students_by_age)
```

Lists are fantastic for **storing sequences** of items in a specific order, but they're not designed for representing relationships between items. When you're dealing with interconnected data or need to express relationships, other data structures are much more suitable.

Dictionaries of sets are brilliant for **expressing relationships** in a structured manner. They allow you to map keys to sets of related values, providing an efficient way to manage associations between distinct elements.

There are many, many other things you can do with lists. Very quickly here are a few that might be of interest:

Default Values with get() Method

The **get()** method allows you to retrieve the value of a key while providing a default value if the key doesn't exist. This prevents errors when trying to access keys that might not be present in the dictionary.

```
#Filename: dic16.py
person = {'name': 'John', 'age': 25}
age = person.get('age', 'Not Available')
# Returns 25
country = person.get('country', 'Not Available')
# Returns 'Not Available'
print (age)
print (country)
```

Copying Dictionaries

Shallow and Deep copies are special subjects and Chapter 13 is devoted to them. So, I'll just mention them here and leave it at that for the mo. But quickly:

Shallow Copy: A shallow copy of a dictionary can be made using the copy() method, which creates a new dictionary with the same key-value pairs as the original.

Deep Copy: For dictionaries with nested structures, you might need a deep copy, which can be created using the copy module.

```
#Filename: dict17.py
import copy
original_dic = {'a': 1, 'b': {'c': 2}}
shallow_copy = original_dic.copy()
deep_copy = copy.deepcopy(original_dic)
```

Combining Dictionaries

Starting from Python 3.9, you can use the '|' operator to merge two dictionaries.

```
#Filename: dict18.py
dict1 = {'a': 1, 'b': 2}
dict2 = {'b': 3, 'c': 4}
merged_dict = dict1 | dict2
print(merged_dict)
# Output: {'a': 1, 'b': 3, 'c': 4}
```

Sorting Dictionaries by Key Values

From Python 3.7 dictionaries are ordered (before they were not). This means that the items in a dictionary maintain the order in which they were inserted. If you iterate over a dictionary, the keys (and their associated values) will be returned in the order they were added. You can sort a dictionary by keys or values and store the results in a list.

```
#Filename: dict19a.py
my_dict = {'b': 2, 'c': 3, 'a': 1}

sorted_by_keys = dict(sorted(my_dict.items()))
sorted_by_values = dict(sorted(my_dict.items(),
key=lambda item: item[1]))
print(sorted_by_keys)
# Output: {'a': 1, 'b': 2, 'c': 3}
print(sorted_by_values)
# Output: {'a': 1, 'b': 2, 'c': 3}
```

Using dict() after sorted() creates a new dictionary that maintains the sorted order. This behaviour relies on dictionaries being ordered. To illustrate the difference between sorting by keys and by values, consider this dictionary:

```
#Filename: dict19b.py
my_dict = {'b': 3, 'c': 1, 'a': 2}

# Sort by keys
sorted_by_keys = dict(sorted(my_dict.items()))
print("Sorted by keys:", sorted_by_keys)
# Output: {'a': 2, 'b': 3, 'c': 1}

# Sort by values
sorted_by_values = dict(sorted(my_dict.items(),
key=lambda item: item[1]))
print("Sorted by values:", sorted_by_values)
# Output: {'c': 1, 'a': 2, 'b': 3}
```

Counting with Dictionaries

Dictionaries are often used to count occurrences of items in a collection.

```
#Filename: dict20.py
text = "hello world"
char_count = {}
for char in text:
```

```
    char_count[char] = char_count.get(char, 0) + 1
print(char_count)
# Output: {'h': 1, 'e': 1, 'l': 3, 'o': 2, ' ': 1, 'w':
1, 'r': 1, 'd': 1}
```

Deleting Items Safely

When deleting a key-value pair, it's safer to use pop() with a default value to avoid errors if the key doesn't exist. Example:

```
#Filename: dic21.py
my_dict = {'name': 'John', 'age': 25}
age = my_dict.pop('age', None)
# Returns None if 'age' is not found
print(my_dict)  # Output: {'name': 'John'}
```

So, whether you're building a recommendation system, analysing network traffic, or solving any problem involving interconnects, having a good grasp of these alternative data structures can really enhance your ability to tackle complex scenarios.

Using Dictionaries over Lists

Here are four reasons:

- **Key-Value Pair Storage**. Dictionaries are the preferred choice when you need to store and access data using **meaningful keys** rather than relying on the position of elements, as is the case with lists. In scenarios where data needs to be represented with descriptive identifiers—such as names, IDs, or labels—dictionaries provide a clear and structured way to organise the information. This makes them particularly useful for representing entities with multiple attributes or properties.

- **Efficient Lookups and Updates.** Dictionaries are efficient for retrieving, updating, or checking data because they are implemented as hash tables, which generally provide **average-case O(1)** performance for lookups. However, the efficiency can degrade in edge cases involving hash collisions, though Python handles these effectively. Contrast with lists: Lists have O(n) time complexity for lookups because you may need to search through every element.

- **Unordered and Non-Sequential Data**. Dictionaries are well-suited for storing ordered but non-sequential data, where the position of elements is not critical. From Python 3.7 onward, dictionaries preserve the order of elements as they were inserted, while still focusing on the association between keys and values. This makes them ideal for managing mappings, configurations, or metadata.

- **Dynamic and Flexible Data Management**. Dictionaries offer flexibility when it comes to modifying data structures dynamically. Adding, updating, or removing elements in a dictionary does not require shifting other data, as would happen in a list. This makes dictionaries particularly useful in scenarios where the dataset is constantly evolving, as you can easily add new key-value pairs or modify existing ones without worrying about maintaining an ordered structure.

The decision between dictionaries and lists hinges on factors like data organisation, access patterns, uniqueness requirements, and the specific operations you intend to perform on the data. Evaluating the characteristics and advantages of each data structure is crucial for selecting the most appropriate one for your specific use case.

While lists are great for maintaining an ordered collection of items, they aren't the most efficient for key-based look-ups due to their linear search nature.

Using data structures like dictionaries (or hash tables) is the way to go when you need to retrieve values based on specific keys quickly. Dictionaries offer constant-time complexity for key-based operations, making them ideal for scenarios where fast look-ups are crucial. So, if you need to associate keys with values and perform frequent look-ups, dictionaries are definitely your best bet!

Questions

1. What is a **dictionary** in Python, and how is it structured?
2. How do dictionaries differ from lists in terms of data organisation and access?
3. How do you create a dictionary, and what syntax is used to separate keys from values?
4. How can you add or modify elements in a dictionary?
5. How do you check if a key exists in a dictionary?
6. What methods can be used to remove items from a dictionary?
7. How do you access all keys or all values in a dictionary?
8. How can you iterate through a dictionary's keys, values, and key-value pairs?
9. How does the get() method work, and why is it useful?
10. What is a shallow copy versus a deep copy in the context of dictionaries?
11. How can you merge two dictionaries in Python 3.9 and above?

10: Sets

A set is an unordered collection of unique elements. Unlike lists or tuples, sets **do not** allow duplicate values, which makes them great for situations where you need to ensure all items in a collection are distinct. They are mutable, meaning you can add or remove elements after creation.

Sets are defined using curly braces {} or the **set()** constructor. For example:

```
my_set = {1, 2, 3}
```

creates a set containing three integers. The order of elements in a set is **undefined**, and elements **cannot** be accessed by index; this is because sets are optimised for fast membership testing rather than storage order.

Sets are good for mathematical set theory applications. Common operations include union, intersection, difference, and symmetric difference. For instance, the union of two sets A and B (A | B) returns a new set containing all elements from both A and B, while the intersection (A & B) gives a set with only the elements that are in both sets. These operations are particularly pertinent in Python because sets are implemented using hash tables, which provide average-case constant time complexity for checking membership (is this element a member of the set?), adding, or removing elements.

The **frozenset** type provides an immutable version of a set, which is useful when you need a set that cannot be modified, for example, as a key in a dictionary.

Sets are versatile and are useful when removing duplicates from a list, as converting a list to a set automatically removes any duplicates. Additionally, sets can be used readily for such as checking whether a particular value exists within a collection. You can also use sets to compare data-sets, find commonalities, or filter unique elements efficiently.

In Summary:

- **Mathematical Set Operations:** Use sets to perform operations like union, intersection, difference, and symmetric difference.
- **Removing Duplicates:** Convert a list to a set to eliminate duplicate values.
- **Membership Testing:** Use sets to quickly check if an element exists within a collection.
- **Comparing Datasets:** Use set operations to find commonalities and differences between datasets.
- **Immutable Sets with frozenset:** Use frozenset when an immutable set is needed, such as when using sets as dictionary keys.

These examples illustrate the versatility and efficiency of sets in Python for various use cases involving collections of data.

Mathematical Set Operations: Union, Intersection, Difference, and Symmetric Difference

This program demonstrates common mathematical operations using sets in Python.

```
#Filename: sets1.py
#Defining two sets
set_a = {1, 2, 3, 4, 5}
set_b = {4, 5, 6, 7, 8}

#Union: all elements in either set
union_result = set_a | set_b
print("Union of A and B:", union_result)
# Output: {1, 2, 3, 4, 5, 6, 7, 8}

#Intersection: elements common to both sets
intersection_result = set_a & set_b
print("Intersection of A and B:", intersection_result)
#Output: {4, 5}

#Difference: elements in A but not in B
difference_result = set_a - set_b
print("Difference of A and B (A - B):", difference_
result)  # Output: {1, 2, 3}

#Symmetric Difference: elements in either but not both
symmetric_difference_result = set_a ^ set_b
print("Symmetric Difference of A and B:", symmetric_
difference_result)  #Output: {1, 2, 3, 6, 7, 8}
```

Removing Duplicates from a List

This program shows how to use a set to remove duplicates from a list, because sets automatically discard duplicate values.

```
#Filename: sets2.py
# Defining a list with duplicate values
list_with_duplicates = [1, 2, 2, 3, 4, 4, 5, 5, 5]

#Converting the list to a set to remove duplicates
unique_set = set(list_with_duplicates)
print("Unique elements from the list:", unique_set)
# Output: {1, 2, 3, 4, 5}

#Converting back to a list if need ordered collection
unique_list = list(unique_set)
print("Unique elements as a list:", unique_list)
#Output: [1, 2, 3, 4, 5] (order may vary)
```

Membership Testing

This program demonstrates how to use sets for fast membership testing to check whether an element exists in a collection.

```
#Filename: sets3.py
# Defining a set of elements
my_set = {"apple", "banana", "cherry"}

# Checking membership using 'in'
if "banana" in my_set:
    print("Banana is in the set.")  # Output: Banana is
in the set.

# Checking membership for a non-existing element
if "grape" not in my_set:
    print("Grape is not in the set.")  # Output: Grape
is not in the set.
```

Comparing Datasets and Finding Commonalities

This program shows how to use sets to compare two datasets and find their common and unique elements.

```
#Filename: sets4.py
# Defining two datasets as sets
dataset_1 = {"apple", "banana", "cherry", "date"}
dataset_2 = {"cherry", "date", "elderberry", "fig"}

#Finding common elements (intersection)
common_elements = dataset_1 & dataset_2
print("Common elements:", common_elements)
# Output: {'date', 'cherry'}

#Finding elements unique to dataset_1
unique_to_dataset_1 = dataset_1 - dataset_2
print("Elements unique to dataset_1:", unique_to__
dataset_1)
# Output: {'apple', 'banana'}

#Finding elements unique to dataset_2
unique_to_dataset_2 = dataset_2 - dataset_1
print("Elements unique to dataset_2:", unique_to_
dataset_2)
# Output: {'elderberry', 'fig'}
```

Using frozenset for Immutable Sets

This program demonstrates the use of frozenset, which is an immutable version of a set. This can be useful when you need to use a set as a dictionary key or when you want a constant set of values that should not change.

```
#Filename: sets5.py
#Creating a frozenset
immutable_set = frozenset([1, 2, 3, 4])
print("Immutable set:", immutable_set)
# Output: frozenset({1, 2, 3, 4})

#add or modify will raise an AttributeError
try:
    immutable_set.add(5)  # This will raise an error
except AttributeError as e:
    print("Error:", e)  # Output: Error: 'frozenset'
object has no attribute 'add'

#Using frozenset as a dictionary key
my_dict = {immutable_set: "This is an immutable set!"}
print("Dictionary with frozenset as a key:", my_dict)
#Output: Dictionary with frozenset as a key:
{frozenset({1, 2, 3, 4}): 'This is an immutable set!'}
```

Modifying Sets

Python provides methods for modifying sets, like **add()** and **update()** to add elements to a set, with update() allowing for the addition of multiple elements from another set or iterable. Removing elements can be done using **remove()**, which raises an error if the element does not exist, or **discard()**, which safely removes an element if it exists but does nothing otherwise. The **pop()** method can also be used, but since sets are unordered, it will remove and return an arbitrary element. The **clear()** method will remove all elements in the set!

Additionally, Python sets support advanced mathematical operations. The **difference()** method, for example, returns a new set containing all elements in one set but not in another, effectively subtracting one set from another. The **symmetric_difference()** method returns elements that are in either one set or another, but not in both, which is helpful for finding non-overlapping elements between two datasets. You can use the **issubset()** and **issuperset()** methods to determine whether a set is a subset or superset of another, respectively.

The methods introduced above are all used in this next program:

```
#Filename: sets6.py
#Create an initial set
my_set = {1, 2, 3}
print("Initial set:", my_set)

#Adding a single element using add()
```

```
    my_set.add(4)
    print("Set after adding an element (4):", my_set)

    #Adding multiple elements using update()
    my_set.update([5, 6, 7])
    print("Set after adding multiple elements (5, 6,
7):", my_set)

    #Removing an element using remove()
    try:
        my_set.remove(7)  # This will succeed
        print("Set after removing element (7):", my_
set)
        my_set.remove(10)  # This will raise a
KeyError
    except KeyError as e:
        print("Error removing element (10):", e)

    #Removing an element using discard()
    my_set.discard(6)  # This will succeed
    print("Set after discarding element (6):", my_
set)

    my_set.discard(10)  # This will not raise an
error
    print("Set after discarding non-existent element
(10):", my_set)

    #Removing/return an arbitrary element using pop()
    popped_element = my_set.pop()
    print("Popped element:", popped_element)
    print("Set after popping an arbitrary element:",
my_set)

    #Clear all elements in the set using clear()
    my_set.clear()
    print("Set after clearing all elements:", my_set)

    #Advanced Mathematical Operations

    #Creating two new sets for mathematical
operations
    set_a = {1, 2, 3, 4, 5}
    set_b = {4, 5, 6, 7, 8}

    #Difference between two sets
    difference_result = set_a.difference(set_b)
    print("Difference (A - B):", difference_result)  #
Output: {1, 2, 3}

    #Symmetric difference between two sets
    symmetric_difference_result = set_a.symmetric_
difference(set_b)
    print("Symmetric Difference:", symmetric_
difference_result)  # Output: {1, 2, 3, 6, 7, 8}

    #Checking subset
    is_subset = {1, 2}.issubset(set_a)
    print("Is {1, 2} a subset of set A?", is_subset)
# Output: True
```

```
    #Checking superset
    is_superset = set_a.issuperset({1, 2})
    print("Is set A a superset of {1, 2}?", is_
superset)   # #Output: True
```

As you can hopefully see, sets provide a flexible, built-in way to manage collections of distinct items, ensuring both performance and clarity in Python programs.

Which One Where?

While lists, dictionaries, tuples, and sets all manage collections of data, they serve different purposes. **Lists** are best for ordered, mutable sequences of items; **dictionaries** for fast key-value pair lookups; **tuples** for immutable, ordered collections; and **sets** for managing unique, unordered elements. As I've said before, choosing the appropriate data structure depends on the specific needs of your application, whether it's maintaining order, ensuring uniqueness, or enabling fast data access. This why it is important to understand how these all work.

Questions

1. Why are sets useful when working with collections of unique elements?
2. Explain how sets are defined in Python. Provide two different ways to create a set.
3. What is a primary advantage of sets when it comes to testing membership of an element in a collection?
4. Describe the union operation on sets. What does it return when applied to two sets A and B?
5. What is the result of the intersection of two sets A and B?
6. What is the difference between using remove() and discard() methods for deleting elements from a set?
7. Explain what a frozenset is and why you might use it instead of a regular set.
8. How can converting a list to a set help in removing duplicate elements from the list?
9. What does the issubset() method do when used with sets in Python?
10. When should you consider using a set instead of a list or dictionary in Python?.

11: Tuples

A tuple is a list's close cousin. Both are ordered collections of elements, but with one major difference: once you create a tuple, you can't change it. It's set in stone (or, as we say in the programming world, it's **immutable**). So, whatever you put in a tuple, you're stuck with it!

Tuples are defined using parentheses ( ), and they can hold elements of different types. Here's an example:

```
my_tuple = (1, "apple", 3.14, True)
```

In this example, my_tuple has four elements: an **integer**, a **string**, a **float**, and a **Boolean**. A nice little mix. Tuples are incredibly **versatile.** They can even contain other tuples.

So Special

No, really, they are. Tuples keep things in the order you define them, so you can always retrieve elements in the same sequence.

Unlike lists, you can't change the structure of a tuple after it's created. However, if a tuple contains mutable objects (like lists), you can still modify those objects themselves.

Just like with lists, you can use indexing to grab individual elements from a tuple. And if you want to slice off a piece of the tuple, that's possible too.

When and How to Use Tuples

Tuples are your go-to when you need a collection of related values that shouldn't change. They're perfect for things like coordinates (x, y), database records, or settings that need to stay consistent.

Here's a quick example showing how indexing and slicing work with tuples:

```
#Filename: tuple1.py
my_tuple = (1, 2, 3, 4, 5)
print(my_tuple[0])  # Output: 1
print(my_tuple[2:4])  # Output: (3, 4)
```

A tuples immutability ensures data integrity and consistency, making them ideal for certain scenarios where you need to keep your data just as it is.

Converting and Switching Between Data Structures

Want to convert a list to a tuple? Just use the **tuple()** function. It takes your list as an argument and gives you back a tuple with the same elements. Here's how it works:

```
#Filename: tuple2.py
my_list = [1, 2, 3, 4]
my_tuple = tuple(my_list)
print(my_tuple)  # Output: (1, 2, 3, 4)
```

And if you ever need to go the other way—from a tuple back to a list—you can use the **list()** function:

```
#Filename: tuple3.py
my_tuple = (1, 2, 3, 4)
my_list = list(my_tuple)
print(my_list)  # Output: [1, 2, 3, 4]
```

Switching between lists and tuples is rather handy, especially when you need to adjust or handle elements in a mutable way with lists, and then lock things down with tuples when you need immutability. For example, you can take a tuple, convert it to a list to make your changes, and then turn it back into a tuple to keep things set in stone.

One key thing to remember is that when you convert a list to a tuple (or vice versa), you're creating a brand-new object. This means any changes you make to the new object won't affect the original one. However, if you save the new object with the same name, the original object will no longer be accessible through that name.

If you use the same name to save the new object, the original data is no longer accessible via that name. This is because the name now points to the new object, and the original object is **orphaned** in memory unless it is referenced elsewhere in your program That is copied and assigned a new name..

Remember, in Python, variables are **references** to objects in memory. When you assign a new object to a variable, the reference **changes** to point to the new object. The original object remains in memory until Python's garbage collector removes it (if no other references to it exist).

Dealing with Nested Structures

When you're working with nested structures (like lists within lists, or tuples within tuples), the conversion process affects only the outer structure. The inner elements stay the same unless you convert them individually. Here's your example:

```
#Filename: tuple4.py
nested_list = [[1, 2], [3, 4], [5, 6]]
nested_tuple = tuple(nested_list)
print(nested_tuple)
#Output: ([1, 2], [3, 4], [5, 6])


nested_tuple[0][0] = 10
print(nested_tuple)
#Output: ([10, 2], [3, 4], [5, 6])
```

In this example, the **tuple()** function converts nested_list to nested_tuple. Notice that while the outer structure is now a tuple, the inner lists remain mutable and can still be changed.

Converting Strings to Lists or Tuples

You can also convert strings into lists or tuples using the list() and tuple() functions. Each character in the string becomes an individual element in the list or tuple:

```
#Filename: tuple5.py
my_string = "Hello"
list_string = list(my_string)
tuple_string = tuple(my_string)
print(list_string)
#Output: ['H', 'e', 'l', 'l', 'o']
print(tuple_string)
#Output: ('H', 'e', 'l', 'l', 'o')
```

Here, we've turned the string "Hello" into both a list and a tuple, with each character becoming a separate element. This can be useful when you need to break down a string into its components and work with them individually.

Converting Tuples to Dictionaries

You might have a tuple that you want to convert into a dictionary. This works great if your tuple is structured as key-value pairs. Here's how you do it:

```
#Filename: tuple6.py
my_tuple = (("key1", 1), ("key2", 2), ("key3", 3))
my_dict = dict(my_tuple)
print(my_dict)
#Output: {'key1': 1, 'key2': 2, 'key3': 3}
```

In this example, my_tuple consists of key-value pairs. By passing my_tuple to the dict() function, we create a dictionary my_dict where each tuple pair is mapped accordingly.

Converting tuples to dictionaries and vice-versa can be useful in a few specific situations, especially when working with structured data:

- **Key-Value Pairing:** Tuples often come in pairs, where the first element is a key and the second is a value. Converting these tuples into a dictionary can make it easier to look up values by their corresponding keys.
- **Faster Lookup**: If you need to frequently access elements by a specific identifier, a dictionary provides faster lookup times compared to a list of tuples.
- **Data Manipulation**: Converting tuples to dictionaries allows for more straightforward manipulation of the data. You can easily add, update, or remove key-value pairs when working with a dictionary.
- **Integration with Functions**: Many Python functions and methods work well with dictionaries, such as **.get(), .keys(), .values(),** and **.items()**. These can make your code more efficient and easier to manage.

For example, if you have a list of tuples representing student names and their scores:

```
students = [('Alice', 85), ('Bob', 90), ('Charlie',
78)]
```

Converting this into a dictionary allows you to access a student's score by their name:

```
student_dict = dict(students)
print(student_dict['Alice'])  # Outputs: 85
```

This conversion is particularly helpful when you need to manage or process the data more effectively.

Just remember that dictionary keys must be unique—if your tuple has duplicate keys, the dictionary will only keep the last key-value pair. And since dictionaries are unordered collections, the order of elements might not match the original order from the tuple.

Tuple as Keys in Dictionaries

Since tuples are immutable and hashable, they can be used as keys in dictionaries. This is especially useful when you need a composite key.

```
locations = {('London', 'UK'): 51.5074, ('New York',
'USA'): 40.7128}
print(locations[('London', 'UK')])  # Output: 51.5074
```

If you attempt to convert a tuple to a dictionary in Python, but the tuple does not contain key-value pairs, you'll encounter an error. Python requires a specific structure when converting a tuple to a dictionary. When converting a tuple to a dictionary, the tuple must consist of iterable pairs (e.g., (key, value) pairs). If the tuple does not contain pairs, Python raises a **ValueError** because it cannot interpret how to map the elements into keys and values.

If your tuple does not have key-value pairs but you still want to convert it to a dictionary, you can manually provide keys:

Use another list or tuple to supply keys for the values in the tuple:

```
tuple_data = (1, 2, 3)
keys = ["a", "b", "c"]
dictionary = dict(zip(keys, tuple_data))
print(dictionary)  # Output: {'a': 1, 'b': 2, 'c': 3}
```

Transform the Tuple Into Key-Value Pairs:

```
tuple_data = (1, "a", 2, "b", 3, "c")
dictionary = dict(zip(tuple_data[::2], tuple_data[1:
:2]))  # Odd indices as keys, even as values
print(dictionary)  # Output: {1: 'a', 2: 'b', 3: 'c'}
```

Add Dummy Keys or Values:

```
tuple_data = (1, 2, 3)
dictionary = {f"key_{i}": value for i, value in
enumerate(tuple_data)}
print(dictionary)  # Output: {'key_0': 1, 'key_1': 2,
'key_2': 3}
```

Tuple Methods

This immutability of tuples restricts the number of methods available for them compared to other data structures like lists. However, the methods that tuples do have are quite useful for basic operations and ensure that tuples remain efficient and consistent in use.

One of the primary methods available for tuples is the **count()** method. This method allows you to count the number of times a specific value appears in the tuple. For instance, if you have a tuple t = (1, 2, 3, 2, 4, 2), calling **t.count(2)** will return 3, indicating that the value 2 appears three times in the tuple. This method is useful when you need to know the frequency of a specific element within a tuple, especially when dealing with repeated values.

Another essential method for tuples is the **index()** method. This method returns the first position at which a specified value occurs within the tuple. For example, given the tuple t = (1, 2, 3, 2, 4, 2), calling **t.index(3)** will return 2, as 3 is located at the third position (index 2 in zero-based indexing). If the specified value is not found, the **index()** method raises a ValueError. This method is particularly helpful when you need to find the location of an element within a tuple.

Beyond these methods, tuples also support operations that are not specific to tuples alone but are generally applicable to sequences in Python. For example, you can use the **len()** function to get the number of elements in a tuple, or the **in** keyword to check if a specific element exists within the tuple. You can also concatenate tuples using the **+** operator or repeat the elements of a tuple using the ***** operator.

While tuples lack the extensive method set that lists or other mutable data structures might have, their simplicity and efficiency make them ideal for situations where a fixed collection of items is needed. The limited set of methods like **count()** and **index()** ensures that tuples remain lightweight and fast, serving as a reliable tool in a Python programmer's toolkit.

Tuple Packing and Unpacking

Tuple Packing refers to the process of combining multiple values into a single tuple. This is done implicitly when you assign multiple values to a single variable, which automatically groups these values into a tuple. For example, when you use 'values = 10, 20, 30', Python packs these three integers into a single tuple 'values', which contains (10, 20, 30). This feature is useful because it allows you to group related pieces of data together without having to manually create a tuple using parentheses. Tuple packing is particularly handy when returning multiple values from a function, as it allows you to package all return values into a single, compact tuple.

Why values = 10, 20, 30 is a Tuple: A tuple can be created without parentheses if multiple items are separated by commas. The commas (10, 20, 30) are what define the tuple, not the parentheses. If values were a list, it would need to be defined using square brackets (values = [10, 20, 30]).Of course, you can confirm the type of values using the type() function:

Tuple Unpacking, on the other hand is the reverse process, where the elements of a tuple are extracted into individual variables. This is done by assigning the tuple to a sequence of variables, which are automatically matched to the corresponding elements of the tuple. For instance, if you have 'coordinates = (10, 20, 30)' and you write 'x, y, z = coordinates', Python unpacks the tuple and assigns 10 to x, 20 to y, and 30 to z. This feature is extremely useful for extracting values from tuples in a clear and concise manner, particularly when dealing with functions that return multiple values. Unpacking makes the code more readable and reduces the need for accessing individual tuple elements by index.

Tuple unpacking can also be extended with the use of the '*' operator, which allows for flexible unpacking. For example, in the statement:

```
a, *b, c = 1, 2, 3, 4, 5,
```

a is assigned 1, c is assigned 5, and b is assigned the remaining values as a list [2, 3, 4]. This is particularly useful when you want to capture a variable number of elements from a tuple, leaving the remaining elements to be handled differently.

Single-Element Tuples

You can actually create single-element tuples, but it can be a bit tricky due to how Python interprets the syntax. Normally, when you enclose a single value in parentheses, Python doesn't treat it as a tuple but rather as an expression with the value inside. For instance, if you use 'single = (5)', Python interprets this as just the integer 5 wrapped in parentheses, not as a tuple. This is because parentheses are used for grouping expressions, and simply enclosing a value in parentheses *does not* automatically create a tuple.

To create a single-element tuple, you need to include a comma after the element, even if it's the only item in the tuple. For example, to create a tuple containing just the integer 5, you would write:

```
single = (5,)
```

The comma is crucial here; it tells Python that you want to create a tuple rather than just a simple expression. Without the comma, Python will not recognise it as a tuple, and instead, it will be treated as a regular integer.

Single-element tuples might seem a weird concept, but they can be quite useful in specific scenarios. For instance, when working with functions that expect tuples as input, you might need to pass a single value in the form of a tuple. Additionally, when using tuples in unpacking operations, maintaining the tuple structure, even with one element, ensures consistency and prevents errors. Single-element tuples are also handy when working with immutable sequences where you want to ensure that even a single value remains unchanged throughout the program's execution.

The takeaway is that when creating a single-element tuple in Python, always remember to include the trailing comma. This small but significant detail ensures that Python interprets your value as a tuple, preserving the tuples properties and behaviour, even when it contains just one element.

Why Choose Tuples Over Dictionaries?

Tuples and dictionaries are both awesome tools in Python, but they serve different purposes and shine in different situations. Let's break down when and why you might want to go with a tuple instead of a dictionary.

Immutable Data

Tuples are like that unchangeable contract—you create it, and it's locked in for life. This makes tuples perfect for storing data that should stay constant throughout your program. On the flip side, dictionaries are mutable, meaning you can add, remove, or change key-value pairs as you go.

Ordered Data

Tuples are all about order. They keep things in the exact sequence you define, which is crucial when the order of elements matters, like in coordinates (x, y). While dictionaries in Python versions 3.7 and later do maintain order, historically, they didn't, so tuples still get the nod when order really counts.

```
#Using a tuple to represent a 2D point with (x, y)
point = (3, 4)  # Order matters (x=3, y=4)
```

Uniqueness

If you want to allow duplicates in your collection, tuples are your mate—they're okay with repeated values. In contrast, dictionaries demand unique keys. If you try to add a duplicate key in a dictionary, it'll just overwrite the existing value. Tuples are great for bundling up multiple values to return from a function. Need to return a name and an age? A tuple has you covered.

```
#Filename: tuple7.py
def get_name_and_age():
    return ("Alice", 12)

name, age = get_name_and_age()  # Unpacking a tuple
print(name)
print(age)
```

Tuples are lean—they're more memory-efficient and can grab your data faster than dictionaries. So if you're dealing with a large collection of data that doesn't need key-based lookups, tuples might be the better choice.

In this world of **cyber security** and **cyber-attacks** and are worried about someone 'accidentally' changing your data, then tuples are your go-to. Because they're immutable, you don't have to worry about any unwanted changes sneaking in.

That said, dictionaries are versatile and useful when you need to associate keys with values for quick look-ups. They're the go-to choice for structured data that needs to be accessed by keys.

Tuples in Object-Oriented Programming (OOP)

In OOP, tuples can be quite handy. For instance:

- **Immutable Attributes:** Tuples can be used to create objects with attributes that you don't want to change after creation. This can help protect the integrity of your objects.

- **Returning Multiple Values:** Methods often return tuples when you need to send back several pieces of information at once.
- **Hashable and Perfect for Keys:** Since tuples are immutable, they're also hashable, which means you can use them as keys in dictionaries or as elements in sets. This makes them great for unique identifiers.
- **Representing Structured Data:** Tuples are also great for storing structured data within objects. For example, a point object in 2D space might use a tuple to store its (x, y) coordinates.

Here's a quick example of using a tuple in a class:

```
#Filename: tuple8.py
class Point2D:
    def __init__(self, x, y):
        self.coordinates = (x, y)

    def get_coordinates(self):
        return self.coordinates

#Usage
point = Point2D(3, 5)
print(point.get_coordinates())
# Output: (3, 5)
```

In this Point2D class, the coordinates attribute is a tuple that holds the x and y values. This tuple is a solid, unchangeable container for the point's coordinates. Here's a neat trick with tuples:

```
my_tuple = (1, 2, 3)
my_dict = {my_tuple: "value"}
print(my_dict[my_tuple])  #Output: value
```

In this example, **my_tuple** is used as a key in the dictionary **my_dict** because it's **hashable**. If you tried using a list instead, Python would throw a TypeError because lists aren't hashable.

So, in a nutshell, tuples are your go-to when you need order, immutability, or a simple, efficient way to bundle and return values. They're also perfect for scenarios where you want to prevent accidental changes or need a reliable key for a dictionary. On the other hand, dictionaries excel when you need the flexibility of key-based look-ups and the ability to change your data on the fly. Choose the right tool for the job, and you'll make your code both cleaner and more efficient!

Tuples vs. Lists:

Tuples and lists are both used to store collections of items, but they serve different purposes due to their distinct characteristics. Indeed, we saw a couple of examples of using list with tuple at the very start of this chapter.

Tuples are immutable, once created, their elements cannot be changed. This ensures data integrity and prevents accidental modifications. Because of this feature, tuples are ideal for scenarios where the data should remain constant, such as when using them as keys in dictionaries or when passing data to functions that should not alter it. Additionally, tuples are more memory-efficient and have a faster creation process compared to lists. This efficiency is particularly beneficial when dealing with large collections of static data. The ability to unpack tuples into multiple variables in a single line is another very useful feature. It enhances code conciseness and readability. Not a bad thing at all!

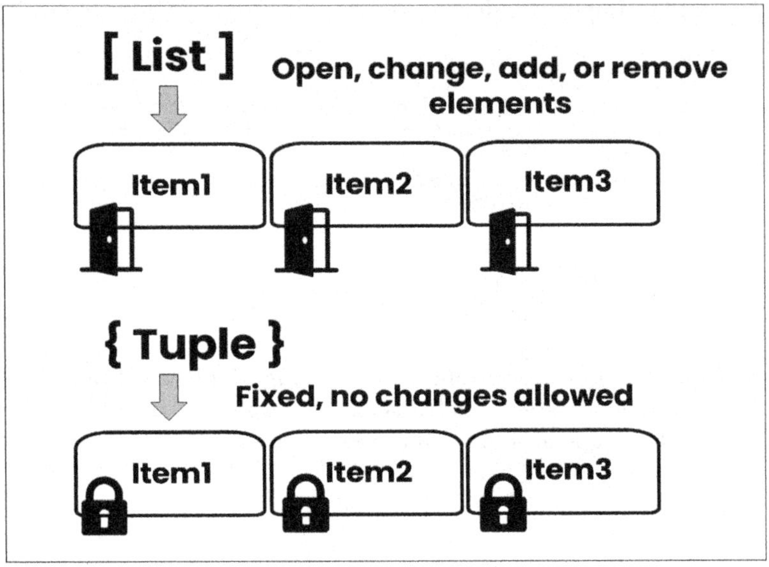

Figure 11a. Lists verse Tuples

As we have learnt, lists are more suitable for tasks that require frequent updates or manipulations, such as filtering, sorting, or transforming data. Lists have a variety of built-in methods, including **append(), remove(), sort(),** and **reverse()**, which allow these operations. Lists also support easy iteration and comprehensions, enabling the creation of new lists from existing ones in a concise and readable manner. Due to their dynamic nature and wide range of functionalities, lists are often the default choice for storing sequences of elements.

The programs 'tuple2' and 'tuple3' demonstrated how to convert a list to a tuple, using the **tuple()** function. It took the list as an argument and returned a tuple containing the same elements: The program looked like this:

```
#Filename: tuple2.py
my_list = [1, 2, 3, 4]
my_tuple = tuple(my_list)
print(my_tuple)  # Output: (1, 2, 3, 4)
```

Conversely, you can use the 'list()' function to convert 'my_tuple' to a list called 'my_list' as we saw in program 'tuple3'

```
#Filename: tuple3.py
my_tuple = (1, 2, 3, 4)
my_list = list(my_tuple)
print(my_list)  # Output: [1, 2, 3, 4]
```

Don't forget, when dealing with nested structures (lists or tuples within lists or tuples), the outer structure is converted, but the nested elements remain unchanged. Each nested structure undergoes conversion to the target type, ensuring a consistent transformation throughout. Demonstrated in 'tuple4'.

Using enumerate()

Loop Through Lists

The enumerate() function is like a multitasking pro—it lets you loop through a list while keeping track of both the index and the value of each element. What you get is an iterable of tuples, where each tuple holds the index and the corresponding value. Here's how it works:

```
#Filename: tuple9.py
#Using enumerate with a list
my_list = [1, 2, 3, 4, 5]

for index, value in enumerate(my_list):
    print(f"Element at index {index}: {value}")
```

This will produce:

```
Element at index 0: 1
Element at index 1: 2
Element at index 2: 3
Element at index 3: 4
Element at index 4: 5
```

Starting enumerate() at a Custom Index

Sometimes, you might want to start your indexing from a number other than zero, here enumerate() has you covered:

```
#Filename: tuple10.py
colors = ['red', 'green', 'blue']

for idx, color in enumerate(colors, start=1):
    print(f"Index: {idx}, Color: {color}")
```

Output:

```
Index: 1, Color: red
Index: 2, Color: green
Index: 3, Color: blue
```

List Comprehension

enumerate() can even be used in list comprehensions, making it simple to create a list of tuples that include both the index and the value

```
#Filename: tuple11.py
missions = ['Perseverance', 'InSight', 'Phoenix']

missions_with_index = [(index, mission) for index,
mission in enumerate(missions)]
print(missions_with_index)


#Output:
#[(0, 'Perseverance'), (1, 'InSight'), (2, 'Phoenix')]
```

As you can see, **enumerate()** is a handy little function that makes it easier to keep track of indexes while looping through the elements of a list. Whether you're working with numbers, strings, or any other data type, enumerate() can help you manage your iterations with style!

The Zipper

The zip function (which we dabbled with in an earlier chapter.) is like a matchmaker for elements from different iterables (like lists or tuples), pairing them up into tuples. Imagine you've got two lists—zip will combine them element by element into neat little pairs. This is handy dandy when you want to loop over multiple sequences at the same time. Here's the go:

Basic Example: How zip Works

```
#Filename: zip1.py
list1 = [1, 2, 3]
list2 = ['a', 'b', 'c']

zipped = zip(list1, list2)
print(list(zipped))
```

When you run this, you'll see:

```
[(1, 'a'), (2, 'b'), (3, 'c')]
```

What's happening here? zip takes the first element of **list1** and pairs it with the first element of **list2** then the second elements, and so on. The result is a zip object—essentially an iterator of tuples. We mentioned this before, earlier in the chapter.

Iterating Over Lists with zip

You can use zip in a loop to walk through multiple lists at once:

```
#Filename: zip2.py
list1 = [1, 2, 3]
```

```
list2 = ['a', 'b', 'c']

for number, letter in zip(list1, list2):
    print(f"Number: {number}, Letter: {letter}")
```

And the output:

```
Number: 1, Letter: a
Number: 2, Letter: b
Number: 3, Letter: c
```

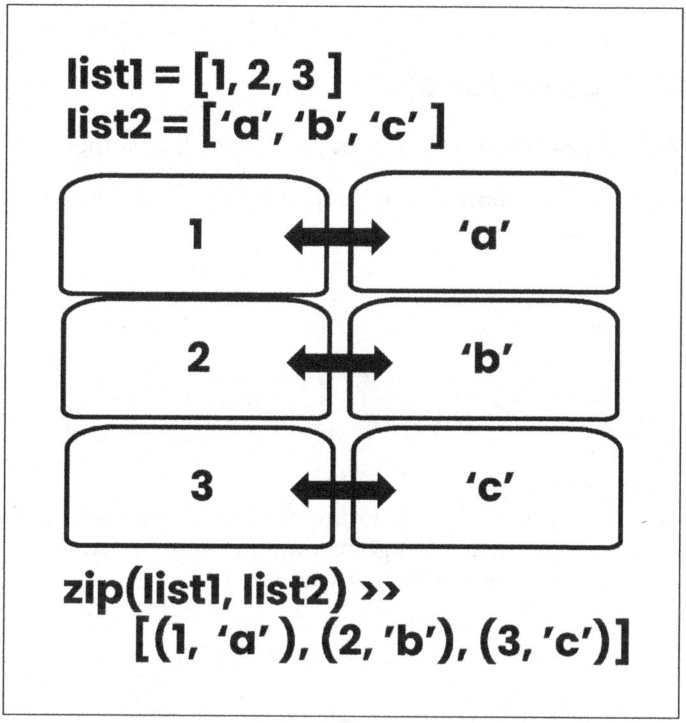

Figure 11b. Illustrating the zip function.

What Happens with Unequal Lengths?

If your lists aren't the same length, zip stops when it runs out of elements in the shortest list:

```
#Filename: zip3.py
list1 = [1, 2, 3]
list2 = ['a', 'b']

zipped = zip(list1, list2)
print(list(zipped))
#Output: [(1, 'a'), (2, 'b')]
```

Here, the third element of list1 is left out because list2 ran out of elements.

Unzipping: How to Reverse a zip

You can even "**unzip**" a zipped object back into individual lists:

```
#Filename: zip4.py
zipped = [(1, 'a'), (2, 'b'), (3, 'c')]

unzipped = zip(*zipped)
list1, list2 = map(list, unzipped)
print(list1)  #Output: [1, 2, 3]
print(list2)  #Output: ['a', 'b', 'c']
```

Practical Uses for zip

- **Parallel Iteration:** Loop over two (or more) lists at the same time.
- **Creating Dictionaries:** You can pair up keys and values from two lists to create a dictionary:

```
#Filename: zip5.py
keys = ['name', 'age', 'city']
values = ['Alice', 25, 'London']

dictionary = dict(zip(keys, values))
print(dictionary)  # Output: {'name': 'Alice', 'age':
25, 'city': 'London'}
```

itertools.zip_longest:

The itertools module gives us **zip_longest**, which doesn't stop at the shortest iterable. Instead, it keeps going until the longest iterable is done, filling in missing values with whatever you specify:

```
#Filename: zip6.py
from itertools import zip_longest

list1 = [1, 2, 3]
list2 = ['a', 'b']

zipped = zip_longest(list1, list2, fillvalue='fill')
print(list(zipped))
#Output: [(1, 'a'), (2, 'b'), (3, 'fill')]
```

Using zip_longest in a Loop

You can use **zip_longest** just like zip, but it keeps going, filling in the gaps:

```
#Filename: zip7.py
from itertools import zip_longest

list1 = [1, 2, 3]
list2 = ['a', 'b']

for number, letter in zip_longest(list1, list2,
fillvalue='fill'):
    print(f"Number: {number}, Letter: {letter}")
```

Summary of zip and zip_longest

Whether you're matching up elements from different lists or creating dictionaries on the fly, zip and zip_longest are handy tools that make working with multiple sequences a breeze!

- **zip:** Combines elements from multiple iterables into tuples, stopping when the shortest one runs out.
- **zip_longest:** Combines elements from multiple iterables, continuing until the longest one is done, filling in missing values as needed.

Exercise

Write a Python program that demonstrates the following tuple-related concepts:

Tuple Immutability: Create a tuple and attempt to modify one of its elements. Handle any exceptions that arise and explain why the error occurs.

Mutable Elements in Tuples: Define a tuple containing a mutable object (e.g., a list). Modify the mutable object and observe how it affects the tuple.

Tuple Packing and Unpacking: Pack three values into a tuple, unpack them into individual variables, and demonstrate swapping values using tuple unpacking.

Tuples as Dictionary Keys: Use tuples as keys in a dictionary to represent coordinates, and display the dictionary's contents.

Using zip() and zip_longest(): Combine two lists into a list of tuples using both zip() and zip_longest(). Handle unequal-length lists by filling in missing values with None.

Your program should use functions to structure each concept and provide clear outputs to explain what's happening at each step.

```
#Filename: 11-exercise-02.py
from itertools import zip_longest

def create_and_modify_tuple():
    print("\n--- Tuple Creation and Immutability ---")
    my_tuple = ("Python", "Raspberry Pi", "Coding", 42)
    print("Original tuple:", my_tuple)
    try:
        my_tuple[0] = "New Value"
    except TypeError as e:
        print("Error:", e)

def tuple_with_mutable_elements():
    print("\n--- Tuple with Mutable Elements ---")
    my_tuple = (1, [2, 3], 4)
    print("Original tuple:", my_tuple)
```

```
    my_tuple[1].append(5)
    print("Modified tuple:", my_tuple)

def packing_and_unpacking():
    print("\n--- Tuple Packing and Unpacking ---")
    packed_tuple = ("apple", "banana", "cherry")
    print("Packed tuple:", packed_tuple)

    a, b, c = packed_tuple
    print("Unpacked values:", a, b, c)

    a, b = b, a  # Swap using unpacking
    print("Swapped values:", a, b)

def tuples_as_keys():
    print("\n--- Tuples as Dictionary Keys ---")
    grid = {
        (0, 0): "Origin",
        (1, 1): "Point A",
        (2, 3): "Point B"
    }
    print("Grid dictionary:", grid)
    for key, value in grid.items():
        print(f"Coordinate {key}: {value}")

def zip_and_zip_longest():
    print("\n--- Using zip() and zip_longest() ---")
    list1 = [1, 2, 3]
    list2 = ["a", "b"]

    zipped = list(zip(list1, list2))
    print("Using zip():", zipped)

    zipped_longest = list(zip_longest(list1, list2,
fillvalue=None))
    print("Using zip_longest():", zipped_longest)

    # Convert back to separate lists
    list1_unzipped, list2_unzipped = zip(*zipped_
longest)
    print("Converted back:")
    print("List 1:", list(list1_unzipped))
    print("List 2:", list(list2_unzipped))

def main():
    print("\n=== Python Tuple Mastery Program ===")
    create_and_modify_tuple()
    tuple_with_mutable_elements()
    packing_and_unpacking()
    tuples_as_keys()
    zip_and_zip_longest()

if __name__ == "__main__":
    main()
```

12: Stacks & Queues

Even before *Homo erectus* or *Homo heidelbergensis* (there's still debate as to who was first and they're not around to tell us), stacks were *en vouge*.

Stacks have been a fundamental part of life and computer systems from the day dot. They're pretty much what you'd imagine: stacks of data or information, like a stack of plates. Picture it: you can keep stacking plates one on top of the other, theoretically forever. But when you want to take a plate off the stack, you'll naturally grab the top one—the last one you placed there. That's why we call this a **LIFO** structure: Last In, First Out.

(If the stack of plates too tall then I'd go for one in the middle. The outcome for a computer driven stack would be the same. Crash.)

Now, if you've heard of a **FIFO** structure (First In, First Out), that's a different kind of data structure, usually referred to as a queue in Python. Think of it as a line of plates lying sideways in a dish rack—the first one in is the first one out. This analogy doesn't quite work for stacks, but it's spot on for **queues**.

Instead of plates, imagine consecutive spaces in memory, like a list or queue. The tricky part is that if you don't keep track of where the first and last spaces are (using indexes), you can run into all sorts of problems when accessing data. In both cases, we're less concerned with knowing the exact location of each item and more focused on being able to access them in the order they were added. We can keep "popping" items off the stack if we maintain the correct order.

For stack operations, you'll often use the **append()** method to push elements onto the stack and the **pop()** method to remove them. Think of it as an internal index specific to this stack, which Python keeps track of to know where we are in the stack. You can largely forget about it.

When you push an item onto the stack, it goes into the next available spot, and the stack pointer (an internal index) moves to the next free space. When you pop an item off, the stack pointer adjusts to point to the newly vacated space. Nothing disappears; it just gets overwritten when something new is added.

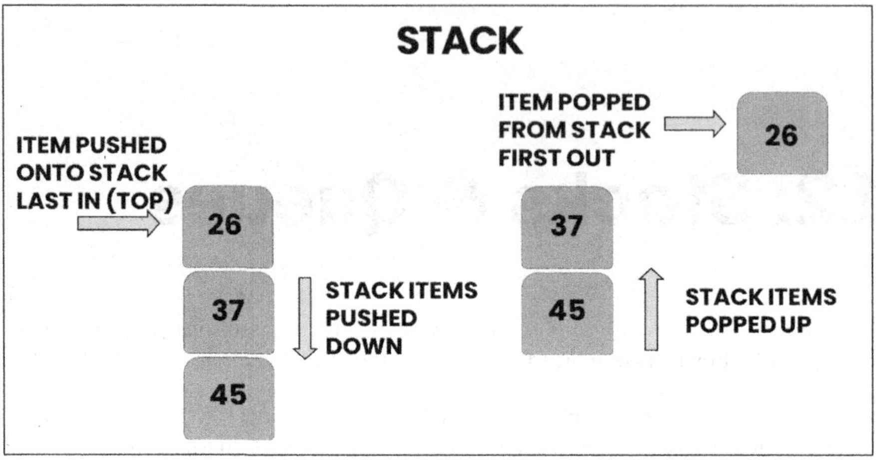

Figure 12a. Last item pushed on the stack (26) is the first item pulled off the stack (26).

Imagine this: you put a banana on the stack, followed by a number. If you don't remember the order, and you take the number off expecting a banana, things could go haywire. So, the order would need to be:

- Banana on
- Value on
- Value off
- Banana off

LIFO Example: Here's a simple Python class that demonstrates how a stack works:

```
#Filename: stack1.py
class Stack:
    def __init__(self):
        self.items = []

    def push(self, item):
        self.items.append(item)

    def pop(self):
        if not self.is_empty():
            return self.items.pop()
```

```
    def peek(self):
        if not self.is_empty():
            return self.items[-1]

    def is_empty(self):
        return len(self.items) == 0

    def size(self):
        return len(self.items)
```

Example of use:

```
stack = Stack()
stack.push(1)
stack.push(2)
stack.push(3)
print(stack.pop())  #Output: 3
print(stack.peek()) #Output: 2
print(stack.size()) #Output: 2
```

This implementation ensures that the last item added to the stack is the first one removed, making it a classic LIFO structure.

Using a List as a Stack or Queue

You can also use a list as a stack in Python by taking advantage of its built-in methods. Here's how:

First, initialise an empty stack:

```
stack = []
```

To add an element to the top of the stack, use the **append()** method:

```
stack.append(element)
```

To remove the top element, use the pop() method:

```
popped_element = stack.pop()
```

To view the top element without removing it, access the last element of the list using index -1:

```
top_element = stack[-1]
```

To check if the stack is empty, use the len() function:

```
is_empty = len(stack) == 0
```

Remember to use append() and pop() to maintain the stack's LIFO behaviour.

First-In-First-Out (FIFO)

A queue is a basic data structure that follows the FIFO principle. In a queue, elements are added to the rear (**enqueue** operation) and removed from the front (**dequeue** operation). The first element added is the first to be removed, which is the opposite of how a stack operates.

Key Characteristics of a FIFO Queue

- **Enqueue:** Adding an element to the rear of the queue.
- **Dequeue:** Removing an element from the front of the queue.
- **Front and Rear:** The front is where elements are removed, and the rear is where new elements are added.
- **Empty Queue:** The state when the queue has no elements.
- **Full Queue:** A state where the queue cannot accept more elements, depending on its implementation.

There are several ways to implement queues in Python, each suited to different scenarios depending on your needs. Let's look at some of the most common types.

Queue Module (Queue Class)

The queue module in Python's standard library provides a **Queue** class, which implements a first-in, first-out (**FIFO**) queue. This is a straightforward way to handle queues, especially when dealing with multi-threaded programs. (A multi-threaded program is a type of software that can execute multiple programs concurrently, allowing different parts of the program to run simultaneously.)

```
#Filename: stack2.py
from queue import Queue

# Creating a queue
my_queue = Queue()

# Enqueue items
my_queue.put(1)
my_queue.put(2)

# Dequeue items
item = my_queue.get()
print(item)
```

In this example, we create a queue, add (**enqueue**) items to it with put(), and remove (**deque**) items with get().

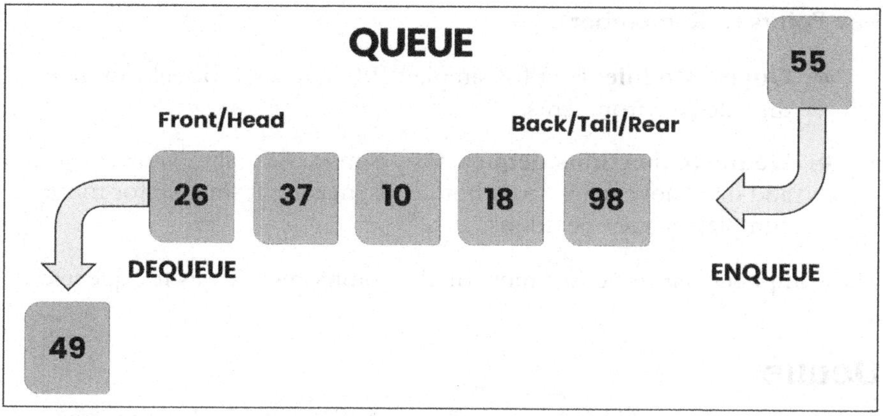

Figure 12b. Enqueue and deque.

Deque (collections.deque)

The deque (double-ended queue) class from the collections module is another efficient way to implement a queue. Deques allow you to add and remove items from both ends, making them more versatile than a regular queue.

```
#Filename: stack3.py
from collections import deque

#Creating a deque
my_queue = deque()

#Enqueue items
my_queue.append(1)
my_queue.append(2)

#Dequeue items
item = my_queue.popleft()
print(item)
item = my_queue.popleft()
print(item)

#Uncommenting the following line would raise an
IndexError
#item = my_queue.popleft()
```

Here, append() adds items to the end of the deque, and popleft() removes items from the front, following **FIFO** order. Note that if you attempt to popleft() from an empty deque, you'll encounter an IndexError, so make sure the deque isn't empty before removing items.

The method **popleft()** is used with the deque data structure from the collections module. It removes and returns the leftmost element of the deque (the element at index 0), making it particularly useful for efficiently implementing queue operations. (popleft() is available only for deque, not for lists.) Note there is **no popright** method, this is what **pop()** does.

Key Points to Remember

- **Queue Module:** Best for simple FIFO queues, especially in multi-threaded environments.
- **Deque (collections.deque):** Offers more flexibility, allowing you to add or remove items from both ends, making it suitable for more complex queue operations.

These implementations cover most of the common use cases for queues.

Deque

A deque (pronounced 'deck') is a double-ended queue, which means you can add and remove elements from both ends—front and back—efficiently. Python's collections module provides the deque class, making it an excellent structure for a variety of tasks like implementing queues and stacks. (Good we're discussing that then…)

Here's how you can implement and use a deque:

```
#Filename: stack4.py
from collections import deque

#Create a deque
my_deque = deque()

#Adding elements to the back
my_deque.append(1)
my_deque.append(2)
my_deque.append(3)

#Adding elements to the front
my_deque.appendleft(0)

#Current deque: deque([0, 1, 2, 3])

#Removing elements from the back
last_element = my_deque.pop()
#last_element will be 3, and the deque becomes:
deque([0, 1, 2])

#Removing elements from the front
first_element = my_deque.popleft()
#first_element will be 0, and the deque becomes:
deque([1, 2])

#Accessing elements by index (similar to lists)
element_at_index_1 = my_deque[1]
#element_at_index_1 will be 2

#Checking the length of the deque
deque_length = len(my_deque)
#deque_length will be 2
```

```
#Iterating through the deque
for item in my_deque:
    print(item)
```

When you iterate through my_deque, the output will be:

```
1
2
```

Key Points About Deques

- You can add elements to the front or back of the deque using **appendleft()** and append(), respectively. Similarly, you can remove elements from the front or back using **popleft()** and pop().
- Deques allow you to access elements by index, just like lists.
- Deques are implemented in a way that makes operations like adding and removing elements from either end very fast—typically in constant time, O(1).

Use Cases for Deques

In addition to **implementing stacks**, deques is clever when it comes to **sliding window problems**, where you need to maintain a subset of elements. A contextual window under which a ticker-tape, for example, passes. Here sliding window operations refer to a approach where a **window** (a subset of elements) moves incrementally over a larger dataset, often maintaining or processing only the elements currently within the window.

Deques are also well-suited for **palindrome checking**. Because deques allow you to access both ends of the sequence, you can easily compare elements from the front and rear to determine if a string or sequence reads the same forwards and backwards. This method is particularly efficient because it avoids the need to reverse the sequence or use additional memory.

Whether you're implementing queues, stacks, sliding windows, or checking palindromes, deques offer a flexible and performance-optimised solution that can simplify and speed up your code. Their versatility makes them an essential part of any Python programmer's toolkit, particularly when performance is a concern.

Another Simple Example Using collections.deque

```
#Filename: stack5.py
from collections import deque

#Create an empty deque
my_deque = deque()

#Push elements to the rear
```

```
my_deque.append(1)    # Deque: [1]
my_deque.append(2)    # Deque: [1, 2]
my_deque.append(3)    # Deque: [1, 2, 3]

#Push elements to the front
my_deque.appendleft(0)   # Deque: [0, 1, 2, 3]
my_deque.appendleft(-1)  # Deque: [-1, 0, 1, 2, 3]

#Pop elements from the rear and front
rear_element = my_deque.pop()
# rear_element = 3, Deque: [-1, 0, 1, 2]
front_element = my_deque.popleft()
# front_element = -1, Deque: [0, 1, 2]
```

Thus, the deque allows you to insert and remove elements efficiently from both ends. The **collections.deque** class is a part of the Python standard library, providing an easy-to-use and efficient implementation of deques.

Exercise: Mastering Stacks and Queues

Write a Python program to implement and demonstrate stacks and queues using both lists and the deque class. Perform the following operations for each implementation:

- Add three items (push/enqueue).
- Show the top (stack) or front (queue) item.
- Remove two items (pop/dequeue).
- Check if the structure is empty.

```
#Filename: 12-exercise-03.py
from collections import deque

# Stack Implementation using List
class Stack:
    def __init__(self):
        self.stack = []

    def push(self, item):
        self.stack.append(item)

    def pop(self):
        return self.stack.pop() if not self.is_empty()
else "Stack is empty"

    def peek(self):
        return self.stack[-1] if not self.is_empty()
else "Stack is empty"

    def is_empty(self):
        return len(self.stack) == 0

# Queue Implementation using deque
```

```
class Queue:
    def __init__(self):
        self.queue = deque()

    def enqueue(self, item):
        self.queue.append(item)

    def dequeue(self):
        return self.queue.popleft() if not self.is_
empty() else "Queue is empty"

    def is_empty(self):
        return len(self.queue) == 0

# Demonstrate Stack and Queue
if __name__ == "__main__":
    # Stack Demonstration
    print("=== Stack Operations ===")
    stack = Stack()
    stack.push(10)
    stack.push(20)
    stack.push(30)
    print("Top of stack:", stack.peek())
    print("Popped item:", stack.pop())
    print("Popped item:", stack.pop())
    print("Is stack empty?", stack.is_empty())

    # Queue Demonstration
    print("\n=== Queue Operations ===")
    queue = Queue()
    queue.enqueue(10)
    queue.enqueue(20)
    queue.enqueue(30)
    print("Front of queue:", queue.queue[0])  #
Accessing front element
    print("Dequeued item:", queue.dequeue())
    print("Dequeued item:", queue.dequeue())
    print("Is queue empty?", queue.is_empty())
```

This program demonstrates the implementation and usage of stack and queue data structures using Python. Here's how it operates:

Stack Implementation: A stack is implemented using a Python list. Key methods:

- push(item): Adds an item to the stack.
- pop(): Removes and returns the top item, or returns "Stack is empty" if the stack is empty.
- peek(): Returns the top item without removing it, or "Stack is empty" if the stack is empty.
- is_empty(): Checks if the stack is empty.

The program demonstrates adding three items to the stack, peeking at the top item, popping two items, and checking if the stack is empty.

Queue Implementation:

A queue is implemented using Python's deque class. Key methods:

- enqueue(item): Adds an item to the end of the queue.
- dequeue(): Removes and returns the front item, or returns "Queue is empty" if the queue is empty.
- is_empty(): Checks if the queue is empty.

The program demonstrates adding three items to the queue, accessing the front item, dequeuing two items, and checking if the queue is empty.

Output:

The program outputs the results of the stack and queue operations, including the items at the top/front, items removed, and whether the structures are empty after the operations.

Key Features:

- Stack: Demonstrates Last In, First Out (LIFO) behaviour.
- Queue: Demonstrates First In, First Out (FIFO) behaviour.
- Efficient Queue: Uses deque for optimal queue operations compared to lists.

13: Deep and Shallow

Copying: We've all done it! We're all familiar with copy or copying something, right? If not you've lived a very sheltered life. These days, there's almost nothing we can't make a copy of. In Python, we have two main techniques to copy data: "shallow" and "deep". These terms might sound fancy, but they just refer to different ways of duplicating objects, especially more complex ones like lists and dictionaries. The big difference between them is how they handle the objects they're copying.

Both types of copying use Python's **'copy'** module, which is part of the standard library, so there's no need to install anything extra.

So, what's the deal with these two? Let's break it down:

Deep Copy: The Whole Package

A deep copy creates a completely independent duplicate of the original object, including everything nested inside it. Imagine you're making a photocopy of a document—it's identical in every way, This is what we're used to when we think of copying something. You start with one item and end up with another that's the same. Even copies of other reference documents that may have been included within it.

Shallow Copy: Just the Surface

A shallow copy, on the other hand, creates a new object, but it doesn't fully duplicate everything inside. Instead, it just copies reference to the nested objects from the original. This means that if you change something in the original list, or in the copy, those changes will appear in both. It's like having a live link between the two—change one, and the other changes too.

For example, if we, shallow copy **original_list** and call it **shallow_copy** and then change the first item in the the shallow_copy list to 50. Since original_ list and shallow_copy are effectively the same item, the value is changed in **both** the original list and the shallow copied list!

Whow!

Hold-up you're probably thinking, if not shouting! How's that work? The deal is that in Python, objects are stored in memory as instances of classes, and the way Python handles object storage is integral to its design and functionality. Here's a breakdown of how Python stores these: objects:

- **Heap Memory:** Python stores objects in a region of memory known as the **heap**. The heap is just a chunk of memory dedicated to storing stuff. When you create an object like a list, dictionary, or even a simple integer, Python allocates heap memory for this object.

Every Python object contains some information, called **metadata**, which is used by Python to manage the object. This metadata typically includes:

- **Reference Count:** The number of references pointing to the object.
- **Type Information:** A pointer to a type object, which defines what kind of object it is (e.g., integer, string, list).
- **Value/Data:** The actual data or value of the object is stored along with the metadata.
- **Object ID:** Every object in Python has a unique identifier, which is its memory address - viz exactly where in the Raspberry Pi memory it is stored.

When you assign an object to a variable, the variable doesn't store the object itself but a pointer to the object's memory location. This means that multiple variables can reference the same object. Makes sense, right?

As we've seen, some objects are immutable, so once created, their state cannot be modified. When you "change" an immutable object (e.g., by adding two integers), Python creates a new object and updates the reference to point to the new object. Conversely when you try and change a mutable object the memory location stays the same, and the changes are applied directly to the object.

Note that both mutable and immutable objects are stored in memory, and variables hold references (pointers) to these objects. When copying mutable objects, shallow copies share references to nested mutable objects, while deep copies create new instances.

Python also applies a similar concept to strings, especially short strings or those used as identifiers, to save memory and improve performance. Python lists are implemented as dynamic arrays. When a list needs more space (e.g., when adding more elements), Python allocates a new block of memory that is larger than necessary and copies the elements over, reducing the frequency of re allocations.

Dictionaries are implemented as hash tables. Remember a **hash table** is a data structure that stores key-value pairs. It allows quick retrieval of a value associated with a given key by using a hash function.)

Keys are hashed to determine where their corresponding values are stored in the table. This is an ultra-efficient way to handle dynamic data.

Another Look at Shallow Copy

Here's a program that provides a visual example, and is followed by some illustrations:

```
#Filename: shallowdeep1.py
import copy
#Original Object
list1 = [[1, 2], [3, 4], [5,6]]
print("Original List:", list1)

#Shallow Copy = list2
list2 = list1.copy()
list2[0][0] = 10
print("Shallow Copied List:", list1)

deep = copy.deepcopy(list1)

#Modify the Deep Copy
deep[0][1] = 99

#Print both Lists
print("Original List:", list1)
print()
print("Deep Copied List:", deep)
print("Original List:", list1)
```

Original Object

Our original list (list1) is a nested list of three elements:

```
[[1, 2], [3, 4], [5,6]]]
```

We then make a shallow copy of the list. This creates a new list, list2, but it **does not** create new copies of the nested lists. Instead, both list1 (the original list) and list2 (the shallow copied list) refer to the same nested lists. Therefore, changes to the nested lists in list2 will also reflect in the original list, list1

This is illustrated in Figure 13a.

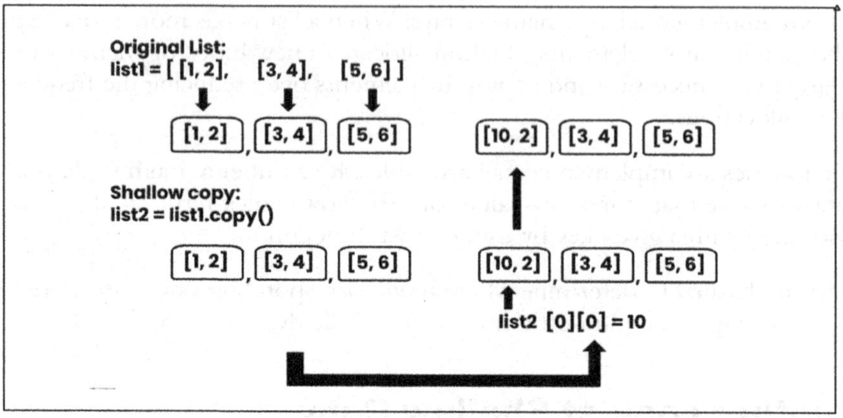

Figure 13a. A shallow copy (list2) of an original list (list1). The first element in list2 is replaced with a '10' and this change also 'seemingly' occurs in the original list1 as they are mirror copies.

Changing an item in the original or copied list will make the identical change in the other list as they are in fact referring to the same data.

We now execute:

```
deep_copy = copy.deepcopy(original_list)

#Modify the Deep Copy
deep_copy[0][2] = 99
```

Here we make a deep_copy of the original list. Remember this original list now has an element changed within it.

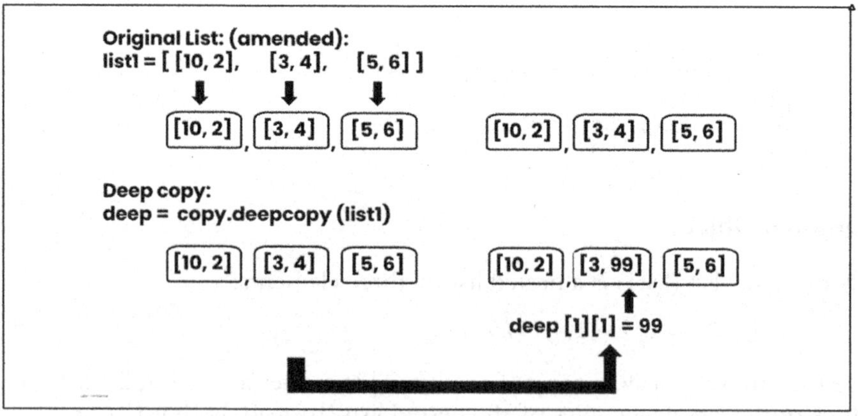

Figure 13b. A deep copy of the shallow copy list.

We now have three versions of the list sitting in memory. The 'original_list', the 'shallow_list' and the 'deep_copy' list. Note that the deep_copy is actioned on the original_list, which has already been modified. We action:

```
deep_copy = copy.deepcopy(original_list)
```

This creates a completely independent copy of original_list, including new copies of the nested lists. As a result, changes to deep_copy do not affect original_list.

```
deep_copy[1][1] = 99
```

This changes the third element of the first nested list in deep_copy. Because deep_copy is independent, this change does not affect original_list.

Final Outputs

The program then makes changes to 'shallow_copy' and 'deep_copy', before printing the contents of all three lists, to give:

```
Original List: [[10, 2], [3, 4], [5,6]]
Shallow List:  [[10, 2], [3, 4], [5,6]]
Deep Copy List: [[10, 2], [3, 99], [5,6]]
```

It is *very* important to remember then that if you wanted to keep an original copy of 'original list' that we actually started with, we would have needed to make an independent copy. However, be careful. Because including a command such as:

```
new_list= original_list
```

Is *not* creating a new, independent copy of original_list. Instead, you are just creating a new reference (alias) to the same list in memory. This means that any changes made to new_list will also affect original_list, and vice versa.

Could get into a pickle here, and this is a common error that often creates puzzles galore for user's new to Python. We must make a deep copy to keep a non-changing copy of the list we started with.

Correct Way to Make an Independent Copy

To create an independent copy of original_list that you can modify without affecting the original, you should use one of the following methods:

Using **copy.deepcopy()** for a deep copy (recommended if your list has nested lists):

```
#Filename: shallowdeep2.py
import copy
original_list = [[1, 2, 3], [4, 5, 6]]

#Create a deep copy
new_list = copy.deepcopy(original_list)
```

Using **copy.copy()** for a shallow copy (only for non-nested lists or when you don't need independent nested objects):

```
#Filename: shallowdeep3.py
import copy
original_list = [[1, 2], [3, 4], [5,6]]

#Create a shallow copy
new_list = copy.copy(original_list)
```

Using Slicing for a shallow copy (suitable for simple lists):

```
#Filename: shallowdeep4.py
original_list = [[1, 2], [3, 4], [5,6]]
#Create a shallow copy using slicing
new_list = original_list[:]
```

Deep Copy: The Real Deal

Now, let me ramble on some more about deep copies. A deep copy doesn't just copy the outer object—it goes all the way down, duplicating every nested object as well. This means changes to the deep copy won't affect the original object at all. It's like taking a snapshot of the data at a moment in time—whatever happens next, your snapshot stays exactly the same.

It's important you understand this copy process, so as not to get into that pickle! In summary:

- **Shallow Copy**: Creates a new object but only copies reference to the nested objects, so changes to nested objects affect both the original and copied objects.
- **Deep Copy**: Creates a completely independent copy of the original object, including all nested objects, ensuring no changes in one affect the other.

If you want complete separation between the original and the copied objects, go for a deep copy. If you're okay with shared references to nested objects, a shallow copy might be just what you need—and it's more efficient in terms of memory and performance.

Here's another example to explore and shows how you can use both shallow and deep copy together:

```
#Filename: shallowdeep5.py
import copy

#Original object
original_list = [1, [2, 3], {'a': 'apple', 'b':
'banana'}]

#Shallow copy
shallow_copy = copy.copy(original_list)
```

```
#Deep copy
deep_copy = copy.deepcopy(original_list)

#Modify the copied objects
shallow_copy[1][0] = 'X'
deep_copy[2]['a'] = 'orange'

#Print all lists
print("Original List:", original_list)
print("Shallow Copied List:", shallow_copy)
print("Deep Copied List:", deep_copy)
```

Breaking It Down

- **Original Object**: The list has three key elements: an integer, a nested list, and a nested dictionary.
- **Shallow Copy**: Uses *copy.copy()* to create a new list with references to the same nested objects.
- **Modification in Shallow Copy**: Changes in the nested list affect both the original and the shallow copy.
- **Deep Copy**: Uses **copy.deepcopy()** to create a completely independent copy of the original object.
- **Modification in Deep Copy**: Changes in the nested dictionary affect only the deep copy, leaving the original untouched.

And there you have it—everything you need to know about shallow and deep copies in Python on your Raspberry Pi!

(You could try drawing this out as done with the previous example.)

Shallow Copy Without the Copy Module

You can create a shallow copy of a list without even touching the copy module? Yep, it's that easy! You can use slicing, which is both simple and efficient. Let me show you how:

```
#Filename: shallowcopy5.py
original_list = [1, 2, [3, 4], 5]
shallow_copy = original_list[:]

#Modifying the nested list in the shallow copy
shallow_copy[2][0] = 'changed'

print(original_list)
#Output: [1, 2, ['changed', 4], 5]
print(shallow_copy)
#Output: [1, 2, ['changed', 4], 5]
```

In this example, original_list[:] creates a new list that contains all the elements of original_list. The [:] notation basically means "copy everything from start to finish," so you get a brand-new list that's a shallow copy of the original.

Breaking It Down

- **original_list[:]**: This slicing operation copies the entire list.
- **shallow_copy**: This is the new list that's a shallow copy of original_list.

A Little Note on Shallow Copies

If the original list contains nested lists (or other mutable objects), the shallow copy will only copy the references to these objects. This means that if you change something in one of the nested objects in the original list, it will also change in the shallow copy—and vice versa.

Why Use the Copy Module?

The copy module is your go-to tool when you're working with more complex data structures, like nested dictionaries, lists of lists, or anything else with multiple levels of nesting. It's great for making sure that changes to a deep copy don't affect the original object or any other copies you've made.

When to Use a Shallow Copy

A shallow copy is perfect when you want to duplicate the structure of an object but don't need to independently copy the nested objects within it. It's efficient and avoids unnecessary duplication, which is especially handy when the nested objects are large, immutable, or aren't going to be modified.

Why You Might Want to Make a Shallow Copy

There are plenty of reasons why you might need to make a shallow copy of something. Let's explore a few common scenarios where a shallow copy is just what you need:

When the Object Contains Immutable Elements: If the object you're copying only contains immutable types, like integers, strings, or tuples, you don't have to worry about accidentally changing shared objects. Why? Because immutable types can't be changed! For example, if you're copying a list of strings, modifying a string in the shallow copy will create a new string, leaving the original untouched.

Quick Duplicate Needed for Read-Only Operations: Sometimes, you need a quick duplicate of an object just for read-only operations. If you're not planning to modify the nested objects, a shallow copy is perfect. For instance, let's say you're copying a list of lists to perform some read-only operations on the outer list. As long as you're not messing with the inner lists, a shallow copy does the job just fine:

```
#Filename: shallowdeep7.py
original = [[1, 2], [3, 4]]
shallow_copy = original.copy()

# Iterate over the shallow copy
for sublist in shallow_copy:
   print(sublist)
# Safe to do, as you're not modifying the inner lists
```

Modify Only the Outer Structure: If your goal is to tweak the outer structure of a composite object—like adding or removing elements from a list—without messing with the inner objects, then a shallow copy is your best bet. For example, if you want to add or remove items from the top level of a list, but leave the inner lists as they are, a shallow copy will work perfectly:

```
#Filename: shallowdeep8.py
original = [[1, 2], [3, 4]]
shallow_copy = original.copy()

shallow_copy.append([5, 6])
# Adds a new list without affecting the original
print(original)
print(shallow_copy)
```

In these cases, a shallow copy is efficient, straightforward, and just what you need to get the job done!

Making a Deep Copy After a Shallow Copy

Even if you start with a shallow copy of an object, you can later make a deep copy of that shallow copy. The deep copy operation will then recursively copy all nested objects within the shallow copy. Example:

```
#Filename: shallowdeep9.py
import copy

#Original object (a list containing other lists)
original = [[1, 2], [3, 4]]

#Perform a shallow copy
shallow_copy = original.copy()

#Now, make a deep copy of the shallow copy
deep_copy = copy.deepcopy(shallow_copy)

#Modifying the shallow copy to show the difference
#This changes the nested list in both original and
shallow_copy
shallow_copy[0][0] = 99  #only affects the shallow_copy
shallow_copy.append([5, 6])

#Modifying the deep copy
deep_copy[0][0] = 42
```

```
#This change does not affect the original or shallow_
copy

print("Original:", original)
print("Shallow Copy:", shallow_copy)
print("Deep Copy:", deep_copy)
```

- **Original Object: A** list of lists, original = [[1, 2], [3, 4]].
- **Shallow Copy:** A new list shallow_copy is created, but it still references the same nested lists as original.
- **Deep Copy:** A completely independent deep_copy is created from shallow_copy. All nested lists are duplicated, so deep_copy and shallow_copy no longer share any references.

Why Would You Do This?

Intermediate Steps: You might want to perform some modifications on a shallow copy first and then decide to create a completely independent deep copy afterwards.

Sometimes you want to avoid the overhead of making a deep copy immediately, and instead, start with a shallow copy, only making a deep copy when necessary.

A deep copy will ensure that all levels of nested objects are duplicated, regardless of whether those objects were initially shallow copies. This allows you to safely modify the deep copy without affecting the original or the shallow copy.

Exercise: Deep and Shallow Copying

This exercise tests your understanding the differences between shallow and deep copying of objects in Python and how it affects the behaviour of mutable and nested data structures.

Understanding Copying Basics:

- Create a list original = [[1, 2], [3, 4]].
- Assign this list to a new variable shallow_copy using the copy module's copy() function.
- Assign this list to another variable deep_copy using the copy module's deepcopy() function.

Shallow Copying:

- Modify an element inside a sublist of shallow_copy.

- Print the original list and the shallow copy.
- Observe and explain how the modification affects both the original and the shallow copy.

Deep Copying:

- Modify an element inside a sublist of deep_copy.
- Print the original list and the deep copy.
- Observe and explain how the modification affects the original and the deep copy.

Solution

```
#Filename: 13-exercise-04.py
import copy

# Step 1: Create the original list
original = [[1, 2], [3, 4]]

# Step 2: Create shallow and deep copies
shallow_copy = copy.copy(original)
deep_copy = copy.deepcopy(original)

# Step 3: Modify shallow copy
shallow_copy[0][0] = 99
print("After modifying shallow_copy:")
print("Original:", original)
print("Shallow Copy:", shallow_copy)

# Step 4: Modify deep copy
deep_copy[1][1] = 88
print("\nAfter modifying deep_copy:")
print("Original:", original)
print("Deep Copy:", deep_copy)
```

Questions

- Why did modifying the shallow copy affect the original list?
- Why did modifying the deep copy not affect the original list?
- In what situations would a shallow copy be sufficient, and when would you need a deep copy?

Output

After modifying the shallow copy, both original and shallow_copy show the change in the nested sublist.

After modifying the deep copy, only deep_copy shows the change, and original remains unchanged.

This exercise reinforces the concept of memory references and object copying in Python, preparing students to handle mutable and nested data structures effectively.

14: Environments +

So, we've agreed that in the Raspberry Pi world, particularly from the Raspberry Pi 5/500 and beyond, virtual environments are **not to be ignored.** They have become essential for managing Python projects. While this isn't strictly necessary for the Raspberry Pi 4 and earlier models, adopting virtual environments is now recommended by the Python-keepers for all versions of Python on the Raspberry Pi.

The **venv** module in Python is a built-in tool designed to facilitate the creation and management of virtual environments. It isolates each project, enabling you to meet the specific requirements of each one, such as running a particular module version tailored to the program's needs. When we created the PyDaily virtual environment in Chapter 04, Thonny effectively used this module to deploy it. That said, the venv module is best installed from the command line ensuring you environments are 'leak free'. Sometimes the system gets upset and very occasionally won't allow modules to be them installed. With a message to the fact that the module is managed 'externally'. It believes it is run in the system environment, and that is probably the case.

You can check that venv is installed by typing at the CLI:

```
dpkg -l | grep python3-venv
```

It is simple enough to create a virtual environment from the Terminal. We already looked at how we do this using Thonny, so you already have a good understanding of how the process works and how the finished article looks. This is handy as you can have more than one virtual environment setup and move from one to another with a couple of simple commands.

We set up a virtual environment called 'PyDaily' earlier. 'This time we'll create a virtual environment called 'DAILY' on the Desktop.

First create the directory through Bash and then the virtual environment with:

```
$ mkdir DAILY
$ python3 -m venv DAILY
```

Now 'DAILY' contains a virtual environment.

- Here:

python3: Invokes the Python 3 interpreter.

-m venv: Directs Python to run the venv module as a script, which is responsible for creating virtual environments.

DAILY: The name assigned to the new virtual environment.

The venv module offers various features and functionalities:

- **Creation of Virtual Environments:** With venv, you can create virtual environments tailored to your project needs. Running a command like the one mentioned creates a new directory within your project, containing a self-contained Python interpreter and a dedicated site-packages directory.
- **Isolation of Dependencies:** Virtual environments are entirely self-contained and do not interfere with the system-wide Python installation or other virtual environments. This isolation ensures that packages and dependencies within a virtual environment do not impact other projects or the system.
- **Activation and Deactivation:** After creating a virtual environment, you can activate it to make it the active Python environment for the current shell session. Activation and deactivation are facilitated by simple commands. The shell prompt will change to indicate the active environment, including its name in parenthesis before the actual prompt. To return to the system's default Python environment, use the **deactivate** command.
- **Package Installation:** Within an activated virtual environment, you can use the pip utility **(see next section)** to install, upgrade, or remove packages. pip scopes packages to the virtual environment and stores them in its site-packages directory, allowing control over project dependencies and avoiding conflicts.
- **Python Version Control:** Besides managing package dependencies, venv lets you control the Python version used for each project. By specifying the desired Python interpreter during virtual environment creation, you ensure compatibility with specific Python versions

required by your project. Of course at this point in the continuum you're unlikely to have any projects, so we're still ahead of ourselves.

- **Portable and Reproducible Environments:** Virtual environments create portable and reproducible setups by isolating project dependencies. This ensures your code runs consistently and can be shared or deployed with confidence.

When creating a virtual environment, the **venv** module generates scripts or executable that enable activation and deactivation, as well as running Python scripts within the environment. These scripts are in the /bin directory.

You can also manage virtual environments using the CLI via the Terminal. To be honest, it is a quicker method once you are used to it. In fact, for simple projects, I use a combination of the Terminal (set to the appropriate virtual environment) and an IDE. I use Geany by default and we'll examine that in Chapter 27.)

To see the files and folder within, type:

```
$ ls -ls
```

To use the virtual environment, you must 'activate' it thus:

```
$ source DAILY/bin/activate
```

From the 'DAILY' directory.

On doing this, you'll see that the virtual environment name is prefixed at the start of the command line to show that you're no longer using the system Python. Instead, you're using the version of Python contained inside your virtual environment!

This will now work completely independent of the system Python.

At this stage, is you don't have the DAILY terminal window open, you might find it easier do so. If so, from the Desktop, right click the DAILY folder and from the drop-down select 'Open in Terminal'

Copy the 'datetime1.py' file into the DAILY folder. Go to the Terminal window of the DAILY environment, and Type at type at the Terminal:

```
python3 datetime1.py
```

And the current date and time will be displayed after the prompt.

Load the '**datetime1.py**' program into Thonny and run it.

Both programs have been run in their own virtual environments. The bottom line is you can have multiple virtual environments running at once. You just need to remember which is which.

Common Issues and Troubleshooting

Sometimes, you can encounter **conflicts** between packages or versions. To resolve these, ensure you are using compatible versions of packages and check the documentation or community forums for advice on handling conflicts.

If a virtual environment becomes **corrupted** (e.g., due to interrupted installations or system changes), it may be necessary to delete and recreate it. Ensure that any critical dependencies or configurations are noted before doing so. (You can also generate a file called 'requirements.txt' to record this information, as well see.)

Virtual environments can grow as packages are installed. Regularly review and clean up unnecessary packages to maintain performance. Tools like **pip-tools** can help manage dependencies more efficiently.

If you are working on a project, especially as you are still learning, keep notes! Keep track of the Python and package versions used in your virtual environments. This helps ensure consistency across different setups and makes it easier to troubleshoot issues or replicate the environment elsewhere.

Deleting virtual environments needs to be done with care and there are some useful ways to manage them and undertake such tasks. We'll get to those.

If you want to create your virtual environment so that it is identical to your system Python, then you can use:

```
python -m venv --system-sitepackages DAILY
```

This would create a copy in the 'DAILY' folder.

APT and PIP

The **Advanced Package Tool** (apt) simplifies the process of installing, upgrading, and managing software packages, ensuring that your Raspberry Pi has access to the latest applications and tools without manually downloading and configuring them.

Installing packages in the Raspberry Pi OS should always be performed using 'apt'. It is the preferred and recommended method. (This is with the system environment not with a virtual environment.)

The use of 'apt' as the preferred method for package management is standard practice across various versions of Raspberry Pi OS, not just with the launch of the Raspberry Pi 5 and Bookworm OS

This requirement was introduced with the launch of the Raspberry Pi 5, attempting to use other methods, such as 'pip,' typically results in errors. As this book covers various versions of the Raspberry Pi, we'll stick to the 'apt' method. This is also the recommended approach for writing Python code.

Packages installed via **'apt'** are certified and ensure faster installation. Additionally, they are specifically tested for the Raspberry Pi OS.

The primary command-line utility for using apt is 'apt-get', though 'apt' command is often used as well:

```
sudo apt install package_name
```

(Note that apt typically requires administrative privileges being root or prefixing with 'sudo' to install or manage packages, as it affects the entire system.)

Pip, on the other hand, can install packages locally within a user's environment without requiring root access.) There are two versions: pip and pip3.

To keep your system up to date, you should regularly update your package lists and upgrade your installed packages. This ensures that you have the latest security patches and feature updates. From a Terminal window type:

```
sudo apt update
```

Followed by:

```
sudo apt upgrade
```

Of course this is something we do regularly as Raspberry Pi users, and the down arrow on the top right of the desktop bar will let you know when an upgrade is available.

Removing a package is simple too:

```
sudo apt remove package_name
```

To remove a package along with its configuration files:

```
sudo apt purge package_name
```

The 'purge' option is much more aggressive than the standard 'remove' command. As its name suggests, it gets rid of everything associated with the package. This beggars the question as to why you wouldn't use it all the time. There are a few reasons:

- The **'remove'** command deletes the package but keeps the configuration files. This can be useful if you plan to reinstall the package later and want to retain your previous configuration settings.

- Keeping configuration files makes for a quicker and easier re installation process if you decide to reinstall the package. Your previous settings will be preserved, so you don't have to configure the package again from scratch.
- Some packages might store **important** data or logs within their configuration directories. Using **purge** would delete this. Using remove avoids this risk, unless you're sure.

The choice between using remove and purge with apt depends on the specific circumstances and user preferences. However, it is generally more common to use 'remove' rather than 'purge'.

The APT package manager receives the user's request and begins the process of managing the installation. APT first retrieves information about the package from the software repositories (a collection of software packages) It of course ensures it exists as well!. Then APT then downloads the actual package files from the repository and installs it.

- **Resolves Dependencies (Installs Required Packages):** APT checks for any dependencies that the package requires and installs them if they are not already present on the system.
- **Verifies Package (Checks Integrity):** APT verifies the integrity of the downloaded package to ensure it has not been tampered with and is safe to install.
- **Installs Software (Places Files in /usr):** The package manager then installs the software, placing the necessary files into the appropriate directories.
- **Configures Software (Sets up System Paths):** After installation, APT configures the software, setting up system paths and other necessary configurations to make the software functional.
- **Completes Installation (Software Ready):** Finally, the installation process is completed, and the software is ready for use.

Interestingly some of these operations are undertaken in parallel rather than sequentially. For example, downloading the package and resolving what its dependencies are.

To clean-up after package removal: After removing packages, you can use:

```
sudo apt autoremove
```

to automatically remove dependencies that are no longer needed. This helps keep your system clean and saves disk space.

You can also search and get information about a package by using:

```
apt-cache search package_name
apt-cache show package_name
```

to search for a package in the APT repositories.

Pip Pip3 Hooray!

pip and pip3 are package management systems used to install and manage software packages into virtual environments. pip is the default package manager for Python 2, while pip3 is the version oft used for Python 3.

This distinction is crucial because packages and libraries might have different versions or compatibility requirements depending on the Python version being used. By explicitly using pip3, you ensure that the packages you install are compatible with Python 3, which helps in avoiding conflicts between versions and maintaining project consistency.

They **streamline** the process of installing libraries and dependencies, making it easier for you to build and maintain Python applications. pip stands for **"Pip Installs Packages,"** and it interfaces with the **Python Package Index** (PyPI), an extensive repository of Python packages. (You'll see this in action when using Thonny to install packages.)

With Python 3, it's safer to use pip3 to ensure that the packages are installed for Python 3. This way, you avoid any confusion about which Python version the packages are being installed for.

From the CLI you would use pip to install a package in a virtual environment thus:

```
python3 -m pip install some_package
```

When you create a virtual environment using python3, the pip command within that environment will correspond to Python 3.x

```
python3 -m venv myenv
source myenv/bin/activate
pip install some_package
```

which fetches the package from the Python Package Index (PyPI) and installs it into your environment.

When you use python3 in a command, it does not automatically mean that the pip command will use pip3.

For upgrading an existing package, you would use:

```
pip install --upgrade package_name
```

If you need to remove a package:

```
pip uninstall package_name
```

will do the job.

pip should be used whenever you require external libraries or tools not included in the **Python Standard Library**. Whether you're starting a new project and need additional functionality, or you're maintaining an existing project that depends on specific packages, pip provides a consistent and efficient method for managing these dependencies. It is particularly useful when working in virtual environments, which isolate your project's dependencies from the global Python installation, ensuring compatibility and preventing version conflicts.

The command

```
python3 -m site
```

will list installed packages, but it does not specifically indicate whether they were installed using pip or pip3. To determine the version of pip used, you can use:

```
pip3 show package_name
```

Or:

```
pip3 list
```

You can check the version of pip and pip3 you have installed with the following commands:

```
pip --version
pip3 --version
```

Ideally you should be consistent and use pip3 unless there is another reason not to do so. (Don't know what that'll be though….)

Running a script with python3 and managing its dependencies with pip3 ensures that your project is using the correct versions of packages, reducing compatibility issues.

Using python3 and pip3 together is a standard practice for managing and executing Python 3 projects. It helps maintain clarity and consistency when working with Python 3 environments.

You can install a **specific packag**e version using:

```
pip install package_name==1.2.3
```

Where 1.2.3 is the version number of the package you require.

Is it Apt for the Raspberry Pi ?

You might find that when trying to install a particular package that it throws an error message in your direction. The reason being that a module may need to have been changed to accommodate the Raspberry Pi and similar systems. There is no hard rule, and sometimes you just need to go through the steps to install what you need.

Installing into a virtual environment is normally straightforward buy sometimes you may find you need to use:

```
pip install python3-<module>
```

If you need the module system-wide (often on a server or if a specific Python package is required by an operating system tool), you might choose:

```
sudo apt install python3-<module>
```

This installs a specific version tested by the OS maintainers for stability with the system's Python version. This is especially the case for common modules that interface with the Pi's hardware or require specific OS-level dependencies.

So, as a rule of thumb, for hardware-related modules and performance-intensive libraries, use:

```
sudo apt install python3-<module>.
```

For general-purpose libraries not tied to the Pi's hardware, using pip within a virtual environment is often a better choice.

If you find yourself floundering, remove everything that may have been installed or part installed before throwing a wobbly. Then start again ensuring your Raspberry Pi OS is fully up to date first.

Questions

1. Why are virtual environments recommended for managing Python projects on the Raspberry Pi, especially from version 5 onward?
2. Describe the function of the venv module in Python and what it provides for managing Python projects.
3. What are the primary steps for creating a virtual environment called DAILY on the Raspberry Pi desktop using the terminal?
4. Explain the difference between activating and deactivating a virtual environment and how to perform these actions.

5. How does a virtual environment maintain isolation of dependencies, and why is this beneficial for managing Python projects?

6. When managing Python package versions, why might specifying the Python interpreter during virtual environment creation be useful?

7. What is the purpose of the apt package manager on the Raspberry Pi OS, and how does it differ from pip?

8. What are the recommended commands for updating and upgrading system packages on a Raspberry Pi using apt?

9. Explain the difference between sudo apt remove package_name and sudo apt purge package_name commands.

10. In which situations would you choose sudo apt install over pip install for installing a package on a Raspberry Pi?

11. What is the purpose of the pip3 command, and when should it be used with Python 3 projects on the Raspberry Pi?

12. How can you install a specific version of a package using pip and why might this be necessary?

13. What are some common troubleshooting tips if you encounter issues with virtual environments or package conflicts on a Raspberry Pi?

15: More Thonny

To paraphrase a well-known saying, "Errors happen." And sometimes, the original saying feels even more accurate! Identifying and fixing these inevitable errors in your code (called **bugs**)can be tricky,, but once you nail the error and correct it, it's soooo satisfying!

There are two types of errors in programming:

- **Syntax Errors**: These happen when you've entered something incorrectly—maybe a typo, a forgotten bracket, or a missing colon.
- **Logical Errors**: These occur when the program runs, but the results aren't what you expected. This often involves incorrect values or calculations, and the issue could be in the code itself or in the values being passed to it.

Thonny gives you a hint through its 'Assistant' window, pointing out the line number where it thinks the error is after your program crashes. Check out this example:

```
#Filename: debugging1.py
#Looping
x = 0
i = 2
for i in range(0, 10, x):
    print(i)
```

Running this will leave the Thonny window looking something like that shown in Figure 15a.:

Figure 15a. Programmer we have a problem.

Figure 15b. Bracket missing.

In the 'Assistant' and 'Shell' windows, you'll see some clear error messages. They show the line number and what's wrong:

```
ValueError: range() arg 3 must not be zero
```

The third argument (referred to as 'arg 3') in the range() function must not be zero. You can see that the third argument is 'x', and 'x' is set to 0 earlier in the code. So, just change the assignment of x in line 5 to:

```
x = 1
```

Now, run the program again. The result appears in the Shell window, and the Assistant window gives you a metaphorical thumbs up—problem solved!

One of the most common errors, especially when you're starting out, is missing or mismatched brackets. Sometimes all you need to do is insert a bracket in the right place. However, pairing off brackets in a program can be tricky. Try this program:

```
#Filename: debugging2.py
#Looping
x = 0
i = 2
for i in range(0, 10, x:
    print(i)
```

Look at the error messages as shown in Figure 15b—they indicate that line 5 is missing a bracket:

```
Unbalanced parentheses, brackets, or braces: '(' at
line 5 is not closed by the end of the line.
```

You might also notice that part of the program is greyed out, which indicates an error before running the program (in this case, lines 5 and 6).

Let's add the bracket back in, but now the colon is missing:

```
#Filename: debugging3.py
#Looping
x = 0
i = 2
for i in range(0, 10, x)
    print(i)
```

In earlier versions of Thonny, the Assistant window might not have pinpointed the exact issue but would highlight the line. In this later version, the error is clearly defined, with the 'hat' symbol showing exactly where the problem is in the shell.

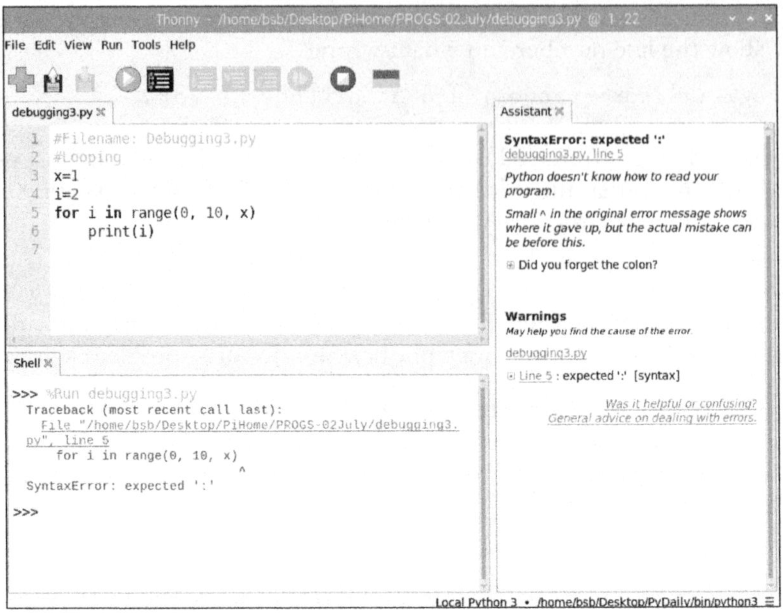

Figure 15c. Sometimes Thonny will point exactly to the issue.

Syntax errors like these are the most common in Python. They happen when your code doesn't follow the language's rules. Double-check for misspelled commands, missing parentheses, commas, semicolons, or quotation marks. Those last four are especially tricky and, in my experience, the most common culprits.

Logical Print Statements: If you're not sure where an error is happening, you can insert print statements at various points in your code to see what values are being assigned to variables or where the code is failing. This is particularly useful for logical errors. Here's a simple example:

```
a = 5
b = 6
c = 7
print(a + b)
```

The result is 11, but you were expecting 12. The issue? You meant to code:

```
print(a + c)
```

Print statements can really help you pinpoint where things are going wrong in your code.

Use a Debugger

While Thonny's Assistant and Shell windows are great for spotting issues, sometimes you need something a bit more sophisticated to really dig into your code, especially when you're dealing with those sneaky logical errors.

A debugger is like a detective tool for your code. It lets you pause the program, inspect what's going on, and figure out why things aren't working as expected. Think of it as a magnifying glass for your code, allowing you to see the inner workings and catch those pesky bugs. Some key features of a debugger, like the one built into Thonny, include:

- **Breakpoints**: These are markers you set in your code where you want the program to pause. When the program hits a breakpoint, it stops running, so you can take a look around—check variable values and see what's happening.
- **Stepping**: This allows you to move through your code one line at a time, or even jump through specific blocks of code. It's a great way to understand how your code flows and where things might be going wrong.
- **Variable Inspection**: With a debugger, you can inspect the values of variables at different points in your code, not just where the program paused. This helps you see how data is being manipulated and identify any unexpected changes.

Debugging in Thonny

Let's break down the basic steps for using a debugger in Thonny:

1. **Set Breakpoints**: Identify areas in your code where you think issues might be happening and set breakpoints there. If you're unsure, start with a few key spots.
2. **Run the Program**: Start your program in debug mode. It will run until it hits a breakpoint or encounters an error.
3. **Inspect Variables**: Once the program pauses, check the values of your variables to see if they match what you expected.
4. **Step Through the Code**: Use the debuggers buttons or function keys to step through your code, line by line, or through specific functions. This lets you watch how your program behaves at each step.
5. **Fix Issues**: Based on what you observe, make corrections to your code to fix any problems you've identified.

6. **Repeat as Needed**: Continue running the program in debug mode, inspecting variables, and stepping through the code until everything works as expected.

The Thonny interface is packed with useful tools for debugging. Across the top of the screen, you'll see several icons, including those for debugging. These icons allow you to peer inside your program and understand what's happening.

Thonny In and Out

The debugging icons in Thonny include:

- **Step In**: This lets you dive into a function or loop, so you can trace the actions of the code within. It's perfect for when you need to understand exactly what's happening inside a specific block of code.
- **Step Over**: This allows you to execute the current line of code and move on to the next one without stepping into any functions that are called on that line. It's great for skipping over code you're not currently interested in.
- **Step Out**: If you're inside a function and want to jump out, this is your go-to. It lets you exit the current function or loop and continue with the next line of code outside of it.
- **Resume**: When you're ready to let your program continue running, click the Resume button to go back to normal execution.

15d. Debugging tools on Thonny menu bar.

Let's look at a sample program to illustrate these concepts:

```
#Filename: debugging4.py
#Demo Stepping

def inner_function():
    x = 2
    y = 3
    z = x + y  #Breakpoint set here

def outer_function():
    a = 5
    inner_function()
```

```
#Main program
outer_function()
```

To start debugging, set a breakpoint by clicking on the line number where you want the program to pause. A **red dot** will appear in the margin. When you run the debugger, it will stop at this point, allowing you to use 'Step In,' 'Step Over,' or 'Step Out' to navigate through your code.

Practical Debugging Example: Finding a Logical Error

Here's a simple program with a logical error. See if you can spot it before running the code:

```
#Filename: debugging5.py
def is_even(n):
    if n % 2 == 1:
        return True
    else:
        return False

number = 4
result = is_even(number)
print(f"Is {number} even? {result}")
```

When you run the program, the output is:

```
Is 4 even? False
```

The problem? The program incorrectly thinks that 4 isn't an even number. The logical error is in this line:

```
if n % 2 == 1:
```

It should be:

```
if n % 2 == 0:
```

The % operator is a **modulo** operator that gives you the remainder of the division of two numbers. Even number should have a modulo value of zero.

You can also use print statements to help debug this issue:

```
#Filename: debugging6.py
def is_even(n):
    remainder = n % 2
    print(f"n = {n}, n % 2 = {remainder}")
    if remainder == 1:
        return True
    else:
        return False

number = 4
result = is_even(number)
print(f"Is {number} even? {result}")
```

Running this version will show you that the condition is incorrect for determining if a number is even.

Fixing the logic to:

```
if n % 2 == 0:
```

will give you the correct result.

Debugging a Factorial Error

Here's a more complex example that involves computing factorials. A factorial is the product of all positive integers less than or equal to a given number. For instance:

```
5! = 5×4×3×2×1 = 120
4! = 4×3×2×1 = 24
3! = 3×2×1 = 6
```

Now, let's look at a program with a logical error:

```
#Filename: debugging7.py
def factorial(n):
    if n == 0:
        return 1
    else:
        return n * factorial(n - 2)

number = 5
result = factorial(number)
print(f"The factorial of {number} is {result}")
```

When run, Thonny will overflow with detail as shown in *Figure 15e.*

Thonny gives you a RecursionError.

This error occurs because the function is decremented ' n' by 2 each time, rather than by 1. The correct line should be:

```
return n * factorial(n - 1)
```

Summary of Debugging Steps

To resolve a logical error, follow these steps:

1. **Understand the Problem**: Know what the program is supposed to do.

2. **Review the Logic**: Check if the logic in the code is correct, especially in conditional statements and loops.

3. **Debug and Step Through**: Use breakpoints and step through the code to watch how variables change and where things go wrong.

4. **Fix the Issue**: Correct the logic and test the program again.

Exercise: What would happen if **number = 6** in the factorial program? Why is this an issue?

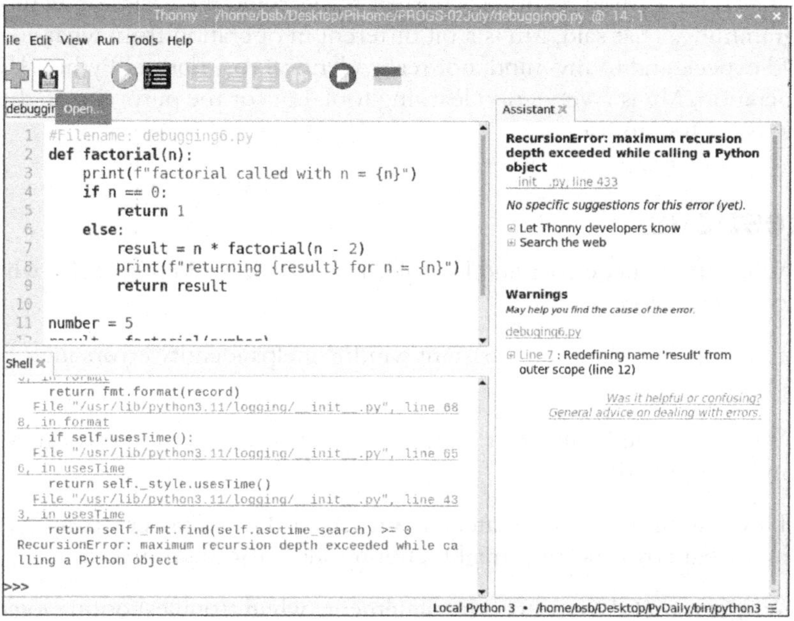

Figure 15e. Output nightmare

Thonny as a Tutor

Thonny's debugger isn't just great for solving problems—it's also a fantastic learning tool. If you don't fully understand a program, try stepping through it with the debugger to see what's happening at each step. You might just find that the process of debugging teaches you more about how your code works!

Mu-tiful

If Thonny is aimed at beginners, then **Mu** is an IDE option that teaches Python in a school friendly manner. It's a good choice for teaching environments, especially those involving children. This is not surprising as its development has been based on educators' feedback from practical use in the program and addressing many of their teaching needs. To that end it delivers, as its target audience includes younger coders and beginners of all ages, especially those working with the Raspberry Pi.

One of Mu's standout features is its intuitive, clutter-free interface. And I mean clutter free – clean as. Mu eliminates unnecessary features that may confuse young newcomers, offering only the essential tools needed to write, run, and debug code. It includes a built-in REPL (Read-Eval-Print Loop), which lets users evaluate Python code snippets interactively.

Mu comes with several helpful modes, each tailored to specific coding activities. The 'Python 3' mode is perfect for learning the basics of Python programming. That said, Mu is a bit different in operation from what you would expect, and to my mind, not really identical to a normal Python IDE in operation. Mu is a very good learning tool, but for the purposes of this book, not a tool to use.

Questions

1. What are syntax errors and logical errors, and how do they differ when it comes to debugging?
2. Explain how Thonny's Assistant window helps identify errors in a program.
3. What does the ValueError: range() arg 3 must not be zero error message indicate in Python?
4. How can missing or unmatched brackets lead to syntax errors in Python, and what error message might Thonny show for this issue?
5. Why is it useful to insert print statements when troubleshooting logical errors? Give an example.
6. Describe how a debugger can help with error handling and the benefits of setting breakpoints in your code.
7. What is the purpose of the 'Step In' and 'Step Over' functions in a debugger, and when would you use each?
8. In the example of the is_even function, what logical error causes the program to give an incorrect result? How would you fix it?
9. Explain the difference between the % (modulo) operator and other operators and how it's used to determine if a number is even.
10. What is a RecursionError in Python, and what caused this error in the factorial example?
11. How can debugging help you understand the program flow and logic, especially for beginners?
12. Why might you encounter an error when running a factorial program with number = 6, and how would you fix it?
13. List the key steps for resolving a logical error in a Python program. Why is each step important?

16: In and Out

Let's be real—**input and output** (I/O) operations are the bread and butter of using a computer. Without them, we'd be stuck with a shiny box of circuits and wires, and that wouldn't be much fun. Over the years, the ways we've handled I/O have changed a lot. From the ancient days of **punch cards** and the screechy sounds of cassette tapes to floppy disks, hard drives, thumb drives, SD cards, and now cloud storage—the world of I/O has come a long way. And who knows, with quantum storage possibly just around the corner, the future looks **zettabyte** fuelled!

We've also come a long way from just typing on keyboards. Nowadays, we're talking to our devices—even those tiny ones on our wrists! It makes you wonder how far off we are from controlling computers with just our thoughts, right? It might sound like science fiction now, but so did the stuff we have now, back in the day.

Today's computers load applications in seconds, a far cry from the minutes we used to wait with cassette tapes. And when it comes to input, it's not just keyboards and mice anymore—we've got touchpads, voice recognition, and who knows what else is coming next.

On your Raspberry Pi, grabbing input from the keyboard is as simple as using the **input()** function. This little function lets you read a line of text typed in, and then hit **<Enter>**, and boom—the text gets stored in a variable for you to play around with. Check out this simple example:

```
#Filename: input1.py
name = input("Enter your name: ")
print("Hello, " + name + "!")
age = input("Enter your age: ")
print("You are " + age + " years old.")
```

When you run this program, it'll ask you to enter your name. Once you've done that, it'll greet you using the name you entered. Then it'll ask for your age (and feel free to fib here), and it'll display that too.

Quick Tip: The **input()** function always gets your input as a string. So, if you need to do any math with the input—like adding numbers—you'll need to convert it to a number using **int()** or **float()**. Here's how you'd do that:

```
#Filename: input2.py
age = input("Enter your age: ")
age = int(age)  # Convert the input string to an
integer

next_year_age = age + 1
print("Next year, you will be " + str(next_year_age) +
" years old.")
```

See what we did here? We converted the user input to an integer so we could add one to it.

Handling Errors and Validation

When you're dealing with user input, it's always a good idea to be cautious. You don't want your program to crash just because someone typed in something unexpected. Imagine getting a program that crashes every time you use it—nobody wants that!

You can use conditional statements or even exception handling to validate and handle different scenarios. For example, when you're expecting a number, you should plan for cases where the user might type in something that isn't a number. This makes your program more robust and gives the user a smoother experience.

Check out this example:

```
#Filename: input3.py
while True:
    try:
        age = int(input("Enter your age: "))
        break  # Break out of the loop if input is
valid
    except ValueError:
        print("Invalid input. Please enter a valid
age.")


print("You are", age, "years old.")
```

Here, the **int()** function tries to convert the input to an integer. If it fails (say the user typed in "twenty" instead of "20"), a ValueError is raised. The try-except block catches this error and prompts the user to try again.

Asking for Multiple Inputs

You can also ask for multiple pieces of information from the user by using several input() calls:

```
#Filename: input4.py
name = input("Enter your name: ")
age = int(input("Enter your age: "))
email = input("Enter your email: ")
print("Name:", name)
print("Age:", age)

print("Email:", email)
```

String Formatting

To make your output look cleaner, you can use string formatting:

```
#Filename: input5.py
name = input("Enter your name: ")
age = int(input("Enter your age: "))

greeting = f"Hello, {name}!"
future_age = age + 10
age_info = f"In 10 years, you will be {future_age}
years old."

print(greeting)
print(age_info)
```

The f"..." syntax is handy for creating strings that can include expressions inside curly braces {}, making your code easier to read and maintain.

Handling Empty Input

By default, **input()** treats an empty input (just pressing <Enter>) as an empty string. If you want to handle empty input differently, just check for it:

```
#Filename: input6.py
name = input("Enter your name: ")
if name:
    print(f"Hello, {name}!")
else:
    print("You didn't enter a name.")
```

In this case, the program checks if name has any content before printing the greeting.

Input to a Dictionary and Tuple

You can also capture input directly into a dictionary:

```
user_dict = {}
key = input("Enter a key: ")
value = input("Enter a value: ")
user_dict[key] = value
```

And if you want the user to keep adding key-value pairs, you can do that in a loop:

```
#Filename: input7.py
user_dict = {}
while True:
    key = input("Enter a key (or press Enter to exit):
")
    if not key:
        break
    value = input("Enter a value: ")
    user_dict[key] = value
```

This little program will keep asking for keys and values until the user presses <Enter> without typing anything.

You can even store user input directly into a tuple:

```
user_input = input("Enter elements separated by commas:
")
user_tuple = tuple(user_input.split(","))
```

For example, if the user enters "1, 2, 3, 4", the tuple will be (1, 2, 3, 4).

Capturing Multiple Inputs at Once

You may find yourself in a situation where you need to grab a bunch of inputs all at once and stash them into a list. You know, like when you're trying to gather everyone's **pizza orders**, and you realise you need a system because "just cheese" isn't the detailed intel you need?

Here's how to wrangle those inputs into a neat little list—because even chaos deserves a bit of organisation:

```
#Filename: input8.py
numbers = input("Enter numbers separated by spaces:
").split()
numbers = [int(number) for number in numbers]
print("You entered:", numbers)
```

In this example, the **split()** method breaks the input string into a list of sub-strings based on spaces. The list comprehension then converts each of those sub-strings into an integer. This is handy when you need to process a bunch of numbers at once.

Default Values in Input Prompts

Sometimes, when asking for user input, you might want to provide a default value so that if the user just hits <Enter>, the program uses a preset value. This is particularly useful for creating more user-friendly programs where users may not always need to provide a custom value.

You can implement this by using the **input()** function along with the **or** operator. If the user input is empty (just <Enter> is pressed), the or operator ensures that the default value is assigned.

Here's how to set up a default value:

```
#Filename: input9.py
name = input("Enter your name (or press Enter for
Guest): ") or "Guest"
print(f"Hello, {name}!")
```

In this example, if the user doesn't enter anything and just presses <Enter>, the program automatically assigns "Guest" to the name variable. This ensures that your program always has a valid input to work with. Of course, you can change "Guest" to any default value you want.

You can apply the same technique to numeric input, although you'll need to handle conversion from string to number:

```
#Filename: input10.py
age = input("Enter your age (or press Enter for 25): ")
or "25"
age = int(age)  # Convert the string to an integer
print(f"You are {age} years old.")
```

If the user doesn't provide any input, the age will default to 25. You then convert the input to an integer using **int()** so you can perform any necessary calculations later.

Reading Numbers with Error Handling

When you're expecting the user to enter a number, it's good practice to handle cases where they might enter something else:

```
#Filename: input11.py
def read_number(prompt):
    while True:
        try:
            return float(input(prompt))
        except ValueError:
            print("That's not a valid number. Please
try again.")

age = read_number("Enter your age: ")
print("You are " + str(age) + " years old.")
```

This function keeps asking for input until the user provides a valid number, making it very user-friendly and robust against errors.

Input with Validation: A Menu Example

You wish the user to select from a list of options. Here's how you can build a simple menu with validation to ensure they pick a valid option:

```
#Filename: input12.py
def display_menu():
    print("Menu:")
    print("1. Start Game")
    print("2. Load Game")
    print("3. Exit")

def get_choice():
    while True:
        choice = input("Enter your choice (1-3): ")
        if choice in ["1", "2", "3"]:
            return int(choice)
        else:
            print("Invalid choice. Please select a
valid option.")

display_menu()
choice = get_choice()

if choice == 1:
    print("Starting new game...")
elif choice == 2:
    print("Loading game...")
elif choice == 3:
    print("Exiting program...")
```

This menu program keeps prompting the user until they choose a valid option, making it more user-friendly and preventing potential errors.

Common Input Mistakes to Avoid

- **Forgetting to Convert Input Types:** Always remember that input() gives you a string, so convert it if you need a number.
- **Not Stripping White Space:** Use the **strip()** method to remove unwanted spaces from your input.
- **Input Assumptions:** Never assume the user will enter the right data. Always add checks and validations to handle unexpected input.

These tips and examples should help you get a handle on input and output in your programs. Whether you're dealing with simple text input or more complex file reading, Python has the tools you need to get the job done smoothly.

Exercise: Using Input and Output

Write a Python program that allows a user to perform basic operations on lists, stacks, and queues. Your program should:

Provide an interactive menu to select between list, stack, and queue operations.

Support the following operations:

- List: Add an element, remove an element by index, display the list.
- Stack: Push an element, pop an element, display the stack.
- Queue: Enqueue an element, dequeue an element, display the queue.
- Display the updated state of the selected data structure after each operation.
- Include an option to exit the program.
- Make your program clear, functional, and user-friendly. Test it with various inputs to ensure it works as expected.3

```
# Filename: 16-exercise-05.py
from collections import deque

def main():
    stack = []
    queue = deque()
    user_list = ["a", "b", "c"]  # Example list

    while True:
        print("\nSelect an option:")
        print("1. Add/Remove from List")
        print("2. Push/Pop Stack")
        print("3. Enqueue/Dequeue Queue")
        print("4. Exit")

        choice = input("Enter your choice: ")

        if choice == "1":
            print("\nList Operations:")
            print("Current list:", user_list)
            print("a. Add an element")
            print("b. Remove an element by index")

            sub_choice = input("Choose an operation: ")

            if sub_choice == "a":
                element = input("Enter an element to
add: ")
                user_list.append(element)
                print("Updated list:", user_list)
            elif sub_choice == "b":
                index = int(input("Enter index to
remove: "))
                if 0 <= index < len(user_list):
```

```
                removed = user_list.pop(index)
                print("Removed element:", removed)
            else:
                print("Invalid index.")
            print("Updated list:", user_list)

    elif choice == "2":
        print("\nStack Operations:")
        print("a. Push an element")
        print("b. Pop an element")
        sub_choice = input("Choose an operation: ")

        if sub_choice == "a":
            element = input("Enter an element to 
push: ")
            stack.append(element)
            print("Updated stack:", stack)
        elif sub_choice == "b":
            if stack:
                print("Popped element:", stack.
pop())
            else:
                print("Stack is empty.")
            print("Updated stack:", stack)

    elif choice == "3":
        print("\nQueue Operations:")
        print("a. Enqueue an element")
        print("b. Dequeue an element")
        sub_choice = input("Choose an operation: ")

        if sub_choice == "a":
            element = input("Enter an element to 
enqueue: ")
            queue.append(element)
            print("Updated queue:", list(queue))
        elif sub_choice == "b":
            if queue:
                print("Dequeued element:", queue.
popleft())
            else:
                print("Queue is empty.")
            print("Updated queue:", list(queue))

    elif choice == "4":
        print("Exiting the program. Goodbye!")
        break

    else:
        print("Invalid choice. Please try again.")

if __name__ == "__main__":
    main()
```

17: File Handling

File handling is all about, not surprisingly, managing files in your programs, and there are a few key operations you'll use often. I'll be honest here. I could fill half this book with file handling in Python, but that would be impractical. In many respects this has been the most difficult chapter to write just for this reason. So, I'm going to cover what I think are the most important aspects of the topic.

So first up, Let's break down these most common file handling tasks, and look at how we can implement them.

Opening, Reading and Writing Files

Before you can do anything with a file, you need to open it. When you open a file, you specify its name and the mode in which you want to access it, such as reading or writing. In Python, for instance, you'd use open('filename.txt', 'r') to open a file in read mode. The 'r' signifies 'read'. There are different modes like 'w' for writing (which creates a new file or overwrites an existing one) and 'a' for appending (which adds content to an existing file).

Once a file is open, you can read its contents. You might use methods like **read()** to grab the entire content at once or **readlines()** to get it line by line. In this context, a "line" is a segment of text ending at a newline character or the end of the file. Understanding this helps when reading files line-by-line and processing text efficiently in Python. In addition readlines() as well, which reads all lines of the file into a list.

Writing to files is where you can create, add or update content. To write to a file, you use methods like **write()** or **writelines().** For instance, file.write('Hello, world!') would add "Hello, world!" to the file. If the file already exists, writing to it can overwrite the existing content if you're in write mode, or append to it if you're in append mode.

Using 'w' mode not only overwrites existing files but also creates a new file if it doesn't exist. Also, it's good to point out that 'r' mode will raise a FileNotFoundError if the file doesn't exist.

The difference between read() and readlines() in Python lies in how they read the content of a file and how they return it. **read()** reads the entire content of the file as a single string and returns the file's content as one large string. **readlines()** reads the entire file but returns each line as a separate string in a list.

If you need to treat the whole file content as one block of text or need to search for patterns or substrings throughout the file, **read()** is the better option. For example, you want to search for a keyword in the entire file:

```
with open('example.txt', 'r') as file:
    content = file.read()
    if "keyword" in content:
        print("Keyword found")
```

For smaller files that can fit into memory comfortably, using read() is practical because it reads everything at once.

If you want to manipulate the entire text in bulk (e.g., replace characters or format text across multiple lines), read() provides the content as a single string, making such operations simpler.

Use readlines(): if you need to handle each line individually, such as parsing a log file or processing each record from a dataset line by line, readlines() is ideal. For instance, you need to count the number of lines or perform an action on each specific line.

```
with open('example.txt', 'r') as file:
    lines = file.readlines()
    for line in lines:
        print(line.strip())  # Process each line
```

For larger files, reading all the content into memory with read() may not be efficient. By using readlines(), you can easily loop through each line, which is more memory-friendly.

When you need the file's line structure to remain intact (i.e., process or print each line separately), readlines() provides this by splitting the file into individual lines.

So to sum up:

- Use read() when you want to load the entire file at once and work with it as a whole.

- Use readlines() when you want to process the file line by line or need the file content as a list of lines.

Closing Files

After you've finished working with a file, you need to close it. Closing a file ensures that all the changes you made are saved and that the file is properly released so other programs can use it. In Python, you'd call **file.close()** to close the file. This step is crucial for preventing data loss and freeing up system resources.

Deleting Files

In Python, you'd use **os.remove('filename.txt')** to delete a file. Be careful with this operation, as once a file is deleted, it's often not recoverable!
That's the general theory, the operations of which is probably familiar to you. The program below, demonstrates the basic file handling operations: opening, reading, writing, closing, and deleting files. This example will guide you through these tasks step-by-step.

```
#Filename: file1.py
import os

#Define the filename
filename = 'example_file.txt'

#Writing to a file
with open(filename, 'w') as file:
    file.write('Hello, world!\n')
    file.write('This is a sample file for file handling
demonstration.\n')

print(f'File "{filename}" created and written to
successfully.')

#Reading from the file
with open(filename, 'r') as file:
    content = file.read()
    print('File content:')
    print(content)

#Appending to the file
with open(filename, 'a') as file:
    file.write('Adding more text to the file.\n')

print('Content appended to file successfully.')

#Reading from the file again to check the appended
content
with open(filename, 'r') as file:
    content = file.read()
    print('Updated file content:')
    print(content)

#Deleting the file
os.remove(filename)
print(f'File "{filename}" deleted successfully.')
```

Here's what's occurring:

Writing to a File: We use with **open(filename, 'w') as file:** to open the file in write mode. The write() method adds text to the file. If the file doesn't exist, it will be created; if it does exist, it will be overwritten.

Reading from the File: Opening the file in read mode ('r') with **open(filename, 'r') as file**: allows us to read its contents using the read() method. This prints out the content of the file to the console.

Appending to the File: We open the file in append mode ('a') with **open(filename, 'a') as file:** The write() method adds text to the end of the file without altering the existing content.

Reading Again: After appending, we read the file content again to verify that the new text has been added.

Deleting the File: We use **os.remove(filename)** to delete the file. This is a permanent action, so be cautious with this operation.

These are the basic file handling operations, but there are many more.

Renaming Files

Renaming a file is straightforward using Python's **os.rename()** function. This operation changes the name of an existing file. It's useful when you need to update file names dynamically.

```
#Filename: file2.py
import os
old_name = 'old_name.txt'
new_name = 'new_name.txt'

os.rename(old_name, new_name)
print(f'File renamed from "{old_name}" to "{new_
name}".')
```

Checking File Existence

Before performing operations, it's often wise to check if a file exists using **os.path.exists().** This helps avoid errors by ensuring that the file you're trying to work with is present.

```
#Filename: file3.py
import os

file_to_check = 'example_file.txt'

if os.path.exists(file_to_check):
    print(f'The file "{file_to_check}" exists.')
else:
    print(f'The file "{file_to_check}" does not exist.')
```

Inserting Data into a File

Inserting data into a file involves modifying the content of the file by adding new data at a specific position. While Python doesn't provide a direct method to insert data into the middle of a file, you can achieve this by reading the file content, modifying it, and writing it back.

Here's an example of inserting text into the middle of a file:

```
#Filename: file4.py
def insert_into_file(filename, position, text_to_insert):
    # Read the original file content
    with open(filename, 'r') as file:
        content = file.read()

    # Insert the new text at the specified position
    new_content = content[:position] + text_to_insert +
content[position:]

    # Write the modified content back to the file
    with open(filename, 'w') as file:
        file.write(new_content)

filename = 'example_file.txt'
insert_into_file(filename, 10, 'Inserted Text ')
print(f'Text inserted into "{filename}".')
```

Bear in mind that this method rewrites the entire file. Inserting data at a specific position always involves rewriting the file since Python doesn't support direct insertion into the middle of a file without reading and rewriting the contents.

So, you may have noticed that we've missed a couple of fundamental file operation including copying and moving files. For some reason unbeknown to me, this is not as simple as it should be in Python and can be fraught with problems. Crazy, isn't it?

Shutil Module

There is a 'safer' method to copy files and this involves using the **shutil module**, which provides a convenient **copy()** function for this purpose. This is handy for creating backups or distributing files. (Yes, it seems crazily strange that there is no simple copy process with Python itself!)

Let's chat about the shutil module. Essentially shutil makes dealing with files and folders simple. We've seen a copy of options and there are methods to take on everything else. It is particularly good for doing things at directory level.

Here's a couple of demo examples. They are all relatively easy to follow, so I won't bore you with any descriptive text.

```
#Filename: file5.py
#Copy File
import shutil

source_file = 'old_name.txt'
destination_file = 'copy_of_old_name.txt'

shutil.copy(source_file, destination_file)
print(f'File copied to "{destination_file}".')

#Filename: file6.py
#Move File
import shutil
import os

source_file = 'example_file.txt'
destination_folder = 'archive/'

# Ensure the destination directory exists
os.makedirs(destination_folder, exist_ok=True)

shutil.move(source_file, destination_folder)
print(f'File moved to "{destination_folder}".')
```

Well, maybe I will.

File Tree Management

shutil simplifies managing file trees. For example, if you need to duplicate a directory structure (say for testing or backups), **shutil.copytree()** is your go-to. It copies an entire directory tree, preserving all the files and sub-directories. It even allows you to apply filters to include or exclude certain files, giving you fine control over what gets copied.

```
#Filename: file7.py
#Copy Tree Directory
#Define the source and destination directories
import shutil
source_dir = 'source_folder'
destination_dir = 'backup_folder'

# Copy the directory tree
shutil.copytree(source_dir, destination_dir)
print(f'Directory {source_dir} has been copied to
{destination_dir}')
```

Replace 'source folder' with the name of the actual source folder (including any path). The named 'backup folder' will be created.

Archiving and Compression

One of the coolest features of shutil is its ability to handle compression and archiving. If you've ever needed to bundle multiple files or directories into a single archive file, shutil has you covered with **shutil.make_archive()**. This function can create zip, tar, and other archive formats with just a few parameters. For instance, if you're working on a project and want to zip up all your work for a quick backup, you'd use this function to create a compressed file, making it easy to transport or store.

And if you need to extract files from an archive, shutil makes it easy too. The **shutil.unpack_archive()** function is perfect for extracting files from zip or tar archives. It's as simple as specifying the archive file and the directory where you want the contents to go. It's a real time-saver when dealing with compressed files.

Shutil offers a **zip method** that will compress your files, and equally an unzip to decompress your files, using **shutil.make_archive()** and **shutil.unpack_archive()** respectively.

Just specify the format (like zip or tar), the directory to be archived, and voilà—your files are neatly packed into a compressed archive. This is great for bundling up multiple files or directories into one neat package, perfect for sharing or storage.

```
#Filename: file8.py
import shutil
import os

def zip_directory(directory_path, zip_name):

    try:
        shutil.make_archive(zip_name, 'zip', directory_
path)
        print(f'Directory "{directory_path}" has been
zipped into "{zip_name}.zip"')
    except Exception as e:
        print(f'Error zipping directory: {e}')

def unzip_archive(zip_path, extract_to):

    try:
        shutil.unpack_archive(zip_path, extract_to)
        print(f'Archive "{zip_path}" has been extracted
to "{extract_to}"')
    except Exception as e:
        print(f'Error extracting archive: {e}')

# Example usage
if __name__ == "__main__":
    # Define paths
    directory_to_zip = 'my_directory'
    zip_file_name = 'my_archive'
    zip_file_path = zip_file_name + '.zip'
    extract_directory = 'extracted_files'

    # Ensure the directory to unzip to exists
    os.makedirs(extract_directory, exist_ok=True)

    # Zip the directory
```

```
    zip_directory(directory_to_zip, zip_file_name)
    # Unzip the archive
    unzip_archive(zip_file_path, extract_directory)
```

Make sure you replace my_directory with the path of the directory you want to zip, and adjust the paths as needed for your setup. This script handles basic errors and prints informative messages, making it easier to track the success or failure of the operations.

Unfortunately the module does not support a password or encryption or password protection. If you want to add a password to a zip file, you can use the **zipfile** module along with third-party libraries like **pyminizip** (the easiest method)or **zipfile** with additional tweaks.

Deleting and Copying a Directory Tree

Use this code to delete a directory and all its contents.

```
#Filename: file9.py
import shutil

# Define the directory to delete
dir_to_delete = 'old_files'

# Delete the directory tree
shutil.rmtree(dir_to_delete)
print(f'Directory {dir_to_delete} and all its contents
have been deleted')
```

Use this code to copy a directory and all its contents.

```
#Filename: file10.py
#Copying a Directory Tree
import shutil

#Define the source and destination directories
source_dir = 'source_folder'
destination_dir = 'backup_folder'

#Copy the directory tree
shutil.copytree(source_dir, destination_dir)
print(f'Directory {source_dir} has been copied to
{destination_dir}')
```

Context Managers

These are a really clever feature that helps you manage resources efficiently and cleanly. They're often used for tasks like opening files, managing database connections, or acquiring locks—essentially, any situation where you need to set up some context and then ensure its properly cleaned up afterwards.

With files you'd need to remember to manually open a file and then close it, which is easy to forget, especially if your code encounters an error. Context managers handle this for you automatically. When you use the **with** statement to open a file, Python ensures that the file is closed once the block of code inside the with statement is done, even if an exception occurs.

Here's a basic example:

```
with open('example.txt', 'r') as file:
    content = file.read()
    print(content)
```

In this snippet, **open('example.txt', 'r')** is a context manager that handles opening and closing the file. You don't need to explicitly call **file.close()**—the context manager does it for you when the block under with is finished.

Context managers aren't just for files, though. They can be used with any resource that needs to be correctly managed.

Error Handling

When working with files, several things can go wrong: the file might not exist, it might be inaccessible due to permissions, or you could encounter unexpected issues during reading or writing. Correct error handling helps ensure your program can respond to these situations without crashing unexpectedly.

Common File Errors

- **FileNotFoundError**: This error occurs if you try to open a file that doesn't exist. It's one of the most common errors and usually means you've got a typo in the filename or the file isn't where you think it is.
- **PermissionError**: If your program doesn't have the right permissions to access a file, you'll get this error. It might happen if you're trying to write to a file in a directory where you don't have write permissions.
- **IOError**: This is a broader error that encompasses issues with file input/output operations, like trying to read from a file that's not open or writing to a full disk.

Handling File Errors with Try-Except

You can use Python's **try-except** blocks to catch and handle these errors. Here's an example:

```
#Filename: file11.py
try:
    with open('example.txt', 'r') as file:
        content = file.read()
        print(content)
except FileNotFoundError:
    print("Oops! The file doesn't exist.")
except PermissionError:
    print("You don't have permission to access this
file.")
except IOError as e:
    print(f"An unexpected I/O error occurred: {e}")
```

Using else and finally

You can also use else and finally clauses with try-except for additional control:

- **else**: Runs if no exceptions were raised in the try block. It's useful for code that should only execute if the file operations were successful.
- **finally**: Always runs, regardless of whether an exception was raised. This is useful for cleanup actions like closing files or releasing resources.

Here's an example:

```
#Filename: file12.py
    with open('example.txt', 'r') as file:
        content = file.read()
except FileNotFoundError:
    print("File not found.")
except PermissionError:
    print("Permission denied.")
else:
    print("File read successfully:")
    print(content)
finally:
    print("Operation completed.")
```

In this example, print("Operation completed.") will always execute, making it ideal for final cleanup tasks or ensuring certain code always runs.

File Permissions

All files come with file permission **codes** which determine what and who they are and what you can and can't do with them.

When you create or modify a file, the operating system saves not just the file, but items of information about the file. This is called 'metadata' which includes information such as the filename, the date and time the file was created or changed, and several settings—known as flags and modes – that determine what can and cannot be done with the file and who, or who not, may access it.

As with file handling this is a big topic so I'm only going to provide detail on this a little bit. Frankly most of it can be skirted around anyway. Because it is programming language independent you may well know about it already.

The following program will list the files in the current directory and display their current attributes. Open in Thonny and open the window right up so that you can read the file info with ease.

```
#Filename: file13.py
#Read and display file information
import os
import stat
from datetime import datetime

def format_permissions(mode):
    permissions = {
        '0': '---', '1': '--x', '2': '-w-', '3': '-wx',
        '4': 'r--', '5': 'r-x', '6': 'rw-', '7': 'rwx'
    }
    return ''.join([permissions[x] for x in
str(oct(mode))[-3:]])

def list_current_directory():
    current_path = os.getcwd()
    try:
        files = os.listdir(current_path)
    except OSError as e:
        print(f"Error: {e}")
        return

    print(f"{'File': <30}{'Permissions': <10}{'Size':
<10}{'Last Modified': <20}")
    print('-' * 70)

    for file in files:
        file_path = os.path.join(current_path, file)
        file_stat = os.stat(file_path)

        permissions = format_permissions(file_stat.st_
mode)
        size = file_stat.st_size
        last_modified = datetime.fromtimestamp(file_stat.
st_mtime).strftime('%Y-%m-%d %H:%M:%S')

        print(f"{file: <30}{permissions: <10}{size: <10}
{last_modified: <20}")

if name __main__==″__main__″
    list_current_directory()
```

The file listing below shows what this looked on my Raspberry Pi–the output from a directory containing the files needed and/or created by executing the above program on my Pi.

The listing will display anything in the current directory, including directories and files.

```
File           Permission      Size  Last Modified
-------------------------------------------------------------
Ascent-Data    drwxr-xr-x      4096  2024-08-08 10:40:55
Deq1.py        -rw-r--r--      795   2024-06-13    09:48:34
Dict1.py       -rw-r--r--      256   2024-06-07    05:51:15
Dict10.py      -rw-r--r--      267   2024-06-07    06:07:43
Dict11.py      -rw-r--r--      288   2024-06-07    06:09:28
Dict12.py      -rw-r--r--      448   2024-06-07    06:19:59
Dict13.py      -rw-r--r--      290   2024-06-07    06:22:07
Dict14.py      -rw-r--r--      438   2024-06-07    06:23:39
Dict15.py      -rw-r--r--      1041  2024-06-07    18:22:05
```

Figure 17a. File Permissions.

The first column is the one with the file names. Here I have sorted these so that the filenames are in alphabetical order with directories shown first. This is then followed by a column listing the file permissions (also referred to as attributes) and size for each file. The final column is the date and time of creation.

You can change file permissions using **os.chmod().** This allows you to set who can read, write, or execute the file, which is essential for security and access control.

```
#Filename: file14.py
import os
import stat

file_to_change = 'example.txt'

#Change file permissions to read/write for owner only
os.chmod(file_to_change, stat.S_IRUSR | stat.S_IWUSR)
print(f'Permissions for "{file_to_change}" changed.')
```

This program uses the stat module translates the results of **os.stat()** (and related functions) into human-readable values. This allows you to interpret the file metadata returned by os.stat() in a meaningful way.

Stat Module

The **stat module** is a part of the standard library and provides tools to interact with and extract information about the file system, specifically file metadata. This module is particularly useful when you need to work with file properties like file permissions or time-stamps and want to process or manipulate them.

Common Use Cases for stat

- Checking file types: Determine whether a file is a regular file, directory, or symbolic link.
- Reading and interpreting file permissions: Display or check file permissions from a program.
- File metadata: Access file size, last modification time, and other important attributes.
- Changing file permissions: Use the constants from the stat module with **os.chmod()** to set specific permissions.
- Cross-platform file handling: Since file permissions and modes are a fundamental part of file systems, the stat module allows for platform-independent code when handling file permissions. The most common use for the stat module is with the **os.stat()** function, which retrieves metadata about a file or directory. The result is an object that contains various attributes, such as file size, creation time, and permissions. The stat module helps in interpreting this data.

```
#Filename: file15.py
import os
import stat

file_info = os.stat('example.txt')

print(f"File size: {file_info.st_size} bytes")
print(f"Last modified: {file_info.st_mtime}")
print(f"File mode (permissions): {file_info.st_mode}")
```

One of the most valuable features of the stat module is working with file permissions, represented in the **st_mode** attribute. This attribute contains both the file type and the permissions (read, write, and execute).

The object returned by **os.stat()** (or **os.lstat()** for symbolic links) has the following useful attributes:

st_mod	File mode (permissions) and type of file.
st_ino	Inode number (an identifier for the file in the file system).
st_dev	Device number (the device that contains the file).
st_nlink	Number of hard links to the file.
st_uid	User ID of the file owner.
st_gid	Group ID of the file owner.

st_size Size of the file, in bytes.

st_atime Last access time (in seconds since the epoch).

st_mtime Last modification time.

st_ctime Last metadata change time

The stat module provides several constants to make interpreting the permissions easier. These constants include:

stat.S_IFDIR	Directory.
stat.S_IFREG	Regular file.
stat.S_IFLNK	Symbolic link.
stat.S_IRUSR	Read permission for the file owner.
stat.S_IWUSR	Write permission for the file owner.
stat.S_IXUSR	Execute permission for the file owner.
stat.S_IRGRP	Read permission for the group.
stat.S_IROTH	Read permission for others.

To check or modify file permissions, you can use these constants in combination with bitwise operations.

```
#Filename: file16.py
import os
import stat

file_info = os.stat('example.txt')

# Check if the file is a directory
if stat.S_ISDIR(file_info.st_mode):
    print("This is a directory.")
else:
    print("This is not a directory.")

# Check if the file is readable by the owner
if file_info.st_mode & stat.S_IRUSR:
    print("The file is readable by the owner.")
```

Working with File Modes and Permissions

The stat module also offers functions like **stat.filemode()**, which converts the file mode into a human-readable string format, showing permissions.

```
#Filename: file17.py
import os
import stat

file_info = os.stat('example.txt')
```

```
# Get the file permissions in a human-readable format
permissions = stat.filemode(file_info.st_mode)
print(f"File permissions: {permissions}")
```

If the file permissions for example.txt were 755, the output would be:

```
File permissions: -rwxr-xr-x
```

This makes it easier to display or log permissions.

Changing File Permissions

You can also use the **os.chmod()** function in conjunction with constants from the stat module to modify file permissions.

```
#Filename: file18.py
import os
import stat

file_to_change = 'example.txt'

# Change file permissions. Read/write for the owner
os.chmod(file_to_change, stat.S_IRUSR | stat.S_IWUSR)
print(f'Permissions for "{file_to_change}" changed.')
```

In this example, the file example.txt is granted read and write permissions for the owner, but no other permissions.

Processing a File

The programs lines below show a complete list of file operations:

```
#Filename: File19.py
file = open('filename.txt', 'mode')
#Modes: 'r', 'w', 'a', 'r+'

content = file.read()
#Reads entire content of the file

lines = file.readlines()
#Reads the file into a list of lines

file.write('This is some text.\n')
file.write('This is the text to append.\n')
file.close()
```

Once you have read the contents of the file, you can do whatever you need and, if required, write it back to the same file or a different file as you wish.

If the data in the file is structured (we'll look at examples of this in the next chapter) you have the option to employ parsing techniques or libraries for extracting meaningful information before passing it to a function.

Handling Large Files

If you are dealing with extensive files that may not fit entirely into memory, I'd recommended reading the file line by line or process it in chunks to avoid memory issues. Equally as the example below shows, read the file in blocks of data.

```
#Filename: file20.py
def process_data(data):
    # Process the data as needed
    print("Data:", data)

with open("large_file.txt", "r") as file:
    for line in file:
        process_data(line)

# Alternatively, process the file in chunks
with open("large_file.txt", "r") as file:
    chunk_size = 1024  #Set the desired chunk size
    while True:
        chunk = file.read(chunk_size)
        if not chunk:
            break
        process_data(chunk)
```

Passing File Objects

Instead of passing the file contents as a string, you can pass the file object itself to the function. This allows the function to read and process the file directly.

```
#Filename: File21.py
def process_file(file):
#Read and process the file directly
    for line in file:
        print("Line:", line.strip())

with open("example.txt", "r") as file:
    process_file(file)
```

By passing the file object, you can process the file incrementally with no need to load the entire contents into memory at once.

These methods offer flexibility when retrieving data from a file and passing it into a function. Select the approach that aligns with your specific use case, considering factors such as file size, data structure, and memory considerations.

Tempfile Module

The **tempfile module** is a handy utility for creating temporary files and/or directories. Given the modules name this makes sense!

These temporary files and directories are useful when you need to store data that doesn't need to remain after your program ends, such as when testing, processing temporary data, or when working with files that you only need to keep for a short duration.

Temporary Files

tempfile.NamedTemporaryFile(): This function creates a temporary file that has a name and can be opened multiple times during the program execution. Once you close this file, it is automatically deleted. This is particularly useful if you need to access the temporary file by name in different parts of your code.

```
#Filename: file22.py
import tempfile

with tempfile.NamedTemporaryFile() as temp_file:
    print(f"Temporary file name: {temp_file.name}")
    temp_file.write(b'Temporary data here!')
    temp_file.seek(0)
    print(temp_file.read())
#File deleted automatically after 'with' block ends
```

tempfile.TemporaryFile(): This function creates a temporary file that doesn't have a name associated with it on the file system, meaning it can only be accessed through the file object returned. The file is deleted as soon as it is closed, which can be convenient for keeping your file system clean.

```
#Filename: file23.py
Import tempfile

with tempfile.TemporaryFile() as temp_file:

   #Write binary ('b') temp data
   temp_file.write(b'Some temporary data')

   #Move file pointer to start
   temp_file.seek(0)
   print(temp_file.read())
```

The file will be deleted when the file object is closed or the program ends.

Temporary Directories

tempfile.TemporaryDirectory(): This function creates a temporary directory that can be used to store temporary files. The directory and all its contents are deleted when the context is exited.

```
#Filename: file24.py
import tempfile

with tempfile.TemporaryDirectory() as temp_dir:
   temp_file.write(b;Some temporary data'
   temp.file.seek(0)

   #Decode to string)
```

```
        print(temp_file.read().decode('utf-8'))
```

You can create files inside this directory as needed. The directory and its contents will be deleted after the '**with**' block ends.

Customising Temporary Files and Directories

You can customise the name, location, and other attributes of the temporary files and directories by passing arguments like prefix, suffix, and dir to the functions.

```
#Filename: file25.py
import tempfile
with tempfile.TemporaryFile()as temp_dir:
    print(f"Temporary Directory: {temp_file.name}")
```

Automatic Cleanup

The tempfile module automatically manages the cleanup of temporary files and directories, reducing the risk of leaving clutter on the file system. This is especially useful when running scripts that create a lot of temporary data.

Questions

1. What are the main modes you can use when opening files in Python, and what does each mode allow you to do?
2. Describe the difference between read(), readline(), and readlines() methods in Python file handling. When would you use each?
3. What is the purpose of using **with open(...)** in Python, and why is it generally preferred over open(...) and close()?
4. Explain the os.remove() function. What precautions should you take when using it?
5. Describe how to insert data into a specific position within a file's content using Python. What challenges are involved in this operation?
6. What is the shutil module used for in Python, and which file operations does it make easier? Provide an example operation.
7. Explain how to compress and extract files using the shutil module in Python. Which functions are used for this?
8. What are file permissions, and why are they important when managing files in Python? How can you change file permissions programmatically?
9. How can you retrieve detailed metadata about a file using the os.stat() function, and what attributes does it provide?

18: CSV and JSON

The csv module is a useful tool for reading, writing, and manipulating data in CSV files. Although CSV stands for "comma-separated values," these files can use other delimiters like semicolons or tabs. By default, the delimiter is a comma, but you can customise this by using the delimiter parameter. You'll often see csv files used for storing structured data in plain text, when you export a spreadsheet or a list into a file, for example.

If you're working on a Raspberry Pi and using **LibreOffice**, you'll find **LibreCalc** to be a great tool for handling csv files. It lets you easily read and write these files, and it also supports other formats like .xls, .xlsx, and .ods, giving you plenty of flexibility.

The csv module offers high-level functions and classes that make parsing and formatting data straightforward. Some of the key tools in this module include **csv.reader** and **csv.writer**, which are great for reading from and writing to csv files. For example:

```
Python,Beginner,Raspberry Pi,Coding,Confidence
```

The module also has **csv.DictReader** and **csv.DictWriter**, which allow you to work with csv data as dictionaries, with each row being treated as a dictionary with column headers as keys. This can be especially useful when you're dealing with data that has named columns. Plus, you can customise how the module handles things like quotes and newlines to better suit your data's needs.

Let's dive into some examples to see how this works in practice. For a couple of these examples, we'll use a csv file called **solarsystem.csv**. You can download this file with the other program file for this book. You can open this in any text editor.

The file of data, as it appears in LibreCalc looks as follows:

Name	Type	Average Distance from Sun (AU)	Diameter (km)	Moons
Mercury	Planet	0.39	4879	0
Venus	Planet	0.72	12104	0
Earth	Planet	1	12742	1
Mars	Planet	1.52	6779	2
Jupiter	Planet	5.2	139820	95
Saturn	Planet	9.58	116460	146
Uranus	Planet	19.2	50724	28
Neptune	Planet	30.05	49244	16
Pluto	Dwarf Planet	39.48	2376	5
Eris	Dwarf Planet	67.67	2326	1
Ceres	Dwarf Planet	2.77	946	0
Haumea	Dwarf Planet	43.22	1595	2
Makemake	Dwarf Planet	45.79	1430	1

Figure 18a. solarsystem.csv file.

Example 1: Reading a CSV File with csv.reader

```
#Filename: csv1.py
import csv

def read_csv_file(file_path, encoding='utf-8'):
    try:
        with open(file_path, 'r', newline='',
encoding=encoding) as csvfile:
            csv_reader = csv.reader(csvfile,
delimiter=',', quotechar='"')

            header = next(csv_reader)
            print("CSV Header:", header)

            for row in csv_reader:
                print("Row:", row)

    except FileNotFoundError:
        print(f"Error: File '{file_path}' not found.")
    except Exception as e:
        print(f"An error occurred: {e}")

csv_file_path = 'solarsystem.csv'
read_csv_file(csv_file_path)
```

Running this script will display the contents of solar system.csv in the Terminal window as lists of strings:

```
CSV Header: ['Name', 'Type', 'Average Distance from Sun
(AU)', 'Diameter (km)', 'Moons']
Row: ['Mercury', 'Planet', '0.39', '4879', '0']
Row: ['Venus', 'Planet', '0.72', '12104', '0']
Row: ['Earth', 'Planet', '1', '12742', '1']...
```

Reading a CSV File with csv.DictReader

```
#Filename: csv2.py
import csv

def read_csv_file(file_path, encoding='utf-8'):
    try:
        with open(file_path, 'r', newline='',
encoding=encoding) as csvfile:
            csv_dict_reader = csv.DictReader(csvfile)

            header = csv_dict_reader.fieldnames
            print("CSV Header:", header)

            for row in csv_dict_reader:
                print("Row:", row)

    except FileNotFoundError:
        print(f"Error: File '{file_path}' not found.")
    except Exception as e:
        print(f"An error occurred: {e}")

csv_file_path = 'solarsystem.csv'
read_csv_file(csv_file_path)
```

The first few lines of output here is:

```
CSV Header: ['Name', 'Type', 'Average Distance from Sun
(AU)', 'Diameter (km)', 'Moons']
Row: {'Name': 'Mercury', 'Type': 'Planet', 'Average
Distance from Sun (AU)': '0.39', 'Diameter (km)':
'4879', 'Moons': '0'}
Row: {'Name': 'Venus', 'Type': 'Planet', 'Average
Distance from Sun (AU)': '0.72', 'Diameter (km)':
'12104', 'Moons': '0'}
Row: {'Name': 'Earth', 'Type': 'Planet', 'Average
Distance from Sun (AU)': '1', 'Diameter (km)': '12742',
'Moons': '1'}
...
```

Key Differences Between the Two Programs:

csv1.py Output (Using csv.reader): This program outputs lists where: Each row from the CSV is read as a list of strings. Column headers are printed separately as a list. Example row output:

```
Row: ['Mercury', 'Planet', '0.39', '4879', '0']
```

csv2.py Output (Using csv.DictReader) This program outputs dictionaries where: Each row becomes a dictionary with keys being column headers and values being the row data. Column headers are shown as a list initially, but the rows are dictionaries. Example row output:

```
Row: {'Name': 'Mercury', 'Type': 'Planet', 'Average
Distance from Sun (AU)': '0.39', 'Diameter (km)':.
'4879', 'Moons': '0'}
```

Data Handling

csv1.py - Data Handling with csv.reader: Rows are Lists: With csv.reader, each row is a list of values. You access data by position/index. This works well for simple datasets where the column order is fixed and known. A **pitfall** of this method is if the column order changes or the dataset grows with more columns, you'll need to update your code accordingly (e.g., by changing the indexes).

csv1.py - Data Handling with csv.DictReader: Rows are Dictionaries: With csv.DictReader, each row becomes a dictionary where keys are the column names, and values are the corresponding row entries. This is more robust if the CSV file structure changes (e.g., if columns are reordered or new ones are added). The advantage here is that you don't need to remember the column index! As long as the column names are consistent, the code works even if the order changes.

Handling Data Integrity Issues

csv.reader: If a row is missing values or has extra columns, you might encounter index out-of-range errors. You need to be very careful with how you index into each row.

csv.DictReader: If a column is missing from a row, the key will exist with a value of None. This makes it more forgiving when working with incomplete or messy data.

With the csv module, you can easily switch between these methods depending on your needs. Whether you're dealing with simple lists or more complex data structures, the csv module has you covered!

Let's break down the structure of the data shown in Figure 18a (earlier). Each row in the csv file corresponds to a planet or celestial body, and each entry in the row is a piece of information about that body. The header row describes what each piece of information represents.

Which One to Use Based on Data Handling Needs?

Use **csv.reader** when:

- The CSV structure is fixed and you know the exact position of each value (e.g., for small, simple datasets).

- Performance is critical (since lists are slightly faster to process than dictionaries).
- You don't need to dynamically access column names.

Use **csv.DictReader** when:

- You need to work with dynamic or messy data (e.g., column order can vary or some columns may be missing).
- The dataset has many columns, and accessing by name makes the code more readable.
- You want to avoid bugs related to hard-coded indexes.

Dictionary of Lists:

You can use a dictionary of lists to store CSV data, especially when you want to organise the data by columns. This structure is useful if you need to access all the data related to a specific category (like all planet names or all diameters). Here's an example:

```
#Filename: csv3.py
planet_data = {
    "Name": ["Mercury", "Venus", "Earth", "Mars",
"Jupiter"],
    "Type": ["Planet", "Planet", "Planet", "Planet",
"Planet"],
    "Average Distance from Sun (AU)": ["0.39", "0.72",
"1", "1.52", "5.20"],
    "Diameter (km)": ["4879", "12104", "12742", "6779",
"139820"],
    "Moons": ["0", "0", "1", "2", "79"]
}
```

This structure allows you to easily access all the data for a specific column. For example, to print all planet names:

```
print(planet_data["Name"])
# Output: ['Mercury', 'Venus', 'Earth', 'Mars',
'Jupiter']
```

The following program extracts planet names and their distances from the Sun from a CSV file, but it uses a simple dictionary of name-distance pairs, not a dictionary of lists.

```
# Filename: csv4.py
import csv

def extract_planet_distances(file_path, encoding='utf-
8'):
    planet_distances = {}

    try:
```

```
        with open(file_path, 'r', newline='',
encoding=encoding) as csvfile:
            csv_reader = csv.reader(csvfile,
delimiter=',', quotechar='"')

            # Skip the header
            header = next(csv_reader)

            # Extract planet names and distances from
the CSV
            for row in csv_reader:
                planet = row[0]  # Name is in the first
column
                distance = row[2]  # Distance from the
Sun (AU) is in the third column
                planet_distances[planet] = distance

        return planet_distances

    except FileNotFoundError:
        print(f"Error: File '{file_path}' not found.")
    except Exception as e:
        print(f"An error occurred: {e}")

# Specify the CSV file path
csv_file_path = 'solarsystem.csv'

# Call the function to extract data
planet_distances = extract_planet_distances(csv_file_
path)

# Print the extracted planet distances
for planet, distance in planet_distance:
        print(f"{planet}: {distance} AU")
```

Explanation:

This program reads the CSV file and extracts planet names and their distances from the Sun (in AU). Although the original CSV contains more data (like diameter and moons), the program only extracts the first and third columns.

The extracted data is stored in a simple dictionary where:

Key: Planet name

Value: Distance from the Sun (AU)

If you run this program with the provided csv data, you'll see something like:

```
Mercury: 0.39 AU
Venus: 0.72 AU
Earth: 1.00 AU
Mars: 1.52 AU
Jupiter: 5.20 AU
Saturn: 9.58 AU
Uranus: 19.22 AU
Neptune: 30.05 AU
Pluto: 39.48 AU
```

```
Ceres: 2.77 AU
Haumea: 43.13 AU
Makemake: 45.79 AU
```

What is JSON?

JSON (JavaScript Object Notation) is a simple but effective data interchange format that is easy to read and write and easy for Python to handle. It is text-based and serves as a **common data format** between applications and systems. In fact, it used almost everywhere that requires data to be moved from a to b across the internet. It also provides an easy 'standardised' way to exchange data between different programming languages. Commonly supported and used in web APIs (see Chapter 39), configuration files, and data storage.

JSON represents data as key-value pairs, like dictionaries or objects in programming languages and is primarily used to transmit data between a server and a web application. JSON data consists of nested structures made up of objects (enclosed in curly braces {}), arrays (enclosed in square brackets []), strings, numbers, Boolean, and null values. Objects contain unordered key-value pairs, where keys are strings, and values can be any valid JSON data type. Here the JSON object has three key-value pairs: "name" with the value "Bob", "age" with the value 30, and "city" with the value " Timbuktu ".

```
{
  "name":"Bob",
  "age": 30,
  "city": " Timbuktu "
}
```

In Python, the **json module** is available to encode (**serialise**) Python objects into JSON format and decode (**deserialise**) JSON data into Python objects. The json module provides functions such as **json.dumps()** to convert Python objects to JSON strings and **json.loads()** to parse JSON strings into Python objects.

JSON and Python work together in a number of ways:

Encoding (Serialisation) Python to JSON:

You can convert Python objects, such as dictionaries, lists, strings, numbers, booleans, and None, into JSON format using the json.dumps() function. This function serialises the Python object into a JSON string representation.

```
# Filename: json1.py
# Encode a Python dictionary into JSON
import json
data = {
    "name": "Bob",
    "age": 30,
    "city": " Timbuktu"
```

```
}
json_data = json.dumps(data)
print(json_data)  # {"name": "Bob", "age": 30, "city":
" Timbuktu"}
```

Decoding (Deserialisation): JSON to Python

You can parse a JSON string into Python objects using the json.loads() function. This function deserializes the JSON string into the corresponding Python data types.

```
# Filename: json2.py
# Decode JSON into a Python dictionary import json

json_data = '{"name": "Bob", "age": 30, "city": "
Timbuktu "}'
data = json.loads(json_data)
print(data)  # {'name': 'Bob', 'age': 30, 'city': '
Timbuktu '}
```

Reading and Writing JSON Files:

Python can read and write JSON data from and to files using the **json.dump()** and **json.load()** functions. These functions work with file-like objects, such as file handles.

```
# Filename: json3.py
# Write Python data to a JSON file

import json
# Write Python data to a JSON file
data = {
    "name": "Bob",
    "age": 30,
    "city": " Timbuktu "
}
with open("data.json", "w") as file:
    json.dump(data, file)

# Read JSON data from a file into Python objects
with open("data.json", "r") as file:
    data = json.load(file)
print(data)  # {'name': 'Bob', 'age': 30, 'city': '
Timbuktu '}
```

So, any system that supports JSON can transfer, exchange and swap data. Easy Peasy. This is especially useful when dealing with APIs, which we discuss in a later chapter, to extract information from a website or data server.

Configuration Files

In addition to data interchange and Web APIs, JSON is also great for configuration files, data storage and data transformation:

- **Configuration Files:** Due to its simplicity and human-readability, JSON is often used for configuration files. Python can read and parse JSON configuration files, allowing you to retrieve settings and parameters for your Python applications or scripts easily. You can modify or update the configuration by manipulating the parsed JSON data in Python.
- **Data Storage:** JSON's lightweight and flexible format for storing structured data. Python can write Python objects to JSON files or databases for persistent storage. Later, you can read and load the JSON data back into Python, enabling you to save and retrieve data for future use.
- **Data Transformation:** JSON can serve as an intermediate format for data transformation or integration. Python's JSON capabilities allow you to convert data between different formats and systems. For example, you can convert CSV data to JSON or transform JSON data into a different structure to meet specific requirements.

Here's a simple Python program that reads a CSV file and converts it into JSON format using the csv and json libraries. This uses the solarsystem file from earlier, converted to csv (with program downloads):

```
#Filename:  json4.py
Program: CSV to JSON Converter
import csv
import json

def csv_to_json(csv_file, json_file):
   data = []

#Open the CSV file for reading
with open(csv_file, 'r') as file:

   # Create a CSV reader object
   csv_reader = csv.DictReader(file)

   # Iterate over each row and add to data list
   for row in csv_reader:
      data.append(row)

# Open the JSON file for writing
with open(json_file, 'w') as file:

   # Convert list to JSON and write it to the file
   print(f"CSV data converted to {json_file}")

# Specify your CSV file and the JSON output file
csv_file = 'solarsystem.csv'
```

```
json_file = 'solarsystem_output.json'

# Call the function to convert CSV to JSON
csv_to_json(csv_file, json_file)
```

The program reads data from a CSV file using Python's **csv.DictReader()**. This method reads each row as a dictionary, with the keys being the column headers. It converts the list of dictionaries into JSON format using the **json.dump()** function and saves the output to a specified file.

The indent=4 argument in **json.dump()** makes the JSON output easier to read by formatting it with a 4-space indentation.

Example CSV (input.csv):

```
name,age,city
Bob,30,Timbuktu
Alice,25,London
Rob,35,Paris
```

Example JSON Output (output.json):

```
[
    {
        "name": "Bob",
        "age": "30",
        "city": "New York"
    },
    {
        "name": "Alice",
        "age": "25",
        "city": "London"
    },
    {
        "name": "Rob",
        "age": "35",
        "city": "Paris"
    }
]
```

Create a CSV file (input.csv) with the data you want to convert and then run the program. The JSON output will be saved in the file specified (in this case, **output.json**).

The program demonstrates a simple way to convert CSV data into JSON, which can be very useful when working with APIs or transferring data between different systems.

JSON config File

A JSON configuration file is used to store settings for applications or systems in JSON format. These settings can be easily loaded, modified, and read and typically contains settings in a structured format, where each setting is represented as a key, and the value can be a string, number, Boolean, array, or nested object. Applications load these settings at run-time and use them to configure various parameters, such as database connections, API keys, logging preferences, and more.

Instead of hard-coding values into the source code, you can modify the config file to adjust settings without altering the main code.

Loading the Config File: Most programming languages have built-in libraries to read JSON files and convert them into dictionaries, objects, or other data structures for use within the application.

```
{
    "app_name": "MyApp",
    "version": "1.0.0",
    "debug_mode": true,
    "database": {
        "host": "localhost",
        "port": 3306,
        "username": "root",
        "password": "password123",
        "db_name": "myapp_db"
    },
    "api_keys": {
        "google_maps": "AIzaSy...12345",
        "weather_api": "f84b3d...56789"
    },
    "logging": {
        "log_level": "INFO",
        "log_to_file": true,
        "log_file_path": "/var/log/myapp.log"
    }
}
```

How to Use a JSON Config File in Python

Here's an example of how you can load and use the settings from a JSON config file in a Python application. (Note this program will not work without the relevant API keys. See Chapter 39 for API applications.)

```
#Filename: json5.py
import json

# Load the config file with error handling
def load_config(config_file):
    try:
        with open(config_file, 'r') as file:
            config = json.load(file)  # Parse JSON into a
Python dictionary
        return config
    except FileNotFoundError:
        print(f"Error: Config file '{config_file}' not
```

```
found.")
            return None
        except json.JSONDecodeError as e:
            print(f"Error: Failed to parse JSON - {e}")
            return None

    # Example usage of the config
    def main():
        config = load_config('config.json')  # Load the JSON
    config file

        if config is None:
            print("Application cannot start without a valid
    config.")
            return  # Exit if config is not loaded

        # Access settings safely with default values
        app_name = config.get("app_name", "UnnamedApp")
 debug_mode = config.get("debug_mode", False)

 db_host = config.get("database", {}).get("host", "localhost")

    api_key = config.get("api_keys", {}).get("google_maps",
"N/A")


    # Use the configuration settings in your application

    print(f"Starting {app_name} in {'debug' if debug_mode
else 'production'} mode...")

    print(f"Connecting to database at {db_host}...")

    print(f"Google Maps API Key: {api_key}")


if __name__ == "__main__":

    main()
```

The **load_config()** function opens the JSON file and parses it into a Python dictionary using the json.load() function. You can then access individual settings from the config dictionary by referencing the appropriate keys. Based on the settings in the config file, the application behaves differently (e.g., runs in debug mode or connects to a specific database).

csv and JSON for Experiments

One of the great uses of csv and JSON is log data coming into the Raspberry Pi. For example, consider you're using a **Raspberry Pi** to read data from a **temperature sensor** (e.g., a DHT22 sensor). You'll log the sensor data into a CSV file for analysis, and you'll manage configuration settings (like sensor thresholds or logging intervals) using a JSON file.

This is how a JSON config file might look in this instance:

```
#Filename: json6.py
{
    "app_name": "TemperatureLogger",
    "debug_mode": true,
    "logging_interval_seconds": 60,
    "sensor_thresholds": {
        "temperature": {
            "min": 15,
            "max": 30
        },
        "humidity": {
            "min": 30,
            "max": 60
        }
    },
    "database": {
        "host": "localhost",
        "port": 5432
    }
}
```

This particular JSON file:

- Sets min/max temperature and humidity thresholds.
- Defines the logging interval (every 60 seconds).
- Stores database connection settings.

You could then log the temperature to csv should you wish.

Handling JSON Errors

When working with JSON you can expect errors not least because you are dealing with data coming from external sources like web APIs. JSON data might be malformed, incomplete, or not match the expected structure, which can cause your program to crash if not properly handled. Fortunately, Python's json module provides mechanisms to catch and handle these errors gracefully. Look back at program **json5.py** and you'll see some good examples in action.

A common error when parsing JSON is **json.JSONDecodeError,** which occurs if the JSON data is incorrectly formatted. This might happen if there are missing commas, unescaped special characters, or mismatched braces in the JSON string. To handle this, you can use a try-except block when calling json.loads() to catch the error and take appropriate action, such as logging the issue or providing a meaningful error message to the user.

For example:

```
#Filename: json7.py
import json

invalid_json = '{"name": "Alice", "age": 25, "city":
"London}'

try:
    print("Parsing JSON...")
    data = json.loads(invalid_json)
   # This raises an error
   except json.JSONDecodeError as e:
    print(f"Failed to parse JSON: {e}")
finally:
    print("This will always run, whether there's an
exception or not.")

print("Program continues after the try-except-finally
block.")
```

The **try...except...finally** block is a mechanism in Python for handling errors gracefully while ensuring that certain code always runs, regardless of whether an error occurs. Here's an explanation:

The try block contains code that might raise an exception. Python attempts to execute this code. If the code runs without any errors, the program moves to the next section after the try block. If an exception occurs in the try block, execution stops at the point of the error, and control is passed to the corresponding except block.

The except block is where you handle exceptions. You can specify the type of exception to catch (e.g., ZeroDivisionError, ValueError) or use a generic except to catch any exception. When an exception is caught:

- The code inside the except block runs.
- The program skips the rest of the try block.
- If no exception occurs in the try block, the except block is ignored.

The finally block contains code that always runs, whether an exception is raised or not. It is commonly used for cleanup actions, such as closing files, releasing resources, or logging.

- If no exception occurs, the finally block runs after the try block completes.
- If an exception occurs, the finally block runs after the except block.

Tying up and matching data can also be an issue: if your code expects a key called "name" but the JSON data is missing that key, a **KeyError** will occur when trying to access it. You can prevent this by using the **.get()** method when accessing dictionary keys, which returns **None** or a default value if the key is missing, rather than raising an error.

19: Path & Pythonpath

When you enter a command on your Raspberry Pi, the Operating System needs to know where to find the necessary programs. Think of it like needing a pint of milk—you need to know where to get it. It might be the corner shop, the chemist, or the petrol station. You probably have a mental list of these locations, and if the first shop doesn't have milk, you try the next one on the list. If none of them have milk, you go without it and let those who need it know. But if you find milk at the first stop, you don't need to visit the others.

Similarly, when you ask your Raspberry Pi to run a program, it looks in specific directories, known to the OS, where the programs are stored. These directories are part of the **PATH** environment variable (not to be confused with Python virtual environments). The PATH is a list of directory locations where the system searches for executables. When you install a program, its location usually gets added to this list.

So, when you type a command, if the program isn't in the current directory, the system searches through the directories detailed in the PATH variable. If it finds the program, it runs it; if not, you'll see a "Command Not Found" error. The order of directories in the PATH matters. If two directories have programs with the same name, the system will run the one in the directory that appears first in the PATH.

If you type:

```
$echo $PATH
```

You'll see something like this:

```
/usr/local/sbin:/usr/local/bin:/usr/sbin:/usr/bin:/
sbin:/bin:/usr/local/games:/usr/games
```

The individual paths are separated by colons. Here's a rough guide to what each means:

- **Local vs. Standard Paths**: Directories like /usr/local are for locally installed software, while /usr/ is for software provided by the OS.
- **System Binaries (sbin)**: Directories with sbin are for system admin tools and usually need root privileges.
- **User Binaries (bin)**: Directories with bin contain executables available to all users.
- **Game Directories**: Directories like /usr/local/games are for storing game executables.

The system searches these directories in the order they're listed in $PATH. If a command exists in multiple directories, the one in the first directory listed will be executed.

Modifying and Adding to the PATH

You can modify the PATH variable to include additional directories where executable files are located. This can be done as a temporary measure within a terminal session or permanently by modifying Raspberry Pi system configuration files.

To add a directory to the PATH variable temporarily for the current terminal session, at the CLI use:

```
export PATH=$PATH:/path/to/directory
```

Replace */path/to/directory* with the directory you want to add. This change lasts **only** for the session; once you close the terminal or log out, the PATH reverts to its default value.

Virtual Environments and $PATH

When working with Python, virtual environments affect the PATH by modifying it so that the Python interpreter and libraries within the virtual environment are isolated from the global Python installation.

How It Works:

- **Creating a Virtual Environment**: When you create a virtual environment (e.g., with venv), it creates a directory that contains a fresh Python interpreter, its own site-packages, and scripts for activating the environment.

- **Activating the Virtual Environment**: When you activate a virtual environment, the PATH variable is modified to prioritise the virtual environment's directories. The directory containing the virtual environment's Python interpreter is added to the beginning of the PATH.

For example, if your virtual environment is at /home/username/myenv, activating it might change your PATH to:

```
/home/username/myenv/bin:/usr/local/sbin:/usr/local/
bin:/usr/sbin:/usr/bin:/sbin:/bin
```

This ensures that when you type python or pip, the system uses the ones in your virtual environment first.

This modification isolates the virtual environment from the global Python installation, meaning you can install different versions of packages in different virtual environments without affecting other projects or the global Python environment.

When you **deactivate** the virtual environment (by running the deactivate command), the PATH reverts to its original state, so the global Python installation is used again.

In summary, virtual environments modify the PATH to ensure that the Python interpreter and libraries within the environment are used instead of the global ones. Activating a virtual environment appends its bin directory to the PATH, and deactivating it restores the original PATH, allowing you to work on different projects with different dependencies without conflicts.

pathlib

pathlib is a handy module in Python's standard library that brings a more user-friendly and intuitive approach to handling filesystem paths. Instead of treating file paths as plain strings, **pathlib** allows you to work with them as **Path objects**. This object-oriented way of dealing with paths makes your code cleaner and easier to understand. **pathlib** was introduced in Python 3.4 and has quickly become the go-to method for working with file paths in Python.

With **pathlib**, paths are represented as **Path objects**, allowing you to perform common path operations with methods and operators. This approach makes your code more readable and concise.

```
from pathlib import Path
#Creating a Path object
p = Path('/home/user/documents')
```

Path Operations: With **pathlib**, you can easily perform various operations on paths, like concatenating them, checking if a path exists, or iterating over files in a directory.

```
# Filename: path1.py
# Joining paths

    from pathlib import Path  # Importing from pathlib

    #Joining paths
    p = Path('/home/user') / 'documents' / 'file.txt'
    print(f"Joined path: {p}")

    #Checking if a path exists
    if p.exists():
         print(f"Path {p} exists.")
    else:
         print(f"Path {p} does not exist.")

# Iterating over files in a directory
directory = Path('/home/user/documents')
if directory.exists():
    print("\nFiles in directory:")
    for file in directory.iterdir():
        print(file)
else:
    print(f"Directory {directory} does not exist.")
```

Path Manipulation: pathlib makes path manipulation straightforward. You can effortlessly get the parent directory, the file name, the file extension, and more.

```
# Filename: path2.py
from pathlib import Path  # Importing Path

# Create a Path object
p = Path('/home/user/documents/file.txt')

# Get the parent directory
print(f"Parent directory: {p.parent}")  # Output: /
home/user/documents

# Get the file name
print(f"File name: {p.name}")  # Output: file.txt

# Get the file extension (suffix)
print(f"File extension: {p.suffix}")  # Output: .txt
```

File Operations: You can also use **pathlib** to perform file operations like reading from and writing to files.

```
#Filename: path3.py
p = Path('/home/user/documents/file.txt')

#Get the parent directory
print(p.parent)  # Output: /home/user/documents

#Get the file name
```

```
print(p.name)   # Output: file.txt

#Get the file extension
print(p.suffix)   # Output: .txt

p = Path('example.txt')
# Filename: path2.py
from pathlib import Path   # Importing Path

# Create a Path object
p = Path('/home/user/documents/file.txt')

# Get the parent directory
print(f"Parent directory: {p.parent}")   # Output: /
home/user/documents

# Get the file name
print(f"File name: {p.name}")   # Output: file.txt

# Get the file extension (suffix)
print(f"File extension: {p.suffix}")   # Output: .txt
#Writing to a file
p.write_text('Hello, World!')

#Reading from a file
content = p.read_text()
print(content)
```

Why Use pathlib?

pathlib simplifies working with file paths and directories, making your code more readable and less prone to errors. **pathlib** is generally recommended over older modules like **os.path**. It offers a more modern and Pythonic approach to handling paths, perfectly aligning with Python's focus on simplicity and clarity.

PTYHONPATH

PYTHONPATH is an environment variable in Python that tells the interpreter where to find the module files you want to import into your Python programs. It's kind of like the PATH environment variable, but instead of helping your system find programs, it helps Python find the modules you want to import and use.

When you use the import statement in Python to bring in a module, Python automatically searches for it in a predefined set of directories. The directories listed in the PYTHONPATH variable are added to this search path.

If you type:

```
echo $PYTHONPATH
```

You probably won't see much—just a blank line. That's because PYTHONPATH isn't always set by default. It's usually configured by root users when there's a need to include extra directories in the search path for modules. That said while root users may set it for system-wide usage, individual users can also set it in their environment without needing root access.

When PYTHONPATH is set, it contains a list of directory paths, each separated by a colon (:), signifying a place where Python will look when you try to import a module. Python goes through the directories in the order they appear in PYTHONPATH. If it finds the module in one of these directories, it imports it. If not, you'll get an ImportError.

When Python tries to import a module, it looks in the following order:

- The directory of the script being run.
- Directories listed in PYTHONPATH.
- The standard library and site-packages. The text doesn't mention that Python always checks the directory of the currently executing script first before moving to PYTHONPATH.

Modifying PYTHONPATH

You can modify PYTHONPATH to include additional directories where you've stored your custom Python modules. This can be done temporarily in a terminal session or permanently by tweaking your system configuration files.

PYTHONPATH is especially handy when you're working with custom or third-party Python modules that aren't installed in the standard library or the site-packages directory. By adding the directory containing these modules to PYTHONPATH, you make sure that Python can find and import them without any hiccups.

PATH vs. PYTHONPATH

While **PATH** and **PYTHONPATH** both involve directory paths, they serve different roles. PATH is used by the operating system to find executable files, while PYTHONPATH is used by Python to locate module files. Keeping these two variables separate helps maintain better organisation and management of both executable files and Python modules.

In short, PATH and PYTHONPATH are like two sides of the same coin. PATH helps your system find programs to run, and PYTHONPATH helps Python find the modules to import into your code.

VIRTUAL_ENV is an environment variable that gets set automatically when you activate a virtual environment in Python. This variable points to the directory of your virtual environment, allowing tools and scripts to easily detect that they are running within a virtual environment and access the necessary resources.

If you ever want to check which virtual environment you're using, just type:

```
echo $VIRTUAL_ENV
```

Keep in mind, though, that you'll need to have your virtual environment activated in the Terminal for this command to work. Once activated, running the command will show you the path to your virtual environment directory.

When working with file and directory paths in Python, you might find a need to modify the $PATH environment variable to include custom directories where your scripts are located. You can do this directly within a Python script using the os module. However, keep in mind that any changes you make to $PATH in a script are only temporary—they'll only affect the current script and any processes it spawns. Once the script finishes, these changes won't persist, and they won't impact the shell that started the script.

Here's how you can do it:

```
#Filename: path4.py
import os

#Get the current PATH
current_path = os.environ.get('PATH')
print(f"Original PATH: {current_path}")

#Define a new directory to add to the PATH
new_directory = "/home/user/my_custom_bin"

#Add the new directory to the PATH
os.environ['PATH'] = new_directory + os.pathsep +
current_path

#Verify the change
print(f"Modified PATH: {os.environ['PATH']}")
```

In this script:

1. **Fetching the Current PATH**: We first retrieve the current value of the $PATH environment variable using **os.environ.get('PATH').**

2. **Adding a New Directory**: We then define a new directory path that we want to add to the $PATH. In this example, it's /home/user/my_custom_bin.

3. **Modifying the PATH**: We update the $PATH by prepending our new

directory to it. We use os.pathsep to ensure the correct separator (a colon on Unix-like systems or a semicolon on Windows) is used.

4. **Verifying the Change**: Finally, we print out the modified $PATH to verify that our change was successful.

Remember, the modification to $PATH in this script will only last as long as the script is running. Once the script ends, the original $PATH in your shell remains unchanged.

Also, when you deactivate a virtual environment, the original PATH is restored, reverting Python back to the global interpreter.

Questions

What is the purpose of the PATH environment variable on the Raspberry Pi, and how does it help locate executable programs?

1. Describe how the directories listed in the PATH variable are organised and prioritised. What happens if a command exists in multiple directories in the PATH?
2. How can you temporarily add a custom directory to the PATH variable in a Terminal session? Write the command to do so.
3. Explain how activating a Python virtual environment affects the PATH variable and why this isolation is useful.
4. What is pathlib, and why is it generally preferred over the older os.path module when working with file paths in Python?
5. Write a small script using pathlib to create a Path object, check if the path exists, and list all files in that directory.
6. What is PYTHONPATH, and how does it differ from PATH? Describe a situation where modifying PYTHONPATH could be useful.
7. Explain the role of the VIRTUAL_ENV environment variable. How can you check its value from the command line, and what information does it provide?
8. How would you modify the PATH variable within a Python script to add a custom directory temporarily?
9. When using a virtual environment, how does deactivating it affect the PATH variable and which Python interpreter becomes active?

20: OS Module

We've talked about the 'os' module a few times, so let's take a closer look at it. The os module is like Python's **toolkit** for interacting with the operating system. It's what you use when you need to manage files, directories, and even processes. Whether you want to create, delete, or change files and directories, the os module has you covered.

The os module also gives you access to environment variables, which can be handy for managing system paths or configuration settings directly in your scripts.

The os module's features can be grouped into a few main categories:

- File Operations
- Working with Paths
- Environment Variables
- Process Management
- Miscellaneous Operations

Let's walk through an example from each category. You should be able to extrapolate how to use the others from this.

Writing a List of Files in a Directory to a List

Here's a program, osm1.py, that creates **a list of all files** in a specific directory. The directory is defined as **/path/to/your/directory**. Just replace this with the path to your directory of the directory you want to catalogue.

```
#Filename: osm1.py
import os
directory_path = '/path/to/your/directory'
file_list = []

try:
    files = os.listdir(directory_path)
    for file in files:
        file_list.append(file)

    print(file_list)

except FileNotFoundError:
    print(f"The directory '{directory_path}' does not
exist.")
except PermissionError:
    print(f"You do not have permission to access the
directory '{directory_path}'.")
```

Listing Directories and Sub-directories

To list all directories and sub-directories, use **os.walk** to take a trip through the directory structure.

```
#Filename: osm2.py
import os

directory_path = '/path/to/your/directory'
directory_list = []

try:
    for dirpath, dirnames, filenames in
os.walk(directory_path):
        directory_list.append(dirpath)

    print(directory_list)

except FileNotFoundError:
    print(f"The directory '{directory_path}' does not
exist.")
except PermissionError:
    print(f"You do not have permission to access the
directory '{directory_path}'.")
```

Directories, Sub-directories, and Files

You can also list all directories, their sub-directories, and all files within them, and store this information in a dictionary:

```
#Filename: osm3.py
import os

directory_path = '/path/to/your/directory'
directory_structure = {}
```

```
try:
    for dirpath, dirnames, filenames in
os.walk(directory_path):
        path_parts = dirpath.split(os.sep)
        current_dict = directory_structure

        for part in path_parts:
            current_dict = current_dict.
setdefault(part, {})
        current_dict['_files'] = filenames

    import json
    print(json.dumps(directory_structure, indent=4))

except FileNotFoundError:
    print(f"The directory '{directory_path}' does not
exist.")
except PermissionError:
    print(f"You do not have permission to access the
directory '{directory_path}'.")
```

Capturing Output

To execute a system command and capture its output, you can use the sub-process module:

```
#Filename: osm4.py
import subprocess

def execute_command(command):
    #Execute a system command and capture its output.
    try:
        output = subprocess.check_output(command,
shell=True, encoding='utf-8')
        return output
    except subprocess.CalledProcessError as e:
        print(f"Error executing command: {e}")
        return None

if __name__ == "__main__":
    command = "ls -l"
    command_output = execute_command(command)

    if command_output is not None:
        print("Command output:")
        print(command_output)
```

Snippets for Common os Module Functions

Here's a quick reference for some commonly used os module functions:

```
#Filename: osm5a.py
#Get the current working directory
import os
cwd = os.getcwd()
print(cwd)

#Filename: osm5b.py
#List files and directories in a directory
files = os.listdir('/path/to/directory')
print(files)

#Filename: osm5c.py
#Create a directory
os.mkdir('/path/to/new_directory')

#Filename: osm5d.py
#Remove a file
os.remove('/path/to/file.txt')

#Filename: osm5e.py
#Rename a file or directory
os.rename('old_name.txt', 'new_name.txt')

#Filename: osm5f.py
#Change the working directory
os.chdir('/new/directory')

#Filename: osm5g.py
#Get a list of environment variables
env_vars = os.environ
print(env_vars)

#Filename: osm5h.py
#Execute a system command and capture its output
output = os.popen('ls -l').read()
print(output)

#Filename: osm5h.py
#Execute a system command and capture its output using
subprocess
import subprocess

try:
    # Execute the command and capture its output
    output = subprocess.check_output(['ls', '-l'],
encoding='utf-8')
    print(output)
except subprocess.CalledProcessError as e:
    print(f"Error executing command: {e}")


#Filename: osm5j.py
#Remove a directory
os.rmdir('/path/to/empty_directory')
```

```
#Filename: osm5k.py
#Copy a file
import shutil
shutil.copy('/source/file.txt', '/destination/')
```

```
#Filename: osm5l.py
#Move a file
shutil.move('/source/file.txt', '/destination/')
```

A few things to note

The functions **os.open()** and **os.popen()** are quite different, as they serve distinct purposes related to file handling and process management. os.open() provides direct control over how a file is opened (e.g., specifying flags like read, write, or create). os.popen() allows you to run shell commands and capture their output or send input to them.

While **os.popen()** can execute system commands, it's recommended to use the **subprocess module** instead for better control and handling of errors., stick to subprocess for consistency and reliability.

os.mkdir() can only create one directory at a time. If you need to create nested directories (for example, /path/to/nested/directory), you should use **os.makedirs()** instead.

```
os.makedirs('/path/to/nested/directory')\
```

The snippet os.rmdir('/path/to/empty_directory') is correct but, if the directory contains files, os.rmdir() will fail. To remove a directory and its contents, you need to use **shutil.rmtree():**

```
shutil.rmtree('/path/to/directory')
```

Environment Variables

Environment variables are key in configuring and operating software in Python. They allow you to manage settings specific to different environments (like development or production) without changing the code. This is especially useful for things like database connection strings or API keys, where you might want to keep sensitive information out of your code base.

To access all environment variables, you can use the **os.environ** dictionary:

```
#Filename: osm6.py
import os

env_vars = os.environ

for key, value in env_vars.items():
    print(f"{key}: {value}")
```

This will print out all the environment variables and their values.

Questions

1. What is the purpose of Python's os module, and what are its main categories of features?
2. Write a Python script using the os module to list all files in a given directory and store them in a list.
3. Explain how the os.walk function works in Python and provide an example where it lists all directories and sub-directories within a specified path.
4. How can you execute a system command within Python and capture its output? Write a sample function to run ls -l and return the result.
5. What are the steps to create a new directory using the os module, and what is the difference between os.mkdir() and os.makedirs()?
6. Describe the difference between os.popen() and subprocess for executing system commands. Which one is recommended, and why?
7. What is the purpose of environment variables, and how can you access and print all environment variables in Python using the os module?
8. Explain how to rename a file or directory in Python using the os module. Create an example that renames old_file.txt to new_file.txt.
9. What function would you use to remove a directory in Python if it's empty, and what function would you use if the directory contains files?
10. Write a short script using the shutil module to move a file from one directory to another.

21: Regular Expressions

The **re module** is designed for working with regular expressions. These are used for searching, matching, and manipulating text based on specific patterns. Regular expressions allow you to define complex search criteria, enabling you to find and process strings that match a given pattern, extract specific parts of strings, or replace segments of text.

As with most modules, the re module provides several functions to perform operations with these patterns. For instance, you can use **re.match()** to determine if a string *starts* with a specific pattern, or **re.search()** to find the first occurrence of a pattern anywhere in a string. If you need to locate all instances of a pattern within a text, **re.findall()** will return a list of all matches. For more advanced tasks, **re.finditer()** allows you to iterate over matches, providing match objects with detailed information about each match.

Beyond just finding patterns, the re module also enables you to manipulate text. The **re.sub()** function is particularly useful for replacing occurrences of a pattern with a different string, which can be helpful in tasks like data cleaning or text formatting. Additionally, **re.split()** can divide a string into a list based on a pattern, offering more flexibility than the standard string **split()** method, which we saw in Chapter 04.

In summary, the re module is a versatile and essential tool for anyone dealing with text processing in Python, providing a way to efficiently search, match, and manipulate strings using regular expressions.

The program example below shows a simple example.

```
#Filename rex1.py
import re
#Define a string
string = "The quick brown fox jumps over the lazy dog"
#Search for the word "fox" in the string
match = re.search("fox", string)
```

```
#Print the result
if match:
    print("Found:", match.group())
else:
    print("Not found")
```

In this example, we imported the **re** module and then defined a string. Using the **re.search() function**, we searched for the word "fox" in the string. The re.search(' function returns a match object if it finds a match and 'None' if no match is found. We then used the match object's 'group()' method to get the matched string.

Regular expressions can also find patterns in strings:

```
#Filename: rex2.py
import re

#Define a string
string = "The quick brown fox jumps over the lazy dog"

#Find all the words in the string
matches = re.findall(r"\w+", string)

#print the result
print(matches)
```

Output:

```
['The', 'quick', 'brown', 'fox', 'jumps', 'over',
'the', 'lazy', 'dog']
```

Here, we used the **re.findall()** function to find all the words in the string. The regular expression '\w+' matches one or more word characters (letters, digits, and underscores). The 're.findall()' function returns a list of all the matched strings.

Useful Functions

The 're' module provides several functions and classes that allow you to work with regular expressions. Here are some of its key features:

re.match(pattern, string): This function tries to match the pattern from the start of the string.

re.search(pattern, string): This function searches the string for the first occurrence of the pattern and returns a match object if we find it. If it doesn't find a match, it returns 'None'.

re.findall(pattern, string): This function returns a list of all non-overlapping matches of the pattern in the string.

re.sub(pattern, repl, string): This function replaces all pattern occurrences in the string with the replacement string repl.

re.compile(pattern): This function compiles the pattern into a regular expression object, allowing for efficient reuse in multiple operations.

MatchObject: This is the object returned by the 'search()' and 'match()' functions. It contains information about the match, including the matched string, the starting and ending positions of the match, and any captured groups.

re.IGNORECASE and **re.MULTILINE**' These flags can modify the behaviour of regular expression matching. 're.IGNORECASE' makes the pattern case-insensitive, while 're.MULTILINE' allows the pattern to match across multiple lines.

re.escape(string): This function returns a string with all special characters escaped, making it safe to use as part of a regular expression pattern.

Common Regular Expressions

Pattern	Description
.	Matches any character except a newline.
^	Matches the start of the string.
$	Matches the end of the string.
*	Matches 0 or more repetitions of the preceding character.
+	Matches 1 or more repetitions of the preceding character.
?	Matches 0 or 1 repetition of the preceding character.
{n}	Matches exactly n repetitions of the preceding character.
{n,}	Matches n or more repetitions of the preceding character.
{n,m}	Matches between n and m repetitions of the preceding character.
[]	Matches any single character within the brackets.
[^]	Matches any single character not within the brackets.
\	Escapes a special character or a sequence (e.g., \d for digits).
|	Matches the pattern before or the pattern after (logical OR).
(...)	Groups patterns for extraction or applying operators.
\d	Matches any digit; equivalent to [0-9].
\D	Matches any non-digit; equivalent to [^0-9].
\w	Matches any word character (alphanumeric or underscore); equivalent to [a-zA-Z0-9_].
\W	Matches any non-word character; equivalent to [^a-zA-Z0-9_].
\s	Matches any whitespace character (space, tab, newline).
\S	Matches any non-whitespace character.
\b	Matches a word boundary.
\B	Matches a non-word boundary.
(?i)	Case-insensitive matching.
(?m)	Multi-line matching; affects ^ and $.

(?s) Dot-all mode; makes . match newline as well.
(?x) Verbose mode; write regexes that are more readable.

Here are some examples of pattern-matching options and meta characters commonly used in regular expressions:

Examples of using character classes in Python's re module:

```
#Filename: rex3.py
import re
#Example 1: Matching vowels
pattern1 = r'[aeiou]'
text1 = 'Hello, World!'
match1 = re.findall(pattern1, text1)
print(match1)  # Output: ['e', 'o', 'o']

#Filename: rex4.py
import re
pattern2 = r'[0-9]'
text2 = 'The price is $25.99'
match2 = re.findall(pattern2, text2)
print(match2)
#Output: ['2', '5', '9', '9']

#Filename: rex5.py
#Example 3: Negation
pattern3 = r'[^aeiouAEIOU]'
text3 = 'Hello, World!'
match3 = re.findall(pattern3, text3)
print(match3)
# Output: ['H', 'l', 'l', ',', ' ', 'W', 'r', 'l', 'd',
'!']
```

In these examples, character classes are used to define sets of characters to match in the texts using the **re.findall** function.

Anchors

Anchors are used to specify the position in the string where a match must occur. There are two anchors:

- ^: Matches the start of a string.
- $: Matches the end of a string.

If the pattern is not found at the specified position, the 're.search' 'function will return 'None'.

```
#Filename: rex6.py
#Demonstrating using the two anchors
import re
def check_greeting(text):
    #Check if the text starts with "Hello" and ends
with "World!"
    pattern = r'^Hello.*World!$'

    match = re.search(pattern, text)
```

```
    if match:
        print('Valid greeting pattern found.')
    else:
        print('Invalid greeting pattern.')

#Test the function with different texts
text1 = 'Hello, World!'
text2 = 'Hello, Universe!'


check_greeting(text1)
check_greeting(text2)
```

This should return:

```
Valid greeting pattern found.
Invalid greeting pattern.
```

This shows how the **^** and **$** anchors are used to specify the position of the pattern within the string.

Groups

Groups provide a neat way to capture and extract sub-patterns within a larger pattern. You create groups by placing part of a regular expression inside parentheses. When a match is found, you can store the contents of the matched groups.

- ( ): Creates a capturing group for extracting a portion of the match.
- (?:): Creates a non-capturing group for grouping but not capturing a portion of the match.

```
#Filename: rex7.py
import re
#Pattern with groups
pattern = r'(\d{3})-(\d{2})-(\d{4})'
#Test string
text = 'Date of birth: 123-45-6789'
#Using re.search to find the match
match = re.search(pattern, text)
#Check if a match is found
if match:
    # Access matched groups using group() or groups()
    full_match = match.group(0)  #Entire match
    group1 = match.group(1)      #Contents first group
    group2 = match.group(2)      #Contents second group

    group3 = match.group(3)      #Contents third group

    print("Full Match:", full_match)
    print("Group 1:", group1)
    print("Group 2:", group2)
    print("Group 3:", group3)
else:
    print("No match found.")
```

In this example:

The pattern (\d{3})-(\d{2})-(\d{4}) defines three groups separated by hyphens.

\d{3}, \d{2}, and **\d{4}** represent sequences of three digits, two digits, and four digits, respectively.

re.search is used to find the pattern in the text.

match.group(1), match.group(2), and **match.group(3)** are used to access the contents of the first, second, and third groups, respectively.

When you run this program, you will see output similar to:

```
Full Match: 123-45-6789
Group 1: 123
Group 2: 45
Group 3: 6789
```

This example demonstrates how groups can be used to capture and extract specific parts of a match within a larger pattern.

Alternation

Alternation is a process that allows you to specify multiple alternatives for a pattern. The pipe character represents it '|'. The pattern matches any of the alternatives. It's akin to the logical OR.

- |: Matches either the pattern on the left or the pattern on the right.

Here's an example:

```
#Filename: rex8.py
import re

#Pattern with alternation
pattern = r'dog|cat'

#Test string
text = 'I have a cat and a dog.'

#Using re.search to find the match
match = re.search(pattern, text)

#Check if a match is found
if match:
    print("Match found:", match.group())
else:
    print("No match found.")
```

In this example: The pattern dog|cat uses the alternation operator | to specify two alternatives: "dog" or "cat."

```
The test string is "I have a cat and a dog."
```

When you run this program, it should produce:

```
Match found: cat
```

This is because the first match encountered in the text is "cat," which satisfies the pattern.

You can extend alternation to include more alternatives, and you can use groups to group parts of the pattern:

```
#Filename: rex9.py
import re

#Pattern with alternation and groups
pattern = r'(apple|orange) juice'

#Test string
text = 'I like apple juice and orange juice.'

#Using re.search to find the match
match = re.search(pattern, text)

#Check if a match is found
if match:
    print("Match found:", match.group(1))
else:
    print("No match found.")
```

Here, the pattern (**apple | orange**) juice uses groups and to match either "apple juice" or "orange juice." The result will be:

```
Match found: apple
```

This shows how alternation is used to create flexible patterns that match different alternatives within a text.

Metacharacters

These are special characters that have a meaning and are used to define the syntax and structure of the pattern. They are not matched as literal characters but serve as operators or modifiers. Metacharacters are useful tools for creating flexible and expressive patterns. Understanding their meanings is essential when working with regex patterns.

```
#Filename: rex10.py
import re

#Sample text
text = "Hello, welcome to the world of Python! 12345.
Email: example@example.com. Visit https://example.com"

#Using different metacharacters in regex patterns
```

```
#Matches any character except newline (.)
matches_any = re.findall(r'H.llo', text)
print(f"Matches any character except newline: {matches_
any}")

#Matches the start of the string (^)
matches_start = re.findall(r'^Hello', text)
print(f"Matches start of string: {matches_start}")

#Matches any digit (\d)
matches_digits = re.findall(r'\d+', text)
print(f"Matches digits: {matches_digits}")

#Matches any word character (alphanumeric + underscore)
(\w)
matches_words = re.findall(r'\w+', text)
print(f"Matches word characters: {matches_words}")

#Matches email pattern (using grouping and character
classes)
matches_email = re.findall(r'[\w\.-]+@[\w\.-]+', text)
print(f"Matches email addresses: {matches_email}")

#Matches a word boundary (\b) for word "Python"
matches_word_boundary = re.findall(r'\bPython\b', text)
print(f"Matches word boundary 'Python': {matches_word_
boundary}")

#Matches either 'Python' or 'world' (| operator)
matches_either = re.findall(r'Python|world', text)
print(f"Matches either 'Python' or 'world': {matches_
either}")

#Matches any whitespace character (\s)
matches_whitespace = re.findall(r'\s', text)
print(f"Matches whitespace characters: {matches_
whitespace}")

#Matches URLs using pattern
matches_url = re.findall(r'https?://[^\s]+', text)
print(f"Matches URLs: {matches_url}")

#Matches non-digit characters (\D)
matches_non_digits = re.findall(r'\D+', text)
print(f"Matches non-digit characters: {matches_non_
digits}")

#Matches non-word characters (\W)
matches_non_words = re.findall(r'\W+', text)
print(f"Matches non-word characters: {matches_non_
words}")
```

Greedy Matching

Greedy matching is the default behaviour of quantifiers. A greedy quantifier matches as much of the input string as possible while still allowing the overall pattern to match. You can denote them by adding '*' or '+' or '?'.' after the character or group to be quantified. For example, '.*' is a greedy quantifier that matches zero or more occurrences of any character:

```
#Filename: rex11.py
import re
text = "abc123def456"
pattern = r'(\D+)(\d+)'
match = re.match(pattern, text)

if match:
    print("Greedy Match:", match.groups())
```

In this example, the pattern '(\D+)(\d+)' captures non-digits followed by digits. The '\D+ 'part is greedy, meaning it matches as many non-digit characters as possible while still allowing the overall pattern to match.

Lazy (Non-Greedy) Matching:

Lazy matching, also known as non-greedy or minimal matching, matches as little of the input string as possible while still allowing the overall pattern to match.

You denote lazy quantifiers by adding *? to the character or group to be quantified, +?, or ?? after the character or group to be quantified:

```
#Filename: rex12.py
import re

text = "abc123def456"
pattern = r'(\D+?)(\d+)'

match = re.match(pattern, text)

if match:
    print("Lazy Match:", match.groups())
```

In this example, the pattern '(\D+?)(\d+)' captures non-digits followed by digits. The '\D+?' part is the 'lazy' portion- it matches as few non-digit characters as possible while still allowing the overall pattern to match.

Choosing between greedy and lazy quantifiers depends on the specific requirements of your pattern. If you want to capture the smallest potential match, use lazy quantifiers. If you want to capture the largest potential match, use greedy quantifiers.

- *?: Matches zero or more occurrences of the preceding pattern in a lazy (non-greedy) way.
- +?: Matches one or more occurrences of the preceding pattern in a lazy (non-greedy) way.
- ??: Matches zero or one occurrence of the preceding pattern in a lazy (non-greedy) way.

- {n}?, {n,}?, {n,m}?: Matches the minimum number of occurrences of the preceding pattern in a lazy (non-greedy) way.

In regular expressions, **escaped characte**rs and special sequences used to represent characters with special meanings or to match specific patterns. Here's an example that shows the use of escaped characters and special sequences:

```
#Filename: rex13.py
import re
text = "The price of the product is $25.99, and the
discount is 10%."

#match a dollar sign and digits
pattern_dollar = r'\$\d+\.\d{2}'

#sequence to match digits and a percent sign
pattern_percent = r'\d+%'

#sequence to match word boundaries find "product"
pattern_word = r'\bproduct\b'

# Search for matches in the text
match_dollar = re.search(pattern_dollar, text)
match_percent = re.search(pattern_percent, text)
match_word = re.search(pattern_word, text)

#Print the results
if match_dollar:
    print("Price Match:", match_dollar.group())

if match_percent:
    print("Discount Match:", match_percent.group())

if match_word:
    print("Word Match:", match_word.group())
```

In this program:

\$\d+\.\d{2} uses escaped characters:

\$ matches a literal dollar sign.

\d+ matches one or more digits.

\. matches a literal dot.

\d{2} matches exactly two digits after the dot.

\d+% uses a special sequence:

\d+ matches one or more digits.

% matches a literal percent sign.

\bproduct\b uses special sequences to match word boundaries:

When you run this program, it should return:

```
Price Match: $25.99
Discount Match: 10%
Word Match: product
```

Exercise: Exploring Regular Expressions

Write a Python program that uses regular expressions to process and manipulate text. Follow these steps:

Lazy vs Greedy Matching:

- Use the string: "The quick brown fox jumps over the lazy dog."

Write two patterns to match:

- A greedy pattern to capture everything between "The" and "dog.".
- A lazy pattern to capture only the shortest segment between "The" and "dog.".

Anchors:

- Use the string: "Python is fun."

Write patterns to:

- Match the word "Python" only if it appears at the beginning of the string.
- Match the word "fun" only if it appears at the end of the string.
- Match the entire string if it starts with "Python" and ends with "fun.".

Pattern Matching in Numbers:

- Use the string: "My favourite numbers are 123, 4567, and 89012."

Write patterns to:

- Match all numbers with exactly 3 digits.
- Match all numbers with more than 3 digits.

Reusable Function:

Write a reusable function test_regex(pattern, text) that takes a pattern and a text, applies the regex, and prints the matches.

```
#Filename: 21-exercise-06.py
import re

def test_regex(pattern, text):
    matches = re.findall(pattern, text)
    print(f"Pattern: {pattern}")
    print(f"Matches: {matches}\n")

if __name__ == "__main__":
    # Lazy vs Greedy Matching
    text_1 = "The quick brown fox jumps over the lazy
dog."
    print("=== Lazy vs Greedy Matching ===")
    test_regex(r"The.*dog", text_1)  # Greedy
    test_regex(r"The.*?dog", text_1)  # Lazy

    # Anchors
    text_2 = "Python is fun."
    print("=== Anchors ===")
    test_regex(r"^Python", text_2)  # Match at the
start
    test_regex(r"fun\.$", text_2)  # Match at the end
    test_regex(r"^Python.*fun\.$", text_2)  # Match
full string

    # Pattern Matching in Numbers
    text_3 = "My favourite numbers are 123, 4567, and
89012."
    print("=== Pattern Matching in Numbers ===")
    test_regex(r"\b\d{3}\b", text_3)  # Match exactly 3
digits
    test_regex(r"\b\d{4,}\b", text_3)  # Match more
than 3 digits
```

22: Exceptions

Let's talk about **exception handling**—it's basically how we manage errors that pop up when our code is running. These errors, called exceptions, can happen for all sorts of reasons: maybe the user gives us some weird input, something goes wrong during execution, or there's an issue with an external resource we're relying on. Whatever the cause, exceptions mess with the usual flow of our code, and that's where exception handling comes in.

Python makes it super easy to handle exceptions with something called a **'try-except' block**. Here's the general idea:

```
try:
    # Code that might cause an exception
    # ...
except ExceptionType1:
    # Code to handle ExceptionType1
    # ...
except ExceptionType2:
    # Code to handle ExceptionType2
    # ...
else:
    # Code that runs if no exception occurs
    # ...
finally:
    # Code that runs no matter what
    # ...
```

So, how does this all work? Well, you wrap the code that might throw an exception inside a **try** block. If something goes wrong, Python immediately jumps to the **except** block that matches the type of error. If everything runs smoothly, and there's no exception, the code in the **else** block (if you have one) gets executed. The **finally** block is the cleanup crew—it always runs, whether an exception happened or not. This is handy for things like closing files or freeing up resources.

Exception handling is all about keeping your program from crashing unexpectedly. By catching these errors, you can show helpful error messages, log the problem, try the operation again, or take some other action to keep things running smoothly.

Here's a quick example to show you how it works:

```
#Filename: exception1.py
try:
    num1 = int(input("Enter the first number: "))
    num2 = int(input("Enter the second number: "))
    result = num1 / num2
    print("Result:", result)
except ValueError:
    print("Invalid input. Please enter valid
integers.")
except ZeroDivisionError:
    print("Error: Division by zero is not allowed.")
else:
    print("No exceptions occurred.")
finally:
    print("Program execution complete.")
```

In this example, if someone types in non-integer values or tries to divide by zero, the specific exceptions (**'ValueError'** and **'ZeroDivisionError'**) are caught, and a friendly error message pops up. If no exceptions happen, the **else block** runs, and the **finally block** always runs at the end, no matter what.

By using exception handling, you're making your code more reliable, better at dealing with unexpected situations, and more user-friendly when things do go wrong.

Handling Multiple Exceptions

Sometimes, your code might encounter different types of errors, and you'll want to handle them in specific ways. Python makes this easy with the except block, which can catch multiple exceptions by listing them in a comma-separated format. This lets you apply different error-handling strategies depending on what goes wrong.

For example:

```
try:
    # Code that might raise exceptions
    # ...
except (ExceptionType1, ExceptionType2):
    # Code to handle both ExceptionType1 and
ExceptionType2
    # ...
```

Handling All Exceptions

If you want to catch any exception, no matter what type, you can use a bare except statement. However, while it might seem convenient, it's usually better to catch specific exceptions so you can handle each one appropriately. Catching everything can sometimes hide bugs or issues you didn't expect.

```
try:
    # Code that might raise exceptions
    # ...
except:
    # Code to handle any exception
    # ...
```

Accessing Exception Details

When you catch an exception, you can grab more information about what went wrong using the keyword. This is really handy for debugging or logging because you can get the error message, type, or even the stack trace.

For example:

```
try:
    # Code that might raise an exception
    # ...
except ExceptionType as e:
    print("An exception occurred:", str(e))
```

Raising Exceptions

Sometimes, you might want to manually trigger an exception to signal that something's not right. You can do this with the **raise** statement. You can raise built-in exceptions or create your own custom ones by subclassing the **Exception** class.

```
For example:
if condition:
    raise ValueError("Invalid input")
```

Exception Chaining

Occasionally, you might catch an exception, do something (like logging it), and then decide to pass it along by re-raising it. You can do this with the raise statement on its own, which preserves the original exception's traceback and context.

For example:

```
try:
    # Code that might raise an exception
    # ...
except Exception as e:
    # Perform some actions
    # ...
    raise  # Re-raise the exception
```

Exception Hierarchy

Exceptions are organised in a hierarchy, meaning they follow a structured relationship. At the top of this hierarchy is the base class **BaseException**, and all other exceptions inherit from this class, either directly or indirectly. Understanding this hierarchy is useful because it helps us know which exceptions are more specific and how to handle them appropriately in our code.

The figure below shows how this hierarchy is structured in Python.

```
BaseException
    >>      SystemExit
    >>      KeyboardInterrupt
    >>      GeneratorExit
    >>      Exception
                >>      StopIteration
                >>      ArithmeticError
                            >>      ZeroDivisionError
                            >>      OverflowError
                            >>      FloatingPointError
                >>      LookupError
                            >>      IndexError
                            >>      KeyError
                >>      ValueError
                            >>      UnicodeError
                >>      ImportError
                >>      OSError
                            >>      FileNotFoundError
                            >>      PermissionError
                >>      TypeError
                >>      NameError
```

Figure 22a. The Python exception hierarchy'

When you catch exceptions using **try-except,** you usually catch subclasses of exception. This is why using except Exception: catches most errors but excludes special cases like **SystemExit** and **KeyboardInterrupt.** Understanding the hierarchy allows you to catch specific errors, handle them differently, and avoid unintentionally catching exceptions that shouldn't be handled.

The program below demonstrates how exception hierarchy handling works. It shows how Python tries to catch the most specific exceptions first before falling back to more general ones.

```
#Filename: exception2.py

def divide(a, b):
    try:
```

```
        result = a / b
        print(f"Result: {result}")
    except ZeroDivisionError:
        print("Error: Division by zero is not
allowed.")
    except TypeError:
        print("Error: Unsupported operand type(s) for
division.")
    except Exception as e:
        print(f"General Exception caught: {e}")
    finally:
        print("Execution finished.")

# Test cases to trigger different exceptions
print("Case 1: Division by zero")
divide(10, 0)

print("\nCase 2: TypeError with string input")
divide(10, "five")

print("\nCase 3: Successful division")
divide(10, 2)
```

The output here will be along these lines:

```
Case 1: Division by zero
Error: Division by zero is not allowed.
Execution finished.

Case 2: TypeError with string input
Error: Unsupported operand type(s) for division.
Execution finished.

Case 3: Successful division
Result: 5.0
Execution finished.
```

ZeroDivisionError: This is caught when attempting to divide by zero, a specific type of error in Python.

TypeError: Raised when unsupported types are used (like trying to divide a number by a string).

Exception: The most general exception, which will catch any other unhandled exceptions.

finally: This block always runs, ensuring that any necessary cleanup (or final tasks) happens regardless of whether an exception was raised.

Wrapping Up

Exception handling is a big part of writing reliable, solid code. By catching and managing errors, you can prevent your programs from crashing unexpectedly, provide helpful feedback to users, and make debugging easier. Understanding and using try-except blocks effectively will definitely improve the quality of your code and help you manage those inevitable bumps in the road.

Common Mistakes Using Exceptions

When you're dealing with exceptions in Python, there are a few pitfalls that can trip you up. Knowing about these in advance can save you a lot of headaches!

Catching All Exceptions Without Specificity

Using a bare except statement to catch all exceptions might seem like a quick fix, but it can actually make debugging a nightmare. When you don't specify the type of exception, it's hard to know what went wrong or how to fix it. Instead, try to catch only the exceptions you expect and know how to handle.

Ignoring Exceptions

Sometimes, you might catch an exception but not do anything about it. This can lead to your program behaving unpredictably because the underlying issue isn't resolved. Always think through how you'll handle exceptions—whether it's showing an error message, logging the problem, retrying the operation, or taking another action. Ignoring an exception should be a last resort, not the norm.

Overusing Exceptions for Flow Control

Exceptions are meant for exceptional situations—things that go wrong, not for regular control flow. If you're using exceptions to manage normal program logic, like you would with if-else statements or loops, it can make your code confusing and harder to maintain. Stick to using exceptions for actual errors.

Catching Too Broad Exceptions

Catching very broad exceptions like Exception or BaseException might seem convenient, but it's often overkill. You could end up catching more than you intended, including errors that you didn't expect. It's better to be specific and only catch the exceptions you're prepared to handle, so your error handling is more precise and informative.

Improper Exception Handling Order

When you're handling multiple exceptions, the order matters—a lot. You should always catch the most specific exceptions first, and the more general ones later. If you mix up the order, the specific exceptions might never get caught because the general one takes precedence. Think of it as filtering out the most detailed issues first before catching the common ones.

Not Providing Enough Information in Error Messages

When an exception happens, the error message you provide is crucial for understanding and fixing the problem. If the message is too vague or generic, it's much harder to diagnose the issue. Make sure to include relevant details, like what went wrong, any related variable values, or even suggestions on how to resolve the issue.

Wrapping Up

Properly handling exceptions is key to writing reliable and maintainable Python code. By being mindful of these common mistakes—like catching exceptions too broadly, ignoring them, or using them for normal flow control—you can ensure your code is more robust and easier to debug. Remember, the goal is to handle exceptions gracefully, provide clear and helpful error messages, and keep your program running smoothly even when things go wrong.

Error Logging

When it comes to handling errors in your Python programs, logging those errors to a file or database can be incredibly helpful. Instead of just showing error messages on the console, logging gives you a record of what went wrong, which makes it easier to track down and fix issues. Python's **logging** module is a great tool for this, offering a flexible system to capture and store error messages.

Here's a simple example of a program that logs errors to a file:

```
# Filename: exception3.py
import logging

def setup_logger(log_file='error.log'):
    # Create logger
    logger = logging.getLogger('error_logger')
    logger.setLevel(logging.ERROR)

    # Create file handler
    file_handler = logging.FileHandler(log_file)
    file_handler.setLevel(logging.ERROR)

    # Create formatter
    formatter = logging.Formatter('%(asctime)s - 
%(levelname)s - %(message)s')
    file_handler.setFormatter(formatter)

    # Add file handler to logger
    logger.addHandler(file_handler)

    return logger, log_file  # Return both logger and 
log file name

def main():
    # Setup logger and get log file name
```

```
    logger, log_file = setup_logger()

    try:
        # Your code that may raise errors goes here
        result = 10 / 0  # Example: division by zero
    except Exception as e:
        # Log the error
        logger.error(f"An error occurred: {str(e)}",
exc_info=True)

    # Read and print errors from log file
    print("\n--- Error Log ---")
    try:
        with open(log_file, 'r') as log:
            print(log.read())  # Print the log file
content
    except FileNotFoundError:
        print("Log file not found.")

if __name__ == "__main__":
    main()
```

Logger Setup: The setup_logger() function sets up a logger named 'error_logger', which is set to log only ERROR level messages. It uses a file handler to direct these messages to a file called error.log. You can change the log file name by passing a different name to the function.

Logging the Error: Inside the main() function, you can put any code that might cause errors. If an error occurs in the try block, it's caught in the except block. The error is then logged using the logger's error() method. By using **exc_info=True**, you ensure that the full stack trace is included in the log, which is incredibly useful for debugging.

How to Use This Program: When you run the script, any errors that happen during execution will be logged to the **error.log file**. Check the Log, to see the logged errors, including the timestamp, error level, and full stack trace.

Benefits

- **Persistent Error Tracking**: Logging errors to a file means you have a record that you can review later, even if the program has terminated.
- **Easy Debugging**: With full stack traces included, you can easily see where things went wrong and address the issue.
- **Customisable Logging**: You can easily extend or modify the logging setup to include more information, log to multiple files, or even send logs to a remote server or database.

Using logging in this way can greatly improve the reliability and maintainability of your Python programs by making error tracking and debugging much easier.

23: Math

Let's dive into something not everyone likes but is pretty essential in the computing world—math. Adding or subtracting numbers is so routine we barely notice it, but without math, loops wouldn't work, and neither would any computer operations. At the heart of it all, computers is binary, working with 1's and 0's—tiny voltages flicking on and off to represent these numbers. No math means no computer, no Raspberry Pi, no nothing!

No surprise then that Python has a **math** module, this is packed with handy operations and functions, perfect for when you need to crunch some numbers without reinventing the isosceles triangle.

So, what's the deal with the math module? It's essential for a few reasons:

- It provides a reliable set of mathematical functions that are useful in fields like scientific computing, engineering, and more. Whether you're doing basic arithmetic, working with trigonometric functions, or tackling logarithms, Python's math module is up to the task. And because these functions are standardised, you can count on them to behave consistently across different applications and platforms.
- The functions in the math module are built with accuracy and efficiency in mind. This means you get **dependable** results whether you're doing something simple or diving into calculus.
- While the math module is, in itself, quite comprehensive, it also plays nicely with other libraries like NumPy and SciPy. These libraries build on top of math to offer even more advanced tools for scientific and mathematical computing. So, if you ever need to go beyond the basics, you're pretty much covered.

Now, even though Python has some built-in mathematical operations, the math module offers a bit extra—**more functions, more constants, and even a little more precision** for those times when you need it.

Here's a breakdown of some basic math operations you can do in Python. These don't need any extra modules, just the standard Python setup. However, keep in mind that these example don't provide a complete overview of every math operation Python can handle, just some of the most common ones.

Example 1: Basic Arithmetic Operations

```
#Filename: math1.py
#Addition (+)
num1 = 10
num2 = 5
addition_result = num1 + num2
print("Addition:", addition_result)

#Subtraction (-)
subtraction_result = num1 - num2
print("Subtraction:", subtraction_result)

#Multiplication (*)
multiplication_result = num1 * num2
print("Multiplication:", multiplication_result)

#Division (/)
division_result = num1 / num2
print("Division:", division_result)

#Exponentiation (**)
exponentiation_result = num1 ** num2
print("Exponentiation:", exponentiation_result)

#Modulus (%)
modulus_result = num1 % num2
print("Modulus:", modulus_result)
```

Example 2: Type Conversion

```
#Filename: math2.py
#Type Conversion: int(x), float(x), complex(real, imag)

#Convert a string to an integer
x_str = "123"
x_int = int(x_str)
print("Integer Conversion:", x_int)

#Convert a string to a floating-point number
y_str = "3.14"
y_float = float(y_str)
print("Float Conversion:", y_float)

#Create a complex number with real and imaginary parts
real_part = 2
imaginary_part = 3
```

```
z_complex = complex(real_part, imaginary_part)
print("Complex Number:", z_complex)
```

Example 3: Summation and Maximum/Minimum Values

```
#Filename: math3.py
#Summation and Maximum/Minimum Values:
#sum(iterable): Computes the sum of elements in an
iterable.
#max(iterable): Returns the maximum value in an
iterable.
#min(iterable): Returns the minimum value in an
iterable.

#Define a list of numbers
numbers = [10, 5, 8, 20, 15]

#Compute the sum of elements in the list
sum_result = sum(numbers)
print("Sum of numbers:", sum_result)

#Find the maximum value in the list
max_result = max(numbers)
print("Maximum value:", max_result)

#Find the minimum value in the list
min_result = min(numbers)
print("Minimum value:", min_result)
```

Example 4: Comparison Operators and Type Checking

```
#Filename: math4.py
#Comparison Operators: <, <=, >, >=, ==, !=
#Type Checking: isinstance(x, type)

#Comparison Operators
num1 = 10
num2 = 5

#Less than (<)
print("Less than (<):", num1 < num2)

#Less than or equal to (<=)
print("Less than or equal to (<=):", num1 <= num2)

#Greater than (>)
print("Greater than (>):", num1 > num2)

#Greater than or equal to (>=)
print("Greater than or equal to (>=):", num1 >= num2)

#Equality (==)
print("Equality (==):", num1 == num2)

#Inequality (!=)
print("Inequality (!=):", num1 != num2)
```

Let's talk about some of the differences between Python's built-in math and the math module:

Functions and Constants: The math module throws in extra goodies like trigonometric functions, hyperbolic functions, and constants like π (pi) and e (Euler's number - no I don't know what it is either. Mrs Google says its "a fundamental mathematical constant approximately equal to 2.71828. It is the base of natural logarithms and arises naturally in various mathematical contexts, particularly in calculus, complex analysis, and number theory. "You do learn something every day even though you still don't know what it means!).

Floating-Point Precision: The math module is tailored for floating-point arithmetic, (math that requires decimal precision) giving you more advanced functions than the basic arithmetic operations Python handles by default.

Trig, Exponential, and Log Functions

Here's how you can use the math module to calculate an exponential and some logarithms:

```
#Filename: math5.py
import math

#Exponential Function
result_exp = math.exp(2)
print(f"Exponential of 2: {result_exp}")

#Natural Logarithm
result_log = math.log(10)
print(f"Natural Logarithm of 10: {result_log}")

#Logarithm to the Base 10
result_log10 = math.log10(100)
print(f"Logarithm Base 10 of 100: {result_log10}")

#Logarithm to Any Base
result_log_custom_base = math.log(8, 2)
print(f"Logarithm Base 2 of 8: {result_log_custom_
base}")

#No Euler's number today.
```

Power Functions and Rounding

When you need to raise numbers to a power, you can either use **math.pow()** or the simpler exponentiation operator ** (two asterisks). Here's a quick comparison:

```
#Filename: math6.py
import math

#Using math.pow()
result_pow_math = math.pow(2, 3)
```

```
print(f"Using math.pow(): 2^3 = {result_pow_math}")

#Using Exponentiation Operator
result_pow_operator = 2 ** 3
print(f"Using Exponentiation Operator: 2^3 = {result_
pow_operator}")
```

Both give you the same result, so use whichever suits your style or needs.

When it comes to rounding, numbers you also have a few options too:

```
#Filename: math7.py
import math

#Rounding
rounded_value = round(5.6)
print(f"Rounded Value: {rounded_value}")

#Ceiling (Round Up)
ceiling_value = math.ceil(5.1)
print(f"Ceiling Value: {ceiling_value}")
```

Tau (τ) – The Circle Constant

Finally, **Tau** (τ). This circle constant is twice **Pi** (π) and can be accessed using **math.tau**. It's especially useful in situations where working with full circles makes more sense:

```
#Filename: math8.py
import math

tau_value = math.tau
print(f"The value of Tau: {tau_value}")
```

Using Math Constants

Here's a quick reminder of how to use some of the constants and functions available in the math module:

```
#Filename: math9.py
import math
#Example usage of math module functions and constants
print(math.sqrt(25))          #Square root function: 5.0
print(math.sin(math.pi/2))    #Sine function: 1.0
print(math.floor(3.7))        #Floor function: 3
print(math.pi)
#Constant for pi: 3.141592653589793
```

With the math module, you've got everything you need for both everyday calculations and those moments when you need a bit more mathematical muscle, or need to impress someone.

Alright, let's clear up a little confusion! While **int** and **dec** might sound like mathematical functions, they're actually not (or a couple of presenters if your

British). They fall into the category of assignment and increment/decrement operators—tools that help you modify the value of variables directly.

Here's the scoop:

- **+= (Add and Assign):** This operator adds the value on the right to the variable on the left and then assigns the result back to that same variable. It's like saying, "Take this number, add something to it, and keep the new total."
- **-= (Decrement):** Use -= to decrease the value of a variable. Subtract the number on the right from the one on the left and put the result in the variable on the left.

These operators are more about programming language mechanics than pure maths, but they're useful, even fundamental to every programming language, even if they may be performed in some different manner. (Some programs use — so be careful not to get too confused.)

How to Use Them

You can easily increment and decrement variables with += and -=, which let you add or subtract in place. Here's how:

```
#Filename: math10.py

#Increment a variable
x = 5
x += 1     #Increment x by 1
print(x)   #Output: 6

#In-place addition
y = 10
y = y + 3 #Increment y by 3
print(y)   #Output: 13

#Decrements a variable
x = 8
x -= 2     #Decrements x by 2
print(x)   #Output: 6

#In-place subtraction
y = 15
y = y - 5  #Decrements y by 5
print(y)   #Output: 10
```

More Math Operations

Now, besides this nifty plus and minuses, let's look at **+** ad **-** on their own:

```
#Filename: math11.py
#Addition
x = 5
y = 3
result = x + y
print(result)  #Output: 8

#Subtraction
x = 10
y = 4
result = x - y
print(result)  #Output: 6
```

I'll stop here for a mo, as you're probably back to the head scratching, asking **didn't you just say** that -= and += do this?

Yes, **-=** and **+=** are related to subtraction, but **-=** and **+=** different purposes.

The - operator is used to subtract one value from **another**. It takes two operands and subtracts the right operand from the left operand, returning the result as a new value. It **does not** modify the original values of the operands. Check out the two examples above. So to be clear:

Subtraction (-) creates a new value without altering the original variables Subtraction Assignment (-=) subtracts a value from the variable and updates the variable in place. Look at how each is used I the previous two programs.

In short, **use -** when you want to subtract values and store the result somewhere else, and **use -=** when you want to subtract and directly update the value of the variable. Examine the next program and see how ***** and ****** and **/** and **//** operate in a like fashion.

```
#Filename: math12.py
#Multiplication
x = 3
y = 5
result = x * y
print(result)  # Output: 15

#Division
x = 10
y = 2
result = x / y
print(result)  # Output: 5.0

#Floor Division (quotient)
x = 10
y = 3
result = x // y
```

```
print(result)  # Output: 3


#Exponentiation (raising x to the power of y)
x = 2
y = 3
result = x ** y
print(result)  # Output: 8
```

Bonus Operations

Don't forget about the **modulus (%)** for remainders, **absolute value (abs())** to get the non-negative value of a number, and **comparison operators** to compare values.

```
#Filename: math13.py
#Modulus (Remainder)
x = 10
y = 3
result = x % y
print(result)  # Output: 1

#Absolute Value
x = -7
result = abs(x)
print(result)  # Output: 7

#Comparison Operators
x = 5
y = 3
is_greater = x > y
print(is_greater)  # Output: True

is_equal = x == y
print(is_equal)  # Output: False
```

The Math Module

The math module, which comes with even more mathematical goodies:

```
#Filename: math14.py
import math

x = 2.3
result = math.ceil(x)
print(result)  #Output: 3

y = 4.7
result = math.floor(y)
print(result)  #Output: 4

z = 5.9
result = round(z)
print(result)  #Output: 6
```

Note: **round()**is a built-in function and **not part** of the math module. But showing it here to complete the sequence.

Here, **ceil()** rounds up to the nearest integer, **floor()** rounds down, and **round()** does what it says on the tin—rounds to the nearest whole number.

Other Handy Functions:

```
#Filename: math15.py
import math

#Square Root
x = 25
result = math.sqrt(x)
print(result)  # Output: 5.0

#Rounding
x = 3.7
result = round(x)
print(result)  # Output: 4

y = 5.2
result = round(y)
print(result)  # Output: 5
```

Trigonometric and Logarithmic Functions

If you're getting into angles or logarithms, the math module can assist. These functions may not be the ones that capture your **imagination** at the off, but they do actually have some really useful uses even in everyday programming. For starters they provide a way to handle and simplify large ranges of values, which is useful in many areas from **data compression** and design to financial modelling and machine learning. They allow management of complex, real-world data in a way that's more intuitive and efficient. I'm not covering that here, but its quiet fascinating to research.

```
#Filename: math16.py
import math

#Trigonometric Functions
angle = math.pi / 4  #45 degrees in radians

sin_value = math.sin(angle)
print(sin_value)  #Output: 0.7071067811865476

cos_value = math.cos(angle)
print(cos_value)  #Output: 0.7071067811865476

tan_value = math.tan(angle)
print(tan_value)  #Output: 1.0

#Logarithmic Functions
x = 100

log_value = math.log(x)
print(log_value)  #Output: 4.605170185988092

log10_value = math.log10(x)
print(log10_value)  #Output: 2.0
```

The **math.sin()**, **math.cos()**, and **math.tan()** functions are great for working with angles in radians, while **math.log()** and **math.log10()** handle natural and base-10 logarithms. This might be a program to display and analogue clock where you need to calculate where the second hand should be for example.

These examples show you just how much you can do with Python's built-in math capabilities and the math module. Whether you're doing simple calculations or diving into more complex stuff, Python's got you covered!

Logical operations in make comparisons and evaluate conditions based on **Boolean** (1s and 0's, True and False, Yes and No) values. There are three main logical operations you'll use.

AND

The **and** operator is all about saying, "I need both of these conditions to be true." If both conditions are **true**, then and returns **True**. But if either one (or both) is false, it returns False. Here's how it works:

A	B	A AND B
True	True	True
True	False	False
False	True	False
False	False	False

OR

The **or** operator is more relaxed. It returns True if at least one of the conditions is true. If both are false, then it gives you False. Here's the truth table.

A	B	A OR B
True	True	True
True	False	True
False	True	True
False	False	False

NOT

The **not** operator is a simple flip switch. It takes one condition and gives you the opposite. If it's true, not makes it false, and if it's false, not makes it true.

A	NOT A
True	False
False	True

Use in Real Code

Logical operations are handy within **if** statements, loops, and anywhere you need to make decisions based on certain conditions. For instance:

```
#Filename: math17.py
#Logical AND
x = 5
y = 10
z = 7

#Check if x is greater than y AND z is less than y
result1 = x > y and z < y
print(result1)  #Output: False

#Check if x is less than y AND z is greater than y
result2 = x < y and z > y
print(result2)  #Output: True

#Logical OR
a = True
b = False
c = True

#Check if a is True OR b is True
result3 = a or b
print(result3)  # Output: True

#Check if b is True OR c is True
result4 = b or c
print(result4)  #Output: True

#Logical NOT
p = True
q = False

#Check if p is NOT True
result5 = not p
print(result5)  # Output: False

#Check if q is NOT True
result6 = not q
print(result6)  # Output: True
```

In these examples, logical operations are used to evaluate conditions and make decisions based on the results. The outcomes can be stored in variables or used directly in conditional statements to control the flow of the program.

More Examples with Everyday Conditions:

```
#Filename: math18.py
#Logical AND
num1 = 15
num2 = 10

#Check if both numbers are greater than 5
result1 = num1 > 5 and num2 > 5
print(result1)  # Output: True

#Check if both numbers are even
result2 = num1 % 2 == 0 and num2 % 2 == 0
print(result2)  # Output: False
```

```
#Logical OR
fruit = "apple"

#Check if the fruit is either "apple" or "banana"
result3 = fruit == "apple" or fruit == "banana"
print(result3)  # Output: True

#Check if the fruit is either "orange" or "pear"
result4 = fruit == "orange" or fruit == "pear"
print(result4)  # Output: False

#Logical NOT
is_raining = False

#Check if it's NOT raining
result5 = not is_raining
print(result5)  #Output: True

#Check if it's NOT sunny
is_sunny = True
result6 = not is_sunny
print(result6)  #Output: False
```

Logical operations are your best friends when it comes to making decisions in your code. They help you determine the truth value of expressions, which is key for controlling program flow, filtering data, and more.

These operators are used to evaluate Boolean values and expressions, making them essential tools in Python programming.

- **AND (and)**: Returns True if both operands are true; otherwise, it returns False. It stops evaluating as soon as it finds a False.
- **OR (or)**: Returns True if at least one operand is true; otherwise, it returns False. It stops evaluating as soon as it finds a True.
- **NOT (not)**: Simply flips the Boolean value—true becomes false and vice versa.

Practical Example: Authentication and Toggling States

not can be particularly useful in everyday programming tasks, such as checking user authentication or toggling a boolean value:

```
#Filename: math19.py
#User authentication example
is_authenticated = False

#Check if the user is NOT authenticated
if not is_authenticated:
    print("Please log in to access the content.")

#Toggling a Boolean variable
flag = True
```

```
# Toggle the value of flag using `not`
flag = not flag

#Check the updated value of flag
if flag:
    print("Flag is True")
else:
    print("Flag is False")
```

In this example:

- **User Authentication**: The **is_authenticated** variable indicates whether a user is logged in. Using not, we can easily check if the user is not logged in and prompt them to log in.
- **Toggling a Boolean Variable**: We can toggle the value of a Boolean variable using **not**, flipping it from true to false or vice versa. This is super handy for toggling settings or flags in your code.

Logical operations like these create flexible, responsive programs that can make decisions based on various conditions. Whether you're controlling program flow, managing authentication, or just comparing values, these operators give you the tools you need to build smart, efficient Python programs.

Bit-wise operators might sound a bit technical, but they're actually quite handy when you want to work directly with the bits of an integer. In reality they're the trues and false of bits. Let's break down what each one does:

- **Bitwise AND (&)**: This operator compares each bit of two numbers and returns a new number where only the bits that were 1 in both numbers stay 1. It's like a gatekeeper that only lets through the bits that are true for both operands.
- **Bitwise OR (|)**: This one is a bit more lenient. It returns a number where the bits are 1 if they were 1 in either of the original numbers. So, it's great for combining bit flags.
- **Bitwise XOR (^)**: Also known as exclusive OR, this operator is a bit picky. It returns a 1 only if the bits in the corresponding positions of the two operands are different. If they're the same, you get a 0.
- **Bitwise NOT (~)**: This operator is all about flipping the script. It inverts all the bits in a number—turning 1s into 0s and 0s into 1s.
- **Left Shift (<<)**: Think of this as pushing the bits to the left, adding zeros on the right. Each shift to the left effectively multiplies the number by two.
- **Right Shift (>>)**: This does the opposite of the left shift. It pushes the bits to the right, filling the left side with zeros (or the sign bit, in

the case of signed numbers). Each shift to the right divides the number by two.

Bit-wise operators are particularly useful when you're dealing with binary data, manipulating bits, or optimising certain algorithms that need low-level bit operations.

Why Use Bitwise Operations?

While you might not need bitwise operations in every Python program, they're really useful in certain scenarios:

- **Flags and Options**: You can store multiple Boolean options in a single integer using bit-wise flags, making your code more memory-efficient.
- **Bit Manipulation**: This is perfect for tasks like setting, clearing, or toggling specific flags or attributes represented in or by a number.
- **Masking and Extracting Bits**: By creating masks, you can isolate or extract specific bits from integers. This comes in handy for tasks like data compression or encryption.
- **Performance Optimisation**: Bit-wise operations can be more efficient than arithmetic operations at the hardware level, which can lead to performance improvements in some algorithms.
- **Integer Compression**: If you need to store and manipulate large sets of integers, bit-wise operations can help compress and optimise this data.
- **Hashing and Hash Functions**: Bit-wise operations are often used in custom hash functions, which are important in data structures like hash tables.
- **Low-Level Operations**: They're essential when you're dealing with low-level data, where understanding the binary representation is crucial.
- **Network Programming**: Bit-wise operations are useful for manipulating IP addresses or handling protocol-specific tasks at the bit level.

Here's an example of bit-wise compression where you pack multiple smaller numbers into a single larger data type by manipulating bits directly. Useful when you want to save memory or transmit data more efficiently.

You can store four 8-bit numbers (each ranging from 0 to 255) into a single 32-bit integer. After all a 32-bit number is four lots of 8-bits. (At this point

I'm assuming you know and can deal with binary numbers.) You can do this by using logical operators as the following example shows.

Program Example: Bitwise Compression to Store Numbers

```
#Filename: math20.py
#Define four 8-bit numbers
num1 = 42     # 00101010
num2 = 150    # 10010110
num3 = 255    # 11111111
num4 = 100    # 01100100

#Compress into a 32-bit integer
compressed_value = (num1 << 24) | (num2 << 16) | (num3
<< 8) | num4
print(f"Compressed value: {compressed_value} (Binary:
{bin(compressed_value)})")

#Decompress back to original numbers
decompressed_num1 = (compressed_value >> 24) & 0xFF
decompressed_num2 = (compressed_value >> 16) & 0xFF
decompressed_num3 = (compressed_value >> 8) & 0xFF
decompressed_num4 = compressed_value & 0xFF

print(f"Decompressed num1: {decompressed_num1}")
print(f"Decompressed num2: {decompressed_num2}")
print(f"Decompressed num3: {decompressed_num3}")
print(f"Decompressed num4: {decompressed_num4}")
```

First we need the four 8-but numbers (or it could be two 16-bit values):

```
num1 = 42     # 00101010
num2 = 150    # 10010110
num3 = 255    # 11111111
num4 = 100    # 01100100
```

Pack the four numbers into a 32-bit integer.

```
Shift num1 by 24 bits (to occupy the highest 8 bits).
Shift num2 by 16 bits.
Shift num3 by 8 bits.
num4 occupies the lowest 8 bits (so no shift is needed
for it).

compressed_value = (num1 << 24) | (num2 << 16) | (num3
<< 8) | num4
```

Decompress the 32-bit integer back into the original 8-bit numbers.

Use bitwise shifts and masks to extract each 8-bit number.

```
decompressed_num1 = (compressed_value >> 24) & 0xFF
decompressed_num2 = (compressed_value >> 16) & 0xFF
decompressed_num3 = (compressed_value >> 8) & 0xFF
decompressed_num4 = compressed_value & 0xFF
```

- **Compression**: You shift the numbers to their respective positions in the 32-bit space, with the highest number (num1) shifted by 24 bits and the lowest (num4) kept as is.
- **Decompression**: You use bitwise shifts to move the packed 32-bit number back to the right, and a mask (& 0xFF) to extract only the 8 bits relevant to each original number.

Questions

1. What is the purpose of Python's math module, and how does it differ from Python's built-in arithmetic operators?
2. Explain how you would convert a string like "123" to an integer and "3.14" to a floating-point number in Python. Why might type conversion be useful in mathematical operations?
3. Provide an example using the math module where you calculate the natural logarithm of a number, and explain what the result represents.
4. Write a Python function that takes two numbers and uses math.pow() and the exponentiation operator ** to raise the first number to the power of the second.
5. Describe the difference between in-place addition (+=) and standard addition (+) in Python. Provide examples to show how each one modifies or doesn't modify the original variable.
6. Explain the purpose of trigonometric functions like math.sin(), math.cos(), and math.tan() in Python's math module. When would these functions be useful in real-world applications?
7.

24: Advanced Functions

By now, you should have a solid understanding of Python functions—how to define them, pass arguments, and return values. But there's much more to functions than meets the eye. In this chapter, we will explore the more advanced aspects of functions in Python. You might want to have a cup of coffee with you…

Functions are one of the most sophisticated tools in a programmer's toolkit. They enable code reuse, promote modularity, and can simplify complex tasks into manageable components. However, to fully harness their ability, it is essential to move beyond the basics and learn some of Python's more sophisticated function techniques.

We will begin with **lambda** functions, which allow you to create small, anonymous functions quickly and efficiently. We'll then look into higher-order functions—functions that can accept other functions as arguments or return them as results. While these concepts might sound complex, they are incredibly useful and can make your code more flexible and elegant.

Next, we'll delve into the intriguing world of **closures**, which allow functions to retain access to variables in their enclosing **scope** even after that scope has completed execution. Closures are particularly useful for creating customised functions dynamically. Alongside closures, we'll explore **decorators**, the perfect feature that enables you to modify or extend the behaviour of functions in a clean and readable manner, without altering their code directly.

We'll also discuss **recursion**, a technique where a function calls itself to solve a problem. Recursion can be a beautiful and effective approach to certain types of problems, but it requires careful consideration to avoid pitfalls such as excessive memory usage. Additionally, we will cover **generators**, which provide a way to handle large datasets efficiently by generating values on the fly, conserving memory and improving performance.

Namespace and Scope

Before we dive into these advanced topics, it is crucial to understand the concepts of **scope** and **namespace**. We'll instigate the analogy function again. You're working in a large organisation where each department has its own files and records. Knowing where to find a specific document requires an understanding of which department it belongs to. Similarly, in Python, scope determines the region of your code where a particular name (such as a variable or function) is accessible, while a namespace acts as a container that maps names to objects.

Grasping the interplay between scope and namespace is fundamental as we move into advanced function techniques. These concepts determine how your functions interact with different variables, whether they are local to a function, global across the entire script, or part of Python's built-in functionality. Understanding this will help you write clearer, more predictable code and avoid common errors related to name conflicts.

Namespace

A 'namespace' is like a container that holds a collection of names, such as variable names, function names, and class names, and connects them to their corresponding objects. It helps manage the names used in a program, preventing naming conflicts and providing a clear context for each identifier.

In Python, an **identifier** is valid if it follows the rules for naming conventions in the language. Valid identifiers must start with a letter or an underscore, followed by letters, digits, or underscores.

The term 'scope' refers to the region of code where a particular identifier is recognised and can be used. Identifiers have a scope, meaning they are accessible only within the boundaries of that scope. Here's a quick overview:

- **Global namespace**: Identifiers defined at the top level of a module or script.
- **Local namespace**: Identifiers defined within a function.
- **Module namespace**: Identifiers within a module.

Combining these concepts, once an identifier is valid, it becomes accessible within specific scopes defined by 'namespaces.' The scope determines where in the code an identifier can be referenced and used. So, an identifier becomes valid when it's defined in a particular scope and accessible only within that scope unless explicitly referenced.

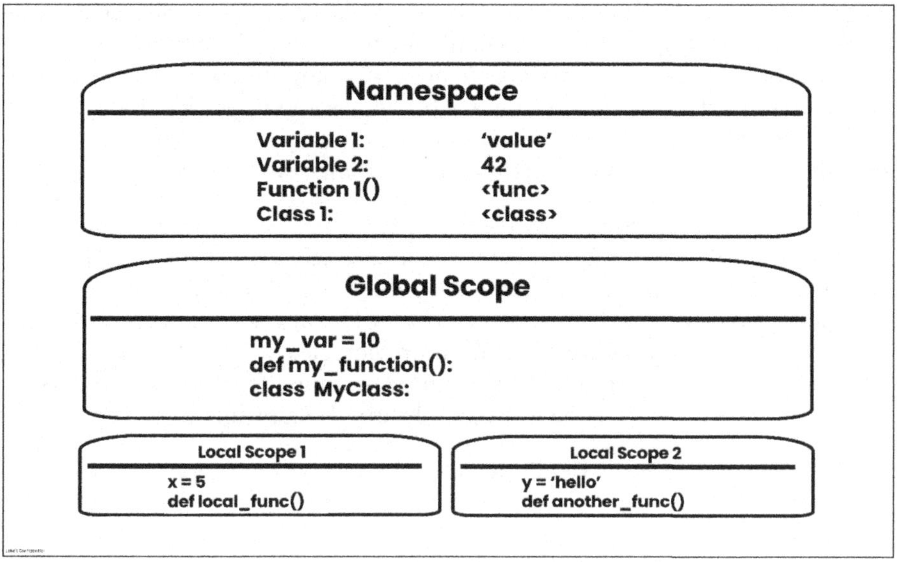

Figure 24a. Namespace, global scope and local scope.

Understanding Variable Scope

Variable scope in Python refers to the region of your code where a variable is recognised and can be accessed. Think of it as the visibility or the "lifetime" of a variable—determining where in your program you can use it and for how long it exists. Scope is crucial because it helps you manage which parts of your program can see or modify a particular variable, preventing conflicts and unintended behaviour in your code.

There are four types of scope in Python:

- local
- enclosing
- global
- built-in

The most specific scope is the **local scope,** which refers to variables defined within a function. These variables are only accessible from within that function; they live and die there. Once the function has finished executing, the local variables are discarded, and any attempt to access them outside of the function will result in an error. This makes local scope perfect for temporary variables that you don't want to affect other parts of your program.

Moving outward, we encounter the **enclosing scope**. This applies when you have nested functions—functions defined within other functions. The inner function has access to the variables of its containing function, or "enclosing" scope, but not the other way around. This allows you to encapsulate behaviour and data more tightly, providing a mechanism for inner functions to utilise the state or variables defined in their enclosing functions.

Next comes **global scope,** which encompasses variables defined at the top level of a script or module. Global variables are accessible from anywhere within the same script or module, making them useful for values that need to be shared across multiple functions or parts of your code. However, using too many global variables can lead to unpredictable code behaviour, especially in larger programs, as they can be modified from anywhere. It is often best to use global variables sparingly and thoughtfully.

Finally, we have the **built-in scope**. This is the broadest scope and includes names that Python itself has defined, like built-in functions (print, len, range, etc.) and exceptions (ValueError, TypeError, etc.). These are available everywhere in your program, regardless of what you are working on. The built-in scope is the last place Python looks when resolving a name.

Understanding variable scope is **essential** for writing clear, maintainable Python code. It helps you manage your variables wisely, ensures that they do not unintentionally interfere with each other, and makes your programs more robust and predictable.

The program below illustrates how variables defined in different scopes are accessible or inaccessible based on their scope:

```
#Filename: scope1.py
#Global variable
global_variable = "I'm a global variable!"

def example_function():
    # Local variable
    local_variable = "I'm a local variable!"

    print(global_variable)  # Accessible within the
function
    print(local_variable)   # Accessible within the
function

#Call the function
example_function()

#Try to access the local variable outside the function
try:
    print(local_variable)  # This will raise an error
except NameError as e:
    print(e)

#Access the global variable outside the function
print(global_variable)
```

Here's what's happening:

- **Global Scope**: The variable global_variable is defined in the global scope, making it accessible both outside and inside the function.
- **Local Scope**: The function example_function creates a local scope where local_variable is defined. This variable is accessible only within the function.

If you try to access local_variable outside the function, you'll get an error because it's not defined in the global scope. Accessing global_variable from within the function is perfectly fine because it's defined globally.

So, identifiers can be valid and accessible within the scope defined by 'namespaces'. Variables and other entities declared within a 'namespace' are typically accessible only within that 'namespace'.

Namespaces also ensure that identifiers within them have unique names, which helps avoid naming conflicts when different parts of a program use similar names. This is fundamental to writing effective and bug-free Python code.

The Lambda Function

A lambda function is a 'small', anonymous function defined using the lambda keyword. Unlike regular functions defined with the def keyword, lambda functions are designed for situations where you need a quick, throwaway function without the need to formally define it. They are sometimes called "inline functions" because they are typically used in a single line of code.

By "small" I mean that these functions are typically limited in size and scope—they are designed to perform simple, single-line operations. A lambda function is small in the sense that it consists of just one expression and does not contain multiple statements or complex logic. Unlike a regular function defined with **def**, which can have multiple lines of code, branching, and extensive functionality, a lambda function is meant to handle straightforward tasks that can be expressed **concisely** in one line.

It's ideal for quick, short operations like basic calculations, data transformations, or passing a simple function as an argument to another function, without the overhead of a more formal function definition.

The syntax for a lambda function is straightforward: lambda followed by a list of arguments, a colon, and an expression that the function evaluates and returns.

For example:

```
result=lambda x, y: x + y
```

takes two arguments, x and y, and returns their sum in the variable **result**. Since they are so concise, lambda functions are particularly useful when you need to pass a small function as an argument to another function, such as in sorting, filtering, or mapping operations.

lambda is used to create small, one-line anonymous functions. It is similar to defining a function with **def**, but it does not require a name.

This lambda function can be assigned to a variable or used directly as an inline function wherever a function is required.

```
#Filename: scope1b.py
#Assigning the lambda function to a variable
add = lambda x, y: x + y
# Using the function
result = add(3, 5)  # Output: 8
print(result)

# Using the lambda function directly
print((lambda x, y: x + y)(10, 20))  # Output: 30
```

This is a concise way to create functions for quick operations without the overhead of defining them explicitly. They are useful for short, throwaway functions that you don't want to define with a full **def** statement. They are commonly used with functions like **map()**, **filter()**, and **sorted()** that require a simple function as an argument.

Here's an example to illustrate how lambda functions work. Suppose we want to sort a list of tuples based on the second element in each tuple:

```
#Filename: scope2.py
#List of tuples
data = [(1, 'apple'), (3, 'banana'), (2, 'cherry')]
sorted_data = sorted(data, key=lambda x: x[1])

print(sorted_data)  # Output: [(1, 'apple'), (3,
'banana'), (2, 'cherry')]
```

In this example, sorted() is a built-in function that sorts the list. The key parameter is used to specify a function that determines the sorting order. Here, we pass a lambda function:

```
lambda x: x[1]
```

that takes each tuple x and returns its second element (x[1]). The sorted() function then uses this lambda function to sort the list by the second element of each tuple.

It' s About Closure

A closure in Python is a unique feature that allows a nested function to "remember" the environment in which it was created, even after the outer function has finished executing. Essentially, closures enable a function to capture and retain access to variables from its enclosing scope, making them available whenever the function is called, even outside their original context. This can be incredibly powerful for maintaining state and creating more dynamic, flexible code.

To create a closure, you need a few key elements: a nested function (a function defined inside another function), an enclosing function that returns the nested function, and at least one variable from the enclosing function that is used in the nested function. When the enclosing function is called, it returns the nested function, which "closes over" the variables from its outer scope, preserving their values.

Closures are useful in many situations, such as when you need to create function factories—functions that generate other functions with specific behaviour. For example, closures can help you create specialised functions that maintain internal state without relying on global variables. They are also helpful in callback functions, where the function you pass needs to remember the context or specific data that it should operate on.

Here's a simple example to illustrate how closures work:

```
#Filename: scope3.py
def multiplier(factor):
    def multiply_by(x):
        return x * factor
    return multiply_by

#Create a closure that multiplies by 2
double = multiplier(2)

#Create a closure that multiplies by 5
triple = multiplier(5)

#Use the closures
print(double(5))  # Output: 10
print(triple(5))  # Output: 25
```

Here, the multiplier function takes a parameter factor and defines a nested function, **multiply_by(x)**, that uses this parameter. When multiplier is called, it returns the multiply_by function, which remembers the value of factor at the time it was created. Thus, when double is called with factor = **2,** it always multiplies its argument by 2, while triple multiplies by 5. The nested function retains access to its enclosing scope's variables, even though multiplier has finished executing.

Closures offer a flexible way to create functions that maintain state or customise behaviour without the need for classes or global variables. They provide a lightweight approach to encapsulation, making your code more modular and reusable while avoiding the pitfalls of shared, mutable state. Understanding closures is essential for writing more sophisticated programs that can handle complex tasks elegantly.

This diagram simplifies the concept of Python closures into three key steps:

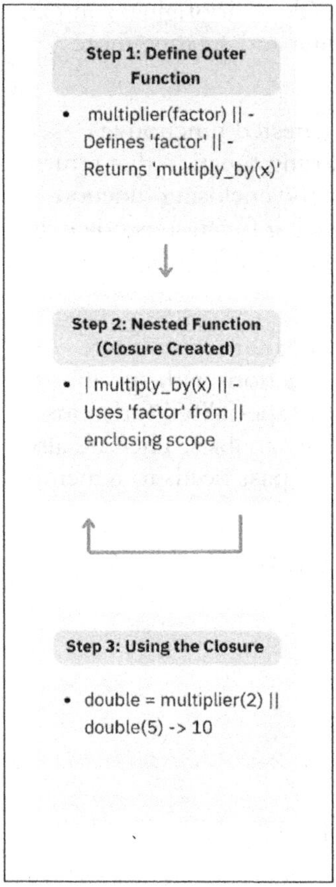

Outer Function: Shows the definition of multiplier(factor) with the variable factor = 2.

Nested Function: Depicts the function multiply_by(x) with an arrow pointing back to factor, demonstrating the retention of the outer variable.

Closure in Action: Illustrates double = multiplier(2) and the use of double(5), producing the result 10.

Figure 24b. Illustrating steps of closure.

Understanding Decorators

Decorators are a very useful tool that allows you to modify or extend the behaviour of functions or methods without altering their actual code. They provide a way to "wrap" a function in another function, enhancing or adding to its functionality in a reusable and clean manner. The most common use of decorators is to enhance or modify the behaviour of functions in a reusable way. Instead of manually modifying the code of each function that requires additional functionality, you can apply a decorator to achieve the same result with much less effort.

Decorators use a special syntax in Python: **@decorator_name**. This syntax is a shorthand that allows you to apply a decorator to a function in a clean and readable way. When Python encounters the @decorator_name line just before a function definition, it passes that function to the decorator and replaces it with the new, decorated function returned by the decorator.

Here is an example showing how a decorator works:

```
#Filename: scope4.py
def my_decorator(func):
    def wrapper():
        print("Something is happening before the
function is called.")
        func()
        print("Something is happening after the
function is called.")
    return wrapper

@my_decorator
def say_hello():
    print("Hello!")

say_hello()
```

In this example, my_decorator is a decorator function that takes another function (func) as its argument. It defines a nested wrapper function, which adds some behaviour before and after calling func. The decorator returns this wrapper function, which effectively replaces **say_hello** with a new function that calls say_hello and adds extra steps around it. When say_hello() is called, it now prints additional messages before and after the original "Hello!" message.

Don't under estimate what can be achieved using decorators.

Logging and Debugging: Decorators can be used to log function calls, input parameters, and output values, which is helpful for debugging or monitoring purposes.

The following program uses the **log_decorator** to demonstrate how it works. In this program, we'll create a couple of simple functions: one that adds two numbers and another that multiplies them. We'll apply the log_decorator to these functions to log their calls, arguments, and return values.

```
#Filename: scope5.py
#Define the log decorator
def log_decorator(func):
    def wrapper(*args, **kwargs):
        # Log the function call details
        print(f"Calling function '{func.__name__}' with
arguments {args} and {kwargs}")
```

```
        # Call the original function
        result = func(*args, **kwargs)

        # Log the return value of the function
        print(f"Function '{func.__name__}' returned
{result}")

        return result
    return wrapper

#Apply the decorator to a function that adds two
numbers
@log_decorator
def add(a, b):
    return a + b

#Apply the decorator to a function that multiplies two
numbers
@log_decorator
def multiply(a, b):
    return a * b

#Main program to call the decorated functions
if __name__ == "__main__":
    # Call the add function
    sum_result = add(5, 3)

    # Call the multiply function
    product_result = multiply(4, 2)
```

When you run the program, you should see output similar to the following:

```
Calling function 'add' with arguments (5, 3) and {}
Function 'add' returned 8
Calling function 'multiply' with arguments (4, 2) and
{}
Function 'multiply' returned 8
```

This demonstrates how the **log_decorator** works by providing detailed logs of each function call, including the function name, arguments, and returned values. The program shows how decorators can be used to add useful functionality, such as logging, without modifying the original function code.

Timing and Performance Measurement: Decorators can be used to measure the time a function takes to execute, which is helpful for performance optimisation.

Here's a practical example that uses the **timer_decorator** to measure the execution time of functions. We'll create a couple of functions: one that calculates the sum of the first n natural numbers and another that finds the factorial of a number. By applying the timer_decorator, we can measure how long each function takes to execute.

```
#Filename: scope6.py
import time

#Define the timer decorator
def timer_decorator(func):
    def wrapper(*args, **kwargs):
        #Record the start time
        start_time = time.time()

        #Call the original function
        result = func(*args, **kwargs)

        #Record the end time
        end_time = time.time()

        #Calculate and print the execution time
        print(f"Execution time for {func.__name__}:
{end_time - start_time:.6f} seconds")

        return result
    return wrapper

#Apply the timer decorator to a function that
calculates the sum of first n natural numbers
@timer_decorator
def calculate_sum(n):
    return sum(range(1, n + 1))

#Apply the timer decorator to a function that
calculates the factorial of a number
@timer_decorator
def factorial(n):
    if n == 0 or n == 1:
        return 1
    else:
        result = 1
        for i in range(2, n + 1):
            result *= i
        return result

#Main program to call the decorated functions
if __name__ == "__main__":
    # Call the calculate_sum function
    print("Sum of first 1000000 numbers:", calculate_
sum(1000000))

    #Call the factorial function
    print("Factorial of 10:", factorial(10))
```

Decorator Definition: The timer_decorator is defined to take a function func as its argument and return a wrapper function. The wrapper function records the time before and after calling the original function (func), calculates the difference, and prints the execution time.

Applying the Decorator: The @timer_decorator syntax is used to apply the decorator to the calculate_sum and factorial functions. This means every time these functions are called, their execution times will be measured and printed.

Main Program: The if __name__ == "__main__": block is the entry point of the script. It calls the decorated functions (calculate_sum and factorial) with example arguments, triggering the decorator's timing behaviour.

When you run the program, you should see output similar to the following:

```
Execution time for calculate_sum: 0.012345 seconds
Sum of first 1000000 numbers: 500000500000
Execution time for factorial: 0.000001 seconds
Factorial of 10: 3628800
```

This output shows how the timer_decorator works by providing detailed logs of each function's execution time. The program shows how decorators can be used to measure performance, and the understanding code behaviour.

How Decorators Differ from Regular Functions

The key difference between decorators and regular functions is that decorators are specifically designed to modify the behaviour of other functions, rather than performing standalone tasks. They allow you to apply reusable patterns of functionality across multiple functions, keeping your code **DRY** (Don't Repeat Yourself) and modular.

Here's a brief description of a few of the more popular decorators available.

@property

Turns a method into a property that can be accessed like an attribute. It allows for controlled access to instance variables by defining **getter**, **setter**, and **deleter** methods. Used: To create read-only or computed properties in a class.

@staticmethod

Defines a method that does not depend on the instance or class state. It does not receive the **self** or **cls** parameter. In Python, getter, setter, and deleter methods are used to control access to attributes (variables) of a class. These methods are commonly associated with properties, allowing you to encapsulate data while still providing a way to retrieve, modify, or delete that data. Used: To create utility functions that logically belong to a class but do not need access to any class or instance-specific data.**@classmethod**

Defines a method that is bound to the class and not the instance. It receives the class (cls) as its first argument, allowing access to class-level attributes and methods. Used: To create factory methods or modify class-level data.

@functools.wraps

A helper decorator to maintain the original function's metadata (name, docstring, etc.) when writing custom decorators. It preserves the decorated function's identity for debugging and introspection. Used: To write custom decorators that do not obscure the identity of the original function.

@dataclass

Automatically generates special methods like __init__(), __repr__(), and __eq__() for user-defined classes, making it easier to create classes that primarily store data. Used: To simplify the creation of classes that are mainly used to store state and have little to no behaviour.

@abstractmethod

Marks a method in an abstract base class as abstract, requiring all subclasses to implement it. Used in combination with the ABC class from the **abc** module. Used: To enforce a contract in subclasses, ensuring that certain methods must be implemented.

@contextmanager

A decorator provided by the **contextlib** module to define a context manager using a generator function. It handles the setup and tear down process automatically. Used: To simplify resource management, such as opening and closing files or network connections.

Understanding Recursion

Recursion is where a function calls itself to solve smaller instances of the same problem. A recursive function is one that solves a complex problem by breaking it down into simpler, more manageable sub-problems of the same type. This process continues until it reaches a base case, a condition that stops the recursion.

Recursion is really useful for problems that have a natural hierarchical structure or can be divided into similar subproblems, such as searching or traversing data structures like trees and graphs, calculating factorials, or generating Fibonacci numbers. It allows for elegant and compact code, making it easier to read and understand in many cases.

A recursive function typically has two main parts:

- **Base Case:** The base case is a condition that stops the recursion. It provides a simple solution for the smallest or simplest instance of the problem. Without a base case, the function would call itself indefinitely, leading to infinite recursion and eventually causing a stack overflow or memory error.

- **Recursive Case**: The recursive case is where the function calls itself with a smaller or simpler version of the original problem. Each recursive call progresses towards the base case, ensuring that the recursion will eventually terminate.

Here's a common demonstration used to illustrate how recursion works, calculating the factorial of a number.

O babysit the keidsA factorial of a number **n** (denoted as **n!**) is the product of all positive integers from 1 to n. For example, 5! = 5 * 4 * 3 * 2 * 1 = 120. The factorial of 0 (0!) is defined as 1.

```
#Filename: scope7.py
def factorial(n):
    # Base case: factorial of 0 or 1 is 1
    if n == 0 or n == 1:
        return 1
    # Recursive case: n * factorial of (n-1)
    else:
        return n * factorial(n - 1)

# Example usage
print(factorial(5))  # Output: 120
```

Let's take a closer look at how the recursive calls are made in the factorial function when n = 5:

```
factorial(5) calls factorial(4)
factorial(4) calls factorial(3)
factorial(3) calls factorial(2)
factorial(2) calls factorial(1)
factorial(1) returns 1 (base case)
```

Then, the results are multiplied back as the recursive calls "unwind":

```
factorial(2) returns 2 * 1 = 2
factorial(3) returns 3 * 2 = 6
factorial(4) returns 4 * 6 = 24
factorial(5) returns 5 * 24 = 120
```

Thus, the final result is 120.

Recursion is ideal for solving complex problems that can be broken down into similar sub-problems, such as finding all permutations of a string or solving the Tower of Hanoi problem. On the pro side, recursion can provide a more elegant solution by eliminating the need for explicit loops and maintaining the logical flow of the problem. On the con side deep recursion, this can lead to high memory consumption and eventually a stack overflow if the recursion depth exceeds the recursion limit, which is effectively amount of memory available for use.

Generator Power

Generators provide a memory-efficient way of generating data on the fly, producing values one at a time and only when required, rather than computing and storing them all upfront. This makes them perfect for working with large datasets or infinite sequences, where storing all the values in memory would be impractical or impossible.

Generators are defined using functions and the **yield** keyword. Unlike regular functions that use return to output a value and terminate, a generator function uses yield to produce a value and pause its execution. The function's state, including local variables and the point of execution, is saved between yields, allowing it to resume where it left off the next time it is called.

When you **call** a generator function, it does not execute the function immediately. Instead, it returns a **generator** object, which is an iterator. You can iterate over this generator object to retrieve values one by one. Each time you iterate, the generator runs until it encounters a yield statement, produces the value, and then pauses, preserving its state. The next time you ask for a value, the generator resumes from where it left off.

This behaviour allows generators to be **incredibly** efficient, especially for tasks where you don't need all the values at once. Generators use less memory because they only produce values as needed, rather than all at once, making them particularly useful for handling large datasets or streams of data.

The following code provides a simple generator function that generates the first 'n' squares of natural numbers:

```
#Filename: scope8.py
def generate_squares(n):
    for i in range(1, n + 1):
        yield i * i

# Using the generator
squares = generate_squares(5)
for square in squares:
    print(square)
```

In this example, the generate_squares function is a generator that yields the square of each number from 1 to n. When you call **generate_squares(5)**, it returns a generator object. As you iterate over this object, the function runs and yields each square value one by one. This approach is much more memory-efficient than creating a list of all squares upfront, especially if **n** is a large number.

Generators are often used to read large files line by line. Instead of loading the entire file into memory, a generator can read and yield each line, reducing memory usage. Other common usages include handling streaming data, such as data from a network connection, logs, or any other data source where the full data set is not available upfront or is too large to fit in memory. They can also be used to create data processing pipelines where data flows from one generator to another, allowing for efficient, step-by-step processing.

Python also supports generator expressions, which provide a compact syntax to create generators, similar to list comprehensions but with round brackets.

LEGB Rule

We've seen that Python goes about its resolution of variable scope in a specific fashion. This is often referred to as the LEGB Rule. When you reference a variable, the interpreter searches for that variable in a specific sequence of scopes: Local, Enclosing, Global, and Built-in. This is what the acronym LEGB stands for.

To recap, when Python encounters a variable name, it follows the LEGB order to resolve it:

- **Local**: Checks if the variable is in the current function or method.
- **Enclosing**: If not found, checks any enclosing functions (in the case of nested functions).
- **Global**: If not found, checks the global scope of the module or script.
- **Built-in:** If not found, checks the built-in scope.

Here's an example that shows LEGB in operation:

```
#Filename: scope9.py
x = 50  # Global scope

def outer_function():
    x = 40  # Enclosing scope

    def inner_function():
        x = 30  # Local scope
        print(x)
# Looks for 'x' in Local scope first

    inner_function()
outer_function()  # Output: 30
```

In this example:

- Python first looks for x in the Local scope of inner_function.
- If it doesn't find it there, it would look in the Enclosing scope (outer_function).
- If still not found, it would look in the Global scope.
- Finally, if it is not found in any of the above, Python would look in the Built-in scope.

Shadowing

Sometimes, a variable in a local scope can **shadow** a variable in an outer scope, meaning that the local variable takes precedence within its scope. This can lead to confusion and errors if not carefully managed.

When this happens, the local variable shadows or overrides the outer variable, meaning that the local variable is used instead of the outer one. While shadowing is not inherently a bug, it can lead to confusion, unexpected behaviour, and hard-to-find bugs, especially in larger or more complex codebases.

```
#Filename: scope10.py
x = 5  # Global variable

def shadow_example():
    x = 10  # Local variable, shadows the global x
    print(x)  # Outputs: 10

shadow_example()
print(x)  # Outputs: 5, global x is unchanged
```

In this example, the **x** inside the shadow_example function shadows the global x, meaning the global x is not affected by changes within the function.

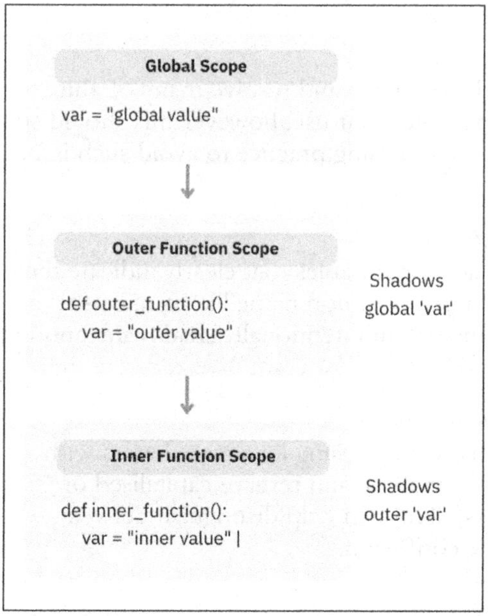

Global Scope: The variable var is defined globally with the value "**global value**".

Outer Function Scope: Inside outer_function, **var** is redefined as "**outer value**", shadowing the global var within the function.

Inner Function Scope: Inside inner_function, **var** is redefined again as "**inner value**", shadowing the var from outer_function within its own scope.

24c. Illustrating Shadowing.

Shadowing Can Be Problematic for several reasons:

- **Accidental Overwrites:** Shadowing can lead to accidental overwrites of important data. For example, if you use a variable name in a local scope that is already defined globally, you might unintentionally change or hide the global value.
- **Confusion and Readability:** Shadowing makes it harder to read and understand code, as it can be unclear which variable is being used. This can cause confusion for anyone reading or maintaining the code.
- **Unintended Behaviour:** When a built-in function or global variable is shadowed, it can lead to unintended behaviour. For instance, if you accidentally name a variable list or str, you override the built-in Python types, which can lead to errors.

While shadowing is not necessarily a bug, it can lead to confusion and unintended behaviour if not managed carefully. By using clear, descriptive names, following naming conventions, avoiding built-in names, and using Linters, you can minimise the risk of variable shadowing and write more readable, maintainable Python code.

Avoid Shadowing

Modules called **Linters** can be used to manage and resolve many of the issues in shadowing. Chapter 26 looks into their use, however this should still not distract from establish a good programming practice to avoid such issues at source.

Use Descriptive Variable Names

Choose meaningful, descriptive names for variables that clearly indicate their purpose. For example, instead of using a common name like **x**, use **user_age** or **total_sum**. This reduces the chance of unintentionally shadowing another variable.

Follow Naming Conventions

Follow Python's naming conventions, such as using lowercase letters with underscores for variable names (my_variable), and reserve capitalised or *camelCase* names for classes (MyClass). This can help distinguish between different kinds of names and reduce confusion.

Use Namespaces Carefully

When using modules or libraries, refer to them explicitly with their namespace to avoid conflicts. For example, instead of using from math import *, use import math and refer to functions as math.sqrt().

Avoid Using Built-in Names

Do not use names that match Python's built-in functions or types (list, dict, str, id, type, etc.). This avoids shadowing built-in objects and keeps your code more predictable.

Use Global Keyword Cautiously

If you intend to modify a global variable inside a function, use the global keyword to declare that you are referring to the global variable. However, use this sparingly, as it can make the code harder to follow.

Limit the Use of Global Variables

Minimise the use of global variables as much as possible. Instead, prefer passing variables as function arguments and returning results from functions. This keeps your code cleaner and reduces the chances of accidental shadowing.

Use Linters or Code Analysis Tools

Use tools like **pylint**, **flake8**, or integrated development environments (IDEs) with built-in Linters to detect shadowing and other potential issues. These tools can provide warnings or errors when variable shadowing is detected.

Built-in Linter Support

Thonny, has basic linting capabilities built-in and can highlight syntax errors, undefined variables, and other issues.

Thonny performs linting automatically, but you can adjust the level of checks under :

```
Tools > Options > General > Editor.
```

Shadowing Example and Resolution

Here's a short program that demonstrates several instances of variable shadowing. In this example, we have variables with the same name used in different scopes, which can cause confusion and unintended behaviour.

```
#Filename: scope11.py
# Global variable
value = 10

def calculate(value):
    # Local variable shadows the global variable
    result = value * 2
    return result

def outer_function():
    value = 5  # Local variable shadows the global
variable
    print(f"Outer function value: {value}")
```

```
        def inner_function():
            value = 3  # Local variable shadows 'value' in
the outer function
            print(f"Inner function value: {value}")

        inner_function()
        print(f"Outer function value after inner: {value}")

# Main program
print(f"Global value: {value}")
print(f"Calculated value: {calculate(7)}")
outer_function()
print(f"Global value after functions: {value}")
```

Output:

```
Global value: 10
Calculated value: 14
Outer function value: 5
Inner function value: 3
Outer function value after inner: 5
Global value after functions: 10
```

In this example the global variable **value** is shadowed by the local variable value in **calculate**. Inside **outer_function**, a new local value is defined, shadowing the global variable. **inner_function** defines another local value, shadowing the value from **outer_function**.

This makes the code harder to read and understand because the same name (**value**) is used in multiple places with different meanings. Here's the same program rewritten to avoid shadowing by using more descriptive variable names:

```
#Filename: scope12.py
# Global variable
global_value = 10

def calculate(input_value):
    # Use descriptive names to avoid shadowing
    calculated_result = input_value * 2
    return calculated_result

def outer_function():
    outer_value = 5  # Clear and descriptive name
    print(f"Outer function value: {outer_value}")

    def inner_function():
        inner_value = 3  # Clear and descriptive name
        print(f"Inner function value: {inner_value}")

    inner_function()
    print(f"Outer function value after inner: {outer_
value}")

# Main program
print(f"Global value: {global_value}")
print(f"Calculated value: {calculate(7)}")
outer_function()
print(f"Global value after functions: {global_value}")
```

Output:

```
Global value: 10
Calculated value: 14
Outer function value: 5
Inner function value: 3
Outer function value after inner: 5
Global value after functions: 10
```

Here the same program avoids shadowing because:

Global variable: Renamed value to global_value to make it clear and avoid confusion.

Function parameters and local variables: Used more descriptive names like input_value, calculated_result, outer_value, and inner_value to make each variable's purpose clear.

Readability and Clarity: The revised program is easier to understand because each variable has a unique name that clearly indicates its role, avoiding any shadowing or ambiguity.

Questions

1. Explain the purpose of Python's lambda functions. When might you use a lambda function instead of a standard function defined with def?
2. What is a higher-order function in Python? Provide an example where a higher-order function can be useful.
3. Describe closures in Python. How does a closure allow a nested function to retain access to variables from an enclosing function?
4. Write a simple closure in Python that multiplies a number by a specific factor. Explain how it retains access to the factor after the outer function has completed execution.
5. What is a decorator, and how does it differ from a regular function? How can decorators help in logging function calls?
6. In the context of decorators, what does @functools.wraps do, and why is it important?
7. Give an example of how the LEGB (Local, Enclosing, Global, Built-in) rule applies to variable scope in Python. How does Python search for variable names in different scopes?
8. What are the four types of variable scope in Python, and what is the difference between each one?

9. Explain the concept of shadowing in Python. Why can shadowing be problematic, and how can it be avoided?

10. Write a recursive function to calculate the sum of the first **n** natural numbers. Explain the role of the base and recursive cases in your function.

11. What is a generator, and how does it differ from a regular function that returns a list? Why are generators more memory efficient?

12. Provide an example where a generator could be used to read a large file line-by-line. Why is this approach preferred overloading the entire file into memory at once?

13. What does the global keyword do, and in what scenarios should it be used cautiously?

14. How does Python's @staticmethod decorator differ from @classmethod, and when might you use each in a class?

15. Discuss one practical use of a decorator for timing a function's execution in Python. Provide an example that uses a decorator to measure how long it takes to run a specific function.

25: Matrix

The whole idea of matrices has fascinated me for years, even though I'm no mathematician. The development of matrix theory was driven by the need to solve various problems in mathematics and beyond. One of the main reasons for diving into matrix theory was to find efficient ways to tackle systems of linear equations. A linear equation is a mathematical statement that shows a straight-line relationship between variables and are fundamental in solving problems involving proportionality, rates, and trends. Matrices quickly became the go-to tool for describing and performing linear transformations in geometry. (A linear transformation is a mathematical function that maps one vector space to another (or itself) while preserving vector addition and scalar multiplication.) They offer a handy way to understand rotations, translations, scaling, and other transformations of geometric shapes.

Matrices are absolutely essential in physics and engineering when it comes to representing and solving problems involving multiple variables. For instance, in quantum mechanics, matrices (or operators) are used to describe quantum states and how they evolve over time. In engineering, matrices help model and analyse systems like electrical circuits, mechanical structures, and control systems.

Matrix theory also played a key role in the development of abstract algebra and the theory of vector spaces. By studying matrices, mathematicians gained deeper insights into linear mappings between vector spaces, leading to a richer understanding of linear algebra and its many applications.

In statistics and data analysis, matrices are invaluable for organising and manipulating data. Techniques like principal component analysis (PCA) heavily rely on matrix computations to reduce and uncover meaningful patterns in large data-sets.

Now, I know for many of us, this might seem like abstract theory, but matrices are a part of computing that captured my imagination. They were brought to us by incredible minds like Arthur Cayley, James Joseph Sylvester, Carl Friedrich Gauss, and William Rowan Hamilton.

Alright, enough history—let's get back to programming.

All that said, I'll just be skirting over matrix in this chapter because they are brilliantly handled by the NumPy module that we'll come across shortly.

At its core, a matrix is just a two-dimensional array of numbers, symbols, or expressions arranged neatly in rows and columns. Each element in a matrix is uniquely identified by its row and column indices. The size of a matrix is determined by how many rows and columns it has, with '

A matrix can have any number of **rows** and **columns,** and the number of rows doesn't have to match the number of columns. For example, if you have a 4x3 matrix, that simply means it has four rows and three columns, like this:

Now, there's often some confusion between arrays and matrices, so let's clear that up. In general, an **array** is a collection of elements stored in contiguous memory locations, and it can have one or more dimensions. Arrays can be one-dimensional (like vectors), two-dimensional (like matrices), or even multi-dimensional. So, while every **matrix** is an **array**, not every array is a matrix.

For example, a 1D array (or vector) in Python might look like this:

```
[5, 10, 15, 20, 25]
```

basically a list.

Index	0	1	2	3	4
Value	5	10	15	20	25

A 2D array (or matrix) could be represented as a list of lists:

```
[[1, 2, 3], [4, 5, 6]].
```

We'll explore a couple of different ways to perform the four basic mathematical operations on matrices: addition, multiplication, subtraction, and division. We'll also touch on scalar operations and techniques to make sure matrix sizes are compatible. We'll revisit these examples when we get to the NumPy chapter, but for now, these programs will help you understand how the basic processes work.

There are two standard approaches to performing matrix operations without relying on a specialist module like NumPy: using nested lists and iterating through the rows and columns. As with many concepts in computing, understanding the basic math behind what you're trying to achieve is really important, and that's exactly what we'll focus on here.

Creating a Matrix Using a Nested List

You can easily represent a matrix in Python as a list of lists, where each inner list stands for a row of the matrix. For example:

```
#Filename: matrix1.py
#Create a 3x3 matrix using nested lists
matrix = [
    [1, 2, 3],
    [4, 5, 6],
    [7, 8, 9]
]
```

In this example, matrix is a list containing three inner lists, each representing a row of the matrix. The elements within these lists are the values of the matrix.

You could also write it more compactly as:

```
matrix = [[1, 2, 3], [4, 5, 6], [7, 8, 9]]
```

Adding Matrices Together

Matrix addition is straightforward when using nested loops. As I mentioned before, you just need to iterate over each element in the matrices and perform the addition "manually." By "manually," I mean you add each corresponding element from the two matrices and store the result in the same position of a third matrix. Here's how you can do it:

```
#Filename: matrix2.py
#Two matrices to add
matrix1 = [
    [1, 2, 3],
    [4, 5, 6],
    [7, 8, 9]
]

matrix2 = [
    [9, 8, 7],
    [6, 5, 4],
    [3, 2, 1]
]
#Create a matrix to store the result
```

```
result = []

#Iterate over each element. Perform element-wise
addition.
for i in range(len(matrix1)):
    row = []
    for j in range(len(matrix1[0])):
        element_sum = matrix1[i][j] + matrix2[i][j]
        row.append(element_sum)
    result.append(row)
#Print the result
for row in result:
    print(row)
```

In this example, we start with **matrix1** and **matrix2,** and we store their sum in a new matrix called **result**. We use **nested loops** to iterate over each element in the matrices and perform the addition. The result is then stored in the result matrix, which we then display. This approach is a great way to get hands-on with how matrix operations work under the hood.

Subtraction

Subtraction of matrices works similarly to addition but with a minus sign instead of a plus. You can subtract two matrices by iterating over their elements with nested loops, just like we did for addition.

```
#Filename: matrix3.py
#Two matrices to subtract
matrix1 = [
    [1, 2, 3],
    [4, 5, 6],
    [7, 8, 9]
]

matrix2 = [
    [9, 8, 7],
    [6, 5, 4],
    [3, 2, 1]
]

#Create a matrix to store the result
result = []

#Iterate over the matrices and perform element-wise
subtraction
for i in range(len(matrix1)):
    row = []
    for j in range(len(matrix1[0])):
        element_diff = matrix1[i][j] - matrix2[i][j]
        row.append(element_diff)
    result.append(row)

#Print the result
for row in result:
    print(row)
```

In this example, matrix1 and matrix2 are given, and we create a new matrix result to store their difference. The nested loops iterate over each element in the matrices, performing the subtraction, which is then stored in result and printed out.

As with addition, it's important to make sure the matrices have the same dimensions before subtracting them. If the number of rows and columns doesn't match, you won't be able to perform element-wise subtraction.

Onwards and Upwards

We'll leave matrices here for now given that we've looked at some basic functions that you can use longhand here to undertake other tasks. As mentioned, will revisit them in the NumPy chapter.

Questions

1. Explain the main motivation behind the development of matrix theory. How did matrices help in solving systems of linear equations and geometric transformations?
2. Describe two practical applications of matrices in fields like physics or engineering. How are matrices useful in these areas?
3. What is the difference between an array and a matrix? Can every array be considered a matrix?
4. How would you represent a matrix as a list of lists in Python? Write a Python code snippet to create a 2x3 matrix using nested lists.
5. If you have a 3x3 matrix [[1, 2, 3], [4, 5, 6], [7, 8, 9]], how would you access the element in the second row and third column?
6. What conditions must be met to add or subtract two matrices? Why is it important to check matrix dimensions before performing these operations?
7. Explain how the element-wise addition of two matrices works using nested loops. What does this approach involve?
8. Given two matrices matrix1 and matrix2 of the same size, explain how you would write code to check if they can be added or subtracted.
9. Why might using a library like NumPy be more efficient for matrix operations compared to using lists and loops in Python?
10. Provide an example where matrix subtraction might be useful in a real-world application. What kind of problem could matrix subtraction help solve?

11. What would happen if you tried to add two matrices with different dimensions? Write code to raise an error if two matrices are not of compatible sizes for addition.

12. How can matrix operations like rotation, scaling, and translation help in computer graphics? Provide an example of one such transformation.

13. How would you explain the importance of understanding basic matrix operations, even if you plan to use a specialised library like NumPy?

26: Linters

Linters might sound like something you'd find in a home renovation project, but in the Python world, they're invaluable tools that help keep your code clean and tidy! Think of a Linter as a proofreader for your code—one that doesn't just check for spelling mistakes but ensures your grammar, style, and even logic are on point.

You may recall *waaaay-back* towards the start of this book, that Thonny did this, even though I didn't explicitly mention it at that point. Thonny has a form of Linter built into its structure and this can certainly help when debugging code. Especially when chasing down issues such as **shadowing**.

But Linters don't just stop at basic errors. They also help enforce coding standards. A Linter can be **customised** as well, so if you prefer to use spaces rather than tabs to indent your code, you can manage that. Linters check that your code follows the standard Python conventions, making it easier to read and maintain.

Who Decides?

Python's programming style is shaped by the Python Enhancement Proposals (PEPs), with PEP 8 being the go-to guide for coding style and conventions. PEPs are like blueprints, offering ideas or changes to Python's language, libraries, or standards. They're created for the Python community and are maintained by the Python Software Foundation (PSF), the Steering Council, and the core development team.

Guido van Rossum (Python's Creator): In the early days, Guido van Rossum, often called the "Benevolent Dictator For Life" (BDFL), made most of the big decisions about Python, including its style. He had the final say on PEPs until stepping down in 2018.

- Python Steering Council: After Guido stepped down, a Steering Council was elected to take over decision-making for Python's evolution, including style guidelines. The council, made up of five members elected by core developers, reviews and decides the fate of PEPs.

- Core Development Team: A team of core developers actively contributes to Python's development. They help write, discuss, and review PEPs, working with the community to keep Python consistent, practical, and user-friendly.

- The Python Community: Everyone in the Python community can get involved by proposing PEPs, including changes to coding style. These proposals are discussed in forums, mailing lists, and at events like PyCon. Community feedback is essential in shaping Python's future.

In short, Python's style is a group effort, starting with PEPs and involving the whole community.Style Documentation

How Is Programming Style Decided?

PEPs are the backbone of how Python's style and features are shaped. They're formal documents that suggest new features or tweaks to Python's language and libraries. When it comes to style, here are two key PEPs:

PEP 8: This is the ultimate style guide for Python code. It lays out rules for things like indentation, naming conventions, and formatting to keep Python code clean and consistent.

PEP 257: This one focuses on docstrings (discussed later), giving guidelines for writing clear and consistent documentation in your code.

How a PEP Comes to Life

- **Drafting and Submission:** Someone spots an area for improvement or a new feature idea and drafts a PEP. They add examples, details, and the reasoning behind the idea, then share it with the Python community.

- **Community Feedback:** The draft gets discussed on platforms like the python-dev mailing list, the Python GitHub repository, or forums. Python users, core developers, and others jump in to give feedback, and the PEP gets revised based on these discussions.

- **Review by the Steering Council:** Once the PEP is polished, the Python Steering Council reviews it. They look at how well it fits with Python's goals, philosophy, and its impact on users.

- **Approval or Rejection:** The council votes. If the PEP is approved, it becomes part of Python's standards (like PEP 8). If rejected, it's archived but could be revisited later.
- **Implementation:** Approved PEPs are put into action by the core development team. The community is notified through updates, documentation, and releases. Tools like pylint and flake8 help developers follow these new guidelines with automated style checks.

PEPs are how Python evolves, with the entire process being a mix of collaboration, feedback, and careful review to keep the language and its style top-notch.

Popular Linters

There are several popular Linters available for Python, each with its unique features and focus. There are no definitive ones that you should use. I suggest you try them for yourself and decide what works best for you.

Pylint: Popular not least because its range of checks. Pylint checks for errors, enforces coding standards, and can even offers suggestions for code improvements.

Autopep8: Can report or automatically format Python code to conform to the PEP 8 style guide.

Flake8: A fast and lightweight Linter that combines the functionality of several Linters.

Black: A "code formatter" that focuses on automatic code formatting according to PEP 8 standards, ensuring consistency across code-bases.

Mypy: Specifically used for type checking in Python, great for ensuring type safety.

Pyflakes: A very lightweight tool focused purely on error detection, without concern for style.

Each Linter has its strengths, so your choice may depend on whether you want a thorough check, a lightweight tool, or something in between. That said the two most popular Linters are: Pylint and Flake8.

Given that Linters tend to do slightly different things then it's natural to use a couple together. Ultimately that selection is down to you. I would suggest playing with a few and deciding what one suits you best. For what it's worth I use Pylint and then it's a toss-up between autopep8 and **Black**. Black normally wins out. That said if I'm writing code for my own benefit then I tend not to use any… (Blasphemy.)

- **Pylint** is primarily used for detecting code quality issues and provides suggestions that you can use to manually correct your code. It also rates you code out of ten! (Not always a good thing.) These changes are listed on the screen for you to make, as you wish.
- **autopep8** will automatically format your Python code to conform to the PEP 8 style guide. It can fix various style issues, like indentation, line length, and whitespace. You can also get it to write the corrected code back to your file or a different file. It will also process a batch of files. In truth most changes are reasonably limited.
- **Black** does what it does. No prompts, nothing, it changes your code formatting to the one it says is best. From a readability point of view it does a good job. Its goal is to make code formatting a non-issue, freeing developers from spending time debating style decisions. Black is often referred to as an "opinionated" formatter because it follows strict formatting guidelines, but many developers appreciate the consistency it provides.
- The are pros and cons of using multiple Linters together, but in my mind the pros outweigh the cons.

Or you may find you need:

```
sudo apt install python3-autopep8
sudo apt install python3-pylint
```

You can install these two Linters into your current environment using:

```
pip install autopep8
pip install pylint
```

Pylint

Pylint will check your code without executing it. It scans your scripts, looking for syntax errors, coding standards violations, and potential bugs. Pylint even provides suggestions for improving your code. Thus the benefits are:

- You'll catch mistakes early
- Learn good coding practices
- Create a higher standard of code
- Make your development process more efficient.

Pylint comes as a module, which is not in the Python Standard Library, so must be installed manually. You can do this into your virtual environment using:

```
pip install pylint
```

Once installed, you can run Pylint from the command line by typing 'pylint' followed by the name of your file:

```
pylint your_script.py
```

Pylint will analyse the code in the specified file and provide a detailed report with error messages, warnings, and suggestions for improvement, including issues related to code style, unused variables, potential bugs and the like.

The tool also provides a numeric score based on the overall quality of the code, allowing you to track improvements over time. (It's pretty finky - sometimes my code, which (mostly) works, will draw a score of 0.0/10 because it's not formatted quiet right. Anything above a 7/10 is awesome!) A typical output from some code might look like this:

I threw the following, 'erroneous' program into it:

```
#Filename: linter1.py
#A simple Python script with several style issues.

def greet(name): print("Hello, " + name + "!"); return
name.upper()


def add_numbers(a, b):
      sum = a + b
      if sum > 10:
            print("Sum is greater than 10")
      else:
            print("Sum is 10 or less")
            return sum


name = input("Enter your name: ")
greeting = greet(name)
print(greeting)

result = add_numbers(5, 6)
print("Result:", result)
```

It returned the following commentary (here's the first few lines only):

```
************* Module pylint1
pylint_test.py:8:15: C0303: Trailing whitespace (trailing-
whitespace)
pylint_test.py:9:16: C0303: Trailing whitespace (trailing-
whitespace)
pylint_test.py:18:15: C0303: Trailing whitespace (trailing-
whitespace)
pylint_test.py:1:0: C0114: Missing module docstring (missing-
pylint_test.py:20:0: C0103: Constant name "result" doesn't
conform to UPPER_CASE naming style (invalid-name)

-------------------------------------------------------------
     Your code has been rated at 1.43/10)
```

As you can see I didn't fare to well in the scoring stakes. Looking at the last line:

20:0 is line 20 of the code, starting at the beginning. It is error code C0103, It is telling me that 'result' should be 'RESULT' as it's a constant (which it isn't to my mind!).

Unfortunately (maybe not…) Pylint itself does not automatically fix any errors it finds, which can be a godsend as it isn't always right. It has a regular habit of stating that variables are constants even when they are in fact, variable. You can actually turn off reporting of various comments back using some additional switches that are available in the module.

Many of the errors pertain to insertion of **docstrings** which we'll look at in Chapter 44. I've not been doing them herein otherwise programs would be excessively long, and loe the code within the script. Docstrings have the ability to provide full descriptions and argument data used to define what a function can do. Using these it is possible to create a full document of the functionality of functions using them. You can think of them as super comments.

As with most modules you can find out more by typing:

```
pylint --help
```

in the terminal. To get a list of error numbers used:

```
pylint - -list-msgs
```

Autopep8 Linter

This Linter is easy to use! It's designed to automatically format Python code to conform to the PEP 8 style guide. autopep8 will scan through a Python program and report on non-conformance issues. This includes, improper indentation, missing spaces, inconsistent line breaks, and other stylistic errors. You can have these issues reported back to you or you can have them automatically update your file.

As mentioned I like to do the latter and then run Pylint for other issues that I then change manually if I want to include them. You can also use the Linter with IDEs to a varying degree, and I'll outline these on upcoming chapters on Thonny and Geany.

autopep8 also offers flexibility with its formatting capabilities. For instance, you can configure autopep8 to ignore specific errors or warnings. Of course this defeats the object of the Linter in the first place!

If you are writing longer programs then you may wish to use these Linters as you develop you code. Linters are not just about the end result. Evaluating as you progress can save much time at the end of the journey. At the very least make you aware of any issues and provide your coding style as you progress.

Format a Python File

To see what autopep8 dislikes about your code (normally, quite a lot) you can run it from the terminal thus:

```
autopep8  your_script.py
```

Using the following script previous file 'pylint_test.py' the result will displayed on the screen. You can retry this to the file using:

```
autopep8 --in-place pylint_test.py
```

This command will automatically fix all PEP 8 violations in the file. We'll maybe. By default, autopep8 only makes safe changes that do not alter the logic of the code. For more extensive formatting, you can use the --aggressive flag:

```
autopep8 --in-place --aggressive pylint_test.py
```

The autopep8'ed file was:

```
#Filename: linter2.py
#A simple Python script with several style and linting
issues.

def greet(name): print("Hello, " + name + "!"); return
name.upper()
def add_numbers(a, b):
      sum = a + b
      if sum > 10:
          print("Sum is greater than 10")
      else:
           print("Sum is 10 or less")
      return sum


   name = input("Enter your name: ")
   greeting = greet(name)
   print(greeting)

   result = add_numbers(5, 6)
   print("Result:", result)
```

So only some minor changes. And pylint was just as damming on it!

If we now pass the file through 'black' we get:

```
#Filename: linter2.py.py
#A Python script with several style and linting issues.

def greet(name):
    print("Hello, " + name + "!")
```

```
    return name.upper()


def add_numbers(a, b):
    sum = a + b
    if sum > 10:
        print("Sum is greater than 10")
    else:
        print("Sum is 10 or less")
    return sum

name = input("Enter your name: ")
greeting = greet(name)
print(greeting)

result = add_numbers(5, 6)
print("Result:", result)
```

Which is much nicer, and the type of formatting I like.

Black Linter

Black is a very opinionated code formatter for Python that aims to simplify the development process by standardising code style. In fact, it's so opinionated, it just makes the changes without any form of discussion! However, it does format it to a predefined set of rules. This means we no longer need to worry about details such as spacing, line breaks, or alignment — Black takes care of that. The idea being to remove the need for discussions around style, offering a strict, consistent, and uniform structure to Python code. I'm all for it.

Black Switches

Black provides several command-line switches and options to customise its behaviour. You can view the available options and help menu by running:

```
black --help
```

This will show a list of switches and options that can be used with Black. Some of the commonly used switches include:

Okay, I was fibbing. You can actually see what Black will change if you use: the - -diff switch:

```
black -diff <filename>
```

In the context of Black, the term "diff" refers to the difference between the original code and the code after Black's formatting rules are applied. Black analyses your code and displays the lines that it would change, highlighting what would be added, removed, or modified.

- Lines to be removed: These are marked with a - (ie, a hyphen).
- Lines or be added: These are marked with a +.

By using --diff, you can make an informed decision about whether to proceed with applying the formatting or not, giving you more control over the process.

That said, my mind is that you just go with it, so you have consistency.

You can use Black via the Python Shell. Ensure that you have Black installed. Load your program into the file editor or save you file. You will need to know the PATH to the directory the file is saved in, if it isn't the current directory.

This will then return with a message, hopefully successful, and the file in the window will have been reformatted as will the file itself.

Tip I have a 'Text Editor' file open on my desktop when programming. This contains one-liners like the black 'path'. So I just copy and paste. This will include other items I forget such as virtual environment commands and so forth.

Questions

1. What is a Linter in Python, and why is it important?
2. What are Python Enhancement Proposals (PEPs), and which is the most influential one?
3. What is Pylint, and how does it help Python developers?
4. What is the difference between Autopep8 and Black in terms of code formatting?
5. Can you use multiple Linters together in Python?
6. How does **Black** differ from other Linters in Python.

27: Geany IDE

If you've double-clicked on a **.py** file, you might have stumbled upon 'Geany Programmer's Edition.' It's one of the options on the Raspberry Pi's Programming Menu. If you haven't tried it yet, go ahead and select it from the Programming menu. Once you're in, use the File menu in Geany to open a file. For example, in the image below, I've opened up Dict1.py.

I have to admit, I'm a fan of **Geany**, definitely more so than Thonny. Now, don't get me wrong—Thonny is a **fantastic** learning tool, especially for beginners getting started with Python. It lets you focus on learning the language without getting bogged down by a complicated interface. It also introduces many concepts that are common to all IDEs, so you'll be able to switch between tools easily as you grow. To my mind there's no better tool to learn with.

But when it comes to day-to-day coding, I prefer Geany. It's not the only alternative, of course. There's Visual Studio (lots of programmers use this especially for collaborative projects), Python's own IDE (IDLE), and others. I like to use Geany alongside an open Terminal window set to the virtual environment I'm using. In addition an open File Explorer window. Do as the image over (**Figure 27a**) shows I have three windows open on my screen. In this respect Geany ticks all the boxes for me—it's clear, simple, and clean. Plus, it supports many other programming languages, not just Python. So, if you ever decide to pick up Java or something else. Geany will also provide you with a programming temples for you to use if you show wish. Any which way Geany's got you covered.

Figure 27b overleaf shows that Geany has three main windows, similar to Thonny. Like Thonny you can add or take away from these by the View menu. The main window is where you write your code.

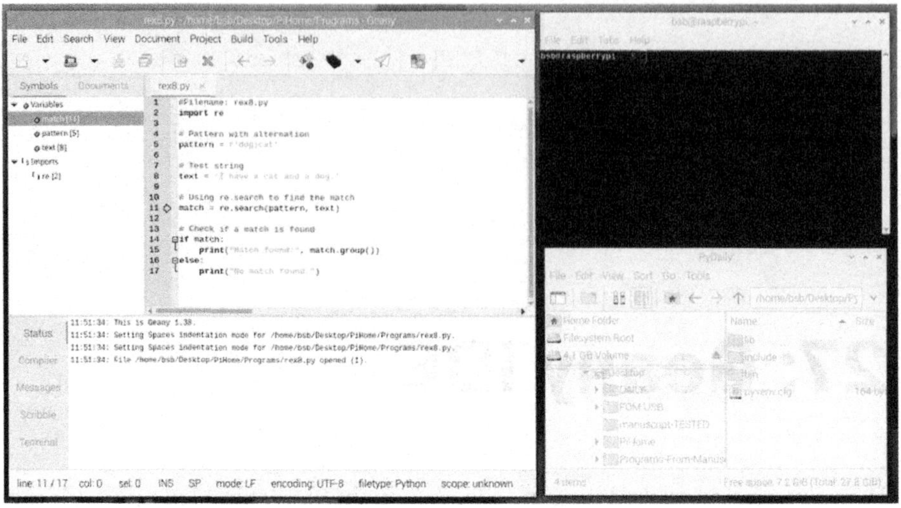

Figure 27a. My preferred programming arrangement using Geany, a Terminal and a File Explorer window.

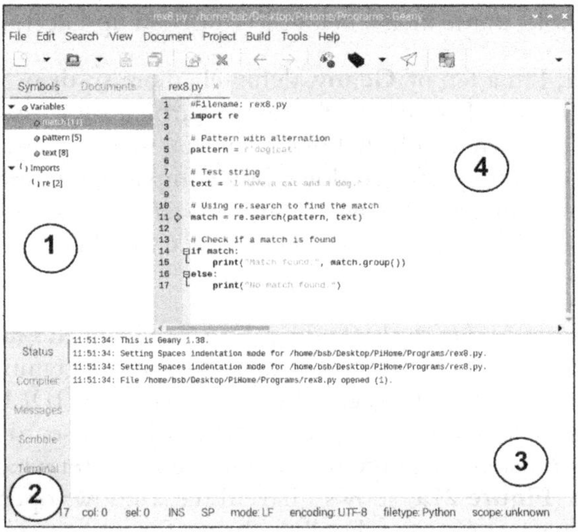

Figure 27b. Geany with some Python code open.

Window 1 has a couple of options. **Symbols** which is in focus in this image and Documents beside it. Documents is fairly self explanatory. It helps you navigate and understand your code's structure with ease.

Symbols provides a list of all items defined or used in the program. In the example above this includes variable and imports. Clicking on a symbol will take you straight to its declaration in the code editor, which is great for jumping between function definitions and calls or quickly reviewing the structure of your classes. You can also collapse and expand sections within the Symbols window to focus on specific parts of your code, making it easier to manage complex projects.

What's more, the **Symbols** window updates dynamically as you code. If you add a new function or modify a class, the window refreshes to reflect these changes, ensuring that you always have an up-to-date overview of your project. This real-time updating feature helps you maintain a clear and organised view of your code-base.

Window 2 has five tabs vertical on the left you can click on and whatever you choose is reflected in **Window 3**.

Status: This shows the current operational state of the application and what Geany is doing or has done with. It.

Compiler: Though Python is an interpreted language, this section may show the results of Python code execution, including any checks for syntax errors.

Messages: This section shows various notifications from the Python interpreter or environment. You might see syntax errors, exceptions, run-time errors, or warnings here, which help identify issues in your code. It's essential for debugging and code correction.

Scribble: This could be a free-form note-taking or scratch area for jotting down ideas, writing temporary Python snippets, or even pseudo code. It's a handy place for brainstorming or drafting quick solutions without affecting your main project files. Its essentially a text editor. Very useful.

Terminal: Exactly as per used everywhere else. A CLI that accesses Bash. You can execute commands in here as you can anywhere else. You can also turn it into a Python Interactive Shell by typing

```
python3
```

into it.

Finally **Window 4** is your program editor. Same as. Geany automatically highlights Python syntax, making your code easier to read. It also suggests code **completions** as you type, which helps you code faster and with fewer errors. Another feature I love is code folding. This lets you hide (or "fold up") functions, for example, by clicking on the small '-' sign to the left of the code. This collapses the code section within the large brace. Pressing the '+' sign that appears afterwards reopens the code. If your code isn't working as expected and you're confident your functions are fine, you can fold them out of the way and focus on the other bits.

Main top menu: The menu options here are very similar to Thonny. Build is probably the least common and is worth a look.

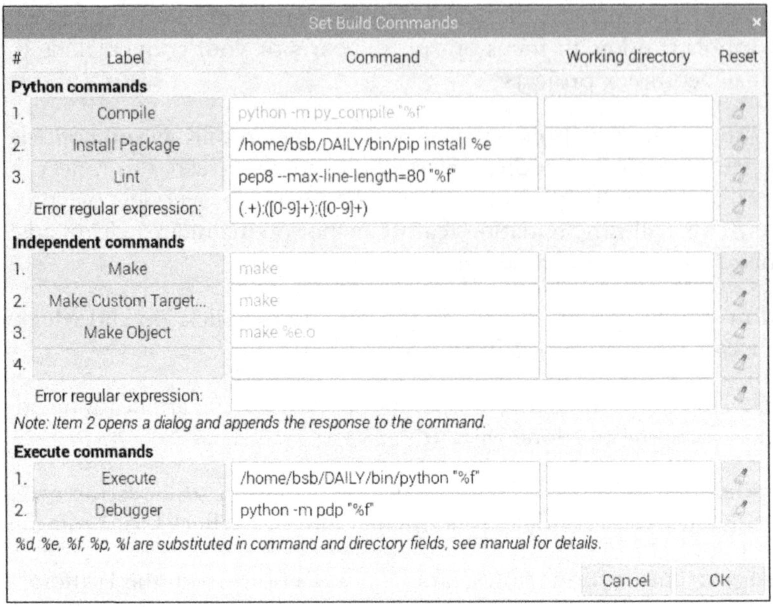

Figure 27c. Set Build Commands Window.

The **Build** menu in Geany is where you manage compiling, running, setting virtual environments and debugging your code. Or more correctly its what you use to determine what runs when you select options in the main window.

As you can see from Figure 27c there are three main sections, 'Python commands', Independent commands', and 'Execute commands'.

Here's a breakdown of the key options in the Build menu, note that some of these work together with others in the Build window. So bear with me.

Compile

Syntax Check: As Python is a semi interpreted language there is no actual compiling other than to bytecode, but what this window does is to ensure that your program is correct and ready to run. This won't run the program, but it will catch syntax errors, which is similar to compiling in languages like C. This checking is done by a Linter (pep8) which we discussed earlier. This particular window is set to:

```
python -m py_compile "%f"
```

The -m flag tells Python to run a module as a script.

The **py_compile module** is part of Python's standard library and is used to compile **.py** files into **.pyc** (Python bytecode) files.

%f is a Geany placeholder that represents the full path of the currently opened file. When you execute this command, Geany substitutes "%f" with the path to the file you're working on.

If there's a syntax error, it will return an error message and point to where the issue lies. This helps catch issues like missing colons, incorrect indentation, or misspelled keywords before running the script.

Execute

Jumping down to the 'Execute commands' section next to Execute is the path to the virtual environment to be used. You'll need to create the virtual environment first using venv, for example. Here the 'DAILY' virtual environment is in use. Below this is the debugger that is to be used.

Popping back up to 'Install Package' in 'Python commands' you can see the directory that 'pip' is used to install packages - here the 'DAILY' virtual environment.

The 'Independent commands' section define how Geany executes the file using the make utility. This creates file called a '**Makefile**'. These are used to define complex build processes, especially when you're working with large projects that have many dependencies or need different build steps. The make command helps automate this by managing which files need to be recompiled.

Debugging with PDB

Debugging code in Python using Geany is straightforward and just requires a little setup. PDB, which stands for **Python Debugger**, is an interactive debugging tool that's built right into Python. As in Thonny, you can set one or multiple breakpoints in your program and then step through the code, checking variable values as the program hits each breakpoint.

Since PDB is part of the Python Standard Library, there's no need to install anything extra. However, you do need to import it when you want to use it and prepare your program by inserting a breakpoint at the point where you want to start debugging. You can do this by adding the line:

```
import pdb; pdb.set_trace()
```

You'll need to insert this line, in your program, wherever you want to set a breakpoint. (And don't forget to save your code before running it for the first time.)

Once your program is ready, head over to:

```
Build -> Set Build Commands
```

In the dialog that pops up, modify the "Execute" command to use PDB. Change it to:

```
python -m pdb "%f"
```

Click OK to save the changes.

Now, to run your script, just press <F5> or go to **Build -> Execute** in Geany. This will start your script and pause execution at the point where you've added:

```
pdb.set_trace()
```

This will open the PDB prompt right in Geany's message window.

At the PDB prompt, you can use various commands to debug your program. For instance, 'n' (next) runs the next line of code, 'c' (continue) resumes execution until the next breakpoint, 's' (step) steps into a function call, and 'q' (quit) stops the debugger and ends the program.

Here's a simple example of a script you might use:

```
#Filename: pdb1.py
def add(a, b):
    return a + b

def main():
    import pdb; pdb.set_trace()
    x = 3
    y = 4
    result = add(x, y)
    print(result)

if __name__ == "__main__":
    main()
```

Running this script in Geany with the **custom** command will start the debugger at the pdb.set_trace() line, letting you step through the code and debug efficiently. When you run this command in Geany, it essentially translates to:

```
python /path/to/your/script.py
```

where */path/to/your/script.py* is the actual path to the script you're working on.

By modifying this command to **python -m pdb "%f"**, you're telling Python to run the PDB debugger on the currently open script in Geany. This allows you to start debugging the script from the beginning or from wherever you've inserted a **pdb.set_trace()** breakpoint.

To print out variable values in PDB, use the **p** command ('p' which stands for "print" and nothing else). For example:

```
p x
```

will print the contents of the variable x. Just make sure the line that initialises x has been executed so that the value exists.

Once PDB is active, you're in an interactive debugging session where you can use various commands to inspect and control the execution of your program. Here are some basic PDB commands:

- n (next): Move to the next line of code.
- c (continue): Continue execution until the next breakpoint.
- q (quit): Quit the debugger and stop the program.
- p (print): Print the value of a variable. For example: p variable_name.
- l (list): List the source code around the current line.

As you step through your code, use these commands to inspect variables and understand how your program is flowing. This will help you identify where things might be going wrong.

If you spot any issues, you can go ahead and modify your code directly in Geany. After making changes, save your file and re-run the script to debug the new version.

Additional Useful PDB Commands

- pp (pretty-print): Like p, but it prints data structures in a more readable format.
- whatis var: Shows the type of the variable var.
- dir(): Lists the attributes of the current scope or an object.
- vars(): Returns the __dict__ attribute for the current scope, containing variable names and their values.
- a or args: Prints the argument list of the current function.
- run: Restarts the Python program being debugged.

Debugging with Geany and PDB is a breeze once you get the hang of it.

Virtual Environments

Setting up a virtual environment in Geany is straightforward, especially if you're already comfortable using the Terminal. We covered this in detail back in Chapter 08, but here's a quick recap. You activate your virtual environment in the Terminal, just as you normally would.

To get Geany to use your virtual environment, you'll need to tweak its build commands. Here's how to do it:

1. **Open Geany** and navigate to **Build > Set Build Commands**.
2. In the "**Python commands**" section, you'll need to update the compile and execute commands to use the Python interpreter from your virtual environment. For example, if your virtual environment is called **DAILY**, you can set the compile command to:

```
DAILY/bin/python -m py_compile "%f"
```

And for the execute command, use:

```
DAILY/bin/python "%f"
```

If your virtual environment isn't named DAILY, just replace DAILY with the name of your actual environment.

To make sure everything is working as it should, create a simple Python script—let's call it **interpreterpath.py**—that prints the path to the Python interpreter and a little message. Run this script using the build command you just configured in Geany. If everything is set up correctly, the output should show the path to the Python interpreter within your virtual environment, along with your message. You could use:

```
#Filename: pdb2.py
import sys

# Print the path to the Python interpreter
print(f"Python interpreter path: {sys.executable}")

# Print a custom message
print("Everything is set up and working correctly!")
```

Following these steps ensures that your Python projects in Geany are using isolated environments, making it easier to manage dependencies and avoid conflicts between projects.

One thing to note: when using Geany, you'll need to reset the Build Command settings if you switch to a different virtual environment. It's a bit of extra work, but it keeps everything running smoothly.

The next chapter shows how you can switch virtual environments in Geany using a projects approach.

Geany Plugins

Geany supports a wide range of plugins that extend its functionality, or perhaps more correctly, provides you with some additional visual aids, such as being able to see a directory tree structure. Others, such as Lipsum insert *Lorem Ipsum* holding text which seems a bit out of place for Python programming.

If you have plug-ins installed you can enable then you go to:

```
Tools>>Plugin Manager
```

Check the box next to the plugins you want to enable.

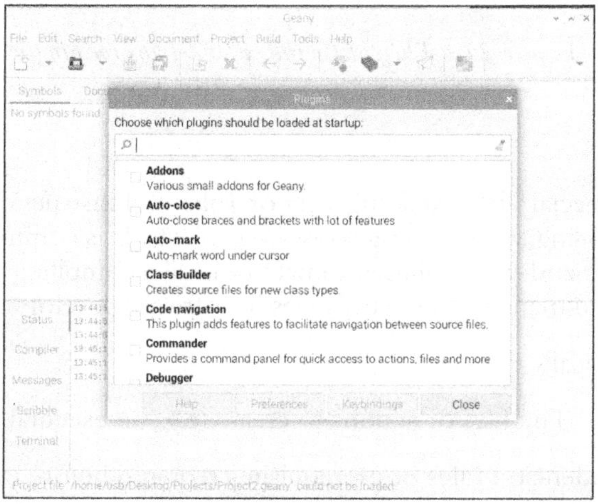

Figure 27d. Geany Plugins available for selection.

Here's an overview of some useful plugins you can install and use with Geany:

Geany-Plugins Collection

The Geany-Plugins collection is a bundle of several useful plugins that are maintained as part of the Geany ecosystem. You can install it easily and it includes many helpful tools. You can install them using:

```
sudo apt install geany-plugins
```

This package includes various plugins, all of which are pretty easy to use but useful Nevertheless, such as spell check, tree manager and split window.

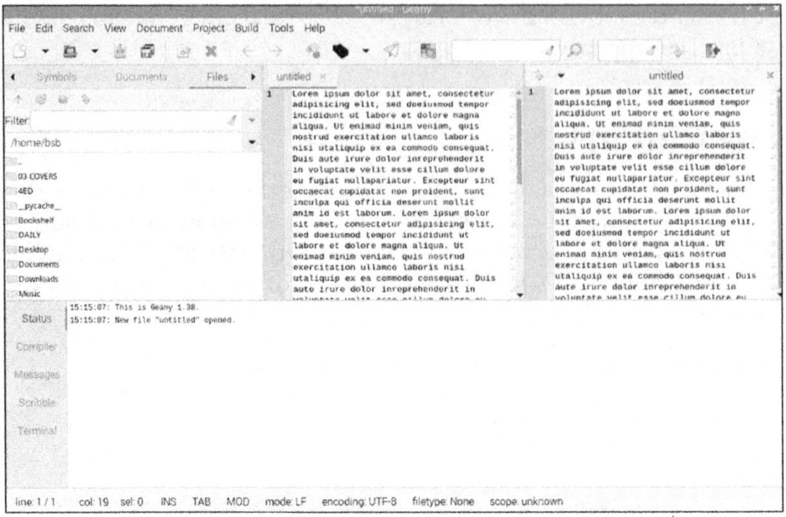

Figure 27e. The split window and Lipsum plugin

Makefile

Makefile is a special file containing a set of rules and instructions for building, compiling, or managing software projects. It is commonly used with the make command-line tool to automate tasks like compiling source code, linking files, and managing dependencies in software development.

A Makefile typically defines:

- Targets: The files or actions to create (e.g., an executable program).
- Dependencies: Files or prerequisites required before target is built.
- Commands: The shell commands to execute to build the target.

Makefiles are covered towards the end of the book.

28: Enviro Switching

It's really easy to create multiple virtual environments and switch between them whenever you need to. While you can do this from Thonny, it's actually simpler to handle it right from the Terminal. Here's how you can use the **venv** module in the Terminal to set things up:

```
python3 -m venv VE1
python3 -m venv VE2
```

Now, we've got two virtual environments: **VE1** and **VE2**.

To activate the first environment, just run:

```
source VE1/bin/activate
```

(Note this assumes that your **Terminal** is open in the VE1 directory.) Once VE1 is activated, you can install the packages you need for your first project. For example:

```
pip install pandas
```

When you're done, deactivate VE1 by typing:

```
deactivate
```

Next, to work in the second environment, activate VE2 with:

```
source VE2/bin/activate
```

Then, install the packages for your second project. For example:

```
pip install matplotlib
```

And when you're finished, deactivate VE2 with:

```
deactivate
```

Now you've got **two** separate virtual environments, each with its own set of packages and dependencies. Anytime you want to work on one of your projects, just activate the corresponding environment, and you're good to go! This way, you can avoid any messy conflicts between projects and make sure each one has exactly the right setup.

To keep track of everything that is any particular environment you can create a **requirements.txt** file. This file will save all the environment's package information, making it easy to recreate the setup later.

```
pip freeze > requirements.txt
```

This command channels the list of installed packages into a requirements.txt file, which will be saved in your virtual environment's main directory. The output might look something like this:

```
numpy==2.0.0
pandas==2.2.0
python-dateutil==2.9.0.post.0
pytz==2024.1
six==1.16.0
tzdata==2024.1
```

This requirements.txt file is very handy—it's like a shopping list for your project's dependencies. You can share it with others to help them recreate the exact environment you're working in. To set up a new environment from a requirements.txt file, you just need to run these commands:

```
python3 -m venv myenv
source myenv/bin/activate
pip install -r requirements.txt
```

The requirements.txt file is your project's way of saying, "Here's everything you need to run smoothly." Each line in the file typically includes the name of a library and its version number, ensuring that everyone uses the same versions. For example:

```
requests==2.24.0
numpy==1.21.2
```

This is crucial because it prevents surprises when someone else tries to run your code with different library versions. By specifying versions, you're making sure your code behaves exactly as expected.

Your Project's Best Friend

The requirements.txt file can be your projects best friend.

- **Consistency**: It ensures that your project's environment is the same for everyone, making collaboration easier.

- **Easy Replication:** If someone else needs to run your project, they can easily recreate your environment with a single command.
- **Version Control:** Specifying version numbers avoids issues that can arise from unexpected updates or changes in libraries.
- **Convenience:** The pip install -r requirements.txt command sets up all the needed libraries in one go—no need to manually install each one.
- **Virtual Environment Friendly:** It works seamlessly with virtual environments, keeping your project's dependencies isolated and organised.

Tips for Using requirements.txt

- **Version Specifiers:** You can use wildcard to allow a range of versions, like requests>=2.20.0,<3.0.0, which means any version from 2.20.0 up to, but not including, 3.0.0.
- **Comments Welcome:** Feel free to add comments in your requirements.txt file to explain why specific versions are used, or create a separate info.txt file for detailed notes.
- **Extras:** If your project has optional features that need extra dependencies, you can define them as extras. For example, requests[security] will install additional dependencies needed for security features.
- **Freezing:** You can freeze your current environment's dependencies into a requirements.txt file by using the **pip freeze** command.
- **Upgrade Strategies:** When upgrading dependencies, you might choose between using **pip install --upgrade** or updating the version directly in requirements.txt. Both have their uses depending on the context of your project.

Think of the requirements.txt file as your project's guidebook. It makes sure everyone is on the same page, using the right tools, and heading in the same direction.

- **Dealing with Extras:** If your project has optional features or additional libraries for different use cases, you can specify them using square brackets in your requirements.txt. For example, matplotlib[PDF] could install extra dependencies needed for PDF support in Matplotlib.
- **Keep It Tidy:** Group your dependencies logically, use comments for clarity, and consider sorting them alphabetically for easy scanning.

- **pipenv Integration:** If you're using **pipenv** for virtual environments, you can generate a requirements.txt file from your pipfile with:

```
pipenv lock -r > requirements.txt
```

It's like getting a snapshot of your pipenv environment.

- **Version Specifiers Demystified:** Understanding version specifiers like ==, >=, and < is key. They define the range of acceptable versions. For instance, requests>=2.26.0 means any version 2.26.0 or higher.

Remember, your requirements.txt file is like your project's travel itinerary, ensuring a smooth journey for anyone who joins in.

Pipenv

Pipenv is a tool for managing project dependencies and virtual environments. It combines the functionality of pip (for installing packages) and virtualenv (for isolating environments) into one streamlined workflow. With Pipenv, you can:

- Automatically create and manage virtual environments for your projects.
- Install and track dependencies using a Pipfile (instead of requirements.txt).
- Lock exact dependency versions in a Pipfile.lock to ensure reproducibility.

You can use simple commands like **pipenv install**, **pipenv shell**, and **pipenv run** for dependency management and running scripts. Pipenv is designed to make Python dependency management easier, more reliable, and more organised.

To Set Up and Use a New Project

```
mkdir my_project              # Create new destination
cd my_project                 # Navigate to the directory
pip install pipenv            # Install Pipenv
pipenv install requests       # Activate environment &
                             #install package
pipenv install black --dev    # Install development
                               #package
pipenv shell                  # Activate the environment
python                        # Start Python interpreter
```

Example Pipfile

After installing requests and black, your Pipfile will look like this:

```
[[source]]
url = "https://pypi.org/simple"
verify_ssl = true
name = "pypi"

[dev-packages]
black = "*"

[packages]
requests = "*"

[requires]
python_version = "3.10"
```

When This Pipfile is in your project directory, running **pipenv install** will:

- Create a virtual environment using Python 3.10.
- Install requests and black (latest versions).
- Maintain dependency tracking in Pipfile.lock.

The Pipfile is neither a script nor typical output. It is a configuration file used by Pipenv to manage your project's dependencies and environment settings. Pipenv uses this file to set up and maintain your virtual environment.

To Remove a Package

```
pipenv uninstall requests
```

Environmental Variable

Python makes it easy to access and work with environment variables—those system-specific variables that store all sorts of useful information like configuration settings, paths, or credentials. These environment variables aren't usually saved as part of your Python code or project files; instead, they're managed at the system level.

For example, if you've got an environment variable called MY_VAR, here's how you can grab its value:

```
import os
my_var = os.environ.get('MY_VAR')
print(MY_VAR)
```

But here's the thing: environment variables don't stick around once your program stops running. They're not saved or preserved between executions—they're just temporary values that are set and managed outside of your Python code, usually via the command line, system settings, or OS-specific scripts.

So, while you can save and manage your virtual environments using tools like **venv** and keep track of your package requirements in a requirements.txt file, environment variables are a bit different. They live at the system level and are accessed or tweaked using the os module, but they're not generally something you save within your project to be reused later.

As you might know, when you're using Thonny, you can easily spot which version of Python you're using by checking the Shell window or glancing at the bottom right-hand corner of the screen.

Folders

Earlier, I mentioned different locations to store your virtual environments. There's no one-size-fits-all rule here—it really depends on your workflow and how you like to keep things organised. That said, here are a few commonly used approaches:

Project-Specific Folders

This method involves keeping each project's dependencies isolated within its own folder. It makes it crystal clear which environment belongs to which project. For example, if you're working on an Astronomy project, you might create a folder called **Astronomy** in your **Documents** folder and place the virtual environment there. The downside? It can lead to a bit of clutter if you have lots of projects.

Centralised Directory

Another approach is to create a centralised directory where all your virtual environments live. You could put this on your desktop or in a neatly named folder. This method makes your environment easy to manage and back up, and it keeps your home directory or project folders less cluttered. The only catch is that it's less intuitive if you've got a lot of projects—you'll need to remember which environment belongs to which project.

Cloud-Based or Version-Controlled Directories

This can be handy for shared or collaborative environments, especially if you're working with a team. Some services even allow version control of environments. However, this approach can be a bit more complex to set up and might depend on external services. I wouldn't recommend diving into this method until you've gained more experience.

My Preference:

Personally, I'm a fan of the centralised approach because it's simple and keeps everything organised. Many developers prefer this method, too. It keeps your home directory tidy and works really well with tools like **virtualenvwrapper**. This tool is fantastic for managing virtual environments and is highly recommended.

So, after proving a few tools to assist you in your management of virtual environments, I'm now going to go through Pythons very only management system. No the past few chapters were **not wasted** as its important to understand how you can do these things for yourself. Now you do...

The WORKON_HOME **environment variable** is used by the 'virtualenvwrapper' tool, which provides a set of shell scripts to manage multiple virtual environments more conveniently.

When you set the WORKON_HOME environment variable, you specify the directory where 'virtualenvwrapper' should create and store all your virtual environments. This makes it easier to manage and locate them.

The following process will ensure that these utilities are available every time you want to create and use a virtual environment.

First install the two files virtualenv and virtualenvwrapper. These should go into the system Python. Install them from the Terminal thus:

```
sudo apt-get install virtualenv
sudo apt-get install virtualenvwrapper
```

.bashrc

You will need to edit your Raspberry Pi configuration file, which is called **.bashrc** Note the 'dot' at the front of the file means it is not visible in normal listings.

You can do this in any text editor, I use Geany. Open a new document and then load the file. This is by going to your **user home directory**, clicking the 'Show Hidden Files' box and then locating the .bashrc file.

The user home directory is:

```
/home/pi
```

If you have changed you user-name then substitute if for Pi. For example, my user-name is 'BSB', so my home directory is:

```
/home/bsb
```

NOTE: **Always be cautious** when editing .bashrc. A mistake in this file can lead to issues with your shell environment. If you encounter problems, you can restore the original .bashrc file by removing or correcting the lines you added. Better still create a backup copy first.

Add the following lines to very end of the Raspberry Pi shell configuration file .bashrc:

```
#Filename: bashrc
#.bashrc additions
#Set the location where virtual environments are stored
export WORKON_HOME=$HOME/.virtualenvs

#Ensure the directory exists
mkdir -p $WORKON_HOME

#Source the virtualenvwrapper.sh script
export VIRTUALENVWRAPPER_PYTHON=$(which python3)
source /usr/share/virtualenvwrapper/virtualenvwrapper.
sh
```

Double check and then save. Now reboot your Raspberry Pi. At this point you may see output showing that various directories are being created.

Now **all your** virtual environments will be created in a directory called '.virtualenvs'. As this directory begins with a 'dot' it will be invisible which makes it 'safe'.

To create a new virtual environment called 'testenv', at the CLI type:

```
mkvirtualenv testenv
```

Within a few ticks the prompt will return, and you'll notice that before the prompt you now have **(testenv)** confirming that the virtual environment has not only been created but also activated!

If you'd like to look at the **.virtualenvs** folder then type the following into the address bar of a file explorer window:

```
/home/pi/.virtualvens
```

Or you can type:

```
echo $WORKON_HOME
```

In a Terminal window to see the directory.

Replace 'pi' with your user directory if it is different. You can see the scripts in the directory that can be used, along with the folders of any virtual environments you have created.

Commands Available

The virtualenvwrapper tool provides these options:

```
mkvirtualenv <env_name>
```

Creates a new virtual environment with the specified name and automatically activates it.

```
workon <env_name>
```

Activates the specified virtual environment, allowing you to work within it.

```
deactivate
```

Deactivates the current virtual environment, returning to the system's default Python environment.

```
lsvirtualenv
```

Lists all virtual environments available in the WORKON_HOME directory.

```
rmvirtualenv <env_name>
```

Deletes the specified virtual environment.

```
setvirtualenvproject <env_name> <project_path>
```

Sets a project path for the specified virtual environment, allowing you to automatically navigate to the project directory when activating the environment.

```
cdvirtualenv
```

Changes the working directory to the project path associated with the currently activated virtual environment.

```
mkproject <project_name>
```

Creates a new virtual environment and sets up a project directory for the specified project name.

The usefulness of these commands should be obvious at a single glance.

Geany Virtual Environment Switching

Having introduced Geany in the last chapter the process of switching environments looked at first sight to be somewhat daunting. It isn't and it's easy to do just that. In fact, once your set-up toy can do with a click of a button. You do this by using project-specific **build** commands'

In the previous chapter we saw that using the Build menu we can fill out some command windows to get where this is and how it gets executed, and even what Linter to use. But to use and change different virtual environments we don't need to edit this all the time. In fact these setting are the system default settings, the ones that are 'set' when you first open Geany.

is an excellent way to manage different virtual environments in Geany, for multiple Python projects without having to manually switch the build settings every time. Here's how you do it.

First create the directories for the virtual environments. In this case I have placed 'Project1' and 'Project2' inside a Projects directory on the Desktop.

```
python3 -m venv /path/to/your/project1
python3 -m venv /path/to/your/project2
```

Do this for as many projects as you need.

In Geany select **Project>New** and enter the project name and specify the project's base directory (where your virtual environment reside).

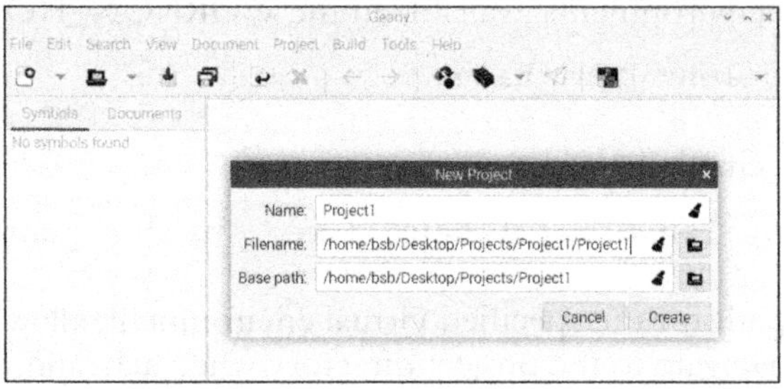

Figure 28a. Setting up a Project for easy switching.

Here you can see that we set the 'Name' field to the name of the project folder. In this case 'Project 1'. Next in the 'Base path' filed we set to the **full** path to the Project. 'Filename' should be then set to the same directory and it will then create a file called 'Project1.geany' when saved.

Now if you look inside the Project1 virtual environment directory it will look a bit like this:

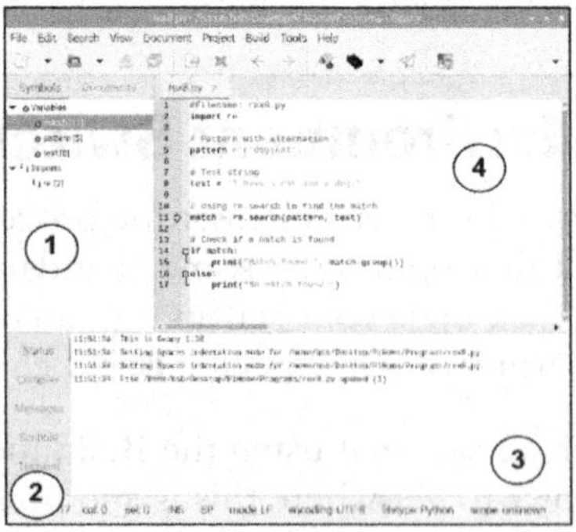

Figure 28b. Project1 virtual environment directory. The .geany file takes care of everything for you.

This contains one extra file you won't have at the moment. Let's create it - 'main.py':

```
#Filename: main.py
#Project1
import sys
print(f"Running {sys.argv[0]} in Project1")
```

Press F5 to execute this program. The output should look as below.

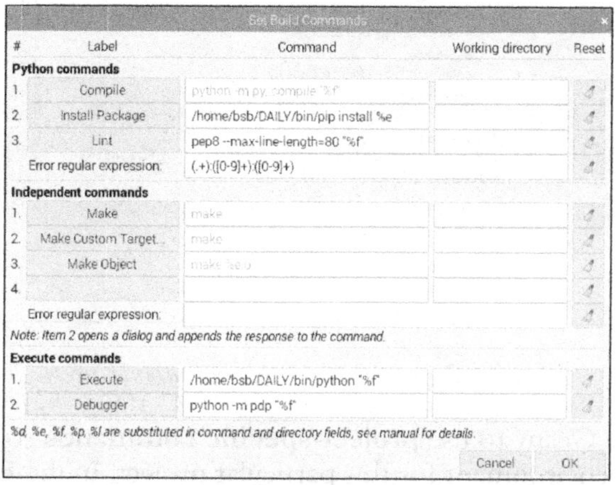

Figure 28c. Output from running 'main.py' in Project1.

You can do the same again to test that Project2 is set up correctly.

The .geany File

The **.geany** is a file, not a folder. It is the project file that Geany creates to store the configuration and settings specific to your project, such as build commands, file patterns, and recently opened files.

When you create a new project in Geany (e.g., Project1), a file named Project1.geany is generated inside the base directory of your project. This file holds all the custom settings related to Project1.

Here's what typically happens:

- When you create a project named Project1, Geany will store the project's settings in Project1.geany.
- This file will be placed in the base directory of your project (in your case, ~/Desktop/Projects/Project1/).

The .geany file tells Geany which build commands, file settings, and open files are associated with the project.

For Project2, a similar file called Project2.geany will be created in ~/ Desktop/Projects/Project2/.

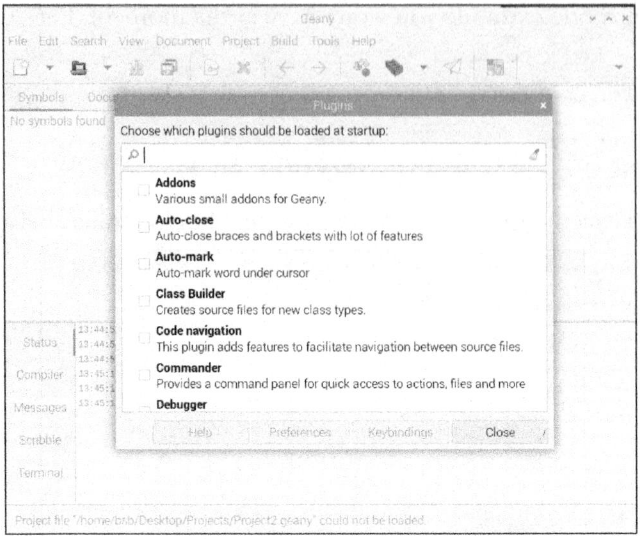

Figure 28d A sample .geany contents file.

Next configure Geany to use **project-specific commands** so it activates the correct virtual environment for this particular project. In the **Execute command** field, enter the command to activate the project's virtual environment and run your Python script, thus:

```
    source /path/to/your/project1/venv/bin/activate &&
python "%f"
```

As always replace **/path/to/your/project1/venv** with the actual path to the virtual environment for this project. Click OK to save this.

Now that the project-specific build commands are configured, you can run your Python script within the project's virtual environment.

Open your Python file in Geany (make sure it's part of the project you just set up). Go to **Build > Execute** or simply press F5.

Geany will now:

- Activate the virtual environment for the project.
- Run your Python script using the Python interpreter from that virtual environment.

The program will execute if you have set this up correctly. If not go back and correct the mistake by checking through.

To switch to another project that has a different virtual environment, Geany will automatically use the project-specific Execute command you set for that project. Do this by opening the other project via **Project > Open** to set the other virtual environments.

To summarise the:

- Create or open your project in Geany.
- Go to **Project > Properties**, then the Build tab.
- Enter the Execute command to activate the project's virtual environment.
- Save the settings.
- Run the script with F5 and Geany will automatically use the correct virtual environment for the project.

The *.geany file (e.g., Project1.geany) is a configuration file where Geany stores all project-specific settings, such as:

- Build commands (e.g., how to run or compile your code)
- File patterns (e.g., which files belong to the project)
- Open files (i.e., which files were open when the project was last saved)
- Project-specific settings (like indentation or compiler flags)

This file is created when you make a new project in Geany, and it's stored in your project's base directory.

The *.geany file is a simple text file in **INI** format, meaning it consists of sections marked by headers in square brackets ([section]) and key-value pairs.

The sections of the file and actions are as follows:

[project]: This section stores the name and base path of the project.

[files] : This section tracks which files are open in the project and which file tab is currently active in the Geany window.

[build_settings]: The project-specific build commands.

[patterns]: This section controls the file types that Geany considers part of the project. You can specify file extensions (patterns) to include in your project.

As you might expect you can actually open and edit this file with any text editor, including Geany itself, to change specific settings. For example, if you want to change the execute command for Project1 to run a different Python script, you would edit the **cmd_execute** line .

How .geany Works

When you run a project in Geany that has a *.geany project file (e.g., Project1.geany), the Build settings are automatically linked to the specific commands and configurations stored in that file. These settings directly affect how Geany compiles, runs, and manages your project. Here's a brief overview of this process:

- **Build Settings in Geany**: When you create a project in Geany and configure it via the Project Properties window (or manually edit the *.geany file), the settings you define—such as custom build, compile, and execute commands—are stored in the *.geany file. Each time you run, build, or compile your project using Geany, it uses these project-specific settings. These are different from the global build settings, which Geany would normally apply to all files not part of a project.

- **How *.geany Affects the Build Menu:** When you have a project open in Geany, the Build commands (Compile, Execute, etc.) behave according to the settings defined in the active project's *.geany file.

- **Specifically -Compile**: When you run the Compile command (F8), it executes the cmd_compile command from your *.geany file. For example, if you have:.**Execute**: When you press F5 (or Build > Execute), it runs the cmd_execute command from your project's settings.

When you're activating a virtual environment, it might look like:

```
cmd_execute=source ~/Desktop/Projects/Project1/venv/
bin/activate && python "%f"
```

This command:

- Activates the virtual environment for Project1.

- Runs the currently open Python file (%f).

- If you have any build steps (like linking object files in C projects), the **cmd_build** command is run when you choose Build > Build from the menu. If no cmd_build is defined, the Build option will simply do nothing.

The *.geany file settings override the global build commands that Geany normally applies for non-project files. This means that when you're working within a project:

- The Compile, Execute, and other build commands will follow the settings from the *.geany file.
- You don't have to manually re-enter commands every time you switch between projects, as Geany will automatically load the relevant commands for the active project.

Switching Between Projects

When you open a different project (Project1.geany or Project2.geany), the Build commands automatically switch to the ones defined for that project. To invoke this switch simply choose the Project (virtual environment) you wish to run from the '**Project>>Open**' drop down.

Summary of Effects

The *.geany file controls all the Build commands (Compile, Execute, etc.) for a specific project.

When you run a Python script or compile a file, Geany follows the commands specified in the *.geany file.

Switching between projects automatically changes the Build commands based on the project's configuration, ensuring that each project's virtual environment and settings are applied.

This setup ensures that your Build settings (like activating the virtual environment) are handled automatically when you switch between projects, streamlining your workflow without manual intervention.

Questions

1. Explain the steps to create and activate a virtual environment using the venv module in the Terminal. How would you activate and deactivate it?
2. Why might it be beneficial to use separate virtual environments for different projects? Give at least two reasons.
3. What is the purpose of a requirements.txt file, and how would you generate one for an existing environment?
4. Describe the process of installing packages from a requirements.txt file into a new virtual environment.
5. What is the WORKON_HOME environment variable, and how does it relate to virtualenvwrapper?
6. List three advantages of using the virtualenvwrapper commands like

mkvirtualenv and workon over manually creating and activating virtual environments.

7. In Geany, what are the steps to set up project-specific build commands, and how do these help in switching virtual environments?
8. Explain how the deactivate command works and when you would use it during a workflow with multiple virtual environments.
9. How can the pip freeze > requirements.txt command help in sharing or replicating a project's environment with others?
10. Why might it be helpful to keep your virtual environments in a centralised directory versus a project-specific directory.

29: sys Module

The 'sys' module is your go-to toolbox for system-level stuff in Python. It gives you a bunch of functions and variables that let you peek into and control different parts of Python and the underlying operating system.

The **sys module** is perfect for helping your Python scripts interact with the operating system. One of the handiest features is managing command-line arguments through **sys.argv**, which makes your scripts more dynamic and responsive to user input. And then there's **sys.path**, which shows you where Python is looking for modules and packages—this is handy for organising your code. The **sys.platform** attribute lets you know which operating system your script is running on, so your code can adapt accordingly. This is key for making your scripts work smoothly across different platforms.

But that's not all—sys lets you dig even deeper. For instance, with **sys.getsizeof()**, you can check how much memory your Python objects are using. There are also advanced features like customising recursion limits with **sys.setrecursionlimit()** and setting trace functions with **sys.settrace()**, which are great for debugging and fine-tuning your code's performance.

The **sys module** really embraces Python's philosophy of keeping things simple yet versatile. It's there to help you navigate the more technical aspects of system-level programming without breaking a sweat.

sys.argv: Lets you access the arguments passed to your Python script, making your scripts more flexible and interactive.

```
#Filename: sys1.py
import sys
#Print command-line arguments
for arg in sys.argv:
    print(arg)
```

Working example: Here's how you might use **sys.argv** to create a simple command-line utility:

```
#Filename: sys2.py
import sys

def calculate_sum(num1, num2):
    """Calculate the sum of two numbers."""
    return num1 + num2

if __name__ == "__main__":
    #Check if the correct number of arguments is
provided
    if len(sys.argv) != 3:
        print("Usage: python script.py <number1>
<number2>")
        sys.exit(1)
        # Exit the script with an error code

    #Extract command-line arguments
    num1 = float(sys.argv[1])
    num2 = float(sys.argv[2])

    #Calculate and print the sum
    result = calculate_sum(num1, num2)
    print("The sum of", num1, "and", num2, "is:",
result)
```

In this script, **sys.argv** helps to create a command-line utility that calculates the sum of two numbers provided as arguments. If the user doesn't give exactly two arguments, the script prints a usage message and exits with an error code.

sys.path: This is your Python script's road map. It tells you where Python is looking for modules and packages. Understanding this can save you a lot of headaches when your imports aren't working as expected.

```
#Filename: sys3.py
import sys

#Print the current Python module search path
print("Current Python module search path:")
for path in sys.path:
    print(path)

#Add a custom directory to the module search path
custom_path = "/path/to/custom/module"
sys.path.append(custom_path)

#Check if the custom directory is now in the module
search path
if custom_path in sys.path:
    print("\nCustom directory added to the Python
module search path.")
else:
    print("\nFailed to add custom directory to the
Python module search path.")
```

```
#Now you can import modules from the custom directory
#Example: import module from the custom directory
try:
    import custom_module
    print("\nSuccessfully imported module from the
custom directory.")
except ImportError:
    print("\nFailed to import module from the custom
directory.")
```

Here, we first print the current Python module **search path** using sys.path. Then, we add a custom directory to this path so Python can find additional modules.

sys.exit(): Need to bail out of your script in a hurry? This function's your best bet. It lets you exit your script gracefully with an optional exit status code. Great for handling errors or just saying, "I'm out!"

```
#Filename: sys4.py
import sys

def process_data(data):
    """Process data and perform calculations."""
    #Example data processing code
    result = sum(data)
    return result

if __name__ == "__main__":
    #Example data to process
    data = [1, 2, 3, 4, 5]

    #Check if the data is empty
    if not data:
        print("Error: No data to process.")
        sys.exit(1)  #Exit script with an error code
    #Process the data
    try:
        result = process_data(data)
        print("Result:", result)
    except Exception as e:
        print("Error processing data:", e)
        sys.exit(1)  #Exit script with an error code

    #Optionally, perform additional tasks here
    print("Script completed successfully.")
    sys.exit(0)  #Exit script with a success code
```

This example shows how sys.exit() can be used to gracefully exit a Python script, with different codes indicating success or failure.

sys.version: Curious about which version of Python you're running? sys. version gives you all the details, which is great for troubleshooting and compatibility checks.

```
#Filename: sys5.py
import sys

#Get Python version information
python_version = sys.version

# Print Python version information
print("Python Version:", python_version)
```

This script will output detailed information about your Python version, which can be helpful for ensuring compatibility with certain packages or scripts.

The **sys module** in Python is incredibly versatile, offering a range of tools for system-level tasks. While it's not the answer to every problem, it provides invaluable support for system-related programming tasks, from debugging and performance tuning to managing command-line arguments and interacting with the OS.

Just remember, these are only a few highlights—the sys module has a lot more to offer when you dig into it.

Questions

1. What is the purpose of the sys.argv in Python?
2. How can you modify the Python module search path using sys.path?
3. How does the sys.exit() function work, and why would you use it?
4. How can you check which version of Python you're running using the sys module?
5. What is the purpose of sys.getsizeof() and how is it useful?

30: abc Module

The abc module, is part of Python's standard library and helps in the creation of abstract base classes. At the heart of this module is the **ABC class** and its metaclass **ABCMeta**.

Here's a fun fact: in Python, classes are actually objects too. They're instances of a metaclass. Normally, Python uses the built-in **type** metaclass to create classes. But if you want to get fancy, you can specify your own metaclass when you define a class. If you don't, Python just goes with type by default. Want to create your own metaclass? Just subclass type and you're good to go!

Now, let's talk about the **ABC** class. The ABC class is used to create abstract classes in Python. Abstract methods or properties, marked with decorators like @abstractmethod or @abstractproperty, are placeholders that must be implemented by any subclass. This ensures all subclasses have consistent behaviour, which is super useful for organising and standardising your code.

Decorators, remember, are like little wands. They let you tweak or extend the behaviour of functions or classes without messing with their actual code. The abc module helps bring structure and clarity to object-oriented design in Python. And just to clarify, a metaclass is a class whose instances are classes themselves. So, while a regular class defines the behaviour and attributes of objects, a metaclass defines the behaviour and attributes of classes.

Here's an example: imagine you have an abstract base class **Shape** with abstract methods like **area()** and **perimeter()**. Any subclass, like **Rectangle**, must provide concrete implementations for these methods. You can't create an object from an abstract class directly—it'll throw a TypeError. This ensures you must implement all abstract methods in a subclass first.

Here's what it looks like in code:

```
#Filename: abc1.py
from abc import ABC, abstractmethod

class Shape(ABC):
    @abstractmethod
    def area(self):
        pass

    @abstractmethod
    def perimeter(self):
        pass
```

In this example, **Shape** is our abstract base class, created using the **ABC** class from the abc module. We've defined two abstract methods, **area()** and **perimeter()**, which every subclass **must** implement. This way, any shape type in your app—whether it's a **Rectangle**, **Circle**, or **Triangle**—will have these essential calculations.

By the way, the **'@'** symbol is how we use decorator syntax. It's a neat way to modify or extend functions, methods, or classes without touching their source code directly. You apply it with the **@decorator_name** syntax right before your function, method, or class definition. Here's an example extending abc1.py:

```
# Filename: abc2.py
from abc import ABC, abstractmethod

class Shape(ABC):
    @abstractmethod
    def area(self):
        pass

    @abstractmethod
    def perimeter(self):
        pass

# Concrete subclass implementing Shape
class Rectangle(Shape):
    def __init__(self, width, height):
        self.width = width
        self.height = height

    def area(self):
        return self.width * self.height

    def perimeter(self):
        return 2 * (self.width + self.height)

# Testing the Rectangle subclass
if __name__ == "__main__":
    # Instantiate the Rectangle with specific dimensions
    rect = Rectangle(3, 4)

    # Test the area and perimeter methods
    print(f"Area of rectangle: {rect.area()}")
    print(f"Perimeter of rectangle: {rect.
perimeter()}")  # Expected output: 14
```

Example: Template Method Pattern

Now, let's look at another example using the **Template Method Pattern**. This design pattern leverages abstract base classes to define a skeleton of an algorithm in a base class, while letting subclasses override certain steps of the algorithm.

```
#Filename: abc3.py
from abc import ABC, abstractmethod

class AbstractRecipe(ABC):
    def prepare(self):
        self.prepare_ingredients()
        self.cook()
        self.serve()

    @abstractmethod
    def prepare_ingredients(self):
        pass

    @abstractmethod
    def cook(self):
        pass

    def serve(self):
        print("Serving the dish")

class PizzaRecipe(AbstractRecipe):
    def prepare_ingredients(self):
        print("Preparing pizza ingredients")


    def cook(self):
        print("Baking the pizza in the oven")

#Usage
pizza = PizzaRecipe()
pizza.prepare()
```

In this example, **AbstractRecipe** defines a template method called **prepare()** that handles the steps of making a dish: preparing the ingredients, cooking, and serving. The **prepare()** method calls abstract methods **prepare_ingredients()** and **cook()**, which sub-classes (like **'**PizzaRecipe**'** here) must implement. This pattern keeps the process consistent across different recipes while letting you customise the details for each dish. **Delicious!**

Let's do a quick recap of each method decorator from the abc module:

- **@abstractmethod**: Marks methods as abstract, requiring subclasses to implement them. This ensures all subclasses follow a consistent interface defined by the abstract base class. For example:

```
#Filename: abc4.py
from abc import ABC, abstractmethod
class Animal(ABC):
    @abstractmethod
    def make_sound(self):
        pass

class Dog(Animal):
    def make_sound(self):
        return "Woof!"

# animal = Animal()  # TypeError: Can't instantiate
dog = Dog()
print(dog.make_sound())  # Output: Woof!
```

- **@abstractproperty**: Defines abstract properties that subclasses must implement, ensuring consistent access to essential data across different subclasses.
- **@abstractclassmethod**: Marks class methods as abstract, meaning subclasses must implement these methods to consistently manipulate class-level data or behaviour within a class hierarchy.
- **@abstractstaticmethod**: Defines abstract static methods that subclasses must implement. This is great for creating utility methods or operations that don't depend on instance or class state.

```
#Filename: abc5.py
from abc import ABC, abstractstaticmethod

class Animal(ABC):
    @abstractstaticmethod
    def description():
        pass

class Fish(Animal):
    @staticmethod
    def description():
        return "Lives in water"

print(Fish.description())  # Output: Lives in water
```

Real-World Scenarios

Abstract Base Classes (ABCs) are particularly useful when you want to ensure that certain methods or properties are implemented in all subclasses. This is great for enforcing a contract or a standard behaviour across various implementations. For example, if you're building a game, you might have an abstract class **Character** with abstract methods like **attack()** and **defend()**. Every character in your game, whether it's a **Warrior** or a **Mage**, must implement these methods. This keeps your code **consistent** and easier to maintain.

While ABCs are great for enforcing structure, they might not always be necessary. If you're working on a smaller project or one that requires a lot of flexibility, using ABCs might add unnecessary complexity. For example, if you're rapidly prototyping or experimenting with different designs, starting with regular classes and later refactoring into ABCs might be a more agile approach.

Metaclasses

A **metaclass** is a class that defines how other classes behave. It's like a blueprint for creating classes, controlling how they are constructed and what attributes or methods they have. You can think of a metaclass as the **class of a class**. In Python, type is the default metaclass, but you can create custom metaclasses by subclassing type to modify or customise class creation.

Here's a simple example of a custom metaclass that enforces all classes to have a particular method:

```
#Filename: abc6.py
#Define a simple metaclass
class MyMeta(type):
    def __new__(cls, name, bases, class_dict):
        print(f"Creating class {name}")
        return super().__new__(cls, name, bases, class_
dict)
# Use the metaclass when defining a class
class MyClass(metaclass=MyMeta):
    def __init__(self, value):
        self.value = value

    def show(self):
        print(f"The value is: {self.value}")

# Create an instance of MyClass
obj = MyClass(42)
obj.show()
```

A metaclass is defined by inheriting from type. The __new__ method in the metaclass is called when a new class is created. In the above example, we print a message whenever a class using **MyMeta** as a metaclass is created.

Using the Metaclass in a Class Definition: The class MyClass is defined with metaclass=MyMeta. When Python encounters this definition, it uses MyMeta to create the class MyClass. As a result, the __new__ method in MyMeta is executed, printing the message "Creating class MyClass".

In the program the metaclass MyMeta intercepted the class creation process and printed a message when the class MyClass was created. This shows how metaclasses allow you to control the creation and behaviour of classes, much like classes control the creation and behaviour of objects.

Custom metaclasses are useful when you need to apply certain rules or checks to the creation of classes. For instance, in a large framework where multiple developers are creating various classes, a metaclass can enforce that all classes meet certain criteria, such as including specific methods or attributes.

In addition, metaclasses allow you to inject additional methods or attributes during class creation, avoiding repetitive code. This is often used in frameworks to provide base functionality to user-defined classes.

You can also ensure that only one instance of a class is created. Using a metaclass, you can control instance creation at the class level, making it easier to enforce a **singleton pattern.** This is a design pattern that ensures a class has only one instance throughout the entire program and provides a global point of access to that instance. It's commonly used to manage shared resources, such as configuration settings, logging, or connection pools. Be aware though that, metaclasses can make you code harder to read and maintain. In reality they are pointless to use in simple tasks where decorators or inheritance would suffice. Use them **only** when simpler techniques fall short,

What Are Decorators Really Doing?

As we saw back in **Chapter 24** (Advanced Functions) Decorators in Python are a way to modify or extend the behaviour of functions or methods. They are applied using the @decorator_name syntax. Under the hood, a decorator is just a function that takes another function and returns a new function with some added (or altered) behaviour.

Here's an example to illustrate a basic decorator:

```
#Filename: abc7.py
def my_decorator(func):
    def wrapper():
        print("Something is happening before the
function is called.")
        func()
        print("Something is happening after the
function is called.")
    return wrapper

@my_decorator
def say_hello():
    print("Hello!")

say_hello()
```

When this is run you get:

```
Something is happening before the function is called.
Hello!
```

```
Something happens after the function is called.
```

This example shows how decorators can be used to wrap additional functionality around an existing function.

Decorators can also be used with classes, as seen with @abstractmethod and other decorators from the abc module. These decorators not only enhance code readability but also enforce structure without altering the original logic of the class or method.

Template Method Pattern

The Template Method pattern is all about defining the skeleton of an algorithm in a base class, while allowing subclasses to fill in the specific details. This pattern is particularly useful when you want to keep the high-level structure of an operation intact but allow for variations in some steps.

Practical Example: Online Order Processing

Imagine an online store where you need to process different types of orders. You could use the Template Method pattern to handle the general flow of processing an order, but allow subclasses to define the specifics of each step:

```
#Filename: abc8.py
from abc import ABC, abstractmethod

class OrderProcess(ABC):
    def process_order(self):
        self.select_items()
        self.pay()
        self.deliver()

    @abstractmethod
    def select_items(self):
        pass

    @abstractmethod
    def pay(self):
        pass

    def deliver(self):
        print("Delivering the items to the customer")

class OnlineOrder(OrderProcess):
    def select_items(self):
        print("Selecting items from the online 
catalog")

    def pay(self):
        print("Paying online via credit card")

class InStoreOrder(OrderProcess):
    def select_items(self):
        print("Selecting items from the store shelf")

    def pay(self):
        print("Paying at the cash register")
```

```
# Example usage
online_order = OnlineOrder()
online_order.process_order()
in_store_order = InStoreOrder()
in_store_order.process_order()
```

Output:

```
Selecting items from the online catalog
Paying online via credit card
Delivering the items to the customer
Selecting items from the store shelf
Paying at the cash register
Delivering the items to the customer
```

This example shows how the Template Method pattern helps maintain a consistent order processing structure while allowing for variations between online and in-store orders.

Common Pitfalls with ABCs

Overusing ABCs: While ABCs can enforce structure, overusing them can lead to unnecessary complexity, especially in simpler projects.

Inconsistent Implementations: Forgetting to implement an abstract method in a subclass can cause run-time errors. Always test your subclasses to ensure they comply with the abstract base class's requirements.

Best Practice

- **Use ABCs Judiciously**: Implement ABCs when you need to enforce a clear contract across multiple classes, but avoid them if flexibility is more important in your project.
- **Combine with Other Design Patterns**: ABCs can be combined with other design patterns, like Strategy or Factory patterns, to create robust, maintainable code.

Questions

1. What is the purpose of the abc module in Python?
2. What is the purpose of the abc module in Python?
3. How can you define an abstract method in an abstract base class?
4. What is the Template Method Pattern and how does it work with abstract base classes?
5. What are decorators, and how are they used in the abc module?

31: datetime Module

The datetime module is pretty neat for working with dates and times, just like you'd expect. It provides classes for representing dates (**date**), times (**time**), and combined date and time information (datetime). It's also handy for handling operations like time intervals and time zones with ease. (But sorry, no SpaceTime—what a shame :-(

One of the key components is the datetime **class**, which is commonly used for representing specific points in time. It allows you to do things like calculate the difference between two dates or add a certain duration to a date and time.

The module also helps with parsing and **formatting** date and time strings, making it easy to switch between string representations and datetime objects. This is particularly useful when dealing with different date and time formats, especially if you're working with data input/output or communicating with external systems.

Another neat feature is how the datetime module handles time zones. You can perform time zone conversions and adjust for daylight saving time, which is crucial if your application needs to work across different graphical locations.

Here are five of the most **useful** functions in the datetime module:

- **datetime.now()**: Returns the current local date and time.
- **datetime.today()**: Alias for datetime.now().
- **datetime.strptime(date_string, format)**: Parses a string representing a date and time according to the specified format.
- **datetime_object.strftime(format)**: Returns a string representing the date and time according to a specified format.

- **datetime.combine(date, time)**: Combines a date object and a time object into a single datetime object.

Other handy functions include:

- **datetime.timedelta(days, seconds, microseconds)**: Represents a duration or the difference between two dates or times.
- **datetime.date(year, month, day)**: Returns a date object.
- **datetime.time(hour, minute, second)**: Returns a time object.
- **datetime_object.date()**: Returns the date part of a datetime object.
- **datetime_object.time()**: Returns the time part of a datetime object.

Now, let's dive into a program that uses datetime.now() to display the current date and time with some formatting:

```
#Filename: datetime1.py
from datetime import datetime

def display_current_datetime():
    #Get the current date and time
    current_datetime = datetime.now()

    #Format the current date and time as a string
    formatted_datetime = current_datetime.strftime("%Y-
%m-%d %H:%M:%S")

    #Display the result
    print("Current Date and Time: {}".format(formatted_
datetime))

#Call the function to display the current date and time
display_current_datetime()
```

In this program:

- We import the datetime class from the datetime module.
- The display_current_datetime function grabs the current date and time using datetime.now().
- The strftime method formats the current_datetime as a string. In this case, the format is "%Y-%m-%d %H:%M:%S", which represents "Year-Month-Day Hour:Minute".
- Finally, the program prints the formatted date and time.

When you run this program, it will output the current date and time in the specified format.

Time Zone Handling with zoneinfo

By default, datetime in Python doesn't have a built-in time zone. When you create a datetime object without specifying a time zone, it's considered "naive," meaning it doesn't contain any information about time zones or daylight saving time.

If you need to work with time zones, Python 3.9 introduced the **zoneinfo** module, which makes it easier to deal with time zones using the IANA (Internet Assigned Numbers Authority) zone database. Here's how you might use it (Note, you may need to install the **tzdata module** to use it.):

```
#Filename:  datetime2.py
from zoneinfo import ZoneInfo
import datetime

# Create a ZoneInfo object for the "America/New_York"
time zone
ny_time_zone = ZoneInfo("America/New_York")

#Get the current date and time in the "America/New_
York" time zone
now = datetime.datetime.now(ny_time_zone)
print("Current time in New York:", now)

#Convert the current time to UTC
utc_now = now.astimezone(ZoneInfo("UTC"))
print("Current time in UTC:", utc_now)
```

This module simplifies working with time zones by providing a standardised interface to access time zone data and perform time zone-related operations. It's a great addition for developers who need to manage datetime data across different time zones.

Comparing Dates and Times

Comparing two datetime objects is straightforward in Python. You can use comparison operators (<, >, ==, etc.) directly with datetime objects to check if one date is before, after, or the same as another. This capability is useful in scheduling, sorting events by date, or validating date inputs.

```
#Filename: datetime3.py
from datetime import datetime

#Create two datetime objects
date1 = datetime(2023, 9, 1, 14, 30)  # September 1,
2023, 14:30
date2 = datetime(2023, 9, 3, 10, 45)  # September 3,
2023, 10:45

#Compare the datetime objects
if date1 < date2:
    print("date1 is before date2")
```

```
elif date1 > date2:
    print("date1 is after date2")
else:
    print("Both dates are the same")
```

You can use this program to:

- Scheduling: Determine if an event is before or after a certain time.
- Sorting: Sort a list of events by their date.
- Validation: Ensure user-inputted dates are valid or in a specific range (e.g., future dates only).

Questions

1. What is the purpose of the datetime module in Python?
2. How do you get the current date and time using the datetime module
3. How can you format a datetime object into a readable string?
4. How can you compare two datetime objects in Python?

32: RPi Graphics

Tkinter is a graphical user interface (GUI) toolkit that's part of the Python standard library, making it an ideal choice for your Raspberry Pi projects. It's known for its simplicity (which you'll soon see), and it lets you easily create interactive desktop applications. While there are other GUI options out there, Tkinter's popularity makes it a solid choice to stick with.

When you're building applications with Tkinter, everything revolves around opening a desktop window where you can use different widgets like buttons, labels, text entry fields, drop-down menus, and more.

Tkinter is event-driven, meaning it responds to actions like button clicks, key presses, or anything you interact with in the application window. Your program needs to watch out for these events and respond accordingly—otherwise, nothing will happen!

Here's a little example to show just how easy it is to open a window on your desktop using Tkinter. The window will be small and might pop up in the middle of your Terminal window—but don't worry, you can drag it around just like any other window. The best part? The code is simple

```
#Filename: gui1.py
import tkinter as tk

#Create a window
window = tk.Tk()

#Set the window title
window.title("My Window")

#Create a label widget to display text
label = tk.Label(window, text="Hello, World!")

#Add the label to the window
label.pack()
#Start the main event loop
window.mainloop()
```

Once your window is open, you can use the widgets in the top right corner to resize or move it, just like any other window. When you're done, simply click the close button to close the window and return to the Terminal.

Let's break down what's happening here: We start by importing the tkinter module and creating a window using **tk.Tk()**. Next, we set the window's title with the **title()** method. We create a label widget to display some text and set its content using the text parameter. The label is added to the window with the **pack()** method, which neatly organises the widget within the window. Finally, we kick off the main event loop with **window.mainloop()**, which keeps the window open and responsive until you close it by clicking the 'x' button.

When you run this code, you'll see a window with a simple label saying "Hello, World!" (And just think, if we could have copyrighted those two words, we'd be rolling in cash by now…)

Let's build on this with a second example. This time, we'll create a window where you can type something into a text box and display it in another part of the window. The code is still straightforward and follows the same easy-to-understand structure:

```
#Filename: gui2.py
import tkinter as tk

def write_text():
    #Get the text from the entry widget
    text = entry.get()

    #Display the text in the label
    label.config(text=text)

#Create a window
window = tk.Tk()

#Set the window title
window.title("Text Display Window")

#Create an entry widget for user input
entry = tk.Entry(window)
entry.pack()

#Create a button to trigger text display
button = tk.Button(window, text="Display Text",
command=write_text)
button.pack()

#Create a label widget to display the text
label = tk.Label(window, text="")
label.pack()

#Start the main event loop
window.mainloop()
```

We start by creating a window and setting its title to "Text Display Window." Then, we add an **Entry** widget where the user can type in some text. When the user clicks the "Display Text" button, the **write_text function** runs. This function grabs whatever text was typed into the entry widget and displays it in the label. The write_text function uses the **get()** method to retrieve the text from the entry widget and updates the label's text using the config() method.

This example is a great demonstration of how easy it is to interact with users by capturing input and displaying results in a Tkinter window. You can take this basic structure and customise it to fit your needs—whether that's adding more widgets or defining additional functions for different actions. Tkinter has a wide range of widgets and functions that make creating interactive desktop applications a breeze!

Tick Tock It's a Clock

This next example is a fun way to display a digital clock, right on your desktop using the awesome datetime module.

The code below pulls out the current date and time components—like the year, month, day, hour, minute, and second—using attributes of the datetime object. It then assigns each of these components to a variable and displays them in a neat format.

Run the code, and you'll see the current date and time pop up in a window on your screen, updating every second. How cool is that?

```
#Filename: gui3.py
#Digital Clock Display
import tkinter as tk
import datetime

#Create a window
window = tk.Tk()

#Set the window title
window.title("Date and Time Display")

#Create a label widget for displaying the date and time
label = tk.Label(window, font=("Helvetica", 24))

#Function to update the label text with the current
date and time
def update_datetime():
    current_datetime = datetime.datetime.now()
    label.config(text=current_datetime.strftime("%Y-%m-
%d %H:%M:%S"))
    window.after(1000, update_datetime)
# Update every second

#Add the label to the window
```

```
label.pack()

#Start updating the label with the current date and
time
update_datetime()

#Start the main event loop
window.mainloop()
```

Let's break it down: First, import the Tkinter and datetime modules, create a window using Tkinter, and set the title to "Date and Time Display." Create a label widget that's going to display the current date and time in a nice, readable format.

The **update_datetime** function is the heart of the operation. It grabs the current date and time using **datetime.datetime.now()**, formats it as a string with the **strftime method** (which lets you decide how the date and time should look), and updates the label's text with this information.

Finally set it to update every second using window.after(1000, update_datetime), ensuring your clock stays accurate and up-to-date.

When you run this code on your Raspberry Pi, you'll see a little window appear on your desktop, displaying the current date and time, ticking away every second.

Now, let's take it a step further and customise the look of your digital clock. We'll tweak the window size, position, and the style of the text:

```
#Filename: gui4.py
import tkinter as tk
import datetime

#Create a window
window = tk.Tk()

#Set the window title
window.title("Date and Time Display")

#Customise the window size and position
window.geometry("400x100+500+300")  # Width x Height +
X offset + Y offset

#Create a label widget for displaying the date and time
label = tk.Label(window, font=("Arial", 24), fg="blue",
bg="white")

#Function to update the label text with the current
date and time
def update_datetime():
    current_datetime = datetime.datetime.now()
    label.config(text=current_datetime.strftime("%Y-%m-
%d %H:%M:%S"))
    window.after(1000, update_datetime)
# Update every 1 second
```

```
#Add padding to the label
label.pack(padx=20, pady=20)

#Start updating the label with the current date and
time
update_datetime()

#Start the main event loop
window.mainloop()
```

Here's what we've added:

- **Window Geometry**: The line **window.geometry("400x100+500+300")** sets the window size to 400x100 pixels and positions it at coordinates (500, 300) on your screen. Feel free to adjust these values to place the window wherever you like. (You can determine the screen dimensions (width and height) of your computer screen using the Tk object's **winfo_screenwidth()** and **winfo_screenheight()** methods. These give you the resolution of the screen in pixels.

- **Label Customisation**: We've jazzed up the label with label = tk.Label(window, font=("Arial", 24), fg="blue", bg="white"). This sets the font to Arial, size 24pt, with blue text on a white background. You can tweak these settings to match your style.

- **Padding**: We added some padding around the label with **label. pack**(padx=20, pady=20), giving it a bit of breathing room from the window edges. **padx** adds space on the sides, and **pady** adds space above and below. Adjust these as needed for a perfect fit.

Run this code, and you'll see a snazzy, customise clock window on your desktop that displays the current date and time, updating every second. It's a simple yet elegant way to keep track of time while you work on your Raspberry Pi!

This next program (gui5.py) is a neat little example that shows how to create a drop-down menu and a button in Tkinter. When you pick an item from the menu and click the button, a new window pops up displaying the selected item. In this case, it's just a window with some text—but you can imagine the possibilities!

The main window is set up with a specific size and position using the geometry method, which places it at 300x200 pixels and positions it at coordinates (500, 300) on your screen.

The magic happens in the **open_new_window function**. This function grabs the selected item from the drop-down menu using **combo.get()**. If you've selected something, it opens a new window titled "Selected Item". The new window is sized and positioned just right, and inside it, a label displays the selected text in a big, blue Arial font on a white background. Here's the code:

```
#Filename: gui5.py
import tkinter as tk
from tkinter import ttk

#Create the main window
main_window = tk.Tk()
main_window.title("Dropdown Menu Example")
main_window.geometry("300x200+500+300")  # Width x
Height + X offset + Y offset

#Function to open a new window with the selected item's
text
def open_new_window():
    selected_item = combo.get()
    if selected_item:
        new_window = tk.Toplevel(main_window)
        new_window.title("Selected Item")
        new_window.geometry("300x100+550+350")
        label = tk.Label(new_window, text=selected_
item, font=("Arial", 24), fg="blue", bg="white")
        label.pack(padx=20, pady=20)

#Create a label for the dropdown menu
dropdown_label = tk.Label(main_window, text="Select an
item:", font=("Arial", 14))
dropdown_label.pack(pady=10)

#Create a combo box (drop-down menu)
combo = ttk.Combobox(main_window, values=["Item 1",
"Item 2", "Item 3"], font=("Arial", 14))
combo.pack(pady=10)

#Create a button to open a new window
open_button = tk.Button(main_window, text="Open",
command=open_new_window, font=("Arial", 14))
open_button.pack(pady=10)

#Start the main event loop
main_window.mainloop()
```

Let's break it down:

- **Dropdown Menu Setup**: We start by adding a label to the main window that says "Select an item:". This is followed by a **combobox** widget, which serves as our drop-down menu. It comes pre-loaded with three items: "Item 1", "Item 2", and "Item 3" (okay, not the most creative names, but they do the job!). The combobox is styled with a 14-point Arial font.

- **Button Action**: Below the combobox, we add a button labelled "Open". When you click it, the button triggers the **open_new_ window** function, which does the rest.

- **New Window Magic**: The open_new_window function checks which item you selected from the dropdown. If you've picked something, it opens a new window titled "Selected Item", sizes and positions it, and displays your selected text in a large, blue Arial font.
- **Keeping It All Running**: The **main_window.mainloop()** line keeps the application running and responsive to whatever you do—whether it's selecting an item or clicking that "Open" button.

This simple but effective program is a great introduction to creating interactive GUIs with dropdown menus and handling events in Tkinter. It's easy to see how you can expand on this to create more complex and engaging applications!

In this next program, we're going to have some fun by creating a simple animation where a line rotates on the screen. Tkinter gives us the tools to create the GUI elements, but we'll use the math module to handle the rotation calculations. The **RotateLineApp** class takes care of the whole process, from creating the window to handling the rotation. The best part? The rotation starts and stops with just a press of a button!

Here's the code:

```
#Filename: gui6.py
import tkinter as tk
import math

class RotateLineApp:
    def __init__(self, root):
        self.root = root
        self.root.title("Rotate Line Example")

        #Create a canvas
        self.canvas = tk.Canvas(root, width=400,
height=400, bg="white")
        self.canvas.pack()

        #Initial coordinates of the line
        self.x1, self.y1 = 200, 100
        self.x2, self.y2 = 200, 300

        # Draw the initial line
        self.line = self.canvas.create_line(self.x1,
self.y1, self.x2, self.y2, width=2, fill="blue")

        #Create a button to toggle rotation
        self.rotate_button = tk.Button(root,
text="Start/Stop Rotation", command=self.toggle_
rotation)
        self.rotate_button.pack(pady=10)

        #Angle for rotation
        self.angle = 0
        self.rotating = False
```

```
    def toggle_rotation(self):
        #Toggle the rotation state
        self.rotating = not self.rotating
        if self.rotating:
            self.rotate_line()

    def rotate_line(self):
        if self.rotating:
            #Increment the angle
            self.angle += 10
            if self.angle >= 360:
                self.angle = 0

            #Convert angle to radians
            radians = math.radians(self.angle)

            #Calculate the center of the line
            cx, cy = (self.x1 + self.x2) / 2, (self.y1
+ self.y2) / 2

            # Translate the line to the origin
            translated_x1 = self.x1 - cx
            translated_y1 = self.y1 - cy
            translated_x2 = self.x2 - cx
            translated_y2 = self.y2 - cy

            #Rotate the line
            new_x1 = translated_x1 * math.cos(radians)
- translated_y1 * math.sin(radians)
            new_y1 = translated_x1 * math.sin(radians)
+ translated_y1 * math.cos(radians)
            new_x2 = translated_x2 * math.cos(radians)
- translated_y2 * math.sin(radians)
            new_y2 = translated_x2 * math.sin(radians)
+ translated_y2 * math.cos(radians)

            #Translate the line back to its original
position
            self.canvas.coords(self.line, cx + new_x1,
cy + new_y1, cx + new_x2, cy + new_y2)

            #Schedule the next rotation
            self.root.after(100, self.rotate_line)

if __name__ == "__main__":
    root = tk.Tk()
    app = RotateLineApp(root)
    Root.mainloop()
```

Breaking it Down

- **Setting Up the Window:** The __init__ method kicks things off by setting up the main window with the title "Rotate Line Example". We create a canvas where the line will be drawn, and we set its initial position using coordinates.
- **Drawing the Line:** The line is drawn with the **create_line** method, and we make it a nice blue colour. The button labelled "Start/Stop

Rotation" is added below the canvas, and it's wired up to trigger the **toggle_rotation** method when clicked.

- **Rotation Logic:** The **toggle_rotatio**n function switches the rotation on and off. When the rotation is on, the **rotate_line** method starts doing its thing. It increases the angle by 10 degrees each time and resetting to 0 after a full rotation, 360 degrees, converts the angle to radians, and then performs some trigonometric calculations to rotate the line around its centre.
- **Animating the Line:** To keep the line rotating, **rotate_line** schedules itself to run again after 100 milliseconds using s**elf.root.after**. This creates a smooth animation loop that keeps the line spinning until you click the button again to stop it.

This program is a great example of how Tkinter can be used to create interactive GUIs with animations in Python. It sets up a simple window with a canvas and a rotating line. A button lets you start and stop the rotation, which is handled using basic trigonometry and a bit of clever scheduling. It's a fun way to see how you can combine GUI elements with mathematical logic to create dynamic visuals!

Organise with Frames

Tkinter frames are invisible containers in the world of graphical user interfaces. Frames help you organise your widgets—like buttons, labels, and text boxes—so everything looks neat and makes sense to the user. They're a bit like those handy little trays people use to keep their desks tidy, making sure everything is in its right place.

The idea behind **Frames** is to give you control over your layout. They act as boundaries within a window, letting you group related widgets together, making it easier to manage and change their arrangement without disturbing everything else. You can nest Frames within each other, like placing smaller boxes inside a bigger box, allowing for more sophisticated layouts. This approach makes your code cleaner and your GUI more organised, which is really helpful as your application grows in complexity

You can align and pack widgets within Frames in various ways, and even control their behaviour—whether they expand, shrink, or stay in one place. This flexibility makes Frames an invaluable tool for building user-friendly, responsive applications that look good no matter the screen size or user's preferences.

Here's an example that demonstrates the use of Tkinter Frames to organise a GUI effectively. In this example, we'll create a small window with two sections: one for user input (a label and entry field) and another for control buttons. This shows how Frames can help keep related widgets together, making the layout clean and easy to understand.

```
#Filename: gui7.py
import tkinter as tk

# Create the main window
root = tk.Tk()
root.title("Frame Example")

# Create a frame for the input section
input_frame = tk.Frame(root, padx=10, pady=10)
input_frame.pack(pady=20)

# Add a label and an entry widget inside the input
frame
label = tk.Label(input_frame, text="Enter your name:")
label.pack(side="left")

entry = tk.Entry(input_frame)
entry.pack(side="left")

# Create another frame for the button section
button_frame = tk.Frame(root, padx=10, pady=10)
button_frame.pack(pady=10)

# Add buttons inside the button frame
submit_button = tk.Button(button_frame, text="Submit")
submit_button.pack(side="left", padx=5)

cancel_button = tk.Button(button_frame, text="Cancel")
cancel_button.pack(side="left", padx=5)

# Start the main loop
root.mainloop()
```

- **Main Window:** We create the main window (root) to hold everything.
- **Input Frame:** This frame (input_frame) is for the input section, containing a label and an entry field. By packing these widgets inside a frame, they stay grouped together, and any changes made to the frame's layout automatically apply to both.
- **Button Frame:** Another frame (button_frame) is created for the control buttons Submit and Cancel. This keeps the buttons aligned and spaced properly, independent of the input section above.

By using frames, the layout remains neat and structured. If you want to change the alignment, padding, or layout, you only have to adjust the frame settings rather than individual widgets. This approach shows how frames can simplify GUI design and management, especially as the complexity of the application grows.

Framing Menus

Let's enhance the previous example by adding a dropdown menu (also known as an **OptionMenu** in Tkinter) to show how frames can be utilised to tie different types of widgets together. This example will have a frame for the user input (name entry and dropdown menu for selecting a country) and another frame for the buttons (Submit and Cancel).

```
#Filename: gui8.py
import tkinter as tk
from tkinter import messagebox

# Function to handle the "Submit" button
def on_submit():
    name = entry.get().strip()   # Get name input
    country = selected_option.get()  # Get selected
country

    if not name:
        messagebox.showwarning("Input Error", "Please
enter your name.")
        return

    if country == "Select Country":
        messagebox.showwarning("Selection Error",
"Please select a valid country.")
        return

    messagebox.showinfo("Submission Successful",
f"Name: {name}\nCountry: {country}")

# Function to handle the "Cancel" button
def on_cancel():
    root.destroy()  # Close the program

# Create the main window
root = tk.Tk()
root.title("Frame Example with Dropdown Menu")

# Create a frame for the input section
input_frame = tk.Frame(root, padx=10, pady=10)
input_frame.pack(pady=20)

# Add a label and an entry widget inside the input
frame
label = tk.Label(input_frame, text="Enter your name:")
label.pack(side="left")

entry = tk.Entry(input_frame)
entry.pack(side="left")

# Add a dropdown menu (OptionMenu) inside the input
frame
options = ["Select Country", "United Kingdom", "United
States", "Australia", "Canada"]

# Create a variable to store the selected option
selected_option = tk.StringVar()
selected_option.set(options[0])  # Set default value
```

```
# Create the dropdown menu and pack it in the input
frame
dropdown = tk.OptionMenu(input_frame, selected_option,
*options)
dropdown.pack(side="left", padx=10)

# Create another frame for the button section
button_frame = tk.Frame(root, padx=10, pady=10)
button_frame.pack(pady=10)

# Add buttons inside the button frame
submit_button = tk.Button(button_frame, text="Submit",
command=on_submit)
submit_button.pack(side="left", padx=5)

cancel_button = tk.Button(button_frame, text="Cancel",
command=on_cancel)
cancel_button.pack(side="left", padx=5)

# Start the main loop
root.mainloop()
```

In easy steps:

- **Main Window:** The main application window (root) is created, where all widgets will be placed.
- **Input Frame:** The frame (input_frame) is used to hold the input widgets. It now contains:
- A Label for the user's name. An Entry widget for the user to type in their name. A dropdown menu (OptionMenu) for selecting a country, created using **tk.OptionMenu,** which provides a predefined list of options to choose from.
- **Dropdown Menu Setup:** options is a list containing the dropdown choices. **selected_option** is a Tkinter **StringVar** that holds the currently selected value from the dropdown.
- The OptionMenu is linked to **selected_option** and is packed next to the entry field, keeping everything neatly aligned.
- Button Frame: Another frame (**button_frame**) is created for the buttons (Submit and Cancel). This frame allows the buttons to be organised separately from the input section.

By using frames, you maintain a clear separation between different groups of widgets—input fields in one frame and buttons in another. This modular approach makes your GUI easier to read, maintain, and modify. The dropdown menu adds interactivity and demonstrates how frames can handle multiple types of widgets while keeping your layout clean and user-friendly.

33: PyGame

Despite what the name might suggest, Pygame wasn't specifically made for the Raspberry Pi. It's actually short for "Python Game" and is a fantastic toolkit for creating video games, multimedia applications, and all sorts of interactive experiences.

Pygame is built on top of **Simple DirectMedia Layer** (SDL), which is a low-level multimedia library. SDL gives you access to essentials like audio, keyboard, mouse, and display controls. Pygame takes all this and wraps it up into a framework that makes these complex tasks much easier to handle—just like any good Python module should.

Whether you're working with basic shapes, custom images, or more complex sprites, Pygame gives you a canvas where your game's visual elements can come to life with minimal fuss.

Pygame is sensitive which can make it difficult to install and use in a virtual environment. There is a bit of history with compatibility. You can verify which versions of Pygame are available for your Python version with:

```
pip install pygame==
```

You can press Tab for version suggestions. Pygame relies on additional system libraries for graphics and sound. These may not be installed or configured properly, particularly on Raspberry Pi OS. You can test if your installation of Pygame is working by typing:

```
python -m pygame.examples.aliens
```

Which should run the Aliens game example included with PyGame.

Unfortunately there is no one size fits all solution and you may have to fiddle a bit to get PyGame to work in a virtual environment. Check error messages that may arise–such as libraries not being installed. Or search around the Python forums

To get started with Pygame on your Raspberry Pi, you can install it your activated virtual environment:

```
pip3 install pygame
```

(Or pip if pip3 doesn't work.)

The example we're about to dive into—**Catch a Falling Star**—is a great little project to get your feet wet with the kinds of techniques you'll need to write an interactive arcade-style game. In this game, you have a paddle at the bottom of the screen that you can move left and right with your mouse. Random blocks (which we'll generously call 'stars') fall from the top of the screen, and your job is to catch these stars with the paddle to score points. Simple, right? Before we jump into the code, it's always a good idea to sketch out what we need to do. Applications that are structured like games can be easily broken down into sections and these tested quite independently of one another. This makes it much easier to debug.

Here's a quick rundown:

1. Set up screen size and colours
2. Create the paddle and make it move
3. Create the falling objects (our 'stars')
4. Make the objects move and detect collisions
5. Update the score when you catch a star
6. Play for a set amount of time

You can code each of these six steps separately to ensure they work adding one by one to test and build towards your overall program

Setup

First things first, we need to import the necessary modules: Pygame for the game functionality and **random** for creating random falling objects. I've also added **import time** so we can put a pause in the program—just to make sure everything is working and you can see what's happening on the screen. Here's the initial code to get us started:

```
#Filename: catch1.py
import pygame
import random
import time
```

```
#Initialize Pygame
pygame.init()

#Constants
SCREEN_WIDTH = 800
SCREEN_HEIGHT = 600
BLACK = (0, 0, 0)
WHITE = (255, 255, 255)
RED = (255, 0, 0)
BLUE = (0, 0, 255)
FONT_SIZE = 36

#Game variables
score = 0
clock = pygame.time.Clock()

#Set up the screen
screen = pygame.display.set_mode((SCREEN_WIDTH, SCREEN_
HEIGHT))
pygame.display.set_caption("Catch the Falling Objects")

#Define fonts
font = pygame.font.SysFont(None, FONT_SIZE)

#Wait for 10 seconds
print("Waiting for 10 seconds...")
time.sleep(5)
print("Done waiting!")
```

Run it and have a look. A quick scan through the code should give you a pretty good idea of what is going on where. Here's what's going on where:

- **Imports**: We start by importing the pygame, random and time modules. The time module is also imported so we can pause the game and see what's going on.
- **Initialisation**: **pygame.init()** gets everything ready to work.
- **Constants**: We define the screen size and some basic colours in RGB format. You can play around with these values to create different colours. Just Google "RGB colour chart" to find the exact values you want.(R=Red, G=Green, B=Blue.)
- **Game Setup:** We set up the screen with the specified dimensions and give it a title using **pygame.display.set_caption().** We also set up a basic font that we'll use later.
- **Pause**: Finally, we add a short pause (five seconds) so you can see that everything is set up correctly before the game moves on.

This code lays the groundwork for the game. And demonstrates how you can build a program in blocks. We've got the screen up and running, colours defined, and the font ready to go. But there's no game yet—let's fix that by adding the paddle.

Paddle Operation

Now, we're going to expand on what we've done by adding a paddle that you can move left and right. The code below handles the paddle's creation and movement:. You'll notice that a significant amount of extra code's been added to achieve this.

```
#Filename: catch2.py
import pygame

#Initialize Pygame
pygame.init()

#Constants
SCREEN_WIDTH = 800
SCREEN_HEIGHT = 600
BLACK = (0, 0, 0)
BLUE = (0, 0, 255)
FONT_SIZE = 36

#Game variables
clock = pygame.time.Clock()

#Set up the screen
screen = pygame.display.set_mode((SCREEN_WIDTH, SCREEN_
HEIGHT))
pygame.display.set_caption("Paddle Movement")

#Define fonts
font = pygame.font.SysFont(None, FONT_SIZE)

#Define player paddle
class Paddle(pygame.sprite.Sprite):
    def __init__(self):
        super().__init__()
        self.image = pygame.Surface((100, 20))
        self.image.fill(BLUE)
        self.rect = self.image.get_rect()
        self.rect.x = SCREEN_WIDTH // 2 - 50
        self.rect.y = SCREEN_HEIGHT - 40

    def update(self):
        pos = pygame.mouse.get_pos()
        self.rect.x = pos[0]
        if self.rect.x > SCREEN_WIDTH - self.rect.
width:
            self.rect.x = SCREEN_WIDTH - self.rect.
width

#Create sprite group
all_sprites = pygame.sprite.Group()

#Create player paddle
paddle = Paddle()
all_sprites.add(paddle)

#Main game loop
running = True
while running:
```

```
        # Keep loop running at the right speed
        clock.tick(30)

        #Process events
        for event in pygame.event.get():
            if event.type == pygame.QUIT:
                running = False

        #Update
        all_sprites.update()

        #Draw / render
        screen.fill(BLACK)
        all_sprites.draw(screen)

        #Flip the display
        pygame.display.flip()

    #Quit pygame
    pygame.quit()
```

Here's what's happening in this section:

- **Main Game Loop**: We've got a loop that keeps the game running at a steady 30 frames per second.
- **Paddle Movement**: The paddle's position is updated based on the mouse's horizontal movement. It stays within the screen bounds, so you can't move it off-screen.
- **Drawing and Updating**: The paddle is drawn on the screen, and we use **pygame.display.flip()** to make sure everything is visible.

With the paddle working, we can now move on to the most fun part: catching those falling stars!

Catch a Falling Star and Scoring

Now it's time to add the falling objects—our stars (albeit squares)—and detect when they collide with the paddle to update the score. Here's the updated code for that:

```
#Filename: catch3.py
import pygame
import random
import time

#Initialize Pygame
pygame.init()

#Constants
SCREEN_WIDTH = 800
SCREEN_HEIGHT = 600
BLACK = (0, 0, 0)
WHITE = (255, 255, 255)
```

```
RED = (255, 0, 0)
BLUE = (0, 0, 255)
FONT_SIZE = 36

#Game variables
score = 0
clock = pygame.time.Clock()

#Set up the screen
screen = pygame.display.set_mode((SCREEN_WIDTH, SCREEN_
HEIGHT))
pygame.display.set_caption("Catch the Falling Objects")

#Define fonts
font = pygame.font.SysFont(None, FONT_SIZE)

#Define player paddle
class Paddle(pygame.sprite.Sprite):
    def __init__(self):
        super().__init__()
        self.image = pygame.Surface((100, 20))
        self.image.fill(BLUE)
        self.rect = self.image.get_rect()
        self.rect.x = SCREEN_WIDTH // 2 - 50
        self.rect.y = SCREEN_HEIGHT - 40

    def update(self):
        pos = pygame.mouse.get_pos()
        self.rect.x = pos[0]
        if self.rect.x > SCREEN_WIDTH - self.rect.
width:
            self.rect.x = SCREEN_WIDTH - self.rect.
width

#Define falling objects
class FallingObject(pygame.sprite.Sprite):
    def __init__(self):
        super().__init__()
        self.image = pygame.Surface((30, 30))
        self.image.fill(RED)
        self.rect = self.image.get_rect()
        self.rect.x = random.randint(0, SCREEN_WIDTH -
self.rect.width)
        self.rect.y = random.randint(-100, -40)
        self.speedy = random.randint(3, 9)

    def update(self):
        self.rect.y += self.speedy
        if self.rect.top > SCREEN_HEIGHT:
            self.rect.x = random.randint(0, SCREEN_
WIDTH - self.rect.width)
            self.rect.y = random.randint(-100, -40)
            self.speedy = random.randint(3, 9)

#Create sprite groups
all_sprites = pygame.sprite.Group()
objects = pygame.sprite.Group()

#Create player paddle
paddle = Paddle()
all_sprites.add(paddle)
```

```
#Main game loop
running = True
while running:
    # Keep loop running at the right speed
    clock.tick(30)

    #Process events
    for event in pygame.event.get():
        if event.type == pygame.QUIT:
            running = False

    #Update
    all_sprites.update()

    # Spawn a new object
    if random.randint(1, 50) == 1:
        obj = FallingObject()
        all_sprites.add(obj)
        objects.add(obj)

    #Check for collisions
    hits = pygame.sprite.spritecollide(paddle, objects,
True)
    for hit in hits:
        score += 1

    #Draw / render
    screen.fill(BLACK)
    all_sprites.draw(screen)

    #Draw score
    text = font.render("Score: " + str(score), True,
WHITE)
    screen.blit(text, (10, 10))

    #Flip the display
    pygame.display.flip()

#Quit pygame
pygame.quit()
```

Now the game is complete! As you can see each time we add an element it seems as though our code doubles in size. Maybe, maybe not? The important things is that the three programs show how you can grow a pygame application and in such a way you can test it before you add the next bit of functionality. Here's a quick breakdown of the final steps:

- **Spawning New Objects**: New stars (falling objects) are randomly generated during each frame of the game. The line **if random. randint(1, 50) == 1:** creates a small chance (1 in 50) that a new object will be spawned each frame, which keeps the game unpredictable and fun. When a new object is spawned, it's added to the **all_sprites** and objects groups so that it will be managed and drawn correctly.

- **Collision Detection**: The program checks for collisions between the paddle and any falling objects using **pygame.sprite.spritecollide(paddle, objects, True)**. This function detects if any of the stars collide with the paddle. If a collision is detected, the star is removed from the screen (thanks to the True parameter), and the score is increased by one.
- **Updating the Display**: After updating the positions of all the sprites (the paddle and the falling stars), the screen is cleared, and the updated sprites are drawn on the screen. The score is then rendered and displayed in the top-left corner of the screen using the blit() function.
- **Game Over**: Finally, after all the stars have fallen and been caught (or missed), the game ends when the player closes the window. pygame.quit() is called to cleanly exit the game.

By now, you should have a fully functional game where you can catch falling stars with a paddle. This project covers many core concepts of game development, from handling user input and sprite management to collision detection and score tracking. With these basics under your belt, you're well on your way to creating more complex games in the future!

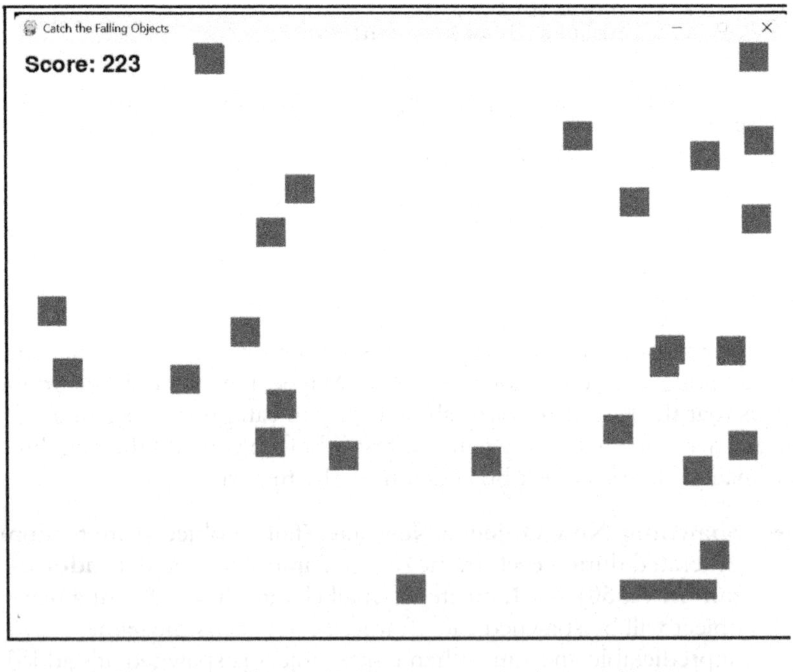

Figure 33a. Catch a Falling Star (in the shape of block).

What's missing though?

Sound

What's a game without some fun sound effects? Luckily, Pygame has got you covered when it comes to adding those satisfying bings, bongs, and more. To get started, you'll need a few sound files. A great place to find free sounds is **freesound.org**. You can browse around, test different sounds, and download the ones you like. Just make sure they're in MP3 or WAV format because Pygame doesn't play nice with FLAC files. Once you've got your sounds, copy them into the same directory where you're storing your game program. (You can store them elsewhere, but just remember to adjust the file path in your code accordingly.)

Let's dip our toes into sound by trying out a basic program that plays an audio file. Here's how it works:

```
#Filename: PygameSound1.py
import pygame
import sys

def play_audio(file_path):
    #Initialize pygame mixer
    pygame.mixer.init()

    #Load the audio file
    pygame.mixer.music.load(file_path)

    #Play the audio file
    pygame.mixer.music.play()

    #Create a basic Pygame window
    pygame.init()
    screen = pygame.display.set_mode((350, 50))
    pygame.display.set_caption("PyGame Audio Player")

    #Main loop to keep the window open and play the
music
    while True:
        for event in pygame.event.get():
            if event.type == pygame.QUIT:
                pygame.mixer.music.stop()
                pygame.quit()
                sys.exit()

        #Refresh the screen
        pygame.display.flip()

if __name__ == "__main__":
    #Specify the path to your WAV or MP3 file
    audio_file_path = 'short_melody.mp3'

    # Call the function to play the audio file
    play_audio(audio_file_path)
```

This little program plays an audio file using just one main function, **play_ audio()**, and a simple main section that calls it. Let's break down how it works:

Initialisation and Audio Playback

We start by importing the necessary modules: pygame for handling audio and graphics, and sys for handling system-level operations like quitting the program.

Inside the **play_audio()** function, we initialise the Pygame mixer module with **pygame.mixer.init()**. This is what allows us to handle audio.

Next, we load the audio file using **pygame.mixer.music.load(file_path)**, and start playing it with **pygame.mixer.music.play()**.

Creating a Simple Pygame Window

Even though the main goal is to play audio, the program also creates a small graphical window using Pygame. We do this by calling **pygame.init()** to set up all Pygame modules, and then we create a window with **pygame.display.set_mode((350, 50))**. This window is titled "PyGame Audio Player" using pygame.display.set_caption().

Event Handling and Program Loop

The program then enters an infinite loop to keep the window open while the audio plays. Inside this loop, we constantly check for events—like clicking the 'x' to close the window.

If a QUIT event is detected, the program stops the music with **pygame.mixer.music.stop()**, quits Pygame with **pygame.quit()**, and exits the script with **sys.exit()**.

The loop also includes **pygame.display.flip()**, which refreshes the window. The window itself doesn't display much, but it stays open while the sound plays.

Main Section and Execution

In the **if __name__ == "__main__":** section, we specify the path to the audio file (audio_file_path = 'short_melody.mp3') and call the play_audio() function to play the file and open the window. The audio file can be either in WAV or MP3 format.

Managing Game State

When creating more complex games, you'll often find it useful to manage different game states. For example, your game might have states like "Main Menu," "Playing," "Paused," and "Game Over." By structuring your game into these **states**, you can better organise your code and make it easier to manage what happens during each part of the game. Typically, you can use a simple state machine pattern, where the game loop checks the current state and calls the appropriate functions or methods for that state.

Optimising Performance

As your game grows in complexity, performance can become an issue, especially on resource-limited platforms like the Raspberry Pi. Here are a few tips to keep your game running smoothly:

- **Limit Frame Rate**: Use **pygame.time.Clock().tick(fps)** to control the frame rate. A common target is 30 or 60 frames per second (fps).
- **Efficient Drawing**: Only redraw parts of the screen that have changed. This can be achieved using **pygame.display.update(rectangle)** instead of pygame.display.flip() when only a small part of the screen needs updating.
- **Sprite Groups**: Use **pygame.sprite.Group()** to manage and update multiple sprites efficiently, as Pygame handles drawing and collision detection more efficiently within these groups.
- **Surface Locking**: If you're performing pixel-level operations, consider locking the surface with s**urface.lock()** before modifying pixels, and unlocking with s**urface.unlock()** afterwards. This can improve performance in certain scenarios.

Handling Different Screen Resolutions

Pygame allows you to create games for different screen resolutions. However, not all screens are the same size or have the same aspect ratio. To ensure your game looks good on different displays, consider the following:

- **Resolution Scaling**: Develop your game at a base resolution and then scale up or down depending on the actual screen size. You can do this by setting a base resolution and then using pygame.transform.scale() to adjust the size of surfaces.
- **Aspect Ratio Handling**: To maintain the correct aspect ratio, you might want to letterbox or pillar box your game (adding black bars on the sides or top/bottom) or dynamically adjust the game layout based on the screen's aspect ratio.

Loading and Managing Assets

Games typically use a variety of assets, including images, sounds, and fonts. Managing these efficiently is crucial for keeping your game organised and performing.

- **Asset Loading**: Load all necessary assets (like images and sounds) at the start of the game to avoid delays during gameplay. You can store these in a dictionary or a custom asset manager class for easy access throughout your game.

- **Spritesheets**: Consider using spritesheets—large images containing multiple smaller images—to reduce the number of image files and improve loading times. Pygame has functions like **Surface.subsurface()** to extract individual sprites from a spritesheet.
- **Lazy Loading**: For large games, you might want to use lazy loading, where assets are only loaded when they are first needed. This can help reduce the initial load time of the game.

Questions

1. What is Pygame and what is its primary use?
2. Why is SDL important in the context of Pygame, and what functionalities does it provide?
3. Describe the general steps needed to install Pygame in a virtual environment.
4. In the "Catch a Falling Star" example, what is the purpose of the pygame.init() function?
5. Explain the purpose of the Paddle class in the game example and how it manages movement.
6. How does the game detect collisions between the paddle and falling objects, and what happens when a collision occurs?
7. What does the pygame.display.flip() function achieve in the game loop?
8. In the "Adding Sound" section, what module function is used to play audio in Pygame, and which audio formats are compatible?
9. What is a state machine pattern, and how might it be useful in managing game states?
10. Rewrite the entire program to include sound. Include pings when a star is caught.
11. With the counter, decrement it when a star is missed. Have a winning score of 100 and play a triumphant sound at this point. If the score reached 0 (zero) play a death march or similar!

Exercise

Expand the program so that it increments the score by one when a star is caught and decrements by one when a star is missed. Find and include a star sprite.

34: Pillow

Pillow is a modern Python library derived from the Python Imaging Library. It is a flexible module for image processing, which handles all the tasks you might expect from a modern day PIL. It handles all populate image formats such as JPEG, PNG, GIF, and BMPP Pillow makes it easy to open, manipulate, and save images with just a few lines of code.

One of the great things about Pillow is that it can handle a wide range of image manipulation tasks. You can resize, crop, rotate, or flip images, and even apply filters like blurring, sharpening, or edge detection. Plus, Pillow lets you draw on images, add text, or modify individual pixels, handy for more advanced image editing, like creating dynamic graphics or applying artistic effects.

Pillow also works well with other libraries and frameworks. It's often paired with web frameworks like **Flask** or **Django** to manage image uploads, resizing, or on-the-fly image creation. In game development or graphical apps, Pillow can be used to create or edit sprites, backgrounds, and other visual elements. For Raspberry Pi projects, it's especially useful when working with displays and sensors to show or modify images, making it a great choice for hobbyists and developers building visual projects on embedded systems.

It's easy to install in a virtual environment:

```
pip install pillow
```

You'll need an image to get started, so find one of the family and have some fun with the examples below. Alternatively, use the spaceman from the downloads

Image Opening and Saving

You can easily load images using the **Image.open()** function, and they can be manipulated within your program.

Saving Images: Images can be saved in different formats using **Image.save()** with options like format specification and quality adjustment.

```
from PIL import Image
image = Image.open("example.jpg")
image.save("example.png", format="PNG")
```

Image Resizing and Cropping

Pillow provides **Image.resize()** to scale images to new dimensions, with optional interpolation methods like NEAREST, BILINEAR, BICUBIC, and LANCZOS. You can extract specific parts of an image using **Image.crop()**, specifying the bounding box as coordinates.

```
resized_image = Image.resize((200, 200))
#Resize to 200x200
cropped_image = Image.crop((100, 100, 400, 400))
#Crop using bounding box
```

Rotating and Flipping

Rotation: Use **Image.rotate()** to rotate images by a given angle (e.g., 90, 180, 270 degrees). Pillow allows flipping images horizontally or vertically using **Image.transpose()**, with options like Image.FLIP_LEFT_RIGHT and Image.FLIP_TOP_BOTTOM.

```
rotated_image = Image.rotate(90)  #Rotate 90 degrees
flipped_image = Image.transpose(Image.FLIP_LEFT_RIGHT)
#Flip horizontally
```

Colour Modes and Conversion

Pillow supports different image modes, such as RGB, RGBA (with transparency), L (grayscale), and CMYK. You can convert images between these modes using **Image.convert()**, which is useful for processing or optimising images for specific outputs.

```
grayscale_image = Image.convert("L")
```

Image Filters and Enhancements

Pillow offers various filters like BLUR, CONTOUR, DETAIL, SHARPEN, and EDGE_ENHANCE, which can be applied using **Image.filter().**

For finer control, you can use the **ImageEnhance** module, which provides options to adjust brightness, contrast, sharpness, and colour balance.

```
from PIL import ImageFilter
blurred_image = Image.filter(ImageFilter.BLUR)
#Apply blur filter
```

Drawing and Text

Using the **ImageDraw** module, you can draw basic shapes (rectangles, circles, lines) or complex graphics on images. The **ImageDraw.text()** function allows you to add text to images, specifying font, size, and position. You can load custom fonts using **ImageFont** to create professional-looking text overlays.

Here's a Python program (two in fact) that demonstrates the use of **ImageDraw** and **ImageFont** functions from the Pillow (PIL) library. This program creates a simple image, draws text on it using a custom font, and draws a rectangle around the text.

In recent versions of Pillow, the **textsize()** method has been depreciated and replaced by **textbbox()** to calculate the bounding box of the text. This following program uses the updated version.

```
#Filename: pil1.py
from PIL import Image, ImageDraw, ImageFont

# Create a blank white image
image = Image.new('RGB', (400, 200), color='white')

# Initialize ImageDraw
draw = ImageDraw.Draw(image)

# Load a font
# Make sure you have a font file in your system; you can
use a TrueType font (.ttf)
# If you don't have a custom font, you can use the
built-in PIL font by omitting the font argument in
`ImageFont.truetype()`
try:
    font = ImageFont.truetype("arial.ttf", 40)  #
Change to any .ttf font file path if needed
except IOError:
    print("Font not found, using default font.")
    font = ImageFont.load_default()

# Define text to be drawn
text = "Hello, Pillow!"

# Get text size to position it properly
text_width, text_height = draw.textsize(text,
font=font)


# Define position
position = ((400 - text_width) // 2, (200 - text_
height) // 2)

# Draw the text on the image
draw.text(position, text, fill="blue", font=font)

# Draw a rectangle around the text
draw.rectangle([position, (position[0] + text_width,
position[1] + text_height)], outline="red", width=2)
```

```
# Save the image
image.save("pillow_text_example.png")

# Show the image (optional)
image.show()
```

Explanation:

Creating a Blank Image: The Image.new('RGB', (400, 200), color='white') creates a blank white image of 400x200 pixels.

Using ImageDraw: ImageDraw.Draw(image) creates a drawing object that allows us to draw on the image.

Loading a Font with ImageFont: ImageFont.truetype("arial.ttf", 40) loads a custom font file (arial.ttf). The 40 is the font size. If you don't have a custom font file, you can use the default PIL font with ImageFont.load_default().

Drawing Text: The draw.text() function draws the text onto the image. You can specify the position, the text itself, the fill colour, and the font.

Drawing a Rectangle: The draw.rectangle() function draws a rectangle around the text. We calculate the coordinates for the rectangle based on the position and size of the text.

Saving and Displaying the Image: The image is saved as pillow_text_example.png and displayed using image.show().

Output: This program generates an image with the text "Hello, Pillow!" centred on it, in blue font with a red rectangle surrounding the text. You can adjust the font and text as needed.

In recent versions of Pillow, the **textsize()** method has been depreciated and replaced by **textbbox() to** calculate the bounding box of the text. I will update the program to use textbbox() instead of textsize() to resolve the

To rewrite the program to use a Google font, you'll first need to download and install a **.ttf font** file from Google Fonts. Once downloaded, you can load it with Pillow's ImageFont.truetype() function and set the desired font size.

Image Rotation

This next program will rotate an image by 180 degrees, ie, flip it upside down. It uses an image that can be found with the program files.

To modify your program to rotate an image by 180 degrees and save it as a PNG file, we can make use of the **rotate() method** from the **PIL.Image** module.

```
#Filename: pil2.py
from PIL import Image

# Load the image (make sure to specify the correct file
path)
image = Image.open("input_image.jpg")  # Replace with
the path to your image file

# Rotate the image by 180 degrees
rotated_image = Image.rotate(180)

# Save the rotated image as a PNG file
rotated_image.save("rotated_image.png")

# Optionally, show the rotated image
rotated_image.show()
```

The Image.open() method is used to load an existing image (input_image.jpg in this case). Make sure to replace "input_image.jpg" with the actual image file path.

The rotate(180) method rotates the image by 180 degrees and save("rotated_image.png") method saves the rotated image as a PNG file. You can change the file name and location as needed.

The show() function is optional, and it will open the rotated image in your default image viewer.

Note: This program occasionally brings up errors across different Raspberry Pi OSs. It can still generate the image operation but the error often arises from the default GNOME-based viewer **image.show().** A simple fix is to install an alternative viewer, such as **feh**. To check which viewer is being used when you call image.show():

```
xdg-mime query default image/png
```

If the result points to a GNOME-based viewer (e.g., eog.desktop), switch it to another viewer:

```
sudo apt-get install feh
```

But as I said if the if the image is displayed correctly and the warning doesn't interfere with the program's functionality, you can safely ignore it.

Image Proportions

Pillow doesn't automatically "sense" or label an image's proportions like 4:3, but you can easily calculate the aspect ratio of an image using its dimensions. Pillow allows you to access the width and height of an image, and from there, you can determine the aspect ratio.

Here's an example of how you can check if an image is in a specific proportion like 4:3:

```
#Filename: pil3.py
from PIL import Image

#Open the image
image = Image.open("example.jpg")

#Get the image dimensions
width, height = image.size

#Calculate the aspect ratio
aspect_ratio = width / height

#Check if the aspect ratio is approximately 4:3
if abs(aspect_ratio - (4/3)) < 0.01:
# Allowing a small tolerance
    print("The image is approximately 4:3.")
else:
    print(f"The image has an aspect ratio of {aspect_
ratio:.2f}")
```

Here's what the code is doing:

image.size returns the dimensions (width, height). By dividing the width by the height, you can find the aspect ratio.

Compare the calculated ratio to common proportions like 4:3 or 16:9. A small tolerance is allowed because floating-point calculations may introduce minor inaccuracies.

Pillow doesn't automatically classify the image's aspect ratio for you, but this simple calculation lets you do that. And you can ensure that a re-sized image isn't squashed up.

Note: I find in the Pillow module the mixture of lowercase and uppercase definitions along with functions starting with a capital letter annoying. But that's me.

Questions

1. What methods does Pillow offer for rotating and flipping images?
2. How can you convert images to different colour modes using Pillow?
3. How do you apply filters in Pillow, and what module allows for more control over enhancements?
4. How can you check if an image has a 4:3 aspect ratio using Pillow?
5. What is Pillow, and what are some of the common image formats it supports?
6. Explain how to resize and crop an image using Pillow, including the method names used.

35: NumPy

NumPy (or Numpy, however you prefer to spell it) is short for **Numerical Python**, and it's like your go-to abacus for handling arrays, matrices, and all things numerical, like linear algebra and data analysis.

NumPy isn't part of Python's standard library. That said in later versions of the OS it is pre-installed as part of the system. However you will need to install it in your virtual environment. Installing should be simple, but sometimes it can be a bit tricky depending on your Raspberry Pi setup. (NumPy can be very finicky installing on the Raspberry Pi. It's important you us the Raspberry Pi version signified as '**python3-numpy**') You might need to try a few options to get it working, but generally to ensure that you have the Raspberry Pi specific version you should use:

```
sudo apt install python3-numpy
```

or

```
pip install numpy
```

into a virtual environment. Once installed, you can check the version of NumPy you're using by running this little program, 'numpy1.py':

```
#Filename: numpy1.py
import numpy as np
print("NumPy Version:", np.__version__)
```

Note is you get a message along these lines:

```
...\site-packages\_distutils_hack\__init__.py can
shadow the library module '_distutils_hack'. Consider
renaming or moving it!
```

suggests that the **_distutils_hack** package in your Thonny installation is interfering with the standard Python environment. This issue occurs because a non-standard package location is being used that may conflict with the library module path, particularly when working with numpy or other packages installed through different methods. It may suggest that you are not working within a virtual environment. In cases such as these try rebooting and reactivating your virtual environment. Once you have it working you should be fine for the long-run. You might also see if you can upgrade your Thonny package, if you are using Thonny.

In Chapter 25, with matrix2.py, we created two arrays and then summed them, which required several steps to get the result. But with NumPy, element-wise operations are much simpler, like this:

```
# Filename: numpy2.py
import numpy as np

# Define matrices using NumPy arrays
matrix1 = np.array([[1, 2, 3],
                    [4, 5, 6],
                    [7, 8, 9]])

matrix2 = np.array([[9, 8, 7],
                    [6, 5, 4],
                    [3, 2, 1]])

# Element-wise addition using the + operator
result_matrix = matrix1 + matrix2

# Print the result
print("Resultant Matrix:")
print(result_matrix)
```

This program imports the NumPy library, defines the matrices matrix1 and matrix2, adds them together element-wise using the + operator, and prints the result. Notice how we display the array in a 3x3 format to make it easier to visualise, but you could also define the array in a list style if you prefer.

Want to subtract one array from another? Just use the subtraction operator for element-wise subtraction:

```
# Filename: numpy3.py
import numpy as np

# Define matrices
matrix1 = np.array([[1, 2, 3], [4, 5, 6], [7, 8, 9]])
matrix2 = np.array([[9, 8, 7], [6, 5, 4], [3, 2, 1]])

# Element-wise subtraction using the - operator
result_matrix = matrix1 - matrix2

# Print the result
print("Resultant Matrix:")
print(result_matrix)
```

Expected Output:

```
Resultant Matrix:
[[-8 -6 -4]
 [-2  0  2]
 [ 4  6  8]]
```

When it comes to matrix multiplication, however, things work a little differently. Unlike element-wise multiplication, where corresponding elements are multiplied, matrix multiplication (or dot product) requires the .dot() method or the @ operator:

```
# Filename: numpy4.py
import numpy as np

# Define matrices
matrix1 = np.array([[1, 2, 3], [4, 5, 6], [7, 8, 9]])
matrix2 = np.array([[9, 8, 7], [6, 5, 4], [3, 2, 1]])

#Perform matrix multiplication using dot
result_matrix = np.dot(matrix1, matrix2)
print("Resultant Matrix (Multiplication):")
print(result_matrix)
```

Resultant Matrix (Multiplication):

```
[[ 30  24  18]
 [ 84  69  54]
 [138 114  90]]
```

Alternatively, you can use the @ operator for matrix multiplication, which is more intuitive. Replace these lines:

```
# Matrix multiplication using the @ operator
result_matrix = matrix1 @ matrix2
```

Matrix multiplication follows different rules than element-wise multiplication. It multiplies the rows of the first matrix by the columns of the second matrix, so the number of columns in the first matrix must match the number of rows in the second.

Now, let's see how you can divide one 3x3 matrix by another using NumPy's element-wise division:

```
# Filename: numpy5.py
import numpy as np

matrix1 = np.array([[10, 20, 30],
                    [40, 50, 60],
                    [70, 80, 90]])

matrix2 = np.array([[10, 8, 3],
                    [5, 50, 4],
                    [5, 6, 10]])

# Element-wise division using NumPy's divide function
result_matrix = np.divide(matrix1, matrix2)
```

```
print("Resultant Matrix (Divide):")
print(result_matrix)
```

The **.divide()** function performs element-wise division between two arrays, meaning each element of the first array is divided by the corresponding element of the second array.

Here's what the output from numpy5.py looks like:

```
[[  1.        2.5      10.   ]
 [  8.        1.       15.   ]
 [ 14.      13.33333333    9.   ]]
```

As you can see, each element in matrix1 is divided by the corresponding element in matrix2, and the result is stored in the resulting matrix. Notice that the decimal point is displayed, even for exact divisions.

Being Mean

NumPy provides tons of mathematical functions for working with arrays. One of the popular ones is calculating the **mean** of a one-dimensional array using **.mean**:

```
#Filename: numpy6.py
import numpy as np

a = np.array([1, 2, 3, 4, 5])

#Calculate the mean of the array
meana = np.mean(a)
print("Mean of array is:", meana)
```

You can also calculate the mean across different axes for multidimensional arrays. For example, calculating the mean along rows or columns for a 2D array.

To that end you can calculate the mean of a multi-dimensional array by specifying the axis parameter to determine along which dimension the mean should be calculated.

Axis 0: Refers to rows, so calculating the mean along axis 0 will compute the mean of each column.

Axis 1: Refers to columns, so calculating the mean along axis 1 will compute the mean of each row.

```
#Filename: numpy7.py
import numpy as np

# Define a 3x3 array
matrix = np.array([[1, 2, 3],
                   [4, 5, 6],
                   [7, 8, 9]])
```

```
# Calculate the mean of the entire array
mean_total = np.mean(matrix)
print("Mean of entire array:", mean_total)

# Calculate the mean of each column (axis 0)
mean_columns = np.mean(matrix, axis=0)
print("Mean of each column:", mean_columns)

# Calculate the mean of each row (axis 1)
mean_rows = np.mean(matrix, axis=1)
print("Mean of each row:", mean_rows)
```

The output should be:

```
Mean of entire array: 5.0
Mean of each column: [4. 5. 6.]
Mean of each row: [2. 5. 8.]
```

mean_total: Calculates the mean of all elements in the array.

mean_columns: Calculates the mean along axis 0, which is across rows (i.e., for each column).

mean_rows: Calculates the mean along axis 1, which is across columns (i.e., for each row).

You can apply the same principle to arrays of higher dimensions by specifying different axes depending on which dimension you want to compute the mean for.

Values as a Variable Name

When working with libraries like NumPy, you'll often see the variable name **values** used. This is a common convention to store and manage data, particularly numerical data. Here's why it's handy:

- **Storage of Data**: **values** is often used to store data that will later be converted into a NumPy array. The name suggests that the data is numerical or array-like.
- **Lists of Data**: Before converting data into a NumPy array, it might be stored as a regular Python list. Naming it 'values' implies that this list holds numerical data that will be processed or analysed.
- **Conversion to NumPy Array**: Data stored in 'values' is often converted to a NumPy array for faster computation and to take advantage of NumPy's functions. For example, if 'values' is a list of numbers, you might convert it like this:

```
#Filename: numpy8.py
import numpy as np

#A list of numbers
values = [1, 2, 3, 4, 5]

#Convert the list to a NumPy array
np_array = np.array(values)

#Now you can use NumPy functions on the array
mean_value = np.mean(np_array)
print(mean_value)  # Output: 3.0
```

Using **values** as a variable name is a convention that signals that the data is numerical or will be processed as such. This makes your code more readable and understandable for others. While **values** is common, it's not mandatory. The name can vary depending on the context, but **values** is often chosen for its clarity in representing a collection of data.

Indexing and Slicing NumPy Arrays

You can slice and dice NumPy arrays just like you would with regular lists. Let's see how that works:

```
#Filename: numpy9.py
import numpy as np

#Creating a one-dimensional NumPy array
a = np.array([1, 2, 3, 4, 5])

#Indexing to get the first element
print(a[0])  # Output: 1

#Slicing to get elements from the second to the fourth
print(a[1:4])
# Output: [2, 3, 4]
```

In this snippet, we create a simple one-dimensional NumPy array **'a'** with the values **[1, 2, 3, 4, 5]**. The first print statement grabs the first element of the array, which is **1**. The second print gives us a slice from the second to the fourth elements, resulting in **[2, 3, 4]**.

But wait, there's more! NumPy has a handy feature that lists don't offer—a **modify** function. This lets you make changes directly to your array elements. To demonstrate how NumPy's modify function works, let's create a program that modifies elements in a NumPy array directly.

```
#Filename: numpy10.py
import numpy as np

# Create a 3x3 matrix using NumPy
matrix = np.array([
    [1, 2, 3],
    [4, 5, 6],
```

```
        [7, 8, 9]
    ])

    print("Original matrix:")
    print(matrix)

    # Modify elements directly using NumPy indexing
    matrix[0, 0] = 10
    matrix[1, 2] = 15
    matrix[:, 1] = [20, 21, 22]

    print("\nModified matrix:")
    print(matrix)
```

Things kick off with the creation of a 3x3 matrix using NumPy's array function. Next we can modifying elements directly, thus:

```
matrix[0, 0] = 10 #modifies the first element.
matrix[1, 2] = 15 #modifies element at 2nd row, 3rd col
matrix[:, 1] = [20, 21, 22] #modifies elements 2ndcol.
```

Finally, the modified matrix is printed to show the changes.

Broadcasting

Broadcasting is one of NumPy's most useful features. It allows you to perform arithmetic operations between arrays of **different** shapes without needing to manually resize or replicate them. This saves time and memory, which is always a positive thing.

When performing operations between arrays, NumPy first compares their shapes element-wise. If the shapes are not identical, broadcasting automatically expands the smaller array to match the larger one so that the operation can be applied on an element-wise basis.

NumPy doesn't, as you may think, copy the smaller array to match the shape of the larger one; instead, it broadcasts it across the larger array. This means that the smaller array is virtually replicated as many times as necessary to match the shape of the larger array. The computation is done as if the arrays were the same size, without the memory overhead of explicitly creating copies.

The 3 Rules of 1 in Broadcasting

Broadcasting follows three specific rules:

Size Mismatch in a Dimension: If the sizes of the arrays differ in any dimension, but one of the arrays has a size of '1' in that dimension, NumPy **stretches** the array with size 1 to match the size of the other array.

Incompatible Dimensions: If the sizes in any dimension do not match and neither array has a size of '1' in that dimension, broadcasting throws an error because the operation cannot be performed.

```
#Filename: numpy11.py
import numpy as np

# Define a 3x3 array with shape (1,3)
array1 = np.array([[1, 2, 3],
                   [4, 5, 6],
                   [7, 8, 9]])

# Define a 1x3 array
array2 = np.array([10, 20, 30])

# Perform element-wise addition with broadcasting
result = array1 + array2

print("Array 1 (3x3):")
print(array1)
print("\nArray 2 (1x3):")
print(array2)
print("\nResult after Broadcasting:")
print(result)
```

This produces the following output:

```
Array 1 (3x3):
[[1 2 3]
 [4 5 6]
 [7 8 9]]

Array 2 (1x3):
[10 20 30]

Result after Broadcasting:
[[11 22 33]
 [14 25 36]
 [17 28 39]]
```

This is calculated thus:

Array 1 has a shape of (3, 3). Array 2 has a shape of (1, 3).

According to the broadcasting rules: Rule 1 is applied: The shape of array2 is "expanded" to match the dimensions of array1. Specifically, array2 is treated as if it were a 3x3 array where the first dimension is broadcast to match the shape of array1. The value [10, 20, 30] is repeated across all rows of array1.

The operation array1 + array2 then adds the values of array2 to each row of array1 element-wise.

See Figure 35a opposite.

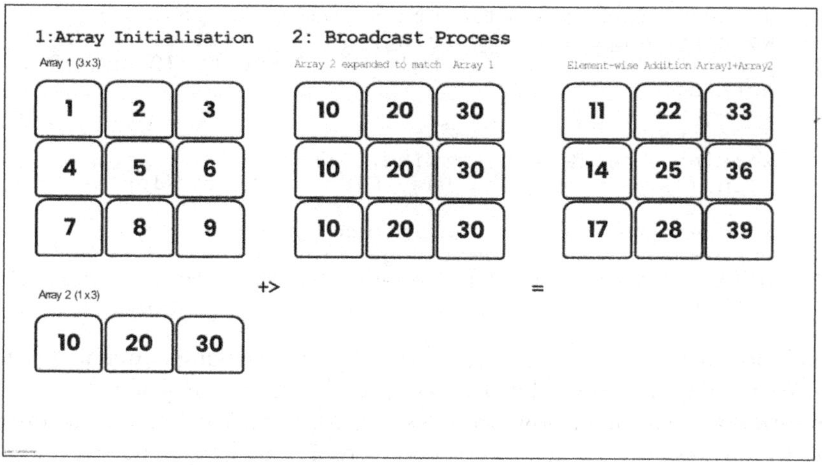

Figure 35a. Adding different size NumPy arrays.

According to the broadcasting rules: Rule 1 is applied: The shape of array2 is "expanded" to match the dimensions of array1. Specifically, array2 is treated as if it were a 3x3 array where the first dimension is broadcast to match the shape of array1. The value [10, 20, 30] is repeated across all rows of array1.

The operation array1 + array2 then adds the values of array2 to each row of array1 element-wise.

Append, Delete, and Insert

NumPy makes it easy to append, delete, and insert data into arrays with some simple array manipulation functions. These operations return new arrays instead of modifying the original array in place, so it's essential to assign the result back to the variable if needed. Let's dive into a program that demonstrates how to perform these operations:

```
# Filename: numpy12.py
import numpy as np

# Start with a simple array
working = np.array([10, 20])
print("Start:", working)

# Append a single element
working = np.append(working, 30.5)
print("Appending:", working)

# Insert a single element
working = np.insert(working, 1, values=25)
# Insert another element at position 2
working = np.insert(working, 2, values=19)
print("After Inserting 25 and 19:", working)
```

```
# Insert multiple elements at multiple positions
working = np.insert(working, [3, 5], values=[9, 12])
print("After Inserting Multiple Elements (9 and 12):",
working)

# Delete the last element
working = np.delete(working, -1)
print("After Deleting Last Element:", working)

# Delete elements at positions 0 and 1
working = np.delete(working, [0, 1])
print("After Deleting Elements at Positions 0 and 1:",
working)
```

Here's how it works: We begin with a simple array working containing [10, 20]. We next append the value 30.5 to the end of the array using **np.append()**. The array now becomes [10, 20, 30.5]. We insert 25 at position 1 and 19 at position 2. Each insertion returns a **new array.** The array now looks like [10, 25, 19, 20, 30.5]. We insert 9 at position 3 and 12 at position 5 in one go. The array expands to [10, 25, 19, 9, 20, 12, 30.5].

We then use **np.delete()** to remove elements. First, we delete the last element, 30.5, shrinking the array to [10, 25, 19, 9, 20, 12]. Then, we delete the first two elements, 10 and 25, leaving [19, 9, 20, 12].

As you can see, these operations are handy and return modified arrays without changing the original array in place.

Copying Arrays in NumPy

When working with NumPy, sometimes you'll want to create an independent copy of an array, while other times, you'll want to reference the original data without duplicating it. This distinction is important for managing memory and controlling whether changes to one array affect another.

Independent Copy with np.copy()

When you use **np.copy()**, you create a new, independent array. Any changes to this new array won't affect the original one because they are stored in separate memory locations.

When working with NumPy, sometimes you'll want to create a copy of an array, while other times, you'll want to reference the original data without duplicating it. This is where the **np.copy()** function comes in, allowing you to choose whether to create a new copy or just reference the original data.

Independent Copy with np.copy()

When you use np.copy(), you create a new, independent array. Any changes to this new array won't affect the original one.

```
# Filename: numpy13.py
import numpy as np

# Original array
original = np.array([1, 2, 3])

# Create a copy of the array
copied = np.copy(original)

# Modify the new array
copied[0] = 10

print("Original array:", original)  # Output: [1 2 3]
print("Modified array:", copied)    # Output: [10  2  3]
```

In this example, the copied array is independent of the original. Changing copied[0] does not affect the original.

Referencing the Same Data

If you don't want to create a new copy and are okay with modifying the original data, you can reference the same data without duplication. This can be useful to save memory.

```
# Filename: numpy14.py
import numpy as np

# Original array
original = np.array([1, 2, 3])

# Create a new array that references the original array
copied = original  # No copying

# Modify the new array
copied[0] = 10

print("Original array:", original)
# Output: [10  2  3]
print("Modified array:", copied)
# Output: [10  2  3]
```

In this case, copied is just a reference to original. Changing copied[0] directly modifies the original array because they share the same memory location.

When to Use Each Method

Use **np.copy()** (independent copy) when:

- You want to make sure the original array stays unchanged, no matter what happens to the new array.
- You need to manipulate the data independently without affecting the original array.
- Memory isn't an issue, and you prefer safety over efficiency.

Use reference (no copy) when:

- Memory efficiency is crucial, and you don't want to duplicate data.
- You're okay with changes in one array affecting the other.
- Performance is key, and you don't need a separate copy of the data.

Array Properties in NumPy

NumPy arrays have several useful attributes that provide information about the array's structure, such as its shape, size, and data type. Here's a program that demonstrates some common array attributes and methods:

```
#Filename: numpy15.py
import numpy as np

# Create a 2D array (3x3) with numbers from 1 to 9
array_2d = np.arange(1, 10).reshape(3, 3)
print("Original 2D Array:")
print(array_2d)

# Reshape the array
reshaped_array = array_2d.reshape(1, 9)
print("\nReshaped Array (1x9):")
print(reshaped_array)

# Calculate statistics
print("\nSum of all elements:", np.sum(array_2d))
print("Mean of all elements:", np.mean(array_2d))
print("Maximum element:", np.max(array_2d))
print("Minimum element:", np.min(array_2d))

# Calculate sums along axes
print("\nSum of each column:", np.sum(array_2d,
axis=0))
print("Sum of each row:", np.sum(array_2d, axis=1))
```

Program Output

```
Original 2D Array:
[[1 2 3]
 [4 5 6]
 [7 8 9]]

Reshaped Array (1x9):
[[1 2 3 4 5 6 7 8 9]]

Sum of all elements: 45
Mean of all elements: 5.0
Maximum element: 9
Minimum element: 1

Sum of each column: [12 15 18]
Sum of each row: [ 6 15 24]
```

When Which?

Use copy=True when:

- You want to make sure the original array stays exactly as it is, no matter what.
- You need a completely independent array that you can modify freely without worrying about the original data.
- Memory isn't an issue, and you'd rather be safe than sorry.

Use copy=False when:

- You want to save memory and avoid unnecessary duplication of data.
- You're okay with changes to the new array affecting the original one.
- Performance is key, and you don't need a separate copy of the data.

Understanding when to use **copy=True** or **copy=False** can help you write more efficient and safer code, depending on your needs.

Common Dot Options for NumPy Arrays

NumPy has loads of handy attributes and methods that can make your life easier. This next program demonstrates the use of methods **.shape**, **.dtype, .size, .ndim, reshape**, and **sum**. The program will create a 2D array (matrix), manipulate its shape, and perform basic calculations on the data:

```
#Filename: numpy16.py
import numpy as np

# Create a 2D NumPy array (matrix) with integers
array = np.array([[1, 2, 3], [4, 5, 6], [7, 8, 9]])

# Display array properties
print("Original Array:")
print(array)
print("\nShape of the array:", array.shape)
# (3, 3)
print("Data type of the array elements:", array.dtype)
# int64
print("Number of elements in the array:", array.size)
# 9
print("Number of dimensions (ndim):", array.ndim)

# Reshape the array from 3x3 to 1x9
reshaped_array = array.reshape(1, 9)
print("\nReshaped Array (1x9):")
print(reshaped_array)

# Calculate sums
print("\nSum of all elements:", array.sum())
print("Sum of each column:", array.sum(axis=0))
print("Sum of each row:", array.sum(axis=1))
```

The program output should look like this:

```
Original Array:
[[1 2 3]
 [4 5 6]
 [7 8 9]]

Shape of the array: (3, 3)
Data type of the array elements: int64
Number of elements in the array: 9
Number of dimensions (ndim): 2

Reshaped Array (1x9):
[[1 2 3 4 5 6 7 8 9]]

Sum of all elements: 45
Sum of each column: [12 15 18]
Sum of each row: [ 6 15 24]
```

The action performed for each of these is:

- **.shape:** Gives the dimensions of the array. In the original 3x3 array, .shape will return (3, 3).
- **.dtype:** The .dtype value may vary depending on your system. For example, it could be int32 on 32-bit systems or int64 on 64-bit systems.
- **.size:** Returns the total number of elements in the array. Here, it's 9, since 3x3 = 9.
- **.ndim:** Returns the number of dimensions the array has. This array has two dimensions (a matrix).
- **.reshape:** Changes the shape of the array. We reshape the original array into a 1x9 array. **reshape** returns a view of the array if possible, meaning changes to the reshaped array may affect the original. If reshaping is not feasible, a copy is created
- **.sum:** Calculates the sum of the array elements. It can compute the total sum or sums along specific axes (rows or columns).

These two programs achieve the same functionality and produce identical outputs numpy15.py is ideal for beginners., while numpy16.py is a concise and direct demonstrations

Methods for Manipulating Array Data

This next program provides some examples of methods used for manipulating array data. This example shows how to manipulate arrays by filling them with values, repeating patterns, and inserting/appending elements.

```
# Filename: numpy17.py
import numpy as np

# Create a 1D array with numbers from 1 to 9
array = np.arange(1, 10)
print("Original Array:")
print(array)

# Use .fill() to replace all elements with a specific
value
array.fill(7)
print("\nArray after .fill(7):")
print(array)

# Create a 2D array and repeat it using .tile()
array_2d = np.array([[1, 2, 3], [4, 5, 6]])
tiled_array = np.tile(array_2d, (2, 2))  # Repeat 2x2
times
print("\nTiled Array:")
print(tiled_array)

# Append elements to the array
array_appended = np.append(array, [10, 11, 12])
print("\nArray after np.append([10, 11, 12]):")
print(array_appended)

# Insert an element at a specific index
array_inserted = np.insert(array, 3, 99)  # Insert 99
at index 3
print("\nArray after np.insert(3, 99):")
print(array_inserted)
```

.fill(): Fills all elements of an array with a specified value. This method modifies the array in-place.

.tile(): Repeats an array along specified dimensions to create a larger array.

np.append(): Appends elements to the end of an array. This creates a new array and does not modify the original.

np.insert(): Inserts elements at a specified index in the array. This also creates a new array without modifying the original.

These two programs only touch the surface of what NumPy is capable of, and if this is your thing you'll find a lot of detail on the NumPy website. Whatever you need to do with arrays there is almost certainly a dot method to help you!

Exploring Data Types (dtypes)

NumPy has a wide range of data types (dtypes) essential for handling different kinds of numerical and non-numerical data efficiently. Let's walk through some of the most common ones:

Integer Types:

int8: An 8-bit signed integer, ranging from -128 to 127.

int16: A 16-bit signed integer, with a range from -32,768 to 32,767.

int32: A 32-bit signed integer, handling values from -2,147,483,648 to 2,147,483,647.

int64: A 64-bit signed integer, covering a vast range from -9,223,372,036,854,775,808 to 9,223,372,036,854,775,807. (Note: On some systems, **int_** may be an alias for either int32 or int64 depending on the architecture.)

Unsigned Integer Types

uint8: An 8-bit unsigned integer, going from 0 to 255.

uint16: A 16-bit unsigned integer, ranging from 0 to 65,535.

uint32: A 32-bit unsigned integer, covering 0 to 4,294,967,295.

uint64: A 64-bit unsigned integer, with a range from 0 to 18,446,744,073,709,551,615.

Floating-Point Types

float16: Half-precision floating-point.

float32: Single-precision floating-point.

float64: Double-precision floating-point (this is the default).

float128: Extended precision floating-point (platform-dependent, and may not be supported on some systems).

In floating-point representation, precision levels (half, single, double, extended) determine the memory used and the accuracy of calculations. For instance, single-precision (32-bit) uses 1 bit for the sign, 8 bits for the exponent, and 23 bits for the fraction. Lower precision reduces memory usage and increases speed at the cost of accuracy.

Complex Types

complex64: A complex number made up of two 32-bit floats (one for the real part, one for the imaginary part).

complex128: A complex number with two 64-bit floats (this is the default for complex numbers).

complex256: A complex number with two 128-bit floats (platform-dependent, and may not be supported on all systems).

Complex numbers are used in fields like engineering, physics, and advanced applications such as quantum mechanics.

Boolean Type

bool_: Represents a Boolean value, which is either True or False.

String Types

string_: Fixed-length ASCII string type.

unicode_: Fixed-length Unicode string type, used when working with Unicode characters.

Other Types

object_: A general-purpose Python object type.

void: Used for arbitrary data types, essentially raw data.

Example Use

Let's see how you can use these different data types in NumPy:

```
# Filename: numpy18.py
import numpy as np

# Integer array
int_array = np.array([1, -2, 3], dtype=np.int32)
print("Integer Array:", int_array, "| dtype:", int_
array.dtype)

# Unsigned integer array
uint_array = np.array([1, 2, 3], dtype=np.uint32)
print("Unsigned Integer Array:", uint_array, "|
dtype:", uint_array.dtype)

# Floating-point array
float_array = np.array([1.0, 2.5, 3.14], dtype=np.
float64)
print("Floating-Point Array:", float_array, "| dtype:",
float_array.dtype)

# Complex number array
complex_array = np.array([1+2j, 3+4j], dtype=np.
complex128)
print("Complex Number Array:", complex_array, "|
dtype:", complex_array.dtype)

# Boolean array
bool_array = np.array([True, False, True], dtype=np.
bool_)
print("Boolean Array:", bool_array, "| dtype:", bool_
array.dtype)

# Unicode string array
unicode_array = np.array(['alpha', 'beta', 'gamma'],
dtype=np.str_)
print("Unicode Array:", unicode_array, "| dtype:",
unicode_array.dtype)
```

```
# Mixed object array
object_array = np.array([1, 'string', 3.14], dtype=np.
object_)
print("Object Array:", object_array, "| dtype:",
object_array.dtype)

# Datetime array
datetime_array = np.array(['2023-10-13', '2024-01-01'],
dtype='datetime64[D]')
print("Datetime Array:", datetime_array, "| dtype:",
datetime_array.dtype)

# Timedelta array
timedelta_array = np.array([1, 2, 3],
dtype='timedelta64[D]')
print("Timedelta Array:", timedelta_array, "| dtype:",
timedelta_array.dtype)
```

Type Conversion

NumPy also makes it easy to convert between different data types. For example, if you need to convert an integer array to floating-point, it's as simple as:

```
# Filename: numpy19.py
import numpy as np

# Integer array
int_array = np.array([1, 2, 3, 4, 5], dtype=np.int32)

# Convert to float
converted_array = int_array.astype(np.float64)
print("Converted Array:", converted_array, "| dtype:",
converted_array.dtype)
```

This produces:

```
[1. 2. 3. 4. 5.] | dtype: float64
```

Why Data Types Matter in NumPy

Choosing the right data type in NumPy isn't just about keeping things organised—it can lead to more efficient memory usage and faster computations, especially when working with large datasets. When creating an array, always consider which **dtype** makes the most sense for your data.

Memory Usage Example

The **.nbytes** attribute in NumPy allows you to determine how much memory an array uses. Let's compare the memory usage of small arrays with different data types:

```
# Filename: numpy20.py
import numpy as np

# Small array of integers with different data types
small_int_array = np.array([1, 2, 3], dtype=np.int8)
```

```
print("Memory used by int8 array:", small_int_array.
nbytes, "bytes")

# Same array with a larger data type
large_int_array = np.array([1, 2, 3], dtype=np.int64)
print("Memory used by int64 array:", large_int_array.
nbytes, "bytes")
```

Output:

```
Memory used by int8 array: 3 bytes
Memory used by int64 array: 24 bytes
```

This example shows how using smaller data types can significantly reduce memory usage.

int8 |■■ (1 byte)

int16 |■■■■ (2 bytes)

int32 |■■■■■■■■ (4 bytes)

int64 |■■■■■■■■■■■■■■■■ (8 bytes)

This chart visually compares the memory usage of different integer types. Here's the memory usage for an array of 1,000,000 elements:

```
int8: 1 MB
int16: 2 MB
int32: 4 MB
int64: 8 MB
```

Why Is This All So Important?

Arrays in Python are widely used because they provide an efficient way to store, manipulate, and process large amounts of numerical data. NumPy is central to this because it brings powerful, optimised tools for working with arrays, enabling high-performance computations and data analysis. Arrays are fundamental for handling numerical and structured data efficient.

Compare a List to a NumPy array.

```
#Filename: numpy21.py
list1 = [1, 2, 3]
list2 = [4, 5, 6]
result = [x + y for x, y in zip(list1, list2)]  #
Element-wise addition
print(result)  # Output: [5, 7, 9]
```

NumPy array:

```
import numpy as np
arr1 = np.array([1, 2, 3])
arr2 = np.array([4, 5, 6])
result = arr1 + arr2  # Element-wise addition
print(result)  # Output: [5 7 9]
```

Why NumPy is Better

Simplicity: NumPy allows operations like addition, subtraction, and multiplication to be expressed in a more concise way.

Performance: NumPy is faster because it uses vectorisation, avoiding the need for Python loops.

Flexibility: NumPy arrays support a wide range of data types and efficient operations on large datasets.

With NumPy, operations are simpler, faster, and more expressive.

NumPy is central because it transforms Python into a sophisticated numerical computing environment, offering speed, flexibility, and a rich set of tools. This is why NumPy is the backbone of scientific computing, data analysis, and machine learning in Python.

Questions

1. How does NumPy simplify matrix addition compared to standard Python?
2. What's the difference between **np.array()** and **np.dot()** when performing matrix operations in NumPy
3. What happens if you attempt element-wise division of two matrices using NumPy and one of the elements in the divisor matrix is zero?
4. How can you check the version of NumPy installed in your Python environment?
5. How does NumPy simplify element-wise addition between matrices compared to standard Python?
6. What is the purpose of the np.dot() function, and how does it differ from the standard + operator in NumPy?
7. What operator can you use as an alternative to np.dot() for matrix multiplication?
8. Describe how element-wise division in NumPy works, and give an example.
9. How can you calculate the mean of an entire matrix or a specific axis in a 2D array?
10. What is broadcasting in NumPy, and why is it beneficial?
11. List the three rules of broadcasting in NumPy and explain each briefly.

36: Pandas

Pandas is an awesome tool for working with structured data, which is data that's organised and formatted in a way that makes it easy to access and search. This kind of data usually lives in homes like tables, spreadsheets, or databases, where every piece of information has its own designated spot in a field or category.

Pandas is built on top of NumPy, allowing it to leverage NumPy's efficiency for handling structured data. Together, Pandas and NumPy form a dynamic duo for data manipulation in Python, with NumPy handling efficient numeric operations and Pandas providing more flexible tools for working with labelled, heterogeneous data.

Pandas Dataframe **v** **Numpy Array**

Index	A	B	C
0	1	4.0	x
1	2	5.1	y
2	3	6.2	z

A	B	C
1	2	3
4	5	6
7	8	9

Figure 36a. Difference Between Pandas DataFrames and NumPy Arrays. This highlights how Pandas handles labelled, heterogeneous data, whereas NumPy arrays are simpler, holding homogeneous data without labels.

One of the key differences between Pandas and NumPy lies in their data structures. NumPy arrays store homogeneous data, meaning all elements must be of the same type (such as all integers or all floats). In contrast, Pandas DataFrames handle heterogeneous data, allowing different types of data (like integers, floats, and strings) to be stored in separate columns, each with its own label. At the core of Pandas is the DataFrame, a two-dimensional table with labelled rows and columns, much like a spreadsheet.

Figure 36a shows a side-by-side comparison between a Pandas DataFrame (with labelled columns and rows, and heterogeneous data types) and a NumPy array (with homogeneous data and no labels).

At the core of Pandas is the DataFrame, a two-dimensional table with labelled rows and columns, much like a spreadsheet. Pandas also offers the **Series** object, which is a one-dimensional array with labelled data. While a Pandas Series is similar to a one-dimensional NumPy array, its ability to handle index labels makes it more useful and versatile for data manipulation.

Creating a Pandas Series

A Pandas Series can be created from various data sources, such as lists, arrays, dictionaries, or even a single value. Once you have a Pandas Series, you can use it for indexing, slicing, arithmetic operations, and more, leveraging Pandas' built-in methods. Here's a simple example of how to create a Pandas Series using a list:

```
#Filename: pandas1.py
import pandas as pd

#Create a Series from a list
data = [1, 2, 3, 4, 5]
series = pd.Series(data)
print(series)
```

Running this code will show you a series with an index (in the first column) and the data (in the second column):

```
0    1
1    2
2    3
3    4
4    5
dtype: int64
```

The index in a Pandas Series allows you to access and manipulate the data more efficiently than in a standard NumPy array.

DataFrames from Different Types of Data

DataFrames can be created from various raw data inputs, whether you're starting with lists, dictionaries, or a CSV file. Here's a program that shows you how to create a DataFrame from a list of lists:

```
#Filename: pandas2.py
import pandas as pd

#Example 1: Creating a DataFrame from a list of lists
data_lists = [
    ['Mercury', 'Terrestrial', '0.39', '0'],
```

```
        ['Venus', 'Terrestrial', '0.72', '0'],
        ['Earth', 'Terrestrial', '1.00', '1'],
        ['Mars', 'Terrestrial', '1.52', '2'],
        ['Jupiter', 'Gas Giant', '5.20', '79'],
        ['Saturn', 'Gas Giant', '9.58', '82'],
        ['Uranus', 'Ice Giant', '19.22', '27'],
        ['Neptune', 'Ice Giant', '30.05', '14'],
        ['Pluto', 'Dwarf Planet', '39.48', '5'],
        ['Ceres', 'Dwarf Planet', '2.77', '0'],
        ['Haumea', 'Dwarf Planet', '43.13', '2'],
        ['Makemake', 'Dwarf Planet', '45.79', '1']
    ]
    columns = ['Planet', 'Type', 'Average Distance from Sun
    (AU)', 'Number of Moons']
    df_from_lists = pd.DataFrame(data_lists,
    columns=columns)
    print("DataFrame from List of Lists:")
    print(df_from_lists)
    print("\n")
```

In this example, **data_lists** contains information about various celestial bodies in the solar system. Each sub-list represents a row in the DataFrame, with values for the planet's name, type, average distance from the Sun (in astronomical units), and the number of moons. The columns argument defines the column names. The resulting DataFrame is structured and labelled, making it easy to work with.

Here the DataFrame is created from a list of lists, which organises the data into rows and columns. Here's a breakdown of the code.

data_lists contains a list of lists. Each sub-list represents data for a specific celestial body in the solar system. The sub-list includes the names of the planet and minor planets and their type. It completes with their average distance from the sun (in astronomical units) and finally the number of moons slipping around them.

columns is a list of strings defining the column names of the DataFrame, corresponding to the information in each sublist of data_lists.
pd.DataFrame() is used to create a DataFrame from the list of lists (data_lists). The columns parameter specifies the column names for the DataFrame. This section prints a string indicating that a DataFrame has been created, followed by the content of the DataFrame. Then finally the data is displayed via some print statements.

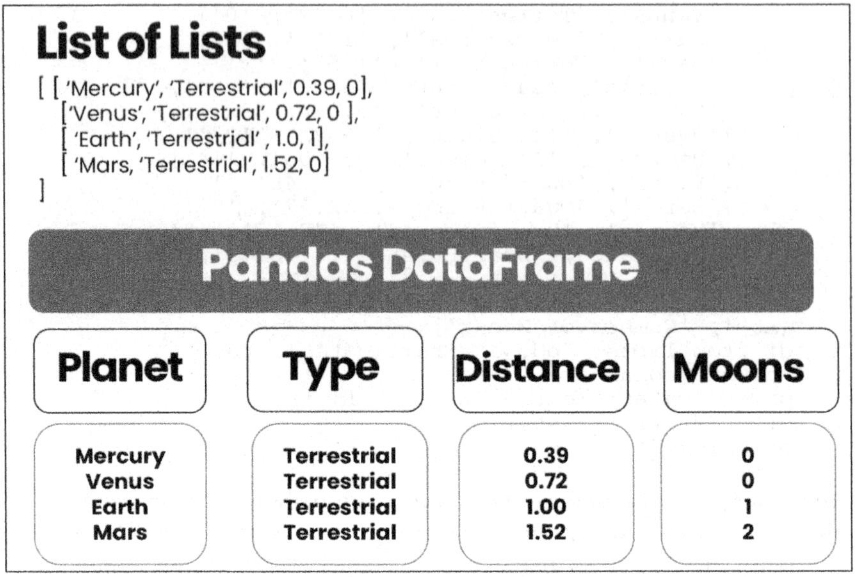

Figure 36b. Converting a list of lists into a DataFrame. At the top the raw data where each sublist represents information about a planet. The raw data is converted into a structured DataFrame clearly labelled columns and row.

In summary then, the code creates a DataFrame and then organises information about planetary and objects, such as their type, distance from the Sun, and the number of moons they have.

Using Pandas, the data is stored in a format that is easy to read and manipulate, allowing for powerful analysis and operations like filtering, sorting, or performing calculations on the data. The great thing is, as with most Python programming its all pretty easy to follow.

Example 1. Creating a DataFrame from a Dictionary

You can also create a DataFrame from a dictionary, where the keys represent the column names, and the values are lists containing the data for each column: Here's a second program using the same data:

```
#Filename: pandas3.py
#Creating a DataFrame from a dictionary
Import pandas as pd
data_dict = {
    'Planet': ['Mercury', 'Venus', 'Earth', 'Mars',
'Jupiter', 'Saturn', 'Uranus', 'Neptune', 'Pluto',
'Ceres', 'Haumea', 'Makemake'],
    'Type': ['Terrestrial', 'Terrestrial',
'Terrestrial', 'Terrestrial', 'Gas Giant', 'Gas Giant',
'Ice Giant', 'Ice Giant', 'Dwarf Planet', 'Dwarf
Planet', 'Dwarf Planet', 'Dwarf Planet'],
    'Average Distance from Sun (AU)': ['0.39', '0.72',
'1.00', '1.52', '5.20', '9.58', '19.22', '30.05',
'39.48', '2.77', '43.13', '45.79'],
```

```
    'Number of Moons': ['0', '0', '1', '2', '79', '82',
'27', '14', '5', '0', '2', '1']
}
df_from_dict = pd.DataFrame(data_dict)
print("DataFrame from Dictionary:")
print(df_from_dict)
print("\n")
```

Here the main difference between this and the previous example is how the data is structured and provided to the Pandas DataFrame constructor: In the previous program there was a list of lists.

In the example above the data is structured as a dictionary, where each key represents a column name, and the corresponding value is a list that contains the data for that column. The DataFrame constructor below directly accepts the dictionary, with each key becoming a column, and the lists within the dictionary are automatically aligned as rows.

Example 3: Creating a DataFrame from a CSV File

You can also create a DataFrame from a CSV file. An example sits below. Here we are able to read a CSV file into a into a DataFrame manipulate it readily and, if required, save it back to CSV.

```
# Filename: pandas4.py
# Creating a DataFrame from a CSV file
# Note: Ensure 'solarsystem.csv' exists in the same
directory or provide the correct path.

import pandas as pd

# Define the CSV file path
csv_file_path = 'solarsystem.csv'

# Create a DataFrame by reading from a CSV file
df_from_csv = pd.read_csv(csv_file_path)
print("DataFrame from CSV File:")
print(df_from_csv)

# Optional: Creating DataFrames from lists and
dictionaries for demonstration
data_from_lists = [
    ['Mercury', 0.33, 2439],
    ['Venus', 4.87, 6051],
    ['Earth', 5.97, 6371]
]
df_from_lists = pd.DataFrame(data_from_lists,
columns=['Planet', 'Mass', 'Radius'])

data_from_dict = {
    'Planet': ['Mars', 'Jupiter', 'Saturn'],
    'Mass': [0.642, 1898, 568],
    'Radius': [3390, 69911, 58232]
}
df_from_dict = pd.DataFrame(data_from_dict)

# Save the DataFrames to new CSV files
df_from_lists.to_csv('output_from_lists.csv',
```

```
index=False)
df_from_dict.to_csv('output_from_dict.csv',
index=False)
```

This code reads data from the CSV file **solarsystem.csv** and organises it into a DataFrame. The **pd.read_csv()** function automatically interprets the first row as the header, and the remaining rows are loaded as data. When saving the DataFrame to a CSV file, the index=False argument ensures that the DataFrame index is not included in the saved file, which is often the desired behaviour when exporting data.

All Together Now

The snippets of text below shows how you can integrate Pandas DataFrames from various sources: lists of lists, dictionaries, and CSV files, and how to save them back to CSV files.

Creating a DataFrame from a List of Lists:

You start with a list of lists (data_lists), where each inner list represents a row of data. The columns variable is used to name the DataFrame's columns, ensuring that the data is properly labelled. By calling **pd.DataFrame(data_lists, columns=columns)**, you generate a DataFrame where the data is neatly organised into rows and columns. This is useful when you already have data in a structured list format.

```
# Filename:pandas5.py
import pandas as pd

# Data represented as a list of lists
data_lists = [
    [1, 'Mercury', 0.39],
    [2, 'Venus', 0.72]
]

# Define column names
columns = ['ID', 'Planet', 'Distance from Sun (AU)']

# Create a DataFrame from the list of lists
df_from_lists = pd.DataFrame(data_lists,
columns=columns)

# Print the DataFrame
print("DataFrame from List of Lists:")
print(df_from_lists)
```

Creating a DataFrame from a Dictionary:

Here, you use a dictionary (**data_dict**) where each key represents a column name, and the values are lists of data for each row in that column. By calling **pd.DataFrame(data_dict),** you create a DataFrame directly from this dictionary. This method is intuitive, especially if your data is already organised by columns.

```
data_dict = {
    'ID': [1, 2],
    'Planet': ['Mercury', 'Venus'],
    'Distance from Sun (AU)': [0.39, 0.72]
}
df_from_dict = pd.DataFrame(data_dict)
```

Reading a DataFrame from a CSV File:

If your data is already stored in a CSV file, you can load it into a DataFrame using **pd.read_csv(csv_file_path).** Pandas will automatically read the first row of the file as the column headers (unless you specify otherwise). Make sure the file path is correct, either by keeping the CSV in the same directory as your script or by providing the full path.

```
df_from_csv = pd.read_csv('solarsystem.csv')
```

Saving DataFrames to CSV Files:

After manipulating or creating a DataFrame, you can save it to a CSV file using the t**o_csv()** method. The **index=False** parameter ensures that the row indices (which Pandas adds by default) aren't written to the CSV unless you want them.

```
df_from_lists.to_csv('output_from_lists.csv',
index=False)
df_from_dict.to_csv('output_from_dict.csv',
index=False)
```

These programs and snippets show how you can create DataFrames from a variety of data formats—whether it's a list of lists, a dictionary, or an external CSV file. It's easy to create DataFrames, which are core to working with tabular data in Pandas.

Once you've created or manipulated data in a DataFrame, saving it back to a CSV is simple, letting you keep a record of your work.

In summary you'll note the following:

- **Creating a DataFrame** from a list of lists, is great for when your data is already organised in that way.
- **Creating a DataFrame** from a dictionary, is a common and intuitive method for structuring data in Pandas.
- **Reading a DataFrame** from a csv file, making it easy to work with data that's already stored in a widely-used format.
- **Saving DataFrames** to new csv files, so you can store the results of your data manipulations.

Data Cleaning

Data cleaning refers to the process of preparing and correcting raw data to make it suitable for analysis. This process involves handling missing values, correcting data types, removing duplicates, and addressing inconsistencies in the dataset. One key question is: how do you decide what to fill gaps with? This depends on the nature of the dataset, the context of the missing values, and how you intend to use the data. There are many approaches, and the right one depends on the type of data you're cleaning.

You can fill gaps with a constant value. In this case if the gaps represent something meaningful, like '0' for missing sales data or 'Unknown' .

When to use: In time series data, where you might assume that the last known value persists (forward fill) or future values give an indication of missing past values (backward fill). This is a good approach:

```
df.fillna(method='ffill')   # Forward fill
df.fillna(method='bfill')   # Backward fill
```

Ideally though, use simple methods (e.g., mean, forward fill) for small amounts of missing data. You can consider more advanced techniques (e.g., interpolation, machine learning) for significant gaps. One thing, however, is that you should *always* keep the context of the missing data in mind and assess how your choice impacts the overall dataset.

Common Data Cleaning Tasks in Pandas

Here are some common tasks involved in data cleaning using Pandas:

- Handling Missing Data: Missing values are filled using the **fillna()** method. For example, missing ages in a dataset can be filled with the mean age of the dataset.

- Removing Duplicates: Duplicate rows are removed with the **drop_duplicates()** method.

- Transforming Data Types: The **astype()** method is used to convert columns to specific data types, such as converting a float to an integer.

- Reshaping Data: A pivot table can be created to summarise the data, such as calculating the average age by department using the **pivot_table()** method.

This next program demonstrates key data manipulation techniques using the Pandas library, focusing on handling **missing** data, removing duplicates, and transforming data types. It begins by creating a sample dataset with missing values and duplicate entries. The dataset, stored in a DataFrame, includes columns for names, ages, genders, and departments.

```
#Filename: pandas6.py
import pandas as pd

#Sample dataset with missing data and duplicates
data = {
    'Name': ['Alice', 'Bob', 'Charlie', 'David',
'Emma', 'Alice'],
    'Age': [25, 30, None, 40, 45, 25],
    'Gender': ['F', 'M', 'M', 'M', 'F', 'F'],
    'Department': ['Sales', 'Marketing', 'Sales', 'HR',
'Marketing', 'Sales']
}

#Creating DataFrame
df = pd.DataFrame(data)

#Display original DataFrame
print("Original DataFrame:")
print(df)
print()

#Handling missing data (filling missing ages with mean)
df['Age'].fillna(df['Age'].mean(), inplace=True)

# Removing duplicates
df.drop_duplicates(inplace=True)

#Transforming data types (converting age to integer)
df['Age'] = df['Age'].astype(int)

#Reshaping data (pivot table to get average age by
department)
avg_age_by_dept = df.pivot_table(index='Department',
values='Age', aggfunc='mean')

#Display cleaned and preprocessed DataFrame
print("Cleaned and Preprocessed DataFrame:")
print(df)
print()

#Display average age by department
print("Average Age by Department:")
print(avg_age_by_dept)
```

Initially, the program displays the original DataFrame to provide a reference before any changes. To address missing data, it calculates the mean age and fills any missing values in the 'Age' column with this mean, ensuring a complete dataset. This is done in a straightforward manner by assigning the filled values back to the 'Age' column directly, avoiding issues related to chained assignments.

The program then removes duplicate rows from the DataFrame to ensure that each record is unique. This step is crucial for cleaning the data and preventing redundancy. Following this, the program transforms the 'Age' column to integer data type, which is necessary for consistent numerical operations and analyses.

The final data transformation involves creating a pivot table to calculate the average age by department. This reshaping of the data helps in summarising and aggregating information efficiently. The **cleaned** DataFrame and the pivot table with average age by department are displayed, showcasing the results of the data cleaning and transformation processes.

The program provides a practical example of essential data pre-processing steps in Pandas. It highlights techniques for managing missing values, removing duplicates, transforming data types, and summarising data, all of which are fundamental for effective data analysis and preparation.

Chained Assignment in Pandas

When you're working with Pandas, you might come across a tricky issue called **chained assignment**. These occur when Pandas is unsure whether it's modifying a view (a reference to the original data) or a copy (a separate version of the data). This ambiguity can result in a **SettingWithCopyWarning,** which means your changes might not affect the original DataFrame as intended.

This happens when you try to modify a DataFrame or series through a sequence of operations, and it can lead to some unexpected behaviour or even slow performance. Chained assignment often sneaks up when you're working with a subset of your data and then applying a method like **fillna()**, **drop()**, or **replace()** with the **inplace=True** argument. What can happen is that instead of updating your original DataFrame, Pandas might create a copy of it, and suddenly, your changes aren't where you thought they'd be!

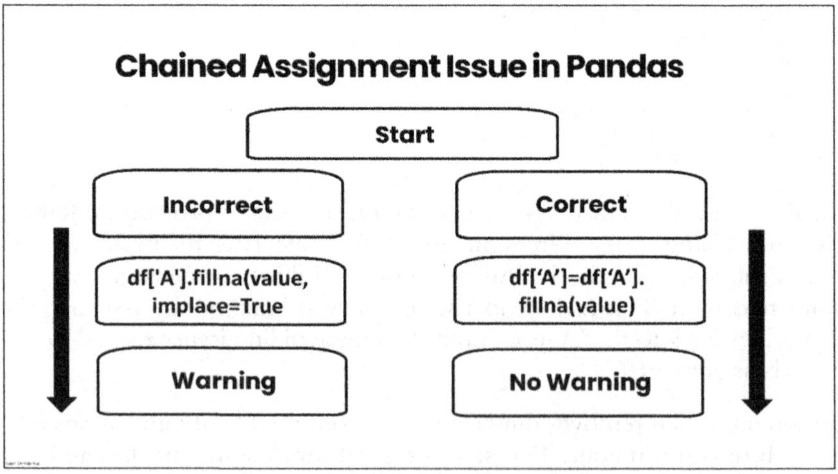

Figure 36c. Avoiding the chained issue assignment in Pandas.

For example, if you write something like this:

```
df[col].method(value, inplace=True)
```

Where **df[col]** is a subset of your DataFrame, you might see a **FutureWarning** from Pandas. This warning is Pandas' way of saying, *"Hey, just so you know, this might not work the way you expect in future versions!"* The **inplace=True** argument might not behave as expected, which is a good heads-up to avoid potential issues.

How to Handle It

Instead of relying on chained assignments, it's better to break down your operations into steps and assign the result explicitly back to your DataFrame or Series. This approach makes your intentions clear and avoids ambiguity. For example, if you want to fill in missing values in the 'Age' column of your DataFrame, you might be tempted to write:

```
df['Age'].fillna(df['Age'].mean(), inplace=True)
```

But this might trigger that pesky chained assignment warning. Instead, try this approach:

First, calculate the mean age:

```
mean_age = df['Age'].mean()
```

Then, fill in the missing values and update the 'Age' column:

```
df['Age'] = df['Age'].fillna(mean_age)
```

By doing it this way, you ensure that the operation is directly applied to the DataFrame without creating a temporary copy that could lead to problems down the road.

Why This Matters

Avoiding chained assignments is key to keeping your code reliable and making sure your data manipulations are doing exactly what you want them to. By using direct assignment methods, you can prevent those annoying warnings and avoid any future compatibility issues with Pandas. If you see a warning about chained assignment, it's a good sign to double-check your code!

Essential Pandas Functionality in Action

Now, let's switch gears and look at a Pandas program that demonstrates some of the essential functionality the library offers. This program covers everything from creating a DataFrame to performing common data inspection and manipulation tasks. Really the program demonstrates each one in use, so you can apply them to your code as you see fit.

```
#Filename: Pandas7.py
import pandas as pd

#Step 1: Create a DataFrame
data = {'A': [1, 2, 3, 4, 5], 'B': [10, 20, 30, 40,
50]}
df = pd.DataFrame(data)

print("Original DataFrame:")
print(df)

#Step 2: Inspecting the DataFrame
print("\nFirst few rows using head():")
print(df.head())

print("\nLast few rows using tail():")
print(df.tail())

print("\nSummary of DataFrame using info():")
print(df.info())

print("\nDescriptive statistics using describe():")
print(df.describe())

#Step 3: Selecting specific columns and rows
print("\nSelecting column 'A' using df['A']:")
print(df['A'])

print("\nSelecting rows using iloc[1:3]:")
print(df.iloc[1:3])  # Select rows by position

print("\nSelecting rows using loc[1:3]:")
print(df.loc[1:3])  # Select rows by label

#Step 4: DataFrame Manipulation
print("\nDropping column 'A' from DataFrame:")
df_dropped = df.drop('A', axis=1)
print(df_dropped)

print("\nAdding a new column 'C' to DataFrame:")
df['C'] = [5, 4, 3, 2, 1]
print(df)

print("\nSorting the DataFrame based on column 'C':")
df_sorted = df.sort_values(by='C')
print(df_sorted)

#Step 5: Handling Missing Data
print("\nHandling missing data:")
df_missing = df.copy()
df_missing.loc[2, 'B'] = None  # Introduce a missing
value
print(df_missing)

print("\nDetecting missing values using isnull():")
print(df_missing.isnull())

print("\nFilling missing values with zero using
fillna():")
df_filled = df_missing.fillna(0)
print(df_filled)
```

```
print("\nDropping rows with missing values using
dropna():")
df_dropped_na = df_missing.dropna()
print(df_dropped_na)

#Step 6: Advanced Data Manipulation
# Creating a new DataFrame for reshaping demonstration
data2 = {'Category': ['A', 'A', 'B', 'B'], 'Type':
['X', 'Y', 'X', 'Y'], 'Value': [10, 20, 30, 40]}
df2 = pd.DataFrame(data2)

print("\nNew DataFrame for reshaping demonstration:")
print(df2)

print("\nPivoting the DataFrame:")
df_pivot = df2.pivot(index='Category', columns='Type',
values='Value')
print(df_pivot)

print("\nStacking the DataFrame:")
df_stacked = df_pivot.stack()
print(df_stacked)

print("\nUnstacking the DataFrame:")
df_unstacked = df_stacked.unstack()
print(df_unstacked)
```

First, we start by importing the Pandas library and creating a simple DataFrame using a dictionary of lists. This DataFrame, called **df**, contains two columns, 'A' and 'B', with some integer values. Here's what the program does next:

Data Inspection:

- View the first few rows using **head()**.
- View the last few rows using **tail()**.
- Get a summary of the DataFrame's structure with **info()**.
- Generate descriptive statistics like the mean, standard deviation, and more with **describe()**.

Selecting and Manipulating Data:

- Select specific columns and rows using **iloc[]** (for positional indexing) and **loc[]** (for label-based indexing).
- Manipulate the DataFrame by dropping a column ('A') and introducing a new column ('C') to play around with sorting.

Handling Missing Data:

- Detect missing values with **isnull()** and **notnull()**.

- Handle missing data by either filling it with a specific value or dropping it from the DataFrame.

Advanced Data Manipulation:

- Reshape the DataFrame by creating a new DataFrame and demonstrating how to pivot the data.
- Stack and unstack data to show how you can transform data structures for better analysis.

These are all vital operations for getting your data ready for analysis or cleaning up messy datasets. Whether you're inspecting data, sorting and filtering it, or even handling missing values, this program shows how Pandas can be your go-to tool for efficient and effective data manipulation.

Exploring Pandas Dot Methods

As you may already have surmised, Pandas is an absolute gem when it comes to data manipulation and analysis in Python. To show off just how handy Pandas can be, let's walk through a program that demonstrates a variety of its "dot methods." These methods let you inspect, manipulate, and even visualise data with ease. Here's the program:

```
#Filename: pandas8.py
import pandas as pd
import numpy as np

#Creating a DataFrame
data = {'A': [1, 2, 3], 'B': [4, 5, 6]}
df = pd.DataFrame(data)
print("Pandas DataFrame:")
print(df)

#Converting DataFrame to a NumPy array
numpy_array = df.to_numpy()

#Performing a NumPy operation: x each element by 2
result_array = np.multiply(numpy_array, 2)

#Displaying the result
print("NumPy Array:")
print(result_array)
```

Data Inspection and Selection

The program starts by creating a simple DataFrame with two columns, 'A' and 'B'. It then converts the DataFrame into a NumPy array using the **to_numpy()** method, which allows you to leverage NumPy's optimised numerical operations. For example, multiplying each element by two using **np.multiply()**.

- **df.head()**: Shows the first few rows of the DataFrame.

- **df.tail()**: Displays the last few rows.
- **df.info()**: Provides a summary of the DataFrame, including the data types and non-null counts.
- **df.describe()**: Generates descriptive statistics like mean, standard deviation, min, and max.

After getting a feel for the DataFrame's structure and content, the program shows how to **select specific data**. You can access parts of the DataFrame by column name (like **df['A']**) or by position using **iloc[]**. Whether you're grabbing a single column or multiple columns, by label or position, Pandas makes it easy. You can access parts of the DataFrame by column name (like df['A']) or by position using iloc[] (position-based indexing). For label-based indexing, use loc[].

Data Manipulation

Next, the program dives into **data manipulation**—the bread and butter of Pandas. Here are some of the things it does:

- **Drop a column**: The df.drop(columns=['A'], inplace=True) method removes the 'A' column from the DataFrame.
- **Rename a column**: The df.rename(columns={'B': 'C'}, inplace=True) method changes the name of column 'B' to 'C'.
- **Sort the DataFrame**: The df.sort_values(by='C', inplace=True) method sorts the DataFrame based on the values in column 'C'.

The **inplace=True** parameter ensures that the DataFrame is modified in place without creating a copy. This is useful when you want to make changes directly to the original DataFrame.

These techniques are essential when you're cleaning up data or getting it ready for analysis.

Handling Missing Data and Aggregation

Handling missing data is a crucial part of any data cleaning process. The program covers this with methods like:

- **df.isnull()**: Detects missing values in the DataFrame.
- **df.fillna(0, inplace=True)**: Fills missing values with a specified value, in this case, 0.
- **df.dropna(inplace=True)**: Removes rows or columns with missing values.

After cleaning up the data, the program moves on to **aggregation** and **grouping**. You can compute summary statistics like the sum and mean of the DataFrame with df.sum() and df.mean(). Plus, you can group data based on a specific column and perform group-wise aggregation using df.groupby('C').sum().

Reshaping and Visualisation

Reshaping data is another handy feature in Pandas, and this program shows how you can:

- **Pivot and unpivot data**: With methods like df.pivot() and df.melt(), you can reshape your DataFrame to fit your analysis needs.
- **Stack and un-stack data**: These methods let you transform your DataFrame's structure, which can be incredibly useful for certain types of data analysis.

Finally, the program wraps up with **data visualisation**. Pandas makes it easy to create quick plots directly from your DataFrame:

- **df.plot()**: Creates a line plot by default.
- **df.hist()**: Generates histograms for each numeric column.
- **df.boxplot()**: Creates boxplots to show the distribution of data.

These visualisations can give you great insights into your data, showing you distributions, trends, and relationships at a glance.

Pandas uses **Matplotlib** under the hood for its plotting capabilities. The **df.plot()** method creates a line plot by default, but you can specify other types of plots, such as bar plots or scatter plots, by setting the kind parameter.

Wrapping Up

This program really shows off the full range of what Pandas can do for data analysis. From inspection and selection to manipulation, reshaping, and visualisation, these methods are a foundation for anyone working with data in Python. Whether you're cleaning up a messy dataset or preparing data for analysis, Pandas has the tools you need to get the job done efficiently and effectively.

DataFrame-NumPy Array Structure Differences

Pandas and NumPy each have their strengths, and when you use them together, you can unlock powerful data manipulation capabilities! Here are some examples that show how Pandas and NumPy can complement each other.

The illustration on the first page of this chapter highlights the basic differences between Pandas DataFrames and NumPy arrays. The following program visually demonstrates these differences:

```
#Filename: pandas9.py
import numpy as np
import pandas as pd

#Creating a DataFrame
data = {
    'A': [1, 2, 3],
    'B': [4.0, 5.1, 6.2],
    'C': ['x', 'y', 'z']
}
df = pd.DataFrame(data)
print(df)

#Creating a NumPy Array
arr = np.array([[1, 2, 3], [4, 5, 6], [7, 8, 9]])
print(arr)
```

This produces an output thus:

```
   A    B  C
0  1  4.0  x
1  2  5.1  y
2  3  6.2  z

[[1 2 3]
 [4 5 6]
 [7 8 9]]
```

Pandas DataFrame: This is like a table with rows and columns, where each column can hold different types of data—integers, floats, strings, etc. In the example above, the DataFrame has three columns: 'A' (integers), 'B' (floats), and 'C' (strings). This flexibility allows you to store and manipulate heterogeneous data types in a labelled format, which is ideal for working with structured datasets where each column represents a different feature.

NumPy Array: is more like a grid or matrix where all the data elements must be of the same type (e.g., all integers or all floats). In our example, the NumPy array is a 3x3 grid of integers. NumPy arrays are highly efficient for numerical computations, but they lack the ability to store multiple data types in the same array, which makes them less suitable for tasks involving mixed data types.

Data Manipulation Together

Now let's see how Pandas and NumPy can work together in harmony:

```
#Filename: pandas10.py

import pandas as pd
import np

#Creating a DataFrame with random data using NumPy
np.random.seed(0)
data = {
    'A': np.random.randint(1, 100, size=10),
    'B': np.random.randint(1, 100, size=10),
    'C': np.random.randint(1, 100, size=10),
    'D': np.random.randint(1, 100, size=10)
}
df = pd.DataFrame(data)

#Display the original DataFrame
print("Original DataFrame:")
print(df)
print()

#Use NumPy to calculate the mean of each column
column_means = np.mean(df, axis=0)
print("Mean of each column using NumPy:")
print(column_means)
print()

#Use Pandas to calculate the sum of each row
row_sums = df.sum(axis=1)
print("Sum of each row using Pandas:")
print(row_sums)
print()

#Add a new column with the sum of squares of each row
using NumPy
df['Sum of Squares'] = np.sum(df**2, axis=1)

#Display the modified DataFrame
print("Modified DataFrame with Sum of Squares column:")
print(df)
```

We start by creating a Pandas DataFrame filled with random data using NumPy. This is a great way to generate data quickly. Next, we use NumPy to calculate the mean of each column in the DataFrame. NumPy's numerical operations are fast and efficient! Then, we use Pandas to calculate the sum of each row. Pandas makes it easy to perform operations along rows or columns. Finally, we add a new column to the DataFrame that contains the sum of squares of each row, calculated using NumPy.

This example shows how you can seamlessly move between Pandas and NumPy, using each library where it shines the brightest.

Moving Data Between Pandas and NumPy

Sometimes you might have a DataFrame in Pandas and want to perform a mathematical operation on it using NumPy. Here's how you can do that:

```
#Filename: pandas11.py
import pandas as pd
import numpy as np

#Creating a sample DataFrame
data = {'A': [1, 2, 3], 'B': [4, 5, 6]}
df = pd.DataFrame(data)

#Converting the DataFrame to a NumPy array
numpy_array = df.to_numpy()

#Performing NumPy operation: multiply each element by 2
result_array = np.multiply(numpy_array, 2)

#Displaying the result
print(result_array)
```

Again, we start with a Pandas DataFrame. We then convert this DataFrame into a NumPy array using the **to_numpy()** method. After that, we apply a NumPy operation to multiply each element by two using **np.multiply()**. Finally, we print out the result.

This shows how easy it is to move data back and forth between Pandas and NumPy, letting you take advantage of the strengths of both libraries.

Key Differences

When you're working with data, it's really helpful to understand the differences between Pandas **DataFrames** and **NumPy arrays**. These differences make each one better suited for specific tasks, so knowing when to use which can save you time and headaches.

Pandas DataFrames:

- **Structure**: DataFrames are inherently two-dimensional but are versatile enough to handle other structures like time-series data or hierarchical indexes (MultiIndex), adding flexibility to how data is organised and .
- **Labels**: They come with labelled rows (known as the index) and columns, which adds flexibility and makes data manipulation and analysis more user-friendly.
- **Data Types**: A DataFrame can hold different types of data (like integers, floats, and strings) all in the same table, which is great when your dataset includes a mix of data types.
- **Built-in Functions**: Pandas offers a wide range of built-in functions

for data manipulation, aggregation, and visualisation, making it a powerhouse for data analysis.

- **Handling Missing Data**: It has robust methods for dealing with missing data, which is crucial when cleaning datasets.
- **Integration**: Pandas plays nicely with other data analysis libraries, such as Matplotlib and **Seaborn** for plotting, and **scikit-learn** for machine learning, making it a central tool in data science workflows.

NumPy Arrays:

- **Dimensions**: NumPy arrays can be of any dimension (1D, 2D, 3D, etc.), so they're incredibly versatile depending on the complexity of your data. Their memory is laid out contiguously, which allows for faster access and computations, especially for large datasets.
- **Data Type**: All elements in a NumPy array must be of the same data type. This requirement makes NumPy arrays more efficient for numerical operations.
- **Performance**: NumPy is optimised for performance, with operations that are typically faster than those in Pandas due to the like nature of the data and the efficient memory layout.
- **Mathematical Operations**: NumPy has extensive support for mathematical and linear algebra operations, which are performed element wise. These operations can also be vectored for even greater efficiency.
- **Broadcasting**: NumPy supports broadcasting, which allows operations on arrays of different shapes in a way that's both memory-efficient and fast.

When to Use Each

- **Pandas DataFrame**: Reach for Pandas when you need label data, are working with a mix of different data types, want to perform data analysis, or are dealing with tabular data where each column represents a different feature or variable.
- **NumPy Array**: Use NumPy when you need to perform numerical computations, work with homogeneous data, or require multi-dimensional array manipulation. It's your go-to for tasks involving heavy mathematical or linear algebra operations.

Understanding these key differences helps you choose the right tool for the job, making your data manipulation tasks smoother and more efficient. Whether you're working with labelled, mixed-type data in Pandas or performing fast, numerical calculations in NumPy, each has its place in your data toolkit!

Exercise: NumPy and Pandas

Write a Python program that demonstrates the following:

Using NumPy:

Create a 2D NumPy array with the following data:

```
[[1, 2, 3],
 [4, 5, 6],
 [7, 8, 9]]
```

Calculate and print:

- The sum of all elements in the array.
- The sum of each row.
- The sum of each column.

Using Pandas:

Create a Pandas DataFrame using the same data as the NumPy array, with column names A, B, and C.

Perform and print the following:

- The mean of each column.
- The mean of each row.
- The total mean of all elements in the DataFrame.

Answer over page.

```
#Filename: 36-exercise-07.py
import numpy as np
import pandas as pd

# NumPy Part
print("=== NumPy Operations ===")
data = np.array([
    [1, 2, 3],
    [4, 5, 6],
    [7, 8, 9]
])

# Total sum
total_sum = np.sum(data)
print("Total Sum:", total_sum)

# Row sums
row_sums = np.sum(data, axis=1)
print("Row Sums:", row_sums)

# Column sums
column_sums = np.sum(data, axis=0)
print("Column Sums:", column_sums)

# Pandas Part
print("\n=== Pandas Operations ===")
df = pd.DataFrame(data, columns=['A', 'B', 'C'])

# Mean of each column
column_means = df.mean()
print("Column Means:")
print(column_means)

# Mean of each row
row_means = df.mean(axis=1)
print("\nRow Means:")
print(row_means)

# Total mean
total_mean = df.values.mean()
print("\nTotal Mean:", total_mean)
```

A 2D NumPy array is created with the given data. The total sum, row sums, and column sums are calculated using np.sum() with appropriate axes.

A Pandas DataFrame is created using the same data, with column names A, B, and C. df.mean() computes the mean for each column. df.mean(axis=1) computes the mean for each row. The total mean is calculated using df.values. mean().

37: Matplotlib Visuals

Matplotlib is primarily used for creating static, animated, and interactive visualisations in Python. It's particularly popular for generating plots, graphs, and charts with the minimum of fuss. Whether its simple line graphs, bar charts, scatter plots, or even histograms and 3D plots, Matplotlib provides the tools to do so! Some of the less obvious tasks include:

- Customising and Enhancing Plots
- Embedding in GUIs
- Exporting to Various Formats
- Animating Data
- Geographical Data Visualisation
- Data Inspection and Debugging
- Creating Dashboards
- Creating Non-Graphical Diagrams
- 3D Plotting and Surface Visualisation
- Layout Design for Figures and Text

One of the key strengths of Matplotlib is its compatibility with other Python libraries like NumPy and Pandas, which are commonly used for data manipulation and analysis.

Customisation is a big part of Matplotlib's appeal. You can tweak almost every aspect of your plots, from colours and line styles to axes labels and legends. This flexibility is ideal for creating publication-quality figures or presentations, where the look and feel of the illustration might be just as important as the data itself.

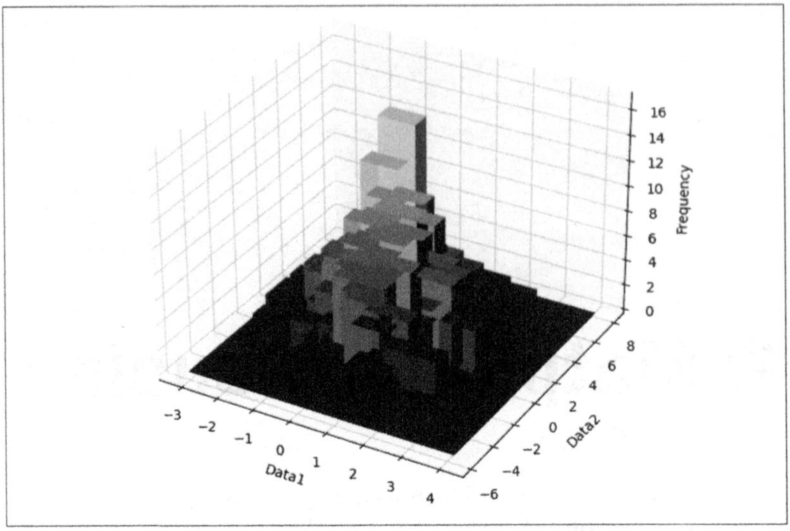

Figure 37a. 3D Plotting with Matplotlib.

Matplotlib also supports animations and interactive features. This can be especially handy when you need to demonstrate changes in data over time or when you want your users to interact with the data by zooming, panning, or hovering over specific points. Though it may not be as interactive as some newer libraries like **Plotly** or **Bokeh**, Matplotlib remains a versatile and reliable choice for most illustrative tasks in Python.

Here are several small programs that create different types of charts using Matplotlib and Pandas, some of which are illustrated.

Line Plot

This program creates a simple line plot showing the trend of some data over time. Ensure you have the relevant modules installed.

```
#Filename: plot1.py
#Line Plot
import pandas as pd
import matplotlib.pyplot as plt

#Sample data for a line plot
data = {'Year': [2015, 2016, 2017, 2018, 2019, 2020],
        'Sales': [250, 300, 350, 400, 450, 500]}

#Convert to a DataFrame
df = pd.DataFrame(data)

#Create a line plot
plt.figure(figsize=(8, 5))
plt.plot(df['Year'], df['Sales'], marker='o',
color='b', linestyle='--')

#Add labels and title
```

```
plt.title('Sales Over Time', fontsize=16)
plt.xlabel('Year', fontsize=12)
plt.ylabel('Sales (in units)', fontsize=12)
plt.grid(True)

#show the plot
plt.show()
```

Bar Chart

This program creates a bar chart showing the sales of different products.

```
#Filename: plot2.py
import pandas as pd
import matplotlib.pyplot as plt

#Sample data for a bar chart
data = {'Product': ['A', 'B', 'C', 'D', 'E'],
        'Sales': [100, 200, 150, 300, 250]}
#Convert to a DataFrame
df = pd.DataFrame(data)

#Create a bar chart
plt.figure(figsize=(8, 5))
plt.bar(df['Product'], df['Sales'], color='green')
#Add labels and title
plt.title('Sales by Product', fontsize=16)
plt.xlabel('Product', fontsize=12)
plt.ylabel('Sales (in units)', fontsize=12)

#Show the plot
plt.show()
```

Scatter Plot

This program creates a scatter plot to visualise the relationship between two variables.

```
#Filename: plot3.py
import pandas as pd
import matplotlib.pyplot as plt

#Sample data for a scatter plot
data = {'Height': [150, 160, 165, 170, 175, 180],
        'Weight': [60, 65, 68, 70, 75, 80]}

#Convert to a DataFrame
df = pd.DataFrame(data)

#Create a scatter plot
plt.figure(figsize=(8, 5))
plt.scatter(df['Height'], df['Weight'], color='red')

#Add labels and title
plt.title('Height vs Weight', fontsize=16)
plt.xlabel('Height (cm)', fontsize=12)
plt.ylabel('Weight (kg)', fontsize=12)
plt.grid(True)

#Show the plot
plt.show()
```

Histogram

This program creates a histogram to show the distribution of values in a dataset.

```
#Filename: plot4.py
import pandas as pd
import matplotlib.pyplot as plt

#Sample data for a histogram
data = {'Age': [22, 25, 29, 33, 35, 40, 45, 50, 55, 60,
65, 70]}

#Convert to a DataFrame
df = pd.DataFrame(data)

#Create a histogram
plt.figure(figsize=(8, 5))
plt.hist(df['Age'], bins=5, color='purple', alpha=0.7)

#Add labels and title
plt.title('Age Distribution', fontsize=16)
plt.xlabel('Age', fontsize=12)
plt.ylabel('Frequency', fontsize=12)
# Show the plot
plt.show()
```

Pie Chart

This program creates a pie chart to show the distribution of market share between different companies.

```
#Filename: plot5.py
import matplotlib.pyplot as plt

# Sample data for a pie chart
labels = ['Company A', 'Company B', 'Company C',
'Company D']
sizes = [35, 30, 20, 15]

# Create a pie chart
plt.figure(figsize=(6, 6))
plt.pie(sizes, labels=labels, autopct='%1.1f%%',
startangle=90, colors=['blue', 'green', 'red',
'yellow'])

# Add a title
plt.title('Market Share Distribution', fontsize=16)

# Equal aspect ratio ensures that pie is drawn as a
circle
plt.axis('equal')

# Show the plot
plt.show()
```

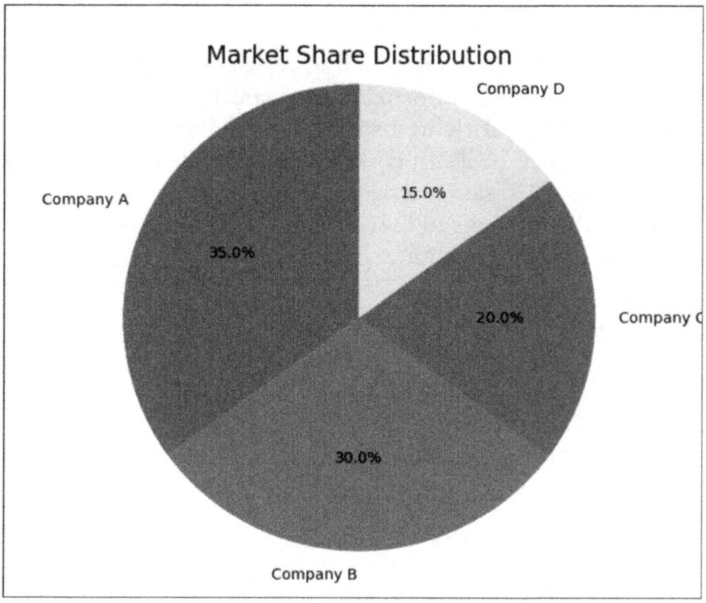

Figure 37b. Pie Chart Plot.

Box Plot

This program creates a box plot to visualise the distribution and spread of data.

```
#Filename: plot6.py
import pandas as pd
import matplotlib.pyplot as plt

#Sample data for a box plot
data = {'Scores': [78, 85, 88, 92, 95, 68, 74, 80, 86,
90]}

#Convert to a DataFrame
df = pd.DataFrame(data)

#Create a box plot
plt.figure(figsize=(8, 5))
plt.boxplot(df['Scores'], vert=False)

#Add labels and title
plt.title('Score Distribution', fontsize=16)
plt.xlabel('Scores', fontsize=12)
#Show the plot
plt.show()
```

Heatmap (Using Seaborn)

This program creates a heatmap to show correlations between different features. Matplotlib works well with Seaborn for more advanced visualisation. To run you'll need to install the **seaborne** module into your virtual environment:

```
pip install python3-seaborn
```

Seaborn is a Python data visualisation library built on top of Matplotlib that makes creating attractive and informative statistical graphics simpler and more intuitive. It is particularly well-suited for handling datasets, especially with Pandas data frames. Seaborn comes with a variety of built-in themes, colour palettes, and visualisation types, making it easier to create plots that are both aesthetically pleasing and informative with fewer lines of code compared to using Matplotlib alone.

```
#Filename: plot7.py
import pandas as pd
import seaborn as sns
import matplotlib.pyplot as plt

# Sample data for a heatmap
data = {'Math': [80, 90, 70, 65, 85],
        'Science': [88, 78, 92, 75, 80],
        'English': [85, 95, 72, 60, 70]}

# Convert to a DataFrame
df = pd.DataFrame(data)

# Create a heatmap
plt.figure(figsize=(6, 4))
sns.heatmap(df.corr(), annot=True, cmap='coolwarm')
# Add a title
plt.title('Correlation Heatmap', fontsize=16)
# Show the plot
plt.show()
```

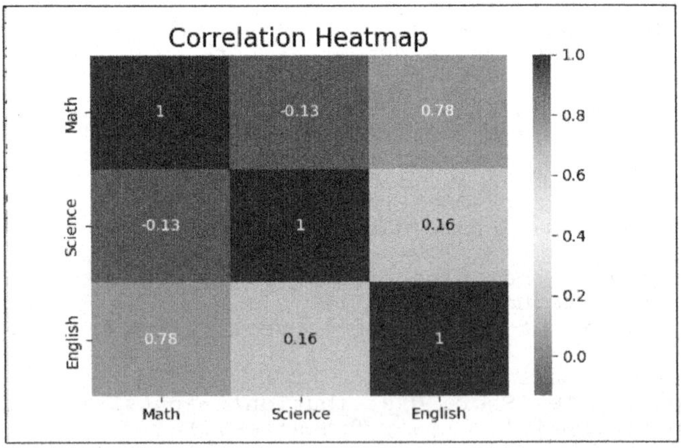

Figure 37c. Correlation Heatmap using the seaborn module.

Colourful 3D Histogram

Here's how you can create a colourful 3D histogram plot using Matplotlib's **mplot3d** toolkit. A 3D histogram can be useful for visualising the distribution of two continuous variables in a 3D space. The image at the start of this Chapter was produced by this program.

- We use NumPy to generate random data for two variables.
- Matplotlib's Axes3D module to create the 3D plot.
- The **hist** function to create a 3D histogram with different colours for visualisation.

Here's the code:

```
#Filename: plot8.py
import numpy as np
import matplotlib.pyplot as plt
from mpl_toolkits.mplot3d import Axes3D

#Generate random data for two variables
data1 = np.random.normal(0, 1, 1000)  # Normally
distributed data (mean=0, std=1)
data2 = np.random.normal(1, 2, 1000)  # Another
distribution (mean=1, std=2)

#Create a figure and a 3D axis
fig = plt.figure(figsize=(10, 7))
ax = fig.add_subplot(111, projection='3d')

#Create the 3D histogram
hist, xedges, yedges = np.histogram2d(data1, data2,
bins=30)

#Construct arrays for the 3D bars
xpos, ypos = np.meshgrid(xedges[:-1], yedges[:-1],
indexing="ij")
xpos = xpos.ravel()
ypos = ypos.ravel()
zpos = np.zeros_like(xpos)

#Width and depth of each bin
dx = dy = np.ones_like(zpos)

#Height (count in each bin)
dz = hist.ravel()

#Colour map (using viridis for a nice colourful plot)
colors = plt.cm.viridis(dz / max(dz))

#Create the 3D bars
ax.bar3d(xpos, ypos, zpos, dx, dy, dz, color=colors,
zsort='average')

# Add labels and title
ax.set_xlabel('Data1')
ax.set_ylabel('Data2')
ax.set_zlabel('Frequency')
ax.set_title('3D Histogram')

#Show the plot
plt.show()
```

What we did:

- **np.random.normal()** generates two sets of random data, each normally distributed with different means and standard deviations.
- **histogram2d()** creates a 2D histogram of the data.
- **bar3d()** is used to generate the 3D bars where the height of each bar represents the count of occurrences in each bin.
- **plt.cm.viridis()** is used to colour the bars based on their height, providing a vibrant, colourful plot.

This will display a colourful 3D histogram where the z-axis represents the frequency of data points falling into each bin, with different colours used to represent different frequencies.

Geographical Representations

To create a geographical data visualisation in Python, we can use **Cartopy**, a library that integrates with Matplotlib for mapping and geographical data visualisation. In this example, we'll use Cartopy to plot a simple map and overlay some geographical data (e.g., population locations).

First, ensure you have Cartopy and Matplotlib installed.

Here's a Python program that uses Cartopy to plot a world map and overlays points representing population centres:

```
#Filename: plot9
import matplotlib.pyplot as plt
import cartopy.crs as ccrs
import cartopy.feature as cfeature

# Step 1: Create a figure with a specific projection (in
this case, PlateCarree for a flat map)
plt.figure(figsize=(10, 6))
ax = plt.axes(projection=ccrs.PlateCarree())

# Step 2: Add map features like coastlines, borders,
and land
ax.coastlines(resolution='110m')
ax.add_feature(cfeature.BORDERS, linestyle=':')
ax.add_feature(cfeature.LAND)
ax.add_feature(cfeature.OCEAN)

# Step 3: Optionally, add gridlines (latitude and
longitude)
ax.gridlines(draw_labels=True)

# Step 4: Plot some sample population centers (latitude
and longitude)
# For example: New York, London, Tokyo, and Sydney
population_centers = {
    'New York': (-74.0060, 40.7128),
    'London': (-0.1276, 51.5074),
```

```
        'Tokyo': (139.6917, 35.6895),
        'Sydney': (151.2093, -33.8688)
}

# Step 5: Overlay these population centers as points on
the map
for city, (lon, lat) in population_centers.items():
    ax.plot(lon, lat, marker='o', color='red',
markersize=8, transform=ccrs.Geodetic())
    # Add city names as annotations
    ax.text(lon + 3, lat, city, transform=ccrs.
Geodetic(), fontsize=12, color='blue')

# Step 6: Show the final map
plt.title('Population Centers on World Map',
fontsize=15)
plt.show()
```

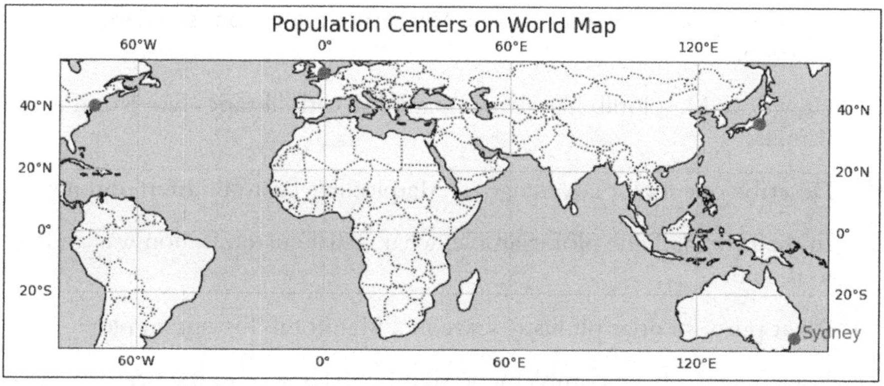

37d. Using the Cartopy library to display maps.

Here's a rough explanation of what's going on. You should now be able to extrapolate from here.

First we setup the map. **ccrs.PlateCarree()** is the projection used to create a flat map of the Earth.

The map includes coastlines, borders, and land and ocean features for context. Next add gridlines to show the latitudes and longitudes for better geographic understanding.

Some example population centres (New York, London, Tokyo, Sydney) are plotted using their latitude and longitude coordinates.

ax.plot() adds red dots at the corresponding geographical coordinates. City names are added using **ax.text()**.

You can extend this by overlaying more complex datasets like temperature zones, earthquake data, or political boundaries.

Questions

1. How can you create a simple line plot in Python using Matplotlib and Pandas?
2. How can Matplotlib be used for 3D plotting, and what are some common use cases?
3. How can Matplotlib be used to create a geographical data visualisation?
4. What are some customisation options available in Matplotlib for enhancing plots?
5. What are some common types of visualisations that Matplotlib can create?
6. Name three less obvious uses of Matplotlib aside from standard charting.
7. How does Matplotlib handle compatibility with libraries like NumPy and Pandas?
8. Describe one major advantage of Matplotlib's customisation options.
9. In the provided line plot example, what visual customisation was added to the line?
10. What purpose does plt.hist() serve in a Matplotlib histogram plot?
11. How does Seaborn complement Matplotlib, as seen in the heatmap example?
12. What is the role of Axes3D in creating a 3D histogram with Matplotlib?
13. How does Cartopy integrate with Matplotlib to create geographical visualisations?

38: Dunder Methods

We've mentioned "**Dunder methods**" a few times already, so let's dive into what they actually are. Dunder methods, also known as "special methods" or "magic methods", are a unique feature in Python that lets you define how objects behave with built-in operations and functions. These methods are named with double underscores at the beginning and end of their names, like **__init__**, **__str__**, and **__add__**. By the way, 'Dunder' stands for "double underscore". If you refer back to Chapter 03 and the section on Programming OOP you'll see that we introduced them there.

Using Dunder methods in a class allows you to customise how objects of that class respond to actions such as creation, string representation, arithmetic operations, and more. One of the most used Dunder methods is **__init__**. It's the constructor method that lets you set up the object's attributes when a new instance is created. For example, when you create an instance of a Person class with **Person("Alice", 30)**, the **__init__** method sets the name and age attributes of that instance to "Alice" and 30, respectively. This is how you 'seed' the values, getting the object ready to use right from the start.

Here's a quick example of a Person class that uses these Dunder methods:

```
#Filename: dunder1.py
class Person:
    def __init__(self, name, age):
        self.name = name
        self.age = age

    def __str__(self):
        return f"{self.name}, {self.age} years old"

    def __repr__(self):
        return f"Person(name={self.name!r}, age={self.
age!r})"
```

```
#Creating instances of the Person class
person1 = Person("Alice", 30)
person2 = Person("Bob", 25)

#Using the __str__ method
print(person1)  # Output: Alice, 30 years old
print(person2)  # Output: Bob, 25 years old

#Using the __repr__ method
print(repr(person1))  # Output: Person(name='Alice',
age=30)
print(repr(person2))  # Output: Person(name='Bob',
age=25)
```

In this example, the **__init__** method initialises the name and age attributes when creating a new Person object. When you create a Person object using **Person("Alice", 30)**, the **__init__** method sets **self.name** to "Alice" and **self.age** to 30.

We also override the **__str__** method to provide a readable string representation of the Person object. So when you print the object, like **print(person1)**, it outputs "Alice, 30 years old".

The **__repr__** method gives an unambiguous string representation of the object, which is especially useful for debugging. For example, **repr(person1)** outputs **Person(name='Alice', age=30)**.

These customisation make your **Person** objects not only functional but also easier to work with and understand in your code.

Let's take another example, this time with a **Car** class, to show the difference between **__str__** and **__repr__**:

```
#Filename: dunder2.py
class Car:
    def __init__(self, make, model, year):
        self.make = make
        self.model = model
        self.year = year

    def __str__(self):
        return f"{self.year} {self.make} {self.model}"

    def __repr__(self):
        return f"Car(make={self.make!r}, model={self.
model!r}, year={self.year!r})"

#Creating instances of the Car class
car1 = Car("Toyota", "Camry", 2021)
car2 = Car("Honda", "Civic", 2020)

#Using the __str__ method
print(car1)  # Output: 2021 Toyota Camry
print(car2)  # Output: 2020 Honda Civic

#Using the __repr__ method
```

```
print(repr(car1))  # Output: Car(make='Toyota',
model='Camry', year=2021)
print(repr(car2))  # Output: Car(make='Honda',
model='Civic', year=2020)

#Using the str() function
print(str(car1))  # Output: 2021 Toyota Camry
print(str(car2))  # Output: 2020 Honda Civic

#Using eval to recreate the object
new_car = eval(repr(car1))
print(new_car)  # Output: 2021 Toyota Camry
```

Here's what's happening:

- The **__init__** method sets up the make, model, and year attributes when you create a new Car object.
- The **__str__** method returns a user-friendly string representation, like "2021 Toyota Camry", when you print the object.
- The **__repr__** method returns a detailed string that can be used to recreate the object, which is useful for debugging.

Using **eval(repr(car1))**, we can recreate the Car object from its __repr__ string, although this should be used with caution since **eval()** can pose security risks if the string contains malicious code.

These examples show how defining **__str__** and **__repr__** gives you clear and useful string representations for different situations—**__str__** for user-friendly output and **__repr__** for detailed, unambiguous representation.

Practical Use

Let's look at how you might use the Person class in different scenarios, like printing user-friendly messages, logging, and debugging:

```
#Filename: dunder3.py
class Person:
    def __init__(self, name, age):
        self.name = name
        self.age = age

    def __str__(self):
        return f"{self.name}, {self.age} years old"

    def __repr__(self):
        return f"Person(name={self.name!r}, age={self.
age!r})"

#Creating instances of the Person class
person1 = Person("Alice", 30)
person2 = Person("Bob", 25)
```

```
#Function to display person details in a user-friendly
manner
def display_person_details(person):
    print(person)  # This uses the __str__ method

#Function to log person details-debugging purposes)
def log_person_details(person):
    with open("person_log.txt", "a") as log_file:
        log_file.write(repr(person) + "\n")  # This uses
the __repr__ method

#Function to simulate a simple registration process
def register_persons(person_list):
    for person in person_list:
        display_person_details(person)
        log_person_details(person)

#Main program
if __name__ == "__main__":
    persons = [person1, person2]
    register_persons(persons)

    # Debugging: printing detailed information about
persons
    for person in persons:
        print(f"Debug info: {repr(person)}")
```

Here's a quick breakdown:

- **__str__** is used for displaying user-friendly information when you print the object.
- **__repr__** is used for logging detailed information, which is helpful for debugging.
- The register_persons function handles both displaying and logging, making sure your Person objects are well-represented in different contexts.

By combining **__str__** and **__repr__**, you get the best of both worlds: clear and concise information for users, and detailed, accurate data for developers.

Why Use Dunder Methods Instead of List

You might wonder why you'd bother with Dunder methods when a simple list of strings could store names and ages. Well, using Dunder methods in a custom class has several advantages:

- **Object-Oriented Approach and Abstraction:** Dunder methods allow you to encapsulate data and behaviour in a single class. This makes your code more modular, as you can group related attributes (like name and age) and behaviour (like how to print or compare objects) in one place.

- **Enhanced Readability and Intent:** With a custom class, it's clear what the data represents and how it should be used. For example, a Person class clearly communicates the intent of the data (i.e., it holds information about a person), whereas a list of strings would require additional context.
- **Flexibility and Extensibility:** Custom classes with Dunder methods allow for easy extension. You can add new attributes or methods to the class (like adding an address or defining custom comparison behaviour) without changing how the class is used elsewhere in your code.
- **Behaviour and Polymorphism:** Dunder methods allow you to define how your objects interact with built-in functions and operators (like printing, addition, or comparison). This means you can treat objects like regular Python types, making your code more intuitive and enabling polymorphism—allowing objects of different types to be treated the same way if they implement the same methods.

So, while a list of strings might work for simple tasks, using custom classes with Dunder methods makes your code more organised, scalable, and maintainable—especially as your project grows.

Remember, don't get too caught up in the terminology. Focus on understanding how these methods work and how they can make your programming life easier.

Operator Overloading:

Dunder methods allow you to overload operators (like +, -, *, etc.) so that objects of your class can behave like built-in types when using these operators.

For example, you can use **__add__** to define how objects of your class should behave when added together using the **+** operator.

```
#Filename: dunder4.py
class Vector:
    def __init__(self, x, y):
        self.x = x
        self.y = y

    def __add__(self, other):
        return Vector(self.x + other.x, self.y + other.
y)
```

```
    def __repr__(self):
        return f"Vector({self.x}, {self.y})"

v1 = Vector(1, 2)
v2 = Vector(3, 4)
print(v1 + v2)  # Output: Vector(4, 6)
```

Custom Comparisons

You can define custom comparison behaviour using Dunder methods like __eq__ (for equality, ==), __lt__ (for less than, <), __le__ (for less than or equal, <=), and others.

This is helpful when you want objects of your class to be comparable using standard comparison operators.

```
#Filename: dunder5.py
class Person:
    def __init__(self, name, age):
        self.name = name
        self.age = age

    def __eq__(self, other):
        return self.age == other.age

    def __lt__(self, other):
        return self.age < other.age

p1 = Person("Alice", 30)
p2 = Person("Bob", 25)
print(p1 == p2)  # Output: False
print(p1 > p2)   # Output: True
```

Callable Objects

By defining the **__call__** method, you can make an instance of a class behave like a function. This can be helpful when you want objects to perform a task when "called" like functions.

```
#Filename: dunder6.py
class Multiplier:
    def __init__(self, factor):
        self.factor = factor

    def __call__(self, value):
        return value * self.factor

times_two = Multiplier(2)
print(times_two(5))  # Output: 10
```

Dunder Methods for Containers

If you're creating custom classes that behave like containers (e.g., lists, dictionaries), you can implement methods like __getitem__, __setitem__, __delitem__, __len__, and __iter__ to customise indexing, length calculation, and iteration.

```
#Filename: dunder7.py
class CustomList:
    def __init__(self):
        self.data = []

    def __getitem__(self, index):
        return self.data[index]

    def __setitem__(self, index, value):
        self.data[index] = value

    def __len__(self):
        return len(self.data)

lst = CustomList()
lst.data = [1, 2, 3]
print(lst[1])    # Output: 2
print(len(lst)) # Output: 3
```

Summary:

Dunder methods are not just useful for creating user-friendly string representations of objects or initialising objects; they offer deep control over how your objects interact with Python's core functionalities. From operator overloading to handling attribute access and making objects iterable, Dunder methods unlock advanced behaviours and enable more Pythonic, readable, and maintainable code.

Questions

1. What is a Dunder method and why is it called "Dunder"?
2. What's the difference between the __str__ and __repr__ methods?
3. What is operator overloading in Python and how do Dunder methods support it?
4. How does the __call__ Dunder method work, and when would you use it?
5. What is the role of the __getitem__ Dunder method?
6. What are Dunder methods in Python, and why are they named this way?

7. What role does the __init__ Dunder method play in a Python class? Provide an example.

8. How do __str__ and __repr__ methods differ, and when should each be used?

9. Explain the purpose of the __add__ method and provide an example of its use in operator overloading.

10. In the context of the Person class, what would be the output of repr(person1) and why?

11. Why might one prefer using a custom class with Dunder methods over a simple list of strings to store related data?

12. How does the __call__ method make a class instance behave like a function? Illustrate with an example.

13. Describe how to make objects of a class comparable using Dunder methods for equality (__eq__) and ordering (__lt__).

14. What are Dunder methods for containers, and how do they allow custom classes to behave like lists or dictionaries?

15. Summarise how Dunder methods contribute to writing more Pythonic and maintainable code.

39: APIs

Application Programming Interfaces (API) allow different software applications to communicate with each other. On the Raspberry Pi, APIs can be used to extend its functionality to interact with external devices, retrieve data from the internet, or serve as a back-end for various applications. Given the Raspberry Pi's affordability, low power consumption, and support for multiple programming languages (especially Python!), it serves as an ideal platform for developing and deploying APIs, especially in projects related to home automation, IoT (Internet of Things), or personal web services.

Why Use APIs on a Raspberry Pi?

APIs can connect your Raspberry Pi to external services, allowing it to:

- Control devices such as lights or sensors in your home automation system.
- Retrieve and display data from a wide variety of external services (e.g., weather data or news feeds).
- Act as a server to communicate with other devices, making the Raspberry Pi the central hub for your IoT setup.

How Organisations Get API Keys

API keys are essential for organisations or developers to interact with various third-party APIs. They serve as a way to authenticate and authorise access to the service and often help track usage for billing and rate limiting purposes.

Organisations need to sign up for an account with the service providing the API. For example, for the OpenWeatherMap API, an organisation would go to OpenWeatherMap's website and create an account. Many APIs offer different pricing tiers, including free tiers with limited usage and paid tiers for more extensive access. Organisations should select the appropriate plan based on their needs (number of requests, available features, etc.).

After signing up, organisations often need to register their application (the app or service that will use the API). This could be as simple as naming the application and describing its purpose.

Generate API Key: Once the application is registered, an API key is usually generated in the developer's account dashboard. This key is unique to the account and must be included in each request to the API for authentication

Configure Usage Limits: Depending on the plan, organisations may configure usage alerts, rate limits, or monitoring to ensure they don't exceed their allowed quota.

Documentation and Examples: The API provider typically supplies documentation on how to use the API, including sample re-quests and explanations of available endpoints, parameters, and responses.

API Key Use:

Security: API keys should be kept private. They are like passwords that provide access to services. Some APIs also allow restricting API key usage to specific IP addresses or domains to prevent misuse.

Usage Monitoring: Most API providers offer a dashboard to monitor how the key is being used, showing the number of requests, errors, and data consumption.

How Users Can Understand API Responses

Once organisations or developers have the API key and access to the API, they need to understand the structure of the data returned by the API to make proper use of it. Here's how users can under-stand the data returned by an API.

Read the API Documentation:

Endpoint Details: API documentation typically lists all the available endpoints (URLs you send requests to) and explains what data each endpoint returns. For example, OpenWeatherMap might have endpoints like **/weather** to get current weather data and **/forecast** for future forecasts.

Parameters: API documentation will also explain the query parameters that need to be passed in the request (e.g., API key, location, temperature units, etc.).

Response Structure: The documentation includes sample responses in JSON (or XML) format, which show the structure of the returned data.

For example, OpenWeatherMap might return a JSON response like this:

```
{
  "coord": { "lon": -0.1257, "lat": 51.5085 },
  "weather": [
    {
      "id": 804,
      "main": "Clouds",
      "description": "overcast clouds",
      "icon": "04d"
    }
  ],
  "main": {
    "temp": 287.84,
    "feels_like": 287.55,
    "temp_min": 287.26,
    "temp_max": 288.47,
    "pressure": 1012,
    "humidity": 79
  },
  "wind": { "speed": 4.63, "deg": 220 },
  "name": "London"
}
```

The API documentation will explain what each field means although it should be reasonably clear, given the information you are seeking.

Inspect Sample Responses:

Use API Testers: Many APIs provide tools or web-based interfaces where developers can make sample requests and inspect the responses. Services like **Postman** also allow you to test APIs by sending requests and viewing the data that comes back.

Run Test Requests: Developers can use tools like curl, Python's requests library, or **Postman** to send API requests and observe the response. The sample response can then be analysed to understand what data fields are available and how they are structured.

Example Python code using the OpenWeatherMap API:

```
import requests

api_key = 'your_actual_api_key'
city = 'London'
country_code = 'gb'
units = 'metric'

url = f"http://api.openweathermap.org/data/2.5/weather?
q={city},{country_code}&appid={api_key}&units={units}"
response = requests.get(url)
weather_data = response.json()
print(weather_data)
```

The output will be in JSON format and will include fields such as temp, humidity, and weather. You can then refer to the documentation to understand the meaning of each field.

Focus on Relevant Data

Depending on your application, you may not need all the data returned by the API. For instance, if you're only interested in displaying the temperature and humidity, you can extract those fields from the response and ignore the rest.

Example of extracting relevant data from the above response:

```
temp = weather_data['main']['temp']
humidity = weather_data['main']['humidity']
description = weather_data['weather'][0]['description']

print(f"Temperature: {temp}°C")
print(f"Humidity: {humidity}%")
print(f"Weather: {description}")
```

Use the API in Development Tools:

Postman: A tool like Postman can help visualise the request and response data more clearly. You can add your API key, set query parameters, and inspect the response, seeing exactly what the server sends back.

Debugging Tools: While developing, you can print the response in the terminal (using print() in Python) or log it to a file to understand the returned data structure.

Check for Rate Limits and Quotas

Understanding the limits of how often you can call the API and how much data you can re-quest is essential. API documentation typically includes details about rate limiting, such as the number of requests allowed per minute or day.

Parse the Data Programmatically

Once the data is understood, it can be parsed in code. In Python, for example, you can access the data in JSON format and extract specific fields (as shown in the previous code). By focusing on the fields relevant to your application, you can make the API data actionable.

Conclusion

- **Getting API Keys:** Organisations can obtain API keys by signing up for an API service, registering their application, and receiving a unique API key that they use for authentication in their API requests.

- **Understanding API Data**: Users can understand the data returned by APIs by reading the API documentation, inspecting sample responses, and using tools like Postman to test re-quests and responses. They can then programmatically extract and manipulate the data they need.

Understanding the documentation and sample responses is key to making effective use of any API. Most API providers offer comprehensive guides, sample code, and tutorials to help developers get started.

OpenWeatherMap Step-by-Step

Here's a follow step by step on how to set-up and interrogate the **OpenWeatherMap** data.

Step 1: Prepare Your Raspberry Pi

Before starting, make sure your Raspberry Pi is up to date:

```
sudo apt update
sudo apt upgrade
```

Step 2: Set Up a Virtual Environment

```
python3 -m venv API        # Create
source API/bin/activate    # Activate
```

I have my own selection of APIs and I keep these scripts grouped in a single directory. I've got a few here for a variety of uses including the ISS and the recent launch of the Europa Space Clipper mission. I also have one for Dad Jokes which those who know me wont be too surprised about.

Step 3: Install Flask and Requests Modules

Install the necessary Python packages (Flask for the web server and requests for handling API requests). For the example below you will need to install the time and requests modules

```
pip install datetime
pip install requests
```

Step 4: Sign Up for an OpenWeatherMap API Key

To collect weather data, you'll need an API key from OpenWeatherMap. You can create a free account which comes with a few restrictions, the most being the number of times you can access it in any period of time. These sort of restrictions won't inhibit the average user.

Go to:

```
https://openweathermap.org/pricing-corp
```

and from here select the 'subscribe for free' option. Add in some details and join. You'll be taken to your page and you'll see your API there. You can generate more APIs if you wish, but not really necessary here, unless you have a team of users all accessing it at once!

Step 5: Write the API Code

Next you can write the code that will access the data. We'll look at how to research this in a bit. But let's see it in action first. Here's the code:

```
#Filename: api_weather
import requests
import time
from pprint import pprint
from urllib.parse import urlencode
from datetime import datetime

# Variables for API key, city, country, temperature
unit, and delay
API_KEY = '<YOU API KEY HERE>'
CITY = 'Sydney'  # Replace with the desired city
COUNTRY_CODE = 'au'  # Replace with the country code
(e.g., 'gb' for United Kingdom)
TEMP_UNIT = 'metric'  # Use 'metric' for Celsius,
'imperial' for Fahrenheit, 'kelvin' for Kelvin
DELAY = 30  # Delay in seconds between API requests

# Function to fetch weather data
def get_weather_data():
    base_url = "http://api.openweathermap.org/data/2.5/
weather"
    query_params = {
        'appid': API_KEY,
        'q': f"{CITY},{COUNTRY_CODE}",
        'units': TEMP_UNIT
    }
    final_url = f"{base_url}?{urlencode(query_params)}"

    try:
        response = requests.get(final_url)
        response.raise_for_status()  # Raise an error
if the request was unsuccessful
        weather_data = response.json()

        # Check if the API returned an error
        if weather_data.get('cod') != 200:
            print(f"Error: {weather_data.get('message',
'Failed to retrieve data')}")
            return None

        return weather_data
    except requests.exceptions.RequestException as e:
        print(f"Error fetching data: {e}")
        return None

# Function to store weather data into a list and
display formatted data
def store_and_display_weather(weather_data, weather_
history):
    if weather_data:
        # Create a structured weather record
        weather_record = {
            "Timestamp": datetime.now().strftime('%Y-
%m-%d %H:%M:%S'),
            "City": weather_data.get('name'),
            "Temperature": weather_data.get('main',
```

```
{}).get('temp'),
            "Humidity": weather_data.get('main', {}).
get('humidity'),
            "Weather Description": weather_data.
get('weather', [{}])[0].get('description'),
            "Wind Speed": weather_data.get('wind', {}).
get('speed'),
        }

        # Append the record to the history
        weather_history.append(weather_record)

        # Print the formatted weather data
        print(f"\nWeather Data for {weather_
record['City']} at {weather_record['Timestamp']}:")
        print(f"Temperature: {weather_
record['Temperature']}°C")
        print(f"Humidity: {weather_record['Humidity']}
%")
        print(f"Weather: {weather_record['Weather
Description']}")
        print(f"Wind Speed: {weather_record['Wind
Speed']} m/s\n")

# Function to display the complete history of weather
data
def display_weather_history(weather_history):
    print("\n--- Weather Data History ---")
    for entry in weather_history:
        print(f"{entry['Timestamp']} - {entry['City']}
| Temp: {entry['Temperature']}°C, "
              f"Humidity: {entry['Humidity']}%,
Weather: {entry['Weather Description']}, Wind:
{entry['Wind Speed']} m/s")

# Main function to run the program
def main():
    weather_history = []  # List to store all weather
data

    print(f"\nFetching weather data for {CITY},
{COUNTRY_CODE} every {DELAY} seconds...")

    while True:
        weather_data = get_weather_data()
        store_and_display_weather(weather_data,
weather_history)
        display_weather_history(weather_history)
        time.sleep(DELAY)

# Run the program
if __name__ == "__main__":
    main()
```

Insert you API key where it is request in the code above. Note that this program is hard coded at first as it sets the city and country within. You can add in other loops to get details from other cities. This program contains various error checking process as well.

How it Works

Here's a detailed description of the programs operation, as it's likely you may have not used API access before.

So, this program is designed to continuously fetch and display weather data from the OpenWeatherMap API at regular intervals. It does so by making HTTP requests to the API and extracting key weather information like temperature, humidity, weather conditions, and wind speed for a specified city. Here's a break down the program's functionality.

Initial Setup and Configuration: At the beginning of the program, several variables are defined:

API_KEY: This holds the OpenWeatherMap API key (which is necessary for authentication).

CITY and COUNTRY_CODE: These specify the city (in this case, Sydney) and the country code (Australia, represented by "au") for which weather data is requested.

TEMP_UNIT: This determines the unit of temperature measurement, set to Celsius (using "metric").

DELAY: This variable defines how often the weather data will be refreshed, set to every 60 seconds.

The function **get_weather_data()** constructs a URL to query the OpenWeatherMap API. It uses the city, country code, and temperature unit as query parameters. The Python requests library is used to send an HTTP request to the API (basically saying 'I want some info from you). If the request is successful (i.e., the response status code is 200), the response data is parsed as JSON. The function checks for errors (like invalid city or API key) and returns None if the request fails.

This function serves as the backbone of the program, allowing it to communicate with the OpenWeatherMap API and retrieve current weather data. The data fetched includes details such as temperature, humidity, weather description, and wind speed.

Storing and Displaying Weather Data: Once the weather data is fetched, the function **store_and_display_weather()** is called. This function creates a weather record, which is essentially a structured dictionary containing the following details:

Timestamp: The current date and time when the data is fetched.

City Name: The name of the city for which the data is retrieved.

Temperature: The current temperature in Celsius.

Humidity: The humidity percentage.

Weather Description: A short description of the current weather conditions (e.g., "clear sky").

Wind Speed: The current wind speed in meters per second.

This record is then appended to the **weather_history** list, which stores all the weather data fetched during the program's execution.

Main Program Loop: In the main() function, the program runs an infinite loop, repeatedly fetching weather data, dis-playing the current data, and updating the weather history. The program pauses for 60 seconds between each data fetch (as defined by the DELAY variable) before making another API request. This loop ensures that the program continuously collects and displays weather information at regular intervals. (You could reduce this to 10 seconds initially so you can see the retrievals frequently at first.)

Summary

In summary, this program interacts with the OpenWeatherMap API to retrieve weather data for Sydney, Australia, at 60-second intervals. It:

- Fetches the latest weather data.
- Formats and displays the data in a user-friendly format.
- Stores the data in a list for future reference.
- Continuously updates the data every 30 seconds, showing both the current weather and historical records.

The combination of these functions ensures the program remains dynamic, providing up-to-date weather information while keeping track of historical data.

This was a typical response for me:

```
2024-10-17 10:52:43 - Sydney | Temp: 20.44°C, Humidity:
61%, Weather: few clouds, Wind: 3.09 m/s
```

A relatively cool day in Sydney.

How Many API keys Needed?

One API Key per API Provider: Most APIs require one API key per provider. For example, if you're using the OpenWeatherMap API, you'll need one API key for that specific service.

If you're using multiple APIs from different providers (e.g.,

OpenWeatherMap for weather data and Google Maps for geolocation), you'll need a separate API key for each provider.

Example:

- OpenWeatherMap API key for weather data.
- Google Maps API key for geolocation and mapping.
- Twitter API key for social media interactions.

Development, Staging, and Production

Separate API keys for each environment (development, staging, production) are often recommended, especially for security and monitoring purposes.

For instance, if you have a development environment for testing and a production environment for live usage, some APIs allow you to generate multiple keys for each. This helps isolate testing from production use.

Rate Limits and Quotas: Multiple API keys from the same provider may be necessary if you have high traffic and need to spread your usage across different keys to avoid hitting rate limits or quotas. Some services allow you to request multiple API keys for the same account.

For example, if the OpenWeatherMap API allows 60 requests per minute on one key and you expect to exceed that, you may need to request additional API keys or upgrade to a higher plan.

Different Projects or Applications: Separate API keys for different projects or applications. If you're building multiple apps or services that use the same API, it's often a good idea to use different API keys for each app. This allows you to monitor usage and debug issues more easily per application.

API Key Expiration and Rotation: Key rotation may require additional API keys. For security, you may want to rotate your keys regularly (e.g., every few months). In this case, you might have one active API key and another one as a backup or in preparation for rotation.

Exercise: Weather History

Create a program that will display the data from this API but keep a record of the highs and lows for the past week and display these on the screen as well.

40: Writing Modules

Creating your own modules in Python is a breeze! After all, a module is just a Python file, so you're already halfway there. Here's a four-step guide to the processes required

1. Open a new file in Geany or Thonny.
2. Define your module's functions, classes, or variables in the file.
3. Think about what arguments each function will need.
4. Save the file with a name that makes sense for what your module does, using '.py' as the extension. That's it! Simple, right? It really is.

There are plenty of reasons why you might want to create your own module. Whether you want to reuse code across multiple projects or just keep things neat and tidy, modules are a great way to package code that you use regularly.

Let's look at a practical example. Suppose you're working on a project that involves prime numbers. You could create a module called **prime** that includes functions for checking if a number is prime and for finding the prime factors of a number. Here's what that might look like:

```
#Filename: modules1.py
#Functions for working with prime numbers

def is_prime(n):
    """Check if a number is a prime number."""
    if n <= 1:
        return False
    if n <= 3:
        return True
    if n % 2 == 0 or n % 3 == 0:
        return False
    i = 5
    while i * i <= n:
        if n % i == 0 or n % (i + 2) == 0:
```

```
            return False
        i += 6
    return True

def prime_factors(n):
    #Return a list of prime factors of a number.
    factors = []
    #Handle 2 separately to allow incrementing by 2 
later
    while n % 2 == 0:
        factors.append(2)
        n //= 2
    #Handle 3 separately to allow incrementing by 6 
later
    while n % 3 == 0:
        factors.append(3)
        n //= 3
    #Check for remaining factors starting from 5
    i = 5
    while i * i <= n:
        while n % i == 0:
            factors.append(i)
            n //= i
        while n % (i + 2) == 0:
            factors.append(i + 2)
            n //= (i + 2)
        i += 6
    #If n is still greater than 2, then n itself is a 
prime number
    if n > 2:
        factors.append(n)
    return factors

#Example usage
if __name__ == "__main__":
    number = int(input("Enter a number: "))
    print(f"Is {number} a prime number? {'Yes' if is_
prime(number) else 'No'}")
    print(f"Prime factors of {number}: {prime_
factors(number)}")
```

In this **prime** module, you've got two main functions:

- **is_prime(n)**: This function checks if a number n is prime. It first handles small numbers and simple cases (like whether the number is less than or equal to 3 or if it's divisible by 2 or 3). For larger numbers, it uses a loop that skips even numbers and multiples of 3 to check for other factors.

- **prime_factors(n)**: This function returns a list of prime factors for the number n. It handles 2 and 3 separately at first, and then checks for other factors starting from 5. If the number left after the loop is greater than 2, it's a prime number itself and gets added to the list.

Once you've saved your **prime.py** file, you can use it in other Python scripts by importing the functions you've created. For example, you could write a script called **prime_test.py** to test it out:

```
#Filename: prime_test.py
from prime import is_prime, prime_factors

number = int(input("Enter a number: "))
print(f"Is {number} a prime number? {'Yes' if is_
prime(number) else 'No'}")
print(f"Prime factors of {number}: {prime_
factors(number)}")
```

This way, you can easily reuse the **is_prime** and **prime_factors** functions across multiple projects, keeping your code neat and organised.

You might also consider placing your modules in a hidden directory (by prefixing the folder name with a dot) or in a specific folder inside your root directory. If you do that, remember to add the location to your path.

Organising Modules

You can place your custom modules in specific directories and use them across multiple projects. If your module is in a different directory, you may need to update your **sys.path** or package it properly by placing it in a package directory (with an **__init__.py** file).

What Functions Are in a Module?

There are plenty of reasons why you'd want to figure out what functions a module provides. The most obvious one is to understand what the module does and how you can use it in your own code. To help with this, Python offers the **dir()** function, which returns a sorted list of all the names defined in a specified module—or in the current module if you don't specify one. These names include functions, classes, variables, and other objects that the module contains.

Here's how you can use the **dir()** function to retrieve the functions provided by a module, like the math module:

```
#Filename: modules2.py
import math

#Get the list of functions in the math module
functions = [name for name in dir(math)
if callable(getattr(math, name))]

#Print the list of functions
for function in functions:
    print(function)
```

The **dir()** function will return everything defined in the module, including variables, classes, and other objects. To filter out just the functions, the code uses a list comprehension along with the **callable()** function to check if each attribute in the module is a function.

Using dir() in this way helps you explore and discover what's available in a module, making it easier to understand its capabilities and use them effectively in your projects.

Let's take this a step further by accessing **additional** information about these functions:

```
#Filename: modules3.py
import math

#Get the list of functions in the math module
functions = [name for name in dir(math) if
callable(getattr(math, name))]

#Print function names and their docstrings
for function in functions:
    func_obj = getattr(math, function)
    docstring = func_obj.__doc__
    print(f"{function}: {docstring}\n" if docstring
else f"{function}: No documentation available.\n")
```

In this example, we first retrieve the list of functions as before. Then, for each function, we use **callable** with **getattr(math, function)** to get the function object itself. callable() ensures that the list of attributes retrieved from the math (or any) module only includes functions. This helps to avoid non-callable objects like constants (pi, e) when you're trying to explore only the available functions.

We then retrieve its docstring (see Chapter 43) using the **__doc__** attribute. If the function has a docstring, we print it; otherwise, we let the user know that no documentation is available.

Running this code will display each function's name along with its docstring, giving you a better idea of what the function does and how to use it.

By exploring the docstrings, you can quickly understand the purpose and usage of the functions provided by a module, making it easier to incorporate them into your own code.

Exercises

Have a go at adding these functions to the **prime** module:

next_prime(n): Returns the smallest prime number greater than **n**.
prev_prime(n): Returns the largest prime number smaller than **n**.
prime_range(start, end): Returns all prime numbers within a range.
prime_gap(n): Returns the gap between two consecutive primes surrounding **n**.

41: Building Websites

Building websites using Python on a Raspberry Pi is a great way to combine both web development and the unique capabilities of the Pi. With frameworks like **Flask** or **Django**, you can set up dynamic, responsive websites that run smoothly on the Raspberry Pi, making it an affordable platform for web experimentation and lightweight hosting. One of the reasons the Raspberry Pi is so appealing for this is its versatility—it can be set up as a web server while also handling tasks like data logging, hardware interaction, or even automation, all integrated into the website.

For beginners, **Flask** is often the preferred choice for creating Python-based websites on the Pi, as the framework it is based on is easy to get a basic site up and running quickly. Note that in this case 'Flask' is correct not 'flask' which might be seen as more accurate.

Flask allows you to handle routes which refers to a URL path that the web application can respond to. It's essentially a way to tell your web server what should happen when a user visits a specific URL. Each route is linked to a specific function (called a **view function**) in your Python code, which dictates what content should be displayed or what action should be taken.

URL stands for **Uniform Resource Locator** and it is the address used to access resources on the internet, such as web pages, images, or files. A URL typically consists of several components, including the protocol (e.g., https), the domain name (e.g., codingpress.com.au), and the path to the resource (e.g., /page1.html).

You can start with simple static pages and easily move into dynamic content. For example, you could use Flask to create a dashboard that displays sensor data from the Raspberry Pi's GPIO pins, making it a great tool for IoT (Internet of Things) projects. Or to display the weather info we saw earlier.

Django, on the other hand, is more feature-rich and is ideal if you're aiming to build larger, more complex applications. With Django, you get more tools out of the box, like user authentication, an admin interface, and database management. However, it's more resource-intensive, so while it can run on the Raspberry Pi, it's a better fit for projects where you need those extra features. The Raspberry Pi's ability to handle both lightweight web frameworks and integrate Python scripts makes it a perfect playground for building custom web applications tailored to your needs.

For the purpose here we'll look at Flask and I'll leave you to explore Django at another time.

Here's a simple step-by-step guide to the process. As always before trying something ensure your fully up to date and get your virtual environment setup. *Note that on Raspberry Pi 4 and before you will need to create your virtual environment using the venv module. Flask illustrates why you should always use venv as it the safest and surest way to install a totally isolated virtual environment, rather than Thonny for example.*

Once that's done install Flask into the virtual environment.

```
pip install flask
```

In your virtual environment create a new directory and call this: **templates**

Create a new file called 'app.py' with the following code. This file should be located in the main directory of the virtual environment:

```
#Filename: app.py
from flask import Flask

app = Flask(__name__)

@app.route('/')
def home():
    return "Hello from Python Unleashed via Flask'

if __name__ == '__main__':
    app.run(host='0.0.0.0', port=80)
```

This script does the following:

- Imports Flask and creates an instance of it.
- Sets up a route (/) that will display a simple welcome message when you visit the root URL of your Raspberry Pi.
- Runs the app on port 80 (the default port for web servers) and makes it accessible from any IP address (0.0.0.0).

On a Raspberry Pi (or any device connected to a network), IP numbers (IP addresses) and ports are key and help identify and communicate with other devices on the network. Let's break them down:

IP Numbers (IP Addresses) An IP address is like the unique postal address for your Raspberry Pi on a network. It allows other devices (like your computer, phone, or another Raspberry Pi) to find and communicate with it.

To run the Flask web server, you'll need to use **sudo** because we're binding to **port 80** (which requires root privileges):

```
sudo python3 app.py
```

A port is like a door on your Raspberry Pi (or any device) that applications use to send and receive data. While the IP address gets you to the correct device, the port number directs the communication to the right service running on that device. On executing you'll get a message in your terminal window detailing the **http://** addresses you can enter. One will provide the page you are after. (Note you will need to use a browser such as Firefox. Chrome is a bit more difficult to use with http addresses.)

If you have a computer on the same network you should be able to enter one of the addresses and also see the page.

Adding HTML templates

To make your website look nicer, Flask can serve HTML templates. Here's how to add some HTML structure:

Create a folder for the HTML templates:

You can add the code for a real website to display a a webpage of pages of your choice. If you haven't already done so create a template folder in the virtual environment:

```
mkdir templates
```

Create an **index.html** file inside the templates folder Note that this is saved as 'index.txt' in the download programs folder. You will need to re-save as 'index.html'. Add this basic HTML code and save.

```
!DOCTYPE html>
<html lang="en">
<head>
    <meta charset="UTF-8">
    <meta name="viewport" content="width=device-width,
initial-scale=1.0">
    <title>My Flask Website</title>
    <style>
        body {
            font-family: Arial, sans-serif;
            background-color: #f4f4f4;
            text-align: center;
```

```
            padding-top: 50px;
        }
        h1 {
            color: #333;
        }
    </style>
</head>
<body>

    <h1>Welcome to the Python Unleashed Book Website!</h1>
    <p>by Bruce Smith @ The Coding Press  codingpress.com.
au</p>
    <p>This site is hosted on a Raspberry Pi using Flask.
</p>
</body>
</html>
```

Save and close the file. Now, modify your **app.py** to render this HTML template instead of just returning a string:

```
Filename: app2.py
from flask import Flask, render_template

app = Flask(__name__)

@app.route('/')
def home():
    return render_template('index.html')

if __name__ == '__main__':
    app.run(host='0.0.0.0', port=80)
```

Save the changes to app.py, and run the Flask app again:

```
sudo python3 app.py
```

Now when you visit your Raspberry Pi's IP address, you should see your custom HTML page!

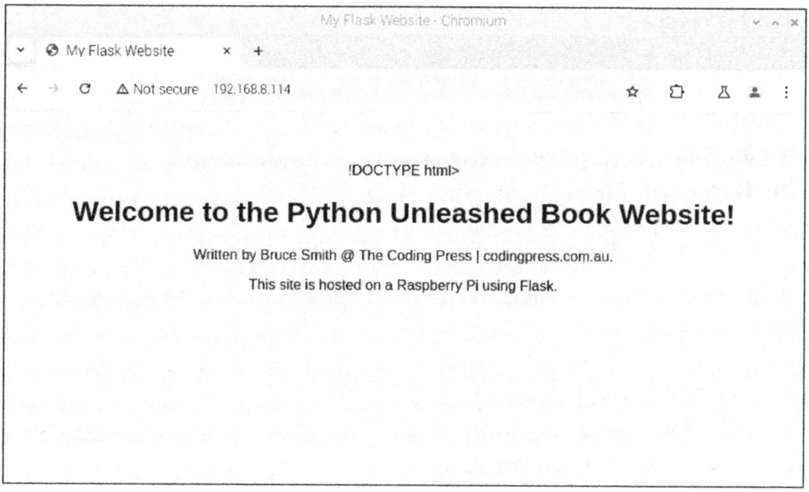

Figure 41a. Custom webpage.

Background Flask

To keep your Flask app running even after you close the terminal, you can use **tmux**, **screen**, or set it up as a service. **tmux** (short for Terminal Multiplexer) is a command-line tool that allows you to create, manage, and switch between multiple terminal sessions within a single window. It's especially useful for tasks that you want to keep running in the background, like when you're running a web server or script on a Raspberry Pi. *This is not a Python program so you need to install it as a system program.* It will be available from within virtual environments though:

```
sudo apt install tmux
```

Start a new tmux session through the Terminal:

```
tmux new -s flask_app
```

Run your Flask app in this session:

```
sudo python3 app.py
```

Detach from the tmux session by pressing CTRL + B, then D. This will leave the Flask app running in the background.

And there you go. Remember **index.html** will always be the web-server goes to when the website is selected. You can name further pages by giving them a meaningful name, or just 'page1', 'page2' etc. Jut remember to add '.html' at the end as the file type.

Questions

1. What are two popular Python frameworks for building websites on a Raspberry Pi?
2. Why is Flask often chosen for beginner web development projects on the Raspberry Pi?
3. What does the @app.route('/') decorator in Flask do?
4. Why might it be beneficial to use a Raspberry Pi for hosting web applications?
5. In Flask, what is the purpose of creating a templates directory?
6. What is the default development port number used by Flask, and how would you access it in a browser?
7. Explain the difference between an IP address and a port when connecting to a Raspberry Pi web server.
8. How can you run a Flask app on the Raspberry Pi so it remains active even if the terminal is closed?
9. What command would you use to install Flask in a virtual environment on the Raspberry Pi?
10. What is the purpose of using render_template() in Flask, and how does it relate to HTML files?
11. Try adding an extra page to this website.

42: Docstrings

Docstrings, short for **documentation strings**, are a feature of Python used to provide an explanation of what a function, method, class, or module does. These strings are normally placed immediately after the definition line (such as after the def or class keyword) and are enclosed within triple quotes **(""" text here """)**. Docstrings serve as the **official** documentation of your code, making it easier for others—and yourself—to understand/remember the purpose, parameters, return values, and behaviour of different parts of the code base.

Unlike regular comments, using '#', which are ignored at runtime, docstrings are stored as an **attribute** of the function, class, or module they document, making them accessible through various means, such as the built-in **help()** function or documentation generation tools like **Sphinx**.

A well-written docstring should provide a brief description of the functionality, detail the parameters (including their types and purpose), describe the return value and its type, and mention any exceptions that the function might raise. For example, a function that calculates the area of a rectangle might have a docstring like:

```
def calculate_area(length, width):
    """
    Calculate the area of a rectangle.

    Parameters:
    length (float): The length of the rectangle.
    width (float): The width of the rectangle.

    Returns:
    float: The area of the rectangle.
    """
    return length * width
```

This docstring clearly explains what the function does, the parameters it expects, and what it returns.

Docstrings are stored as metadata, they can be accessed at runtime to provide help and documentation directly within Python. This makes them a core part of Python's philosophy of being readable and user-friendly.

In addition, docstrings can be leveraged by automatic documentation generation tools like **Sphinx**, which can convert them into structured documentation formats, such as HTML or PDF, providing a professional and maintainable way to document larger projects.

Sphinx

Sphinx is a documentation generation tool for that utilises docstrings embedded in Python code, and has become a popular choice for generating comprehensive, easy-to-navigate, and aesthetically pleasing documentation for all kinds of software projects. It can convert plain text files, into various output formats such as HTML, PDF, ePub, and more. It is extensible in that it supports a wide range of plugins and themes to format the look and functionality of its output.

Key Features of Sphinx

- **Automatic API Documentation:** Sphinx can automatically extract documentation from your Python code, including docstrings, modules, functions, classes, and methods. It ensures that the documentation stays in sync with your code.

- **Cross-Referencing:** Sphinx provides cross-referencing capabilities, allowing you to create links between different parts of your documentation. This includes linking to functions, classes, modules, and even external resources. This feature ensures that readers can easily navigate through the documentation and find related information quickly. It's a bit like the Contents list at the beginning of this book, or the index.

- **Support for Multiple Formats:** Sphinx can generate documentation in a variety of formats, including HTML for web-based documentation, allowing with the ability to create PDFs, ePub for e-book readers, and more.

- **Theming and Styling:** Sphinx supports multiple themes and custom styles, allowing you to create documentation that aligns with a style or branding you wish to use.

Using Sphinx

To use Sphinx, you need to install it first into your virtual environment using pip:

```
pip install sphinx
```

After installing Sphinx, you can set up a new documentation project:

```
sphinx-quickstart
```

This will guide you through the setup process, asking questions about the project's name, author, and desired configurations. It will generate a basic directory structure with essential files like **conf.py** (configuration file) and **index.rst** (the main document file).

Worked Example

Let's go through a step-by-step guide to creating and viewing documentation from the docstrings listed in **doctest.py file** listed below. This guide assumes you have Sphinx installed in your activated virtual environment.

Step 1: Write Docstrings in doctest.py

First, make sure your Python file (doctest.py) contains correctly formatted docstrings. Here's a simple example of how you might structure your Python code with docstrings:

```
#Filename: doctest.py

def example_function(param1, param2):
    """
    This is an example function.

    :param param1: The first parameter.
    :param param2: The second parameter.
    :return: The sum of param1 and param2.
    """
    return param1 + param2

class ExampleClass:
    """
    This is an example class.
    """

    def __init__(self, value):
        """
        Initialize the class with a value.


        :param value: The value to initialize with.
        """
        self.value = value

    def get_value(self):
        """
        Get the value of the instance.

        :return: The value of the instance.
        """
        return self.value
```

Step 2: Create a Sphinx Documentation Directory

Navigate to your project directory and create a new directory for the Sphinx documentation in your environment

```
mkdir docs
cd docs
```

Step 3: Initialise Sphinx

Run the following command to initialise a new Sphinx project in the docs directory (Note I normally set myself up in the 'bin' directory to keep these directories out of the way. Not sure if that is good programming practice, but suits me!):

```
sphinx-quickstart
```

This command will prompt you with a series of questions. Most are in regards you project. If you're sure then simply hit <Enter>.

Here are some suggested answers:

```
Separate source and build directories: n (yes)
Project name: Enter your project name (e.g., Magic
Documentation)
Author name: Bruce Wayne
Project release: Enter the version of your project (e.g.,
0.1)
Language: Enter your preferred language (e.g., en for
English)
```

This process creates a basic directory structure and configuration files for Sphinx. If you have create the 'docs' directory in here you should find folders called '_Templates' and '_Static' and '_build' plus a couple of extra files.

Step 4: Configure conf.py for Auto-Documentation

Open the 'bin' directory (or wherever you decided to pack them) and load the 'config.py' file into an IDE. You need to modify it to enable the autodoc extension and set up the path to your source code.

Make the following changes to conf.py by commenting them:

```
import os
import sys
```

Ensure that PATH is set to to reach your source code - uncomment the line:

```
sys.path.insert(0, os.path.abspath('.')(/home/bruce/
Desktop/MyEnv1'))
```

This will search the current directory Which , in my case is where I am working, before searching the directories in sys.path)

Enable the autodoc extension: by locating the following line in conf.py:

```
# extensions = []
```

Uncomment it and add 'sphinx.ext.autodoc' on to it so the line reads:

```
extensions = ['sphinx.ext.autodoc']
```

Step 5: Create a .rst File for Your Module

In the docs/source directory, create a new reStructuredText (.rst) file named **magic.rst** (or the name of you program you are documenting), with the following content:

```
Magic
=====

.. automodule:: magic
   :members:
```

This tells Sphinx to automatically generate documentation for all the members (functions, classes, etc.) in the docstring.py file.

Step 6: Update index.rst

Open the index.rst file in the docs/source directory. Add a reference to magic so that it is included in the table of contents:

```
.. toctree::
   :maxdepth: 2
   :caption: Contents:

   magic
```

Step 7: Build the Documentation

To build the HTML documentation, navigate to the docs directory and run the following command:

```
make html
```

This command generates HTML files in the docs/build/html directory.

Step 8: View the Generated Documentation

Open the Generated Documentation: Navigate to the build/html directory and open index.html in your web browser. You can do this by double-clicking the file or using the **open** command in the terminal.

Check Your Docstrings: Look for the entry for sphinx_test in the table of contents and click on it. You should see the documentation generated from the docstrings in magic.py.

Here's an image of the webpage and also a look inside at the docstring generated by sphinx.

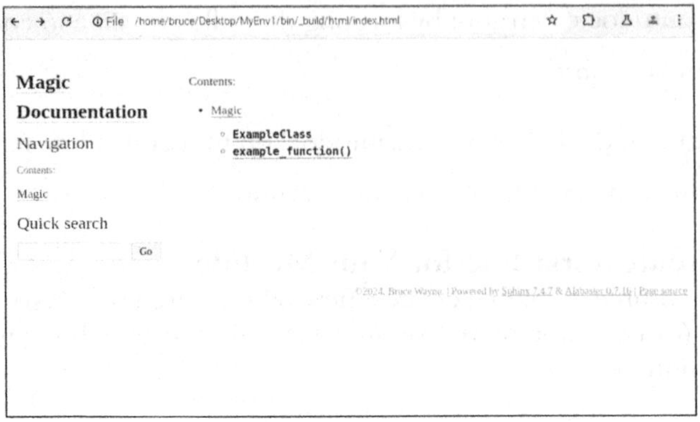

Figure 42a: Home page of Magic Documentation.

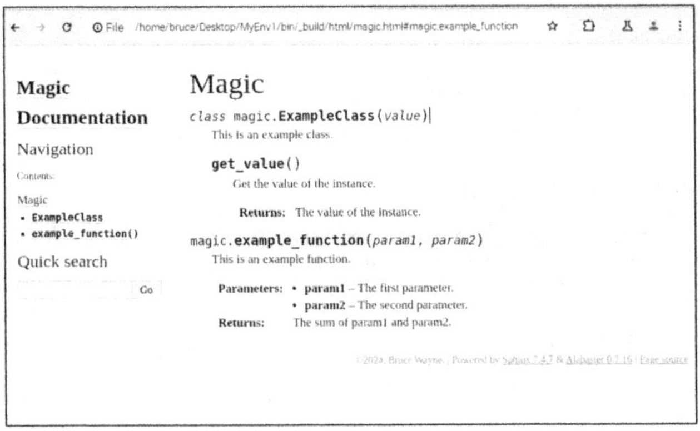

Figure 42b. Definitions and documentation.

Step 9: Troubleshooting Common Issues

Check the **sys.path** in conf.py: Make sure the directory where magic.py is located is correctly added to sys.path or specified.

Rebuild the Documentation: If changes aren't appearing, run:

```
make clean
```

and then **make html** to rebuild the documentation from scratch.

Ensure Your Virtual Environment is Active: If using a virtual environment, activate it before running **make html** to ensure all dependencies are available.

Exercise

1. Create a docstring document for the **prime** module we created earlier.

43: GPIO and HATS

The Raspberry Pi 5 brings one of the biggest architectural shifts in the Pi's history. It changes how peripherals are wired up and how we, as programmers, interact with GPIO devices and HATs (Hardware Attached on Top). Many pre-Pi 5 add-on boards that behaved perfectly on a Pi 4 may not work out-of-the-box on a Pi 5. Here's why, what to use instead, and how to move forward with clean, modern Python.

If you're new to peripheral hardware on the Raspberry Pi, two implementations of it matter:

- GPIO (General-Purpose Input/Output): the 40-pin header that lets your Pi control LEDs, read buttons, and talk to sensors and motors.
- HATs ("Hardware Attached on Top"): add-on boards that plug into that header (they literally sit on top like a hat) to add features such as audio, sensors, relays, displays and RFID. A tiny EEPROM on the HAT identifies it so the Pi can apply the right settings at boot.

These hats are additional add-ons that you can purchase for the pi. Por indeed design and construct for yourself as a Maker.

On the Raspberry Pi itself the GPIO header itself hasn't fundamentally changed since the early 40-pin Pis; what has changed is the way GPIO is managed on the Pi 5, and the number and variety of HATs (which keeps growing — have a quick search; there's something for everyone).

The Hardware Shift

Broadcom SoC on earlier boards: Up to (and including) Raspberry Pi 4/400, Broadcom SoCs such as the BCM2711 handled almost everything inside one package: CPU, GPU, RAM controller, and the I/O blocks (USB,

Ethernet, GPIO). On Pi 3, USB and Ethernet often sat behind a LAN9514 hub/controller via USB 2.0 — simpler, but bandwidth-limited.

RP1 Southbridge on Raspberry Pi 5: Pi 5 moves many peripheral and I/O duties to a new custom RP1 Southbridge. The 40-pin header is physically familiar, but the underlying controller and driver model are different. This modular design frees the main SoC and sets the stage for future performance gains — but it also means some older GPIO software no longer applies.

Practical impact: the once-ubiquitous RPi.GPIO library isn't supported on Pi 5. Use **libgpiod** (Python bindings) directly, or — much nicer — a high-level wrapper such as GPIO Zero, which chooses an appropriate backend automatically.

The Raspberry Pi 5 release introduced a different geography for the i/o devices that made many of the pre Raspberry Pi 5 GPIO modules redundant. Thus, while modules work on Raspberry Pi 4 models and before, they may not work on the Raspberry Pi 5. This is because of the different hardware that the Raspberry Pi 5 now uses and is likely to be continued on subsequent release, though we'll have to wait and see at the time of writing. Let's have a look at the reasons why. The standard software used to access the Raspberry Pi 4 would work on Raspberry Pi 5.

Practical impact: the once-ubiquitous RPi.GPIO library isn't supported on Pi 5. Use **libgpiod** (Python bindings) directly, or — much nicer — a high-level wrapper such as GPIO Zero, which chooses an appropriate backend automatically.

This is one of the biggest architectural shifts in the Pi's history; it changes how peripherals are wired up and how we write GPIO code. Some add-ons that behaved perfectly on a Pi 4 may not work out-of-the-box on a Pi 5 until their software is updated — the fix is usually to adopt the modern libraries above and follow the vendor's latest instructions.

The boot config file

On Raspberry Pi OS Bookworm, the boot config is /boot/firmware/config.txt (older images use /boot/config.txt). The Pi's firmware reads this before Linux starts and applies your settings, for example to:

- turn features on/off: I^2C, SPI, UART, camera stack
- load HAT overlays (e.g. an audio HAT's driver)
- tweak HDMI modes, GPU memory split, performance options

It's just key=value lines (optionally inside [sections]). After editing, reboot.

Pins: What They Are

Each metal post on the 40-pin header is a pin. Some pins are power (5 V, 3V3), some are ground (GND), and the rest are GPIO you can control in software.

They follow two numbering schemes:

- Physical (BOARD): counts the pins 1–40.
- BCM (Broadcom): uses names such as GPIO 17, GPIO 27.

Most Python examples use BCM. For instance, LED(17) means GPIO 17 (which happens to be physical pin 11).

Some pins also provide I²C, SPI, and UART buses. If those aren't in use, the pins can still act as general-purpose I/O.

On the Blink

If you have a suitable board attached (with LEDs and Buttons) or have attached these directly to the GPIO you can control them. The Hello World of GPIO interfacing is to blink or turn on and off an LED via software. You toggle a GPIO HIGH/LOW to flash an LED.

```
from gpiozero import LED
from time import sleep

led = LED(17)              # BCM numbering
while True:
    led.on();  sleep(1)
    led.off(); sleep(1)
```

GPIO Zero auto-selects a backend (on Pi 5 it typically uses **lgpio**). To force one for a run:

```
GPIOZERO_PIN_FACTORY=lgpio python3 blink.py
```

A 'low-level explict blink would look like this:

```
import gpiod, time

# Discover your chip first with: gpiodetect  /  gpioinfo
CHIP_NAME = "gpiochip4"   # adjust to your system
PIN_BCM   = 17

with gpiod.Chip(CHIP_NAME) as chip:
    line = chip.get_line(PIN_BCM)
    line.request(consumer="blink", type=gpiod.LINE_REQ_
DIR_OUT, default_val=0)
    try:
        while True:
            line.set_value(1); time.sleep(1)
```

```
            line.set_value(0); time.sleep(1)
    finally:
        line.release()
```

Low-level is wordier because you open the chip, choose a line, request it, then drive values — but it's precise and portable across Linux boards.

Action on Action

This is where we might get the action of one item to action another. In this case using a push-button to toggle a LED on and off.

```
from gpiozero import LED, Button
from signal import pause

led = LED(17)
btn = Button(27)
btn.when_pressed  = led.on
btn.when_released = led.off
pause()
```

When the button is pressed, the LED turns on; when released, it turns off.

On a higher plane we might use sound detector to blink an LED.

PWM LED (soft brightness)

This routine will dim a LED using pulse width modulation. With PWM we switch the pin very quickly and vary the duty cycle (percentage of time it's on). Your eye averages the pulses, so 20% looks dim; 80% looks bright.

```
from gpiozero import PWMLED
from time import sleep

led = PWMLED(18)          # hardware-PWM friendly,
others work too
led.value = 0.3           # ~30% brightness
sleep(2)
led.pulse(fade_in_time=1, fade_out_time=1, n=5,
background=False)
```

HAT Software: Vendor Code vs Your Own

Most HATs provide:

- EEPROM + overlay so Linux exposes the hardware cleanly at boot
- A Python library and examples so you can use the board immediately

Always run the supplier's example first to prove your wiring and setup. Then either reuse it or write your own to:

- combine HATs (e.g. RFID tap → play a chime on an audio HAT)
- add logging, retries, clearer errors, or a command-line interface
- modernise older examples (RPi.GPIO >GPIO Zero, /boot/config.txt > /boot/firmware/config.txt)

Common HAT Patterns

Audio HATs (DACs / amplifiers)

Enable an overlay, reboot, smoke-test with ALSA; then play audio from Python.

```
# /boot/firmware/config.txt
dtoverlay=hifiberry-dacplus

aplay /usr/share/sounds/alsa/Front_Center.wav

import sounddevice as sd, soundfile as sf
data, sr = sf.read("track.wav"); sd.play(data, sr);
sd.wait()
```

Camera (Picamera2, modern stack)

```
from picamera2 import Picamera2
cam = Picamera2(); cam.start(); cam.capture_file("photo.
jpg"); cam.stop()
```

Sensors & automation (I²C/SPI)

```
from PiicoDev_BME280 import PiicoDev_BME280
from PiicoDev_Unified import sleep_ms

bme = PiicoDev_BME280()
while True:
    t,p,h = bme.values()
    print(f"{t:.1f}°C {p:.1f} hPa {h:.1f}%"); sleep_
ms(2000)
```

RFID (I²C)

```
from PiicoDev_RFID import PiicoDev_RFID
r = PiicoDev_RFID()
print("Scan a tag...")
while True:
    if r.tagPresent():
        print("Tag:", r.readID())
```

From here you can play a chime on an audio HAT, open a relay, or log attendance.

Using Virtual Environments with Raspberry Pi HATs

Virtual environments are a valuable tool when working with Raspberry Pi HATs (**Hardware Attached on Top**). HATs are add-on boards that expand the Pi's functionality, enabling interaction with sensors, motors, displays, and other peripherals. Each HAT may require specific libraries and dependencies, which could conflict with each other or the base system. Virtual environments help isolate these dependencies, ensuring a clean and conflict-free development environment.

By creating a virtual environment for a Raspberry Pi project involving a HAT, you can install all necessary Python packages specific to that HAT without affecting the global Python environment. This is especially useful when working on multiple projects or experimenting with different HATs that may require different versions of the same library. For example, one project might need an older version of a GPIO library while another uses a newer version. Virtual environments allow you to manage these dependencies independently.

While HAT modules themselves don't use virtual environments, these environments are crucial for managing the software associated with projects involving HATs.

HATs often bring their own Python libraries. Keep projects clean by isolating dependencies:

```
python3 -m venv ve-hat
source ve-hat/bin/activate
pip install gpiozero picamera2 piicodev
```

Now a Audio-HAT demo won't clash with a RFID project.

Key Features of GPIO Zero

Abstracted API: GPIO Zero hides low-level hardware details, letting you write the same code for different Raspberry Pi models. For example, whether you're using a Pi 4 or Pi 5, the library handles hardware differences seamlessly.

Support for Multiple Backends: GPIO Zero works with backends like RPi.GPIO, lgpio, and pigpio. On a Raspberry Pi 5, where RPi.GPIO is incompatible, GPIO Zero automatically switches to a compatible backend like lgpio or pigpio. On a Pi 4, it might default to RPi.GPIO.

Simplified GPIO Operations: GPIO Zero eliminates the need for direct interaction with hardware or underlying libraries. You can perform common tasks, such as controlling LEDs or reading sensor inputs, without worrying about back-end details.

Streamlined Code: By abstracting complexity, GPIO Zero allows you to write less code while achieving the same functionality. It simplifies GPIO interactions compared to libraries like RPi.GPIO, making your programs easier to write and maintain.

GPIO Zero is the ideal library for managing GPIO on Raspberry Pi, especially when working with different models or transitioning to newer hardware. It keeps code simple, functional, and adaptable.

The Big Switch: Nice and Easy

GPIO Zero is able to work with multiple GPIO libraries, and simplifies many tasks, so you might find that you can write less code while achieving the same functionality. Equally, you'll find your code will generally become more streamlined, and you won't need to make your programs more complex.

You will not need to write fundamentally different programs to use GPIO Zero, but the way you interact with the GPIO pins will be much simpler compared to libraries like RPi.GPIO.

Here's how GPIO Zero differs and simplifies things:

High-Level API:

GPIO Zero provides a higher-level, object-oriented interface. Instead of writing detailed setup and cleanup code, you create objects representing hardware components like LEDs, buttons, or sensors. This makes your code cleaner and easier to understand. He's an example:

Using RPi.GPIO:

```
import RPi.GPIO as GPIO
import time

GPIO.setmode(GPIO.BCM)
GPIO.setup(17, GPIO.OUT)

try:
    while True:
        GPIO.output(17, GPIO.HIGH)  # LED on
        time.sleep(1)
        GPIO.output(17, GPIO.LOW)   # LED off
        time.sleep(1)
finally:
    GPIO.cleanup()
```

Using GPIO Zero:
from gpiozero import LED

```
from time import sleep

led = LED(17)

while True:
    led.on()
    sleep(1)
    led.off()
    sleep(1)
```

Notice how GPIO Zero doesn't require explicit pin setup or cleanup, making the code simpler and more readable.

Installation

Install the library in your virtual environment using:

```
pip install gpiozero
```

Enable GPIO Permissions: Running GPIO operations may require superuser privileges. To avoid using sudo with the virtual environment, add your user to the gpio group:

```
sudo usermod -aG gpio your_username
```

Replace **your_username** with your Raspberry Pi username. Log out and log back in for the changes to take effect.

Compatibility

Most 40-pin HATs work across Pi 2/3/4; the first 26 pins remain backward-compatible with the older 26-pin header era. Alt-functions sometimes differ, but rarely break typical HAT use.

Device-tree overlays are how you enable drivers for audio, displays, RTCs, etc.—a short call-out box explaining overlays + config.txt is very helpful for readers.

For teaching code, recommend GPIO Zero on Pi 4 and earlier (it'll default to RPi.GPIO or pigpio), so students can later run the same scripts on a Pi 5 with minimal/no edits.

44: Makefile

A **Makefile** uses a language called **Make**, which is associated with the build automation tool make. This language is a specialised scripting format designed to manage dependencies and automate tasks, commonly used for compiling The build automation tool make is a widely used utility for managing the build process of software projects. It automates the compilation and linking of code and can be used for other repetitive tasks like testing, packaging, or deployment. and linking code, but it can be extended to perform various other tasks.

Makefiles define rules where each rule has:

- A target: What you want to build (e.g., an executable file).
- Dependencies: Files required to build the target.
- Commands: Shell commands to execute for building the target.

A make file is a plain text file, so can be written in any text editor. The file is saved without an extension and is named makefile. Here's an example of its use. Save the content above in a file named **Makefile** in the root directory of your Python project.

```
#Filename: makefile
#Variables
PYTHON = python3
VENV_DIR = venv
DEFAULT_TARGET = .

.PHONY: help
help:
@echo "Makefile for Python project"
@echo "Usage:"
@echo "  make venv              - Create a virtual
environment"
@echo "  make install           - Install runtime
dependencies"
```

```
@echo "  make format file=<file_or_dir> - Format a
specific file or directory with Black"
@echo "                             (default: current
directory)"
@echo "  make clean            - Remove temporary files
and the virtual environment"

# Create a virtual environment
.PHONY: venv
venv:
@echo "Creating virtual environment..."
[ -d $(VENV_DIR) ] || $(PYTHON) -m venv $(VENV_DIR)

# Install dependencies
.PHONY: install
install: venv
@echo "Installing runtime dependencies..."
$(VENV_DIR)/bin/python -m pip install numpy pandas
black

# Format code
.PHONY: format
format:
@if [ -z "$(file)" ]; then \
  echo "Formatting the current directory with Black...";
\
  $(VENV_DIR)/bin/black $(DEFAULT_TARGET); \
else \
  echo "Formatting $(file) with Black..."; \
  $(VENV_DIR)/bin/black $(file); \
fi

# Clean up
.PHONY: clean
clean:
@echo "Cleaning up..."
rm -rf $(VENV_DIR)
find . -type d -name '__pycache__' -exec rm -rf {} +
find . -type f -name '*.pyc' -delete
```

In the terminal, navigate to your project directory and run with 'make'.

make venv - Create a virtual environment"

make install - Install run-time dependencies imcluding modules

make format file=<file_or_dir> - Format a specific file or directory with Black

make clean - Remove temporary files and the virtual environment"

Dependencies:

You can also use a a **requirements.txt** file l for **make install**.

For more information check: https://www.gnu.org/software/make/manual/

45: A Final Word

Congratulations on completing this book! While you've covered a wealth of Python concepts and applied them to real-world problems, this is just the beginning of your journey. There is a lot of information and detail in this book. You will almost certainly need to use it as a reference guide.

Don't forget that **practice makes perfect**. You will need to devote time and energy to go further. You wouldn't expect to learn to become a chess ninja but taking a few lessons. You need to delve into the detail and understand how to become better by putting hours of practice in. You might need to set aside time to:

- Set aside time daily or weekly to code.
- Revisit previous concepts and build upon them.
- Work on personal projects to test your skills.

Take on example practice tasks such as

- Recreate a project you've already done but add a new feature.
- Try solving problems on coding platforms. Check out other languages and convert their exercises into Python.

Your Python journey doesn't end here—it's a lifelong adventure. By practising regularly, staying connected with the community, and exploring new topics, you'll continue to grow as a programmer. Whether it's a simple script to automate a task or a complex IoT project on a Raspberry Pi, the skills you've learned in this book will serve as your foundation for future success.

I have covered an awful lot of ground in this book. Frankly, I have 200 or so more pages that I could include. They most likely will make for a second book in due course. One particular subject I have not covered is **PyTest**. Some may be disappointed or critical. PyTest is an excellent tool for modern testing, but it's not always necessary or ideal for every situation. You have to consider your project's complexity and existing infrastructure before adopting PyTest. While PyTest is a popular and clever testing framework, it might not be the best choice for every situation.

Not least, there is a steep learning curve, and it often requires multiple plugins. The simple case is that the most important thing is to learn to code correctly, debug issues, and implement solutions yourself. Do this, and PyTest is redundant for most purposes. Python also has **unittest**. You have enough knowledge to investigate this yourself.

Discovering New Modules and Blogs

Python's Standard Library is extensive, but its ecosystem of third-party libraries is even larger. Explore these to expand your capabilities.

Visit PyPI (Python Package Index) to discover thousands of libraries. (*https:/ /pypi.org/*)

Use the pip search command to find packages related to your needs:

```
pip search <keyword>
```

Subscribe to Python blogs or newsletters, such as Python Weekly. (*https:// www.pythonweekly.com/ subscribe*)

The Python and Raspberry Pi communities are incredibly active and welcoming. Engaging with these communities is one of the best ways to learn and solve problems. Like: *https://forums.raspberrypi.com*

The Python Documentation is the ultimate reference: *https://docs.python.org.* Here Library-specific documentation often includes examples and tutorials to get started.

And don't forget to check out

```
www.codingpress.com.au
```

Or:

```
www.brucesmith.info
```

for more Python books later in 2025.

Remember, the Python community is vast and supportive, and there's always something new to learn. So, keep coding, keep exploring, and enjoy the endless possibilities that Python offers!

Happy Python Coding.

INDEX

D

J

K

T

U

V

Made in the USA
Monee, IL
05 November 2026

67812861R00275